MW00784718

Blas na Gàidhlig

The Practical Guide to Scottish Gaelic Pronunciation

Michael Bauer

Akerbeltz

Published by Akerbeltz, Glasgow

First published worldwide in 2011

Copyright © Michael Bauer 2011

The right of Michael Bauer to be identified as author of this work has been asserted by him in accordance with the Copyright, Designs and Patents Act 1988.

British Library Cataloguing in Publication Data

A CIP record for this book can be obtained from the British Library

All rights reserved. No part of this publication may be reproduced, stored on a retrieval system, or transmitted in any form or by any means, electronic, mechanical, photocopying, recording, or otherwise without either the prior written permission of the Publishers or a licence permitting restricted copying in the United Kingdom issued by the Copyright Licensing Agency Ltd, 90 Tottenham Court Road, London W1P 0LP. This book may not be lent, resold, hired out or otherwise disposed of by way of trade in any form of binding or cover other than that in which it is published, without the prior consent of the Publishers.

Designed and typeset by Akerbeltz
Cover Design by Rob Wherrett
Illustrations by Jim Daily
Graphics digitisation by Chris Szigeti

ISBN 978-1-907165-00-9

More information on the material in this book may be obtained at:

www.akerbeltz.eu

Do mo céile airron caic
naċ ṡaḃ a pàiṡeaḋ
⁊
do ḃ'oiḋe cànanaċar na Ṡàiḋliṡ
ar ḟeaṁ a ḃa aṡam a-ṅiaṁ,
Rob Ó Maolalaiṡ

Ṡu roḃ mìle maċ aṡaiḃ

Gaelic and Irish have one of the oldest continuous writing traditions in Europe. The Gaelic script used above that, amongst other things, uses a dot above consonants to indicate lenition instead of an **h** and the Tironian Ampersand ⁊ instead of & began to appear in the 6th century in Ireland. It was in use in Scotland up until the 18th century and in Ireland up until the 1940s.

Contents 1

I.   Foreword

Welcome to the Practical Guide to Gaelic Pronunciation! This course will help you on your way to learning really good Gaelic by getting you over the first hurdle: the pronunciation of Gaelic.

This is perhaps the most important hurdle. The grammar of Gaelic is relatively easy but the sounds present a complex and seemingly daunting challenge to a learner. As a result pronunciation is often sidestepped or 'left till later' - an approach that will seriously affect the ability to understand native Gaelic and communicate effectively.

This book will take you through the sounds of Gaelic step by step. Once you have mastered the sounds it will then introduce you to the way in which these sounds interact. There will also be plenty of exercises on the way, sound files to go with the examples and exercises.

This book does not intend to 'tell native speakers how to pronounce their Gaelic' - it is primarily a tool for Gaelic learners or tutors. Native speakers already have native pronunciation. However, this book can of course be used by people teaching Gaelic to adults who want to teach a more mid-ground form of Gaelic pronunciation or by native speakers who want to find out more about the way this fascinating language works.

Great care has been taken to present a difficult topic in a user friendly way. This book has grown organically out of materials that have evolved over many classes of teaching good pronunciation to Gaelic learners. There has been many a request to put all this material together in a single publication supported with audio material. If you've had the pleasure before, you may recognise some of the material but a lot of it will have changed considerably over time as I have striven to make it easier to understand and learn. So this is not a linguistic essay but a book designed to help the learner or teacher of Gaelic find their way through the sounds of the language. In this sense, it is 'Gaelic Pronunciation Made Easier'.

Beir buaidh!

Michael "Akerbeltz" Bauer, Glasgow 2011

II.   Structure of the book

There are several sections to this book.   Each section contains both illustrated explanations with examples and exercises.

1	**The first section deals with some general but important points:** ▪ How do we learn languages? ▪ Why are small languages 'special cases' for learners? ▪ Learner motivation and aims and their effect on the role of pronunciation ▪ The role of dialects and standard language ▪ Some technical issues surrounding sounds
2	**The second section looks at the sounds of Gaelic:** ▪ What are the sounds? ▪ How do you make them accurately?
3	**The third section looks at sounds in a wider context:** ▪ How do these sounds interact with each other? ▪ Other pronunciation issues such as intonation, stress, lenition…
4	**The fourth section looks at the way Gaelic is normally written:** ▪ How does the system work and where does it come from? ▪ Issues you need to be especially aware of like 'helping vowels' ▪ A step by step guide to reading Gaelic

The Wordlist:

The sixth section contains a wordlist of some basic Gaelic vocabulary you are likely to need as a beginner with the pronunciation for each word including the different forms a word can show up in.

The Guide:

The last section is the Guide to Gaelic Pronunciation, a step-by-step guide that allows you to unlock the full potential of the brilliant spelling system Gaelic has.

So there's a logical progression through the book which I suggest you follow initially, at least for the first two sections. These lay the foundations for your pronunciation and give you the necessary skills to use this book. Once you have covered those sections, you can continue following the progression or jump between topics that interest you particularly.

PART 1

Learning a Language

III.   Learning a language

It is no big secret that children find it much easier than adults to learn a language fluently. And for children it doesn't even matter how 'odd' the language is. All they need is enough exposure to the language (or even languages) around them.

But does that mean that as adults we can learn the same way?

Linguists have studied the way we learn languages, both as adults and as children for a long time now. I'll spare you all the research details and just sum up. Linguists might not all agree on how exactly children learn languages but almost all agree that we are born with the ability to acquire a native language (or even more than one).

They have studied this over and over again, especially in immigrant communities where you find families with children moving to a different country with a different language. As it turns out, if you are fully immersed[1] in a language without much in the way of formal teaching, the results are drastically different for children and for adults.

As a young child (before the age of about 10), if you're exposed enough to a language, you will grow up speaking that language as a native language. No one, not even 'native' native speakers will be able to tell the difference. Take a British expat family with young children in Spain. If both the adults and the children are immersed in Spanish, the children will grow up to speak perfect Spanish but for the adults this immersion alone is no guarantee that they will ever get a good command of the sounds and structure of the language.

---

[1] This means learning the language simply by listening to other speakers and gradually picking your way through the language without much in the way of classes, books etc.

That's the reason why in communities which are trying to resurrect their language very young children can be successfully immersed in a language playgroup and become native speakers without thinking about it. The Māori in New Zealand realised this and invented the modern idea of the *Kōhanga Reo*, the language nest, in the 1980s where they immersed children in playgroups. The mothers would attend while pregnant so her babies could be exposed to the sounds even before birth and once they were born, they would hear nothing but Māori in these language nests.

Because this tapped into the way **children** learn languages naturally, it worked really well. Their success did not go unnoticed and the concept was copied many times, first by the Hawaiians who set up their *Pūnana Leo,* the Salish with their *Snq̓ʷiíq̓ʷo,* the Quechua with the *Runa Shimi Cusha*, the *Keelepesä* in Estonia for Vorõ speakers, *Kielâpiervâl* for Inari Sámi right down our very own *Sgoiltean Àraich* here in Scotland. The list is long.

All this means that...

before the age of 10, **Children:**	beyond the age of 10 and certainly after puberty, **Adults:**
▪ if fully immersed, will grow up speaking any language on this planet as native speakers	▪ will not automatically become fully fluent in a new language even if fully immersed
▪ do not have to think about learning a new language and so do not require formal teaching such as vocabulary lists or grammar exercises	▪ require formal teaching such as vocabulary lists or grammar exercises if they wish to become good speakers of a new language
▪ will automatically have good pronunciation	▪ will not necessarily have good pronunciation without proper instruction
⇒ Given the right input, children pick up a new language 'just like that'.	⇒ Even with the right input, adults need to put in some hard work.

So does that mean you've no chance as an adult before you have even started? No because given the proper training (and some hard work) you can largely overcome this problem even as an adult.

Fine-tuning your tongue with the help of this book will also help you overcome the obstacle that most Gaelic learners face on top of everything else - a lack of opportunities to use the language. Unless you're lucky and living in one of those few areas where you will hear a lot of Gaelic spoken every day, you're unlikely to have a lot of opportunities to 'immerse' yourself in the language.

Training your tongue is about as frustrating as learning how to ski. As adults we've been staying upright and moving for years. Now you have to learn it all over again. And as with skiing, it has its frustrations and embarrassing moments but it can most certainly be done as long as you keep working at it!

This also means you can't skip steps – how good an idea is it to head straight for the black run without having learned how to lock your skis and brake?

IV.   Why is pronunciation more important for Gaelic learners?

Think about the main differences between the world of Gaelic and the world of English for a moment. Where do you find Gaelic and where do you find English in the 21st century?

English	Scottish Gaelic
• has some 375 million native speakers	• has less than 60,000 native speakers
• has some 750 million fluent learners (⇒ more fluent learners than native speakers)	• has maybe 500-1000 fluent learners (⇒ less than 2% of all fluent speakers)
• is a major international language spoken all over the world in hundreds of countries	• is a minority language spoken only in Scotland and tiny emigrant communities
• number of speakers increases every year	• (still) has a decreasing number of speakers
• has a major presence in the media, education, entertainment, science, business, international politics & government...	• not seen or heard in the media much, struggling in education, little in entertainment, almost none in business or science...
	• even struggles in communities where it used to be strong up until recently

As a result, most English speakers are used to hearing lots of foreign accents and do not expect people to have perfect English. On the other hand, people who speak Gaelic fluently are almost always native speakers and generally are not used to learners or 'foreign' accents.

Now when we're speaking we rarely ever make fully grammatical sentences. We start a sentence. Change our mind half way through. Or we never finish. We break rules left right and centre... but one thing we never really do is come up with 'unnatural' pronunciation in our native language. Even when we're half asleep!

Listen to people from foreign countries working in your area. You probably notice their accent before you worry about how they string the words together. You may have to ask them to repeat themselves. It can be as difficult for you to understand a heavy Polish accent speaking English as it is for an Englishman to understand someone from the Gorbals. Or for you to understand a Brummie. We can't even make out the words they are using - so whether they have perfect grammar or not doesn't even enter the question. In the same way, when you are learning Gaelic, a native speaker will easily forgive somewhat messy grammar but will find it a lot more difficult to accept what you may think is 'roughly the right pronunciation' but to them barely understandable or not at all.

This is a serious issue and bad pronunciation can lead from anything like simply not being understood, amusement and behind-the-back ridicule to degrees of social exclusion[2]. And it will almost always cause native speakers to stop speaking Gaelic with you and switch over to English instead. Kind of defeats the objective doesn't it?

Importantly you have to get it right straight away. If you learn words with a bad pronunciation now and try and 'sort it out later', you'll never get there. You just can't edit your memory the way you can edit a written dictionary.

LEARNING GOOD PRONUNCIATION AT THE VERY BEGINNING
WILL SLOW YOU DOWN INITIALLY
BUT THE REWARD WILL BE INFINITELY BETTER GAELIC

---

[2] This doesn't mean strong foreign accents are bad but simply that a lot of people who aren't "interested in languages" find them hard to cope with.

V.   The Gaelic Granny Syndrome

"There's something else Master, something elusive" as Obiwan Kenobi puts it. This has to do with motivation and the reasons for learning a language.

Imagine you're Jarosław, a young Pole who is learning English in his home town because he wants to work in a UK hotel during the summer to fund his university studies at Warsaw University. There are 12 other young Poles like him in his evening class who want to go and work somewhere in the British Isles. What is their motivation for learning and what kind of English will they most likely be aiming for? Fireside English? Conversational English? Business English? Scientific English? BBC English? Stage English?

In most cases, our Polish friends need enough English to be able to work in an English-speaking environment. Understanding Chaucer and Shakespeare is probably not high on their list of priorities. Neither is 100% perfect grammar or pronunciation. For most, it is just a working language, a tool to use to make their way in the world.

Now take Jim in Glasgow who is learning Gaelic. He signed up for an immersion course at Stow College a few months ago because his grandparents always spoke Gaelic with each other when he visited them

during the summer on the island but never to him or his mother. Or Alistair who is on the same course because he believes that as a Scot you should speak either Scots or Gaelic (or maybe even both). Or Mórag, who, in spite of her Gaelic background, stopped speaking Gaelic at the age of 5 when her parents moved to Dunfermline and she had no one else to speak Gaelic with any more.

Or Kenny, the pensioner whose teacher washed his mouth with carbolic soap when he spoke Gaelic in school in his youth and who, perhaps unsurprisingly, never spoke Gaelic again.

So what about our friends learning Gaelic? How many of them are learning Gaelic purely to earn a living? Or are they doing it because they, in the broadest sense, are trying to regain their 'native' language, perhaps even to pass it on to their children? For most, the motivation is broadly in that area. That makes them very different from our Polish friends and gaining a good command of the language to be able to speak, understand and read it for its own sake is much more important for them. This is a very different sort of motivation which makes good pronunciation so much more important for them.

VI.   Dialect or standard?

Human language isn't uniform. No two sentences, even if spoken by the same person, are ever exactly the same. The way we say things depends on a great number of things - where we grew up, where we went to school, where we're working, who we're living with, who we are talking to, our age and gender, whether we're writing or speaking, when we are talking, how drunk we are, how angry or affectionate, how much background noise there is… the list is endless.

Because of this great variation, languages which have some form of official function often develop a 'standard' for very

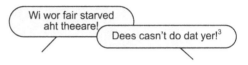

practical reasons. If you are writing laws, you need to be specific, if you're writing an essay, you want to make sure the person who's going to read it will understand you. If you're giving an election speech in Liverpool, speaking Broad Yorkshire might get you some laughs but not much in the way of comprehension or votes.

And although no one really speaks or writes 100% standard language, it is a common goal that people can aim for and be confident that if they get somewhere near it, people who are aiming for the same goal will understand them and, if they stay within what's acceptable for native speakers, not sound odd or foreign.

---

[3]   Broad Yorkshire for 'we were really cold out there' and Brizzle for 'you can't do that'.

For learners it has another benefit - it keeps them from cracking up. Imagine a learner of English who starts with a teacher who insists on teaching the students Broad Yorkshire in Liverpool while everyone around them speaks Scouse. The student then moves to London and continues with a teacher who speaks Glaswegian while their new partner speaks Cockney with them all day long. Confusing or what?

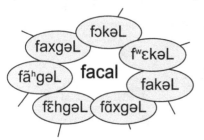

This is too often the case for Gaelic learners - they move from a teacher who is a Harris speaker to a Lewis speaker, then to a Skye speaker and finally to someone from Argyll or the other way round...

For the same reason that it would be confusing to a learner of English to move from dialect to dialect, we will not be presenting you with a course in any particular dialect of Gaelic but a common denominator. 'Common Gaelic Pronunciation' if you want to put it that way.

This means that if you pronounce things the way suggested, you will not end up speaking a particular Gaelic dialect - instead of pure Lewis Gaelic, pure Harris Gaelic, pure Uist Gaelic, pure Skye Gaelic or even pure Argyll Gaelic, you will learn a pronunciation that is recognisably good Gaelic to any native speaker and will be easily understood by most Gaelic speakers. It has this advantage because your Gaelic pronunciation will be 'somewhere in the middle' between today's dialects, rather than at (potentially) opposite ends.

The only catch is that people will not be able to tell where you are from and you will get puzzled looks and questions like "so which island were your parents from?" But that is a much better question to have to answer than "Say that again?"

This 'Standard Gaelic' isn't a concept I have invented as such either - most surviving dialects of the West Highlands and the Hebrides are actually slowly meeting somewhere in the middle of their own accord, the result being what you could call West Highland Gaelic.

VII. Style? What style?

Another question that one must consider is that of style. We constantly adapt our style of speaking depending on the situation and who we're talking to in our native language. Do you talk the same way to your mother as you do to your children's teacher? Does the style you use with your boss differ from how you speak to someone who just put a brick through your window? Or would you explain the way to the station to a Japanese tourist struggling with English in the same style you would give directions to the people from your village?

The bad news is that in our native languages, we learned gradually which style was appropriate and when as we were growing up, over a long period of time. When we're learning a new language, we're not only faced with new words, sounds and grammar but also the question of style.

This is not only a question of choice of words or phrases, it also affects the way we pronounce things which is why we must consider it here.

So what styles do we have? Well, oversimplifying things vastly, we shall say three:

Formal Gaelic: for example in church, parliament, at a reading competition, reciting poetry…

Everyday Gaelic: most everyday settings, at home, speaking to neighbours, your children's teachers…

Colloquial Gaelic: in the pub with your mates, at a céilidh, chatting up someone…

To make life as easy as possible, I will present you with 'Everyday Gaelic'. That means it's a style in the middle in terms of its pronunciation - neither overly formal nor overly colloquial. By going for the middle ground, you are the least likely to offend or amuse anyone. At the worst, you might sound a little colloquial (in a very formal setting) or a little formal (in a very colloquial setting) but never really totally out of place.

It also means that once you have mastered this style, it will be reasonably easy for you to explore the other styles. You may want to learn how to be more colloquial or how to be very formal, you may want to explore a particular dialect. No matter which direction you ultimately want to head in, this is the best starting point for you.

VIII.   The transcription system

The normal Gaelic writing system is very regular, much more so than the system English uses. But it can also be confusing and (apparently) misleading to a beginner. Often you will think you know how to pronounce a word - and still be way off. You need to know about 250 rules to be able to read the normal writing system with accuracy. For example there's:

> **(e)a** is [au] before **nn**, **ll**, **rr** or **m** except if followed by a vowel

Not rocket science and overall, not a lot of rules compared to English but it's still a bit much when you're just starting and several of them seem somewhat obscure at first sight.

But all you need to know to be able to read Gaelic in (proper) phonetic spelling are 37 symbols in a system called the 'International Phonetic Alphabet' (or IPA for short). Many of these symbols will be familiar so it's even less work and a lot more reliable!

Learners often use - or are confronted with - a method of indicating pronunciation called 'Adopted Pronunciation'. This tries to use English letters, syllables and words to imitate the sounds of Gaelic. It may look a lot easier than bothering with the IPA but sadly it just doesn't work. English and Gaelic are just too different for such a system to work. For example, you would make at least three serious mistakes in the simple phrase *ciamar a tha thu* if you wrote it as *kimmer uh ha oo*. This may not sound like a lot but if you get these mistakes ingrained and stack up enough, there will come a day when you can handle all the grammar but will still have real difficulties speaking to and understanding native speakers. Or even other learners who have memorised a different set of mistakes.

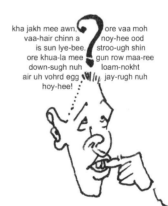

kha jakh mee awn, vaa-hair chinn a is sun lye-bee. ore khua-la mee down-sugh nuh air uh vohrd egg hoy-hee! ore vaa moh noy-hee ood stroo-ugh shin gun row maa-ree loam-nokht jay-rugh nuh

As the IPA has been specifically constructed by linguists to enable them to correctly write down sounds in any language on the planet, it is the most uniform and efficient tool for this task. Don't worry, we won't be studying the hundreds of symbols the IPA has, simply those that we need for Gaelic.

This also means that you should not invent your own system for writing Gaelic pronunciation. If you already are using one, then you should switch over to the IPA. No system that you will ever come up with will be as accurate and you will lose the vital details that you are trying to capture! It would be like using two empty tins and a bit of string instead of buying an industry-standard mobile phone.

While we're on the topic of how we write things - you will probably notice that this book does not follow the latest guidelines on how to spell Gaelic. Instead, I'm using a much more 'traditional' orthography. The reason is simple.   The traditional orthography (while not without its own shortcomings) is usually much more accurate at indicating the correct pronunciation of a word than any set of new rules drawn up in the last 50 years. As this book is intended as a study aid for good pronunciation for adults and not as a guide to SQA sanctioned spelling, I have chosen those spellings that are most helpful in terms of pronunciation if more than one variant exists. But more on that later.

IX.   Letter or sound?

We must be careful to distinguish between letters and actual sounds. In a language written with an alphabet, we sometimes have a confusing situation where one letter can be pronounced in several different ways or combines with other letters to give an entirely different sound - or even letters which have no sound at all!

θruː

rʌf

lɒx

goːst

through

rough

lough

ghost

The Phonetic Alphabet does away with all that confusion by introducing a simple rule:

> One symbol represents one sound only - no exceptions

Therefore a [g] in phonetic writing always represents a [g] sound, unlike in the English spelling system where the letter **g** can stand for [g] [dʒ] or even [f] when it combines with an **h**!

To show that symbols are representing phonetic transcription rather than just letters, we place them in square brackets, for example [gɪliː] for *ghillie*.

X.   Still 'all sound same'?

As we grow up, we learn how to pick apart the sounds that we have in our native language and how to make them just by hearing them over and over again. But again this ability disappears once we hit puberty.

In English for example we learn how to make and perceive the difference between [l] and [r] as this distinction is vital. Think of words like *lead* and *read*, *light* and *right*. In Japanese on the other hand [l] and [r] are considered variants of the same sound. Because of that, it is very difficult for Japanese people to learn how to both hear and pronounce these sounds correctly and to their ears, *Karate* and *Kalate* sound exactly the same and announcing an *election* in public may result in worried looks. And, similarly, to many Germans ears *we three kings* sounds pretty much the same as *wee free kings,* even though most Scots would disagree.

Meeting a totally new sound is a bit like being introduced to a fruit you've never seen before. You will normally try and relate it to the closest known fruit you're familiar with - that's why in the early days of exotic fruits and vegetables tomatoes were 'love apples', kiwis were 'Chinese gooseberries' and why a pineapple has this rather odd name.[4] Or even amusingly, why early cookery books talked about 'Italian rarebit' - something you and I would call a pizza!

---

[4] Because you're dying to know - it's called 'contact induced lexical development' by linguists!

Not just in English either. French has the *pomme de terre* (earth apple, ie potato) and German the *Apfelsine* (China apple, ie orange). Or on the other side of the pond Lakhóta[5] has *šúkawakhá* (mystery dog, ie horse), Cheyenne *ma'aetano'e* (iron bowstring, ie gun) and Yup'ik *atsarpak* (big berry, ie apple).

So in the ears of a non-native, foreign sounds are all too easily related to the nearest equivalent. French *tu* becomes *too*, German *München* becomes *Munshin* and Gaelic *uisge* becomes *ishkey*. Sometimes the outcome can be hilarious. In Eastern Canadian Inuktitut, the word 'onion' turned into *uaniujaq* - a word which also means 'smell of armpit'!

Some languages, Spanish for example, are a little more forgiving about bad pronunciation like this but Gaelic is definitely not one of them.

A very small number of adults can still hear 'new' distinctions and say them correctly and we'd all love to be in that select group of people but most of us unfortunately aren't.

But this is where we can cheat a little - even though some linguists would happily kick me for suggesting this to you. Because (in Gaelic) we can generally rely on context to supply us with the exact meaning of a potentially ambiguous sentence, you can to some extent get away with not quite being able to <u>hear</u> the difference.

But as long as you learn when you have to <u>make</u> which sound, no one will ever know because all <u>they</u> can hear is your good pronunciation!

Of course this doesn't mean you shouldn't try to but if you have to make a choice, you're better off being able to say the sounds correctly rather than hear them.

---

[5] Formerly called the Sioux, which comes from the middle bit of the word *naadowe<u>si</u>wag* in the Ottawa language. Ok, technically the Sioux call themselves the *Očhéthi Šakówį* 'the Seven Council Fires' but most English speakers know them as the Lakhóta. Or rather the 'Lakota' in bad spelling.

PART 2

The Sounds of Gaelic

XI.   Unit structure

At this point, we will begin to look at the sounds of Gaelic. Which sounds does Gaelic have and how do we make these sounds properly? Right now we're not interested in how Gaelic is written or how the letters represent sounds, simply the sounds themselves.

Once we have learned and practised the sounds we can then move on and explore how Gaelic represents these sounds in writing.

In the part where we deal with the sounds, each new sound will have:

- A large example of the IPA symbol used for this particular sound and the name of the sound and pictures which show you what your lips and your tongue are doing

- A detailed explanation of what your mouth is doing for this sound and what you need to pay attention to

- Exercises to help you make this sound and practise it

XII.   Time to loosen up!

Now after the leisurely read through my rambling introduction we're striding towards the nitty-gritty stuff. Before we get there, here's something I'd like you to do before you get started to help you relax, focus and 'open your mind'. This is especially good for you if you happen to think 'you're bad at languages' or were 'really put off languages by a bad teacher of French'…

Believing things like that can be a massive stumbling block when trying to learn a new language. So let's start out by getting you in the right frame of mind and relax a bit - this book won't bite!

Breathing, physical exercise and mental focus (not on 'the topic' itself) are the key things that can help you do just that. There are any number of different ways in which you can do that either alone, with someone else or a group.

It may seem a little odd to you to start off learning a language by doing some exercises which have apparently nothing to do with language but trust me, it helps. Professionals who teach people how to deal with

challenges and stress and even phobias use such techniques. And if you feel self-conscious about it, there's nothing that keeps you from doing them when nobody is looking or listening!

1) Breathing and Exercises

Stand up and breathe in for 8 counts, hold for 16 counts and breathe out for two counts. Repeat 10 times.

Then do a little light exercise. If you have some favourite ones you do anyway (for example push-ups), try those. Otherwise stand up, stretch your hands as high as you can and hold for a count of 10. Then relax. Then lock your hands in front of you with your palms facing out and stretch as far forward as possible, hold for a count of 10 then relax. Stand up and face forward. Raise your shoulders then roll them back and down again. Repeat five times. Then do the same only roll them forward this time.

You can also come up with your own 'exercises' to suit yourself. Any form of moderate exercise will work, including sex!

2) Affirmation

Saying something affirmative about the task in hand can really help you overcome any fears or stress you might have.

For example, say "Learning is fun, when I learn I grow" rhythmically for 5 minutes. Another affirmation might be "my mind can learn a language well - I did it once[6], I can do it again"

3) Wind Down

Focus on a point in time in the future when you will have mastered Gaelic pronunciation. Imagine it in the present tense. Feel the joy, feel proud of your achievement and imagine the praise from fellow learners, your teachers and Gaelic speakers as you confidently demonstrate your expertise.

Now we're ready to roll!

---

[6] Your native language(s)!

1.   The vowels or Tongue Twisters Part 1

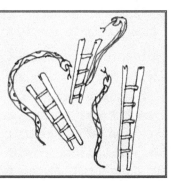

If you got here without reading the previous chapters, go back and start again! They are very important!

Ok, 'what's a vowel?' is a perfectly legitimate question. We can broadly split the sounds of a language into two main groups, vowels and consonants. In a nutshell, any letter you couldn't possibly sing in the alphabet song without adding another sound to it (kay, gee, eff...) is a consonant and anything else is a vowel (e, i, o...).

Luckily only about 4 of the 11 vowels in Gaelic pose any serious problem to speakers of English, Scottish English or Scots because there is a considerable overlap between the languages. There are some issues though, such as vowel length, which you need to pay attention to as they 'work' differently in Gaelic.

Vowel length means that Gaelic has short and long vowels. Unlike in English, the length of the vowel can change the meaning of a word in Gaelic. Scots will be familiar with this concept as the length of a vowel does make a difference in Scots and Scottish English[7]:

Short	Long
brood [brʉd]	brewed [brʉːd]
crude [krʉd]	crewed [krʉːd]
need [nɪd]	kneed [niːd]

---

[7] The famous SVLR (Scottish Vowel Length Rule). Well, it's famous amongst linguists anyway.

Either way, you must make sure that in Gaelic your long [aː] is about twice as long as your short [a] and so on. Otherwise you might turn the word for a stick, which has a short [a], into a boat, which has a long [aː]. There's no hard and fast rule which says a long vowel has to be this many milliseconds long – some Gaelic speakers have very long long vowels, some have them a bit shorter. As long as your long vowels are about twice as long as your short ones, you're doing fine.

1.1   The schwa or lazy e [ə]

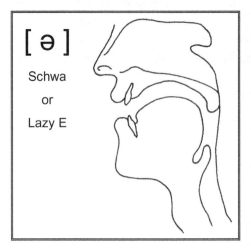

[ə]

Schwa

or

Lazy E

The technical name for this symbol, schwa, comes from the Hebrew שוא (šĕwā) which means 'nought', a name for one of the small dots that are used as diacritics[8] in Hebrew. One of its uses in Hebrew is to mark the [ə] sound which is why German philologists borrowed the word from Hebrew as a name (hence the German looking spelling). At some point people in my pronunciation workshops decided to rename this symbol Lazy E because of the way it is made. It doesn't really matter what you call it as long as you know which sound it is you mean!

This is by far the most common vowel in Gaelic and very easy to make. It also occurs in English and Scots where it is also one of the most common vowels.

It is the most boring vowel you could possibly imagine. You make this vowel by simply relaxing absolutely everything in your mouth and going *uh* [ə], right in the middle of your mouth. This occurs in Scots words like *bannock* [banək], *paircel* [pɛrsəl], *raveri* [reːvɐrɪ] and in Standard English words like *the* [ðə], *shiver* [ʃɪvə] and *cedar* [siːdə].

If you're unsure of what Standard English is, think of the kind of BBC English you hear on the national news today and you're not far off.

---

[8] A diacritic is a little symbol (such as dots, lines, hooks and circles) that is placed on, next to, in or under a letter to modify it or distinguish it from a similar letter. French for example uses dots, lines and hooks as diacritics, so you get c and ç, a and á, i and ï and so on.

✎ **Exercise 1.**

Say the following words[9]:

the [ðə]   shiver [ʃɪvər]   under [ʌndər]   cedar [siːdər]

Now say the last part of each word again (if you pronounce the r at the end, then also drop that):

the [ðə]   ..ve [və]   ..de [də]   ..da [də]

Now repeat only the vowel:

[ə]   [ə]   [ə]   [ə]

✎ **Exercise 2.**

Say the following nonsense syllables out loud:

mə	mamə
amə	ulə
anə	kanə
punə	əm

Because it's a somewhat unusual shape, trace the letter a few times below to get used to the symbol. It doesn't really matter which way round you write it as long as you're happy with it:

---

[9] On the recordings these are spoken with a Highland accent but unless stated otherwise, the examples will work for most varieties of English.

Progress Report									
5%									
ə	iː	i	ɪ	eː	e	ɛː	ɛ	aː	a
ɔː	ɔ	oː	o	ɤː	ɤ	uː	u	ɯː	ɯ

Having reached this point, you will be able to pronounce the following Gaelic words (all consonants used in the Progress Reports are pronounced as they would be in Scottish English or Scots for the time being):

Gaelic	Meaning	Gaelic	Meaning
ə	his/her	nə	in his
nən	in their	mə	about

Not a lot so far but don't worry, I can promise a steep learning curve! But even at this stage you already have an advantage over people who are ignoring pronunciation for the most part because many Gaelic learners mispronounce all of the above words.

The schwa is actually one of the most common vowels in the world's languages. You may not have considered this before but not every language uses all possible speech sounds [10] or indeed the same subset. Some have lots of vowels, some have rather less but, perhaps unsurprisingly, every language needs at least one vowel and if it has very few vowels, then the schwa is often one of them.

The Arrernte language from the Mparntwe [11] region for example has only two vowels, [a] and - you guessed it - the schwa. But, before you buy your ticket, it has plenty of consonants to make up for the lack of vowels.

---

[10] A sound used in language, in contrast to other sounds we can make that are not used in language, such as gnashing your teeth or coughing.

[11] Ok, Alice Springs in Australia to most people.

1.2   Long [iː], short [i] and the lazy i [ɪ]

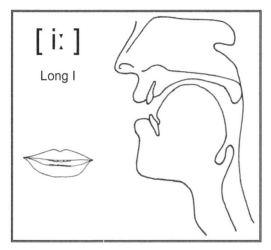

[iː]

Long I

The colon [ː] after a phonetic symbol tells you that the sound is long. This means that [iː] is a long vowel sound. You get this sound in Scots words like *dee* [diː], *gie* [giː], *reive* [riːv], *jeel* [dʒiːl].

In Standard English you get this sound in words like *bee* [biː], *see* [siː] and *tea* [tiː].

Now just to remind you, remember that in the Phonetic Alphabet one symbol always represents just the one sound so [iː] is always just a long [iː] sound like in *bee* [biː]. It will never ever represent the [aɪ] sound that you get in words like *kite* [kaɪt] which, as you can see, would be [aɪ] in phonetic writing. It will take some time to get used to the idea because you're just so used to the letter **i** being [aɪ] but once you get over that, it'll be easy.

So, make sure the [iː] is nice and long and made towards the very front of your mouth.

✎ **Exercise 3.**

Say the following words:

bee [biː]   see [siː]   tea [tiː]   flea [fliː]

Now repeat only the vowel:

[iː]   [iː]   [iː]   [iː]

✎ Exercise 4.

Say the following nonsense syllables out loud.

i:	hi:
pi:	i:m
mi:	mi:n
fi:	li:

❊ ❊ ❊ ❊ ❊ ❊ ❊

[i]

Short i

The [i] sound is pronounced the same as [i:] only shorter. This is not the same sound as in Scots and Standard English words like *runny* [rʌnɪ]. Such words have a very relaxed [ɪ] vowel made further back in your mouth (which we will meet in a moment) but this short [i] must be made towards the very front of your mouth, exactly in the same place as long [i:].

In fact, [i:] and [i] are the most front vowel sounds that you can get. If you moved your tongue any further forward in your mouth than it already is for [i:] and [i], you will be entering the realm of French kissing!

✎ Exercise 5.

Say the following words:

bee [bi:]   see [si:]   tea [ti:]   flea [fli:]

Say them again but now make the vowel about half as long and without changing the position of your tongue:

[bi]   [si]   [ti]   [fli]

Now repeat only the vowel:

[i]   [i]   [i]   [i]

✎ **Exercise 6.**

Say the following nonsense syllables out loud:

i	hi
pi	imə
mi	minə
fi	miʃə

❋ ❋ ❋ ❋ ❋ ❋ ❋

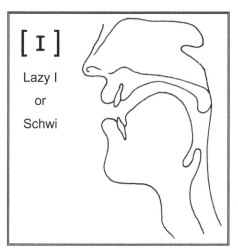

[ɪ]

Lazy I

or

Schwi

This vowel also exists in Scots, for example in *sleekit* [sliːkɪt], *inks* [ɪnks], and *canny* [kanɪ] and in Standard English words like *honey* [hʌnɪ], *money* [mʌnɪ] and *grainy* [greinɪ] - any short i sound in either language really. Just a word of caution: if you pronounce the above words with a vowel that sounds very different from the vowel in the Gaelic examples below, then just ignore the examples, this vowel varies quite a bit in Scots and English.

It is the 'relaxed' version of the [i] vowel. This means that in order to make this sound, you have to say [i] but relax the muscles of your mouth while saying it. Hence the name 'Lazy I'.

Schwi, by the way, is really just a pun on schwa because it's as relaxed as the [ə], just in a slightly different place in your mouth.

You may have already asked yourself why [ə] and [ɪ] only appear short in Gaelic. This has something to do with the way Gaelic treats stress (where the emphasis goes in a word). But more on that a lot later.

✎ Exercise 7.

Say the following words:

  honey [hʌnɪ]   money [mʌnɪ]   grainy [greːnɪ]   comfy [kʌmfɪ]

Now drop the first part:

         [nɪ]   [nɪ]   [nɪ]   [fɪ]

Now repeat only the vowel:

         [ɪ]   [ɪ]   [ɪ]   [ɪ]

✎ Exercise 8.

Say the following nonsense syllables out loud:

    imɪ   mamɪ

    emɪ   ilɪ

    anɪ   kanɪ

    pinɪ   mulɪ

Progress Report									
→20%									
ə	iː	i	ɪ	eː	e	ɛː	ɛ	aː	a
ɔː	ɔ	oː	o	ɣː	ɣ	uː	u	ɯː	ɯ

The number of words you can say is already going up quite steeply. Let's have a look at what else you can say now:

Gaelic	Meaning	Gaelic	Meaning
mi	I	iːm	butter
mil	honey	miːm	my butter
miːlə	a mile	i	she
miːn	fine	iː	Iona

1.3   Long [eː] and short [e]

[eː]

Long E

Scots speakers have this sound (see examples) and shouldn't have any problem in making it. Some examples are *dae* [deː], *gaed* [geːd], *knave* [neːv], *faither* [feːðər].

In Standard English this long [eː] sound doesn't exist on its own. The short version of this vowel only appears in the [eɪ] diphthong in words like *day* [deɪ], *grey* [greɪ] or *say* [seɪ].

✎ **Exercise 9.**

Say the following words:

      day [deː]   may [meː]   say [seː]   hey [heː]

Now repeat only the vowel:

      [eː]   [eː]   [eː]   [eː]

✎ **Exercise 10.**

Say the following nonsense syllables out loud:

eː	heː
meː	eːm
peː	feːm
leː	leːʃ

❊ ❊ ❊ ❊ ❊ ❊ ❊ ❊

[e] Short E	This is the same sound as [e:], only shorter. Scots speakers should have no problem with this short vowel as it exists in Scots: *graith* [greθ], *stane* [sten], *danger* [dendʒər], *bele* [bel].

In Standard English this short vowel only appears in the [eɪ] diphthong in words like *day* [deɪ], *grey* [greɪ] or *say* [seɪ].

This is a short vowel. As Gaelic has both the short [e] and the long [e:], make sure that you do not draw out the short [e] too much.

🖎 **Exercise 11.**

Say the following words:

day [de:]   may [me:]   say [se:]   hey [he:]

Now say the first part of each word again:

[de]   [me]   [se]   [he]

Now repeat only the vowel:

[e]   [e]   [e]   [e]

🖎 **Exercise 12.**

Say the following nonsense syllables out loud:

e	he
me	emə
pe	fe
le	leʃ

Progress Report									
		➔30%							
ə	iː	i	ɪ	eː	e	ɛː	ɛ	aː	a
ɔː	ɔ	oː	o	ɣː	ɣ	uː	u	ɯː	ɯ

Ok, let's have a look what new words and phrases you can add to your repertoire of perfect Gaelic now:

Gaelic	Meaning	Gaelic	Meaning
feːm	need	feːmɪ mi	I have to
leː mi	I jumped	heːn	self
eːʃ	(a) lack	ə leːnə	his shirt
eːv	shout!	leːv mi	I read

1.4   Long [ɛ:] and short [ɛ]

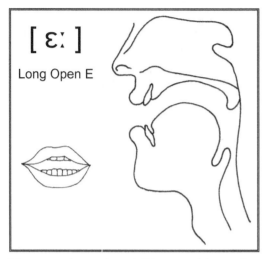

[ɛ:]

Long Open E

Again, Scots speakers are in luck here because they have the long [ɛ:]. It shows up in words like *neve* [nɛ:v], *refer* [rəfɛ:r], *air* [ɛ:r], *flether* [flɛ:ðər].

In Standard English only the short [ɛ] vowel occurs in words like *bed* [bɛd], *said* [sɛd] and *says* [sɛz]. So you can also get this long sound simply by making the short [ɛ] longer.

You can also arrive at this sound by saying [e:] and opening your mouth wider while saying it.

Ο Παρθενώνας

The Parthɛnon

Because there are two main **e** sounds in the world's languages (the closed [e] and this open [ɛ]) linguists had to shop around for a second symbol when they devised phonetic writing. They eventually settled on the Greek letter for **e**, the epsilon.

✎ Exercise 13.

Say the following words:

     bed [bɛ:d]   said [sɛ:d]   shed [ʃɛ:d]   dead [dɛ:d]

Now say the first part of each word again but this time draw out the vowel:

     [bɛ:]   [sɛ:]   [ʃɛ:]   [dɛ:]

Now repeat only the vowel:

     [ɛ:]   [ɛ:]   [ɛ:]   [ɛ:]

✎ Exercise 14.

Say the following nonsense syllables out loud:

     ɛ: hɛ:

     mɛ: mɛ:ʃ

     pɛ: kɛ:

     lɛ: lɛ:ʃ

❋❋❋❋❋❋❋❋

[ɛ] Short Open E	This vowel exists both in Scots and Standard English. Scots examples are *leather* [lɛðər], *raik* [rɛk], *het* [hɛt], *serve* [sɛrv] and in English *bed* [bɛd], *said* [sɛd] and *says* [sɛz]. This is a short vowel so remember to keep the [ɛ] shorter than the [ɛ:].

✎ Exercise 15.

Say the following syllables:

     [bɛ:d]   [sɛ:d]   [ʃɛ:d]   [dɛ:d]

Now repeat them but keep the vowel short:

     [bɛ]   [sɛ]   [ʃɛ]   [dɛ]

Now repeat only the vowel:

     [ɛ]   [ɛ]   [ɛ]   [ɛ]

✎ Exercise 16.

Say the following nonsense syllables out loud:

ɛ	hɛ
mɛ	fɛ
pɛ	kɛ
lɛ	lɛmə

Progress Report									
→40%									
ə	iː	i	ɪ	eː	e	ɛː	ɛ	aː	a
ɔː	ɔ	oː	o	ɣː	ɣ	uː	u	ɯː	ɯ

You can now add the following to your list:

Gaelic	Meaning	Gaelic	Meaning
mɛː mɛː	baa baa!	mɛr	lively
fɛr	a man	ɛ	he
ə vɛn	his wife	ə hɛn	his grandpa
ɛr	East	ʃɛr	East(ward)

You will have noticed something about most of the sounds we've done so far: they're all made towards the front of your mouth. Try and run

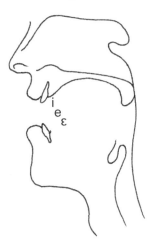

through them again: [i] [iː] [e] [eː] [ɛ] [ɛː]. Pay attention to where the sounds are made and you'll notice your tongue is in the front part of your mouth.   And the only thing you're changing as you're moving from [i] to [e] to [ɛ] is opening your mouth progressively wider and pushing your tongue <u>down</u> a bit further.

That's why linguists call them front vowels. Now you're justified in saying 'so what' at this point in time but just keep this idea at the back of your head.   You'll get big brownie points later if you do because this idea is fundamental to many things in Gaelic, from things to do with sounds right down to the way it is written.

And, as you may have correctly guessed by now, all the remaining vowels are going to be called back vowels because, well, they're made towards the back of your mouth.

That's the way vowels are 'logically' grouped together by linguists and also the reason why I am introducing them in this order and not as a-e-i-o-u, the way they are ordered in the alphabet.

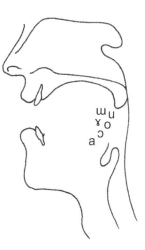

1.5   Long [aː] and short [a]

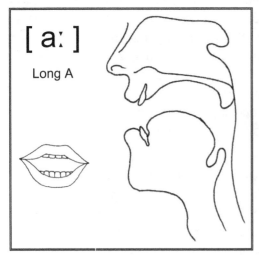

[aː]

Long A

For Scots, this is another easy one because Scots has both the long and short clear [a] vowels, for example in *baa* [baː], *haar* [haːr], *gar* [gaːr], *maa* [maː].

And although this is an extremely common vowel all over the world, for speakers of English this sound is a bit tricky because it doesn't occur in Standard English. This sound does occur in many northern varieties of English, for example in Broad Yorkshire *abaht* [əˈbaːt], *aht* [aːt], *rahnd* [raːnd].

In Standard English short [a] occurs only in the [aɪ] diphthong in words like *dive* [daɪv], *night* [naɪt] and *rye* [raɪ].

This long Gaelic [aː] is different from the apparently long **a** in English words like *father* [fɑːðə], *bath* [bɑːθ] and *master* [mɑːstə]. English [ɑː] in these words is made at the very back of your mouth. Of all vowels in any language, it's the furthest back. Relative to that, Gaelic [aː] on the other hand is made not quite as far back. So if you only have the [ɑː] sound, make this sound, keep it going and then try to literally move the whole sound forward by moving your tongue towards the front of your mouth.

✎ Exercise 17.

Say the following words:

    dive [daɪv]   night [naɪt]   rye [raɪ]   lie [laɪ]

Now say the first part of each word again and draw out the [a] vowel:

        [daː]   [naː]   [raː]   [laː]

Now repeat only the vowel:

        [aː]   [aː]   [aː]   [aː]

✎ Exercise 18.

Say the following nonsense syllables out loud.

    aː   haː

    paː   kaː

    maː   vaː

    faː   aːv

By the way, did you know that most of our letters have a totally bizarre history? The letter **a** for examples goes back to a pictogram for 'ox' used in the middle east thousands of years ago by a bunch called the Proto-Canaanites who had nicked the original idea from the Egyptians.

Egyptian   Proto-C.   Greek   Etruscan   Latin

The Proto-Canaanite word for ox was something like *'ālep.* It was then borrowed by the Phoenicians in the 11th century BC who called it *'aleph.* Being more concerned with trade than carving stone columns, these master traders cut it down to some twenty symbols to do their book-keeping with - the first real alphabet.

Then the Greeks nicked *'aleph* and called it *alpha.* Next in line were the Etruscans of Northern Italy who imported it for the [a] sound. When the Romans took over from the Etruscans, they too decided an alphabet was a good thing and used it to write Latin. And from Latin it spread all over the world. A widely travelled ox, wouldn't you say?

❋ ❋ ❋ ❋ ❋ ❋ ❋ ❋

[a]

Short A

This, again, is the same as the previous long sound only shorter. Easy for Scots speakers as it occurs in words like *bannock* [banək], *quart* [kwart], *cran* [kran], *sclaff* [sklaf].

In Standard English short [a] only occurs in the [aɪ] diphthong in words like *dive* [daɪv], *night* [naɪt] and *rye* [raɪ]. As before, northern varieties of English do have the short [a] as well, for example *mafted* [maftɪd], *ganzey* [ganzɪ], *addle* [adl] in Broad Yorkshire.

✎ Exercise 19.

Say the following words:

dive [daɪv]   night [naɪt]   rye [raɪ]   lie [laɪ]

Now say the first part of each word again:

[da]   [na]   [ra]   [la]

Now repeat only the vowel:

[a]   [a]   [a]   [a]

✎ Exercise 20.

Say the following nonsense syllables out loud:

a	ha
pa	ka
ma	va
fa	af

Progress Report

➔50%

ə	iː	i	ɪ	eː	e	ɛː	ɛ	aː	a
ɔː	ɔ	oː	o	ɤː	ɤ	uː	u	ɯː	ɯ

We're now exactly half way through the vowels and can add some more words and even a few short – but full – sentences:

Gaelic	Meaning	Gaelic	Meaning
af af	bow wow!	hamə	ham
ha mi ma	I am good	aːlə	an atmosphere
amər	a basin	aːlan	a meadow
fal	a pigsty	va mi ma	I was good

1.6   Long [ɔː] and short [ɔ]

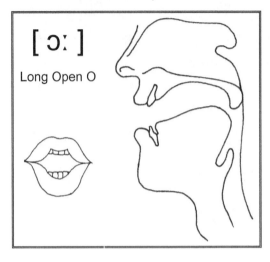

[ɔː]

Long Open O

As we saw with **e** sounds, again there are two main types of **o** sound that occur in the languages of the world. Gaelic has both. This one is called the 'Open O' because it requires you to open your mouth relatively wide. Because of this obvious 'opening', the symbol for this sound is simply an **o** with an opening.

For a change, Scots does not have this vowel but you can also get there by saying [oː] (see 1.7) and opening your mouth wider while saying it. The result will be [ɔː].

This vowel occurs in Standard English words like *thaw* [θɔː], *vault* [vɔːlt] and *oral* [ɔːrəl].

✎ Exercise 21.

Say the following words:

thaw [θɔː]   drawn [drɔːn]   lawn [lɔːn]   pawn [pɔːn]

Now say the first part of each word again:

[θɔː]   [drɔː]   [lɔː]   [pɔː]

Now repeat only the vowel:

[ɔː]   [ɔː]   [ɔː]   [ɔː]

✎ Exercise 22.

Say the following nonsense syllables out loud:

ɔː	hɔː
kɔː	pɔː
mɔː	ɔːl
fɔː	fɔːʃ

❊❊❊❊❊❊❊❊

[ɔ]

Short Open O

The short version of the 'Open O' doesn't occur in either Scots or English. It does appear in the [ɔɪ] diphthong in Standard English words like *toy* [tɔɪ], *joy* [dʒɔɪ] and *boil* [bɔɪl]. So you can either work your way through to this sound by starting with [ɔɪ] or alternatively you can start with [ɔː] and make it shorter, about half as long.

✎ Exercise 23.

Say the following words:

thaw [θɔː]   drawn [drɔːn]   lawn [lɔːn]   pawn [pɔːn]

Repeat the first part of each word but with the vowel only half as long:

[θɔ]   [drɔ]   [lɔ]   [pɔ]

Now repeat only the vowel:

[ɔ]   [ɔ]   [ɔ]   [ɔ]

✎ Exercise 24.

Say the following nonsense syllables out loud:

ɔ	hɔ
kɔ	pɔ
mɔ	ɔl
fɔ	fɔʃ

ə	iː	i	ɪ	eː	e	ɛː	ɛ	aː	a

Progress Report									
ə	iː	i	ɪ	eː	e	ɛː	ɛ	aː	a
ɔː	ɔ	oː	o	ɤː	ɤ	uː	u	ɯː	ɯ
→60%									

Both [ɔ] and [ɔː] are common in Gaelic but as we haven't covered the consonants yet, we can only add a few example words on this occasion.

Gaelic	Meaning	Gaelic	Meaning
ʃɔ	this	ə vɔl	his rage
kɔr	condition	ə hɔl	his wish
vɔnə valə	from the town	rɔnə valə	before the town

1.7   Long [o:] and short [o]

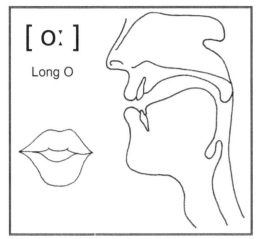

[o:]

Long O

This is the second **o** sound Gaelic has. And since it requires your mouth to be more closed and rounded than for [ɔ:], the symbol is the unbroken letter **o**.

Scots have this long round [o:] sound and shouldn't have any problems. Some examples are *brose* [bro:z], *hose* [ho:z], *jo* [dʒo:] and *stove* [sto:v].

This sound doesn't occur in Standard English at all. It isn't too difficult to make though as it resembles [ɔ:] closely. The only difference is that your mouth is not as wide open as for [ɔ:] so your lips are really rounded. If you're having any trouble with this sound, imagine you're kissing someone while saying this sound.

✎ **Exercise 25.**

Say the following words:

    stove [sdo:v]   hose [ho:s]   brose [bro:s]   low [lo:]

Now say the first part of each word again but make really round lips at the same time:

        [sdo:]   [ho:]   [bro:]   [lo:]

Now repeat only the vowel:

        [o:]   [o:]   [o:]   [o:]

✎ **Exercise 26.**

Say the following nonsense syllables out loud and make sure that your lips go really round for this sound:

oː	hoː
poː	koː
moː	voː
foː	foːl

Ok, last footnote on the history of the alphabet. Three guesses why the letter **o** is round? Because it comes from a pictogram for 'eye':

Egyptian   Proto-C.   Phoenician   Greek

All our letters are nothing but a banal sounding list of everyday items (well, everyday items thousands of year ago) so when you recite your ABC you're really just going 'ox, house, camel, door...'

It was a success story though. Apart from ultimately developing into the Latin alphabet, it also gave rise to the Arabic, Hebrew and Cyrillic writing systems and possibly even the writing systems of the Indian subcontinent.

✳ ✳ ✳ ✳ ✳ ✳ ✳ ✳

[o]	Short close [o] is pronounced the same way as long close [oː], only shorter.
Short O	It occurs in Scots words like *cot* [kot], *toll* [tolʸ], *hoch* [hox] and *flocht* [flox] but not in Standard English.

The best way of getting there if you do not have this close [o] sound is by starting with the long round [oː] and the making it shorter.

Alternatively you can start with the short [ɔ] and close your mouth a bit when saying it.

🔖 **Exercise 27.**

Say the following syllables from the previous exercise:

[sdoː]   [hoː]   [broː]   [loː]

Now repeat them but make the vowel only half as long:

[sdo]   [ho]   [bro]   [lo]

Now repeat only the vowel:

[o]   [o]   [o]   [o]

Progress Report

ə	iː	i	ɪ	eː	e	ɛː	ɛ	aː	a
ɔː	ɔ	oː	o	ɤː	ɤ	uː	u	ɯː	ɯ

→70%

Having covered the two *o* sounds of Gaelic, we've only got three more vowels to go and the words now really begin to pile up:

Gaelic	Meaning	Gaelic	Meaning
komə	indifferent	moː moː	moo moo!
ov ov	oh dear!	moːr	big
ə voː	his cow	koː	who?

1.8   The [ɣ:] and [ɣ]

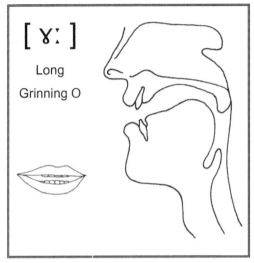

[ɣ:]

Long

Grinning O

Now we're getting into the realm of the exotic. From the point of view of Scots and English anyway.

In fact, it's quite rare amongst the languages of the world.

Geographically the closest (of the major languages) to have this sound is Estonian, then Thai! So if you don't happen to know any native Gaelic speakers, time for some Tom Yam (which incidentally translates as 'boiled-mixed') at your local Thai place and hope for a patient (or bored) waiter/waitress.

And before you start thinking this is just too weird for words, the principle behind the difference between [o:] and [ɣ:] is common. English too has a vowel pair which uses it. The vowels in the words *pun* [pʌn] and *pawn* [pɔ:n] for example are the same[12] except that for [ʌ] your lips are spread (as if you're grinning slightly) and for [ɔ:] they are rounded.

[pʌn]   [pɔ:n]

So, even if you don't like Thai food it isn't too difficult to learn how to make this sound. Gaelic [ɣ:] is like the close [o:] with only one difference - for [ɣ:] you need to have spread lips.

---

[12] Yes, well spotted - the vowel length is also different but in terms of the way the vowel is made, the only difference is the lip rounding.

To make this sound, simply say [oː] (and keep it going) and grin hard at the same time (without moving your tongue!). This will automatically spread your lips into the right position for [ɣː]. This may seem decidedly weird at first but it produces exactly the sound you're aiming for. And if you ever have trouble remembering how to make this sound, go back to the [oː] and grin.

Initially you should really exaggerate the lip spreading. As time passes you will adjust to a more natural degree of spreading.

Do not let yourself be tempted to sidestep this vowel or the [ɯ] vowel (see 1.10). In spite of their oddness (from a Scots/English point of view anyway) they are extremely common in Gaelic and cannot be avoided.

✎ Exercise 28.

Say the following syllables from the previous chapter:

    [sdoː]   [hoː]   [broː]   [loː]

Now repeat them and grin hard at the same time:

    [sdɣː]   [hɣː]   [brɣː]   [lɣː]

Now repeat only the vowel:

    [ɣː]   [ɣː]   [ɣː]   [ɣː]

✎ Exercise 29.

Say the following nonsense syllables out loud and make sure that you are grinning while saying this sound:

ɣː	hɣː
kɣː	pɣː
mɣː	mɣːʃ
fɣː	fɣːl

❄❄❄❄❄❄❄❄

[ɤ]	Same as the [ɤ:] vowel, only short.
Short Grinning O	You can either start with [ɤ:] and make it shorter to get [ɤ] or you can start with short [o] and grin while saying it.

Going between pairs such as [po] and [pɤ] is a good exercise to get your mouth accustomed to moving in this way. As a rule of thumb, if practising these new sounds makes your jaw hurt after a while, you're doing it right. It's like going to the gym after not having been for a long time. Eventually, you'll get (back) into it and the same is true of making new sounds.

✎ Exercise 30.

Say the following syllables from the previous chapter:

[sdo]   [ho]   [bro]   [lo]

Now repeat them and grin hard at the same time:

[sdɤ]   [hɤ]   [brɤ]   [lɤ]

Now repeat only the vowel:

[ɤ]   [ɤ]   [ɤ]   [ɤ]

✎ Exercise 31.

Say the following nonsense syllables out loud and make sure that you are grinning while saying this sound:

ɤ   hɤ

kɤ   pɤ

mɤ   mɤʃ

fɤ   fɤl

Again this is a slightly unusual letter so trace the letter a few times below to get used to it. Note that this symbol does not go below your line of text:

Progress Report									
ə	iː	i	ɪ	eː	e	ɛː	ɛ	aː	a
ɔː	ɔ	oː	o	ɤː	ɤ	uː	u	ɯː	ɯ

➜80%

This sound is fairly common in Gaelic but because we're still short on consonants, we can't add any new Gaelic words right now.

1.9   Long [uː] and short [u]

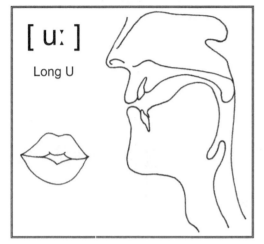

[uː]

Long U

This vowel occurs in Standard English words like *zoo* [zuː], *food* [fuːd], *loo* [luː].

The main characteristic of this sound is that the front of your tongue is very low down. The back of your tongue is raised up high and your lips are nice and round.

Common Mistake: Scots speakers (and speakers of Scottish English[13]) must be careful with this sound. Instead of [uː] some speakers have the [ʉː] sound where the tongue is in the middle the mouth (a **u** sound which sounds almost like the German **ü** vowel). You must make sure that your tongue is quite far back in your mouth (not so far that you start gagging but not far off that point). The same applies to the short [u].

Some Scots examples are *oor* [**u**ːr], *flooer* [fl**u**ːr], *roose* [r**u**ːz], and *doo* [d**u**ː].

---

[13] Scots and Scottish English aren't the same thing but it's difficult to draw a clear line between the two, because the speech of many people is somewhere in between the two. If your everyday language sounds pretty much like what you hear on BBC Scotland everyday, then you're most likely a speaker of Scottish English. If you speak more like Rab C Nesbitt, then you probably speak something closer to Scots.

✎ Exercise 32.

Say the following words:

      zoo [zuː]   moo [muː]   loo [luː]   brew [bruː]

Now repeat only the vowel:

        [uː]   [uː]   [uː]   [uː]

✎ Exercise 33.

Say the following nonsense syllables out loud:

uː	huː
fuː	uːʃ
muː	kuːm
kuː	uːl

Ok, I lied. One more thing about our alphabet. Did you know that the letter **u** is a fairly recent addition to our alphabet? In Roman times there was only one letter representing both [u] and [v] and it was up to the reader to figure which was which. That's why Julius Caesar shows up as GAIVS IVLIVS CAESAR on inscriptions  rather than as GAIUS IULIUS CAESAR. Only in the 14th century people began to use a rounded form of V to distinguish the [u] sound from the [v] sound in writing. That was actually the Goths, believe it or not.

❀❀❀❀❀❀❀❀

| [u]
Short U | You get the short version of this vowel in Scots words like *cooch* [kutʃ], *outgang* [utgaŋ], and *groof* [gruf]. |

This vowel doesn't exist in Standard English as a short vowel. But as with all these long-short pairs, it is the same as [u:] only short.

🔊 Exercise 34.

Say the following syllables from the previous exercise:

      [zu:]   [mu:]   [lu:]   [bru:]

Now say them again but make them only half as long:

      [zu]   [mu]   [lu]   [bru]

Now repeat only the vowel:

      [u]   [u]   [u]   [u]

🔊 Exercise 35.

Say the following nonsense syllables out loud:

u	hu
fu	ful
mu	umə
ku	pu

Progress Report									
ə	iː	i	ɪ	eː	e	ɛː	ɛ	aː	a
ɔː	ɔ	oː	o	ɣː	ɣ	uː	u	ɯː	ɯ

➔90%

Now we **can** add some new words **and** we've only got one more set of vowels to go!

Gaelic	Meaning	Gaelic	Meaning
uːmɪ	a blockhead	ful	blood
uːr	new	ə ruːn	his secret
kuːl	a corner	uməm	about me
kuː	a dog	u	an egg

1.10   The [ɯː] and [ɯ]

[ɯː]

Long
Grinning U

Ok, we're down to the last vowel sound. Not a very common sound in Europe, the nearest languages that also have it are in the Near East. This, incidentally, is not implying that there is a link between these languages.

In any case, this sound doesn't exist in Scots or English. Since you have understood the principle behind making [ɤː], it isn't difficult to make. As before, you need to start with a different sound, in this case [uː]. Keep it going and grin hard (without moving your tongue at all) while you're saying it. Again this will spread your lips wide and produce exactly the sound you are aiming for.

Really exaggerate the lip spreading and as time passes you will adjust to a more natural degree of spreading.

✎ **Exercise 36.**

Say the following syllables from the previous chapter:

[zuː]	[muː]	[luː]	[bruː]

Now repeat them and grin hard at the same time:

[zɯː]	[mɯː]	[lɯː]	[brɯː]

Now repeat only the vowel:

[ɯː]	[ɯː]	[ɯː]	[ɯː]

✎ Exercise 37.

Say the following nonsense syllables out loud and make sure that you are grinning while saying this sound:

ɯː	ɯːm
pɯː	kɯː
mɯː	mɯːl
fɯː	fɯːl

❊❊❊❊❊❊❊❊

[ɯ]

Short Grinning U

Last sound and for good measure you'll learn how to say sushi like a true native speaker of Japanese.

You can start with long [ɯː] and simply make it shorter. Or, you can start with short [u], grin hard while saying it which will give you short [ɯ].

As we mentioned before, [ɤ] and [ɯ] are odd sounds from an English point of view but they are very normal and common in Gaelic so you have to master them. So what about the sushi? Well, the short **u** in sushi is exactly this sound so in good Japanese, it is pronounced [sɯʃi]. So next time you're ordering some, you can impress the waiter with your perfect [ɯ].

✎ Exercise 38.

Say the following syllables from the previous chapter:

[zu]	[mu]	[lu]	[bru]

Now repeat them and grin hard at the same time:

[zɯ]	[mɯ]	[lɯ]	[brɯ]

Now repeat only the vowel:

[ɯ]	[ɯ]	[ɯ]	[ɯ]

✎ Exercise 39.

Say the following nonsense syllables out loud and make sure that you are grinning while saying this sound:

ɯ	nɯ
pɯ	kɯ
mɯ	ɯl
fɯ	fɯl

Another weird letter (an upside down **m** really) so trace the letter a few times below to get used to it:

The good news is that you've now studied all the Gaelic vowels there are - well done indeed!

| Progress Report |||||||||||
★★★100%★★★										
ə	iː	i	ɪ	eː	e	ɛː	ɛ	aː	a
ɔː	ɔ	oː	o	ɤː	ɤ	uː	u	ɯː	ɯ

As this is a common vowel, we can now add quite a lot of new words to our list. Here are a few of them:

Gaelic	Meaning	Gaelic	Meaning
ɯːn	one	mɯːr	an officer
ɯːm	bend!	rɔ vɯː	too foolish
kɯːlə	narrowness	ɯːl	of lime
fɯːvər	a blade	ɯːnan	one person

1.11   More vowel exercises

🐾 Exercise 40.

In this exercise you will hear different words and syllables. Each set of exercises focuses on hearing the difference between closely related sounds.

- Listen to the recordings of the word/syllables.

- Indicate which sound it was you heard.

- Check your results against the key and then listen again and repeat.

Vowel Set 01

	[e]	[eː]	[ɛ]	[ɛː]
01				
02				
03				
04				
05				
06				
07				
08				
09				
10				

Vowel Set 02

	[o]	[o:]	[ɔ]	[ɔ:]
01				
02				
03				
04				
05				
06				
07				
08				
09				
10				

Vowel Set 03

	[a]	[a:]	[ɛ]	[ɛ:]
01				
02				
03				
04				
05				
06				
07				
08				
09				
10				

Vowel Set 04

	[i]	[iː]	[ə]	[e]
01				
02				
03				
04				
05				
06				
07				
08				
09				
10				

Vowel Set 05

	[ɯ]	[ɯː]	[u]	[uː]
01				
02				
03				
04				
05				
06				
07				
08				
09				
10				

1.12 Are you feeling lucky?

Ok, time for a pat on the shoulder and an Islay Malt. That's it, you have all the vowels of Gaelic under your belt now. That wasn't so bad, was it?

Gaelic does have quite a lot of vowels, 20 altogether. If you compare the languages of the world you will find that the smallest number of vowels anywhere is 2 (remember Arrernte?) to moderate cases like Cantonese (7 vowels). The largest number is 24 in !Xū, a Bushman language from Southern Africa, which has 141 sounds in all, the largest set in the world! English is about average with 11 vowels. Not that that makes it any easier but put in perspective, you could have been worse off.

If you want to know what a Bushman language actually sounds like or if you don't believe that is actually possible, get the film *The Gods Must Be Crazy* on DVD!

There are vowels out there which are a lot more complicated to make than the handful we have in Gaelic. Like those where you have to learn how to constrict your pharynx (really deep down in your throat) to make certain vowels, for example in Arabic. Or you could be going for Cantonese, in which case you would have to cope with 7 tones on the 7 vowels.

So, in true Scottish fashion, Rest and Be Thankful! You can now move to the next stage - the consonant sounds.

2.   The consonants

It is important to understand some basic things about how we make sounds because Gaelic has a large number of consonants which are radically different from English consonants. Without knowing what to do with your tongue and the rest of your mouth, there is only a very remote chance that you will get all these sounds right.

We will begin with the familiar and explore the ways in which we make sounds by looking at some English examples.   Then, when we understand what goes on in our mouths, we will move on to the Gaelic consonants.

2.1   How to make a consonant

The way we make sounds is very much like making sounds by blowing into an empty glass bottle. Take a smaller bottle and you get a higher sound, take a larger bottle and you get a deeper sound. Fill part of the same bottle with water and you get a different sound.

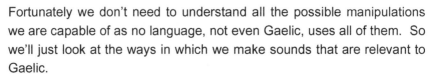

When we humans speak, we basically blow air out from our lungs. If you do just that, you get a very basic [h] sound. You can then manipulate the area above your throat in hundreds of ways to change the sound. You could close your lips for example and they suddenly blow them open. What you then get is a [p] sound.

Fortunately we don't need to understand all the possible manipulations we are capable of as no language, not even Gaelic, uses all of them. So we'll just look at the ways in which we make sounds that are relevant to Gaelic.

On the next page is a picture of the so-called vocal tract. All this means is 'the bits of your body you use for making sounds'. For humans, that is the space between your vocal chords (inside your throat) and your lips and nostrils.

Generally, we use two things to make a speech sound: our tongue and some other part of our mouth (for example our lips). The important points both for Gaelic and English are your:

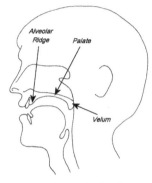

- lips

- teeth

- alveolar ridge (sometimes also called the 'gum ridge'), the bony ledge behind your teeth

- palate (mostly the hard part in the middle of your mouth)

- velum (the back part of your (soft) palate which has 'the dangly bit' hanging from it); its anatomical function is to block off your nasal cavity from your mouth. You may have had the unpleasant experience of coughing while eating getting something lodged 'behind your nose' or even come out via your nose. That happened because when you coughed, your velum got caught out and didn't block properly.

In terms of your tongue, we need to distinguish the following areas:

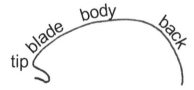

- tip of the tongue (= the very tip of your tongue)

- blade of the tongue (= the front third of your tongue)

- body of the tongue (= the middle part of your tongue)

- back of the tongue (= the far back of your tongue)

Let's look at some examples from English now. When you say the examples, pay attention to which part of your mouth you are using when making these sounds.

■   Labial Sounds

These sounds are made using your lips - or your teeth and your lip, hence the name labial. Examples are:

bee [biː]   moo [muː]   pooh [puː]   foe [fəʊ]   vow [vaʊ]

■   Dental Sounds

These sounds are made at or between your teeth, hence the term dental (think of *dentist*). Examples are:

the [ðə]   thin [θɪn]

■   Alveolar Sounds

These sounds are made at your upper gum ridge (alveola). This is the bony ridge behind your teeth. Touch your upper teeth with your tongue and slide it back - it's the little ridge a bit further back from your teeth. English has a lot of alveolar sounds:

| no [nəʊ] | to [tʊ] | do [dʊ] | so [səʊ] |
| zip [zɪp] | shin [ʃɪn] | rude [ruːd] | lee [liː] |

■   Palatal Sounds

These sounds are made at your palate, hence the term palatal. For most palatal sounds you use the blade or body of your tongue rather than the tip. English has only one true palatal sound but Gaelic has a lot of them as you'll see shortly.

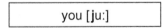
you [juː]

- Velar Sounds

These sounds are made at the far back of our mouth using the back of the tongue and your velum, hence the name velar sounds. Or, looking at it differently, it's the bit of your mouth that meets your tongue for the [g] or [k] sounds. Depending on where you're from, you'll have 3 or possible 4 velar sounds in your English:

goo [guː]	coot [kuːt]	bingo [bɪŋgəʊ]	loch [lɔx]

- Nasal Sounds

A sound is nasal when air escapes through your nose rather than your mouth. English has three nasal sounds:

moo [muː]	no [nəʊ]	bingo [bɪŋgəʊ]

And yes, well spotted. A sound can be in more than one category. For example, [m] is both a labial and a nasal sound.

✎ Exercise 41.

Decide where the underlined sounds are made in the following words:

	labial (lips)	dental (teeth)	alveolar (tooth ridge)	palatal (palate)	velar (at the back)	nasal (nose)
si̱p						
f̱lit						
ti̱me						
c̱reel						
ẏoung						
eeḻ						
ġone						
ḏish						
bon̲n̲y						
bot̲h̲er						
ḇairn						
r̲ain						
stic̲k̲						
wid̲t̲h						
mer̲r̲y						
ba̱g						
t̲his						
m̲ush						
bu̲n̲g						
ġob						
w̲eek						
ḵirk						
hiv̲e						
loc̲h̲						
cousi̱n						

2.2   The consonants of Gaelic

There are various ways in which one can order the consonants of Gaelic into groups. When teaching the sounds of Gaelic this is often done alphabetically but in many ways this is really unhelpful because the order of the letters in the alphabet is rather arbitrary. Because, as you now know, the order was cooked up thousands of years ago.

For example, you could order the consonants of English alphabetically: b, c, ch, d, f, g, h, j, k, l, m, n, p, r, s, sh, t, th, v, w, x, y, z. To someone who already speaks the language and learned their 'letters' in school, that makes perfect sense. But if you're new to the language and are trying to understand the important distinctions between these sounds, it makes a lot more sense to order them in logical groups. Logical in the way they are made, for example: p ~ b (**p**at ~ **b**at), t ~ d (**t**uck ~ **d**uck), k ~ g (**k**ill ~ **g**ill), ch ~ j (**ch**oke ~ **j**oke), f ~ v (**f**ew ~ **v**iew), s ~ sh (**s**in ~ **sh**in), th ~ th (**th**igh ~ **th**y) and so on.

Because it makes sense to order them into such groups when we are learning new sounds, that is exactly what we will do in this book.

2.3   The Gaelic plosives

The first group of sounds we will look at are called plosives. The word is connected to the word 'explosive' because in order to make them, you block your vocal tract somewhere (for example by closing your lips) which it then suddenly 'explodes' open again. This 'explosion' causes a sound. Very much like a pop-gun.

Say the English word **p**ig and pay attention to what your lips are doing for the **p**. First, they both come together to close off your mouth and then they suddenly explode to make the **p**. Hence the term plosives. English has a number of these: **p**oo, **b**ooh, **d**o, **t**wo, **k**ill, **g**ill…

So all the sounds in the first section (after we sort out the issue of voicing in the next section) are going to involve your mouth going pop in some fashion.

2.3.1   Voicing

This has nothing to do with the voicing you get with certain musical instruments like organ pipes where you try to get the pitch/tone/colour right. Or very little anyway.

When it comes to making speech sounds, voicing has something to do with vibrations (or lack of them) in your throat. Start by putting your hand on your throat and saying fff. You will notice that there is no vibration in your throat. For that reason, [f] is considered to be a voiceless sound.

Now do the same with vvv. You will notice that there is vibration this time. For exactly that reason we consider [v] to be a voiced sound. Alternate the two a few times to get a feel for the difference: fff vvv fff vvv fff vvv.

You can also experience this by putting your fingers in your ears tightly and saying vvv. You will hear a strong buzzing noise whereas for fff you won't hear anything.

These vibrations are produced in your throat by two muscles called vocal chords. These can either vibrate or sit still when you make a speech sound. If they vibrate, they make the buzzing noise, the 'voicing'. It's like a flesh and blood version of a chanter reed - if you've never seen one in action ask a friend who has bagpipes to get the reed out and demonstrate.

This voicing effect is most notable with sounds like fff and vvv because you can keep them going but it also happens with other sounds. You can easily feel this difference by placing your hand on your throat and saying word pairs like **g**ood and **c**ould. Pay close attention to the g and c. You will notice that in **g**ood your throat is producing the vibration throughout the word whereas in **c**ould there is no vibration until you reach the *ould* bit. Hence [g] is a voiced sound and [k] is a voiceless sound. In Gaelic on the other hand b d and g are voiceless[14]. I'll explain in a moment how you can make these sounds quite easily.

The concept of voicing is important. Because for almost all speech sounds (certainly in Gaelic[15], English and Scots) you use air from your lungs coming past these muscles in your throat, it's one of the most basic ways in which human languages differentiate sounds. You can easily see the effects of this by considering a few examples from English where getting the voicing wrong will totally change the meaning of a word: ho**p** ~ ho**b**, pi**g** ~ pi**ck**, ba**d** ~ ba**t**…

I will explain later how and why that is even more important for Gaelic but for now all that is important is that you understand the basic principle of voicing – vibration on or off in your throat.

---

[14] Or 'devoiced'. Both terms mean pretty much the same thing, at least for our purposes here and fortunately we don't have to settle the scientific debate on which term is better!

[15] As opposed to sucking air in to make a sound. Interestingly, the 'Highland Gasp' is an example of a European language using exactly this mechanism. Gaelic is such a treasure trove of interesting linguistics!

2.3.2   P sounds

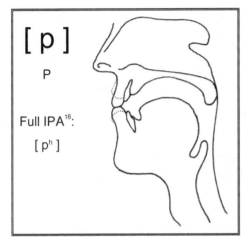

[p]

P

Full IPA[16]:

[pʰ]

This sound shouldn't be problematic because you get it in English and Scots. The [p] sound occurs in Scots words like *pairt* [pɛrt], *puir* [peːr], *pavie* [peːvɪ], *plowt* [plʌut] and in English words like *pig* [pɪg], *puff* [pʌf] or *pad* [pad].

Notice the puff of air after the [p]? This puff is called aspiration and is important because (seen from the English point of view) it shows up in unexpected places in Gaelic.

To make sure you are getting this sound right, hold a piece of paper close to your mouth and say *pen*. There should be a puff of air moving the paper. If your paper doesn't move at all, practice until it does.

✎ **Exercise 42.**

Hold your hand in front of your mouth (to check for the puff of air) and say the following words out loud:

pig [pɪg]   puff [pʌf]   pad [pad]   pin [pɪn]

Now repeat the first part of every word:

[pɪ]   [pʌ]   [pa]   [pɪ]

---

[16] We'll be using a slightly simplified version of the IPA to make the phonetics less 'cluttered' but without losing any accuracy for the purposes of this course. I will just list the full IPA symbol once for each sound for the benefit of people who have a lot of experience reading full IPA.

✎ Exercise 43.

Say the following words and nonsense syllables out loud:

panə	pɔnə
pɛnɪ	pinɪ
pumə	puːmə
pul	pɔl

❈ ❈ ❈ ❈ ❈ ❈ ❈ ❈

[pj]

PJ

Full IPA:

[pʰj]

The second sound also occurs in Scots and English.

Its two sounds close together really[17]: a [p] followed by a [j] (the same sound you get in *yes* [jɛs].

Scots has this sound in *peuch* [pjux], *pewl* [pjuːlʸ] and *peuther* [pjutər] and English in words like *puce* [pjuːs], *pew* [pjuː] and *pubic* [pjuːbɪk].

✎ Exercise 44.

Hold your hand in front of your mouth (to check for the aspiration) and say the following words out loud:

puce [pjuːs]   pew [pjuː]   pubic [pjuːbɪk]

Now repeat the first part of every word:

[pjuː]   [pjuː]   [pjuː]

Now repeat only the [pj] sound:

[pj]   [pj]   [pj]

---

[17] Something linguists call a 'unitary sound'.

✎ Exercise 45.

Say the following words and nonsense syllables out loud:

pjɔ	pjɔː
pju	pjuː
pjaː	pjɔ
pja	pjau

Progress Report

➜5%

p pj	b bj	t tʲ	d dʲ	k kʲ	g gʲ
m mj	ŋg ŋʲgʲ	N Nʲ n	L Lʲ l	R r rʲ	f fj
v vj	s ʃ	x ç	ɣ ʝ j	h hj	

Up until now we were quite restricted in what we could say because even though we had covered all the vowels, we only had 8 consonants to work with which you could say from the start. This means that from now on with each consonant our repertoire of words which we can say will really expand.

Gaelic	Meaning	Gaelic	Meaning
pian	pain	əm parav	Cape Wrath
pilə	a pill	panə	a pan
puh	a puff	pɔlan	pollen

Ready for another bit of trivia? P sounds are amongst the most common consonants in the world's languages. Nonetheless, Gaelic managed to misplace this sound early in its history and has only recently re-acquired it. *Fadó fadó* as the Irish would say, there once was a language called Proto-Indo-European. This was the ancestor language of all modern Indo-European languages, from Portuguese, Icelandic and Irish to Russian, Kurdish, Persian and Bengali, spoken some 5000 years ago somewhere near the Black Sea. Linguists have worked out that this language had 12 stop consonants (the ^{h} indicates a very breathy sound and the ^{w} something called lip rounding):

p	t	k	k^w
b	d	g	g^w
b^h	d^h	g^h	g^{hw}

The first thing the Celts did was reduce the system by merging the third row with the second row, leaving us with:

p	t	k	k^w
b	d	g	g^w

They then got carried away and in something called Late Common Celtic, they also dropped the [p]:

	t	k	k^w
b	d	g	g^w

Now this is where it gets interesting. Old Brythonic (the ancestor of Welsh, Cornish and Breton) took the [k^w] and turned it into a **p** because the ^{w} bit made it sound very much like a **p**.

p	t	k	
b	d	g	g^w

That's why Welsh, Cornish and Breton have had a [p] for quite some time now.

The Gaels had other ideas. They decided that [p] was just too cumbersome and did away with it, end of story.

For example, the word for father has **p, b, f** or **v** in most Indo-European languages: English *father*, German *Vater*, French *père*, Greek πατέρας, Kurdish *bav* and so on. But no such thing in Gaelic and Irish *athair* [ahərʲ] or Manx *ayr* [e:ar].

In addition to that, they also merged last two columns, so [kʷ] became [k] and [gʷ] became [g]:

	t	k
b	d	g

So, no chance of a [p]. That's why, in the early days, when Irish borrowed words which had a [p] in them, it turned them into [k] instead. So Latin *Patricius* became Coċṗaiʒe, *Pascha* 'Easter' became Cáirc and *pallium* 'cloak' gave us caiLLe 'veil' and hence caiLLeċ 'woman of religion' - and our modern *cailleach* 'old woman'.

Through a combination of borrowing words with **p** (and keeping the **p**) and something called backformation (see 4.5.3) Irish, Gaelic and Manx got the [p] back but to this day, [p] is not a very common sound (just count the number of pages in your Gaelic dictionary that begin with **c** and those with **p**...) and for the most part occurs in loanwords. It's also a fun way to see the relationship between Welsh words and Gaelic words. If you see a Welsh word with a **p**, substitute that with **c** or **ch** (or drop it) and see if it looks familiar: *pump ~ còig, pysgod ~ iasg, plant ~ clann, pren ~ crann, Pasg ~ Càisg, pedwar ~ ceithir, pen ~ ceann, pwy ~ có, pesychiad~ casad, pryd ~ cruth, pryf ~ cruimh...*

You may have heard people talk about Gaelic, Irish and Manx being 'Q-Celtic' and Welsh, Breton and Cornish being 'P-Celtic'. That's what that is about, the former have **c** or **q** (for example Irish *cúig*, Gaelic *còig*, Manx *queig*) where the latter have **p** (for example Welsh *pump*, Breton *pemp* Cornish *pymp*). But back to the topic of pronunciation.

2.3.3   B sounds

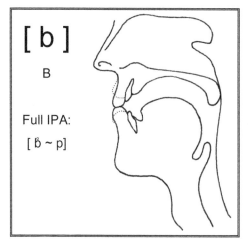

[b]

B

Full IPA:

[b̥ ~ p]

This sound doesn't occur on its own in English. Yes, I know that sounds weird but you'll see in a moment what I mean by that.   There are different ways of getting to the correct pronunciation.

The technical name for this sound is 'devoiced b'. You will remember from the section on voicing (2.3.1) that voiced means that your vocal chords are vibrating.   Now English and Gaelic **b** are similar but not the same. For the English **b** your vocal chords are vibrating, it's a voiced sound. But for Gaelic **b** there is no vibration, so it's a voiceless sound.   So the 'chanter reed' in your throat isn't doing anything for this sound.

Method 1: There is one place where this sound occurs in English - in combination with **s**: *speed* [sbi:d], *spike* [sbaɪk], *spoon* [sbu:n].   The same also applies to Scots: *spae* [sbe:], *speir* [sbir], *sprack* [sbrak], *spraich* [sbrex].   Start by saying one of these words and gradually dropping all other sounds until you are left only with the [b].

sbi:d ⇒	sbi: ⇒	sb ⇒	b
sbaɪk ⇒	sbaɪ ⇒	sb ⇒	b
sbu:n ⇒	sbu: ⇒	sb ⇒	b

Method 2: The other way of getting there is by constricting your throat so no air can pass through. Hold your Adam's apple with your hand so you can feel the constriction. Then, without releasing the constriction say b. The result will be [b]. Some people find it helpful to imagine that their throat is 'missing' and to produce this [b] with their lips only.

You will know that you're making the right sound if you hold one hand on your throat and the other in front of your mouth and can feel neither vibration in your throat (for the **b**) nor a puff of air.

To a native speaker of English, this [b] will sound like something halfway between a **b** and a **p** - which it is, so that's what you are aiming for.

This may sound like nit-picking but having a voiceless [b] is vital to Gaelic pronunciation and if you get it wrong and make it too 'soft', it's a clear giveaway of bad pronunciation.

✎ **Exercise 46.**

Say the following words and nonsense syllables out loud.

ba	bo:
abə	obə
kab	ubə
bi:b	buɯ:

❋ ❋ ❋ ❋ ❋ ❋ ❋ ❋

[bj]

BJ

Full IPA:

[b̥j ~ pj]

This sound is exactly like [b] except that it is followed by a [j] sound (just what we had with [pj] earlier).

This sound also occurs in Scots *speuchan* [sb̥juxən], *spue* [sb̥ju:] and *speug* [sb̥jug] and in English after *s: dispute* [dɪ'sb̥ju:t], *spew* [sb̥ju:], *spurious* [sb̥juərɪəs].

Start by saying one of these words and gradually dropping all other sounds until you are left only with the [bj].

dɪsbjuːt	sbju ⇒	sbj ⇒	**bj**
sbjuː	sbju ⇒	sbj ⇒	**bj**
sbjʊərɪəs	sbjʊə ⇒	sbj ⇒	**bj**

As with [b] you will know that you're making the right sound if you hold one hand on your throat and the other in front of your mouth and can feel neither vibration in your throat (for the **b**) nor a puff of air.

✎ Exercise 47.

Say the following words and nonsense syllables out loud:

bju	bjuː
bja	bjaː
bjɔ	bjɔː
bjo	bjoː

Progress Report

➜10%

p pj	**b bj**	t tʲ	d d	k kʲ	g gʲ
m mj	ŋg ŋʲgʲ	N Nʲ n	L Lʲ l	R r rʲ	f fj
v vj	s ʃ	x ç	ɣ ɟ j	h hj	

Good news! We're getting to the stage now where we can only give you example words because there are just so many things that you can pronounce now that I can't list them all here.

Gaelic	Meaning	Gaelic	Meaning
ɔːban	a little bay	bjɔːl	oral
baːn	white	bjɔː	alive
boː	a cow	bruː	a belly
boban	a daddy	maːb	vilify!

2.3.4   T sounds

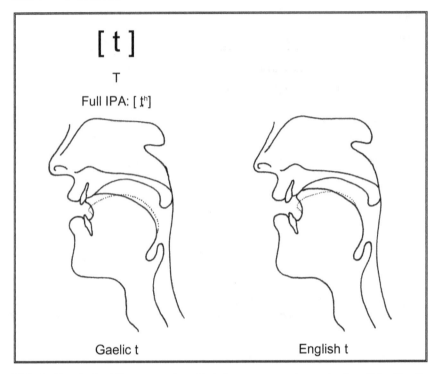

[t]

T

Full IPA: [tʰ]

Gaelic t   English t

This is the first of five sounds which form a very important unit in Gaelic on a different (linguistic) level. It is part of a group of sounds called the dentals which all have one thing in common: your tongue touches your (upper) teeth when making these sounds.

Fortunately it is the easiest thing in the world to remember which sounds are dental in Gaelic. Just take the word dental and underline all the consonants: DeNTaLS. These are the Gaelic dental sounds. Handy, isn't it?

Now, the first sound of this group we're looking at does not exist in English and it goes by the technical name of 'dental t'. It is similar to English t, for example in *tea* [tiː] but for Gaelic t your tongue must touch the base of your upper teeth. Both for English and Gaelic t there is a puff of air after the t sound (called aspiration, by the way).

To your ears (unless you happen to be a native speaker) this may sound exactly like a Scots or English **t** but that to a native speaker the difference will be very obvious. Remember, to most Germans, saying [s] or [f] instead of **th** sounds perfectly reasonable but native speakers of English probably wouldn't agree.

🖎 **Exercise 48.**

Say the following words and nonsense syllables out loud:

ta	ta:
tumə	tu:mə
tɔum	tomə
tan	tanə

✻✻✻✻✻✻✻✻

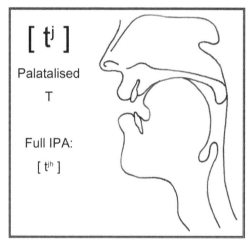

[tʲ]

Palatalised

T

Full IPA:

[tʲʰ]

This sound doesn't occur in Scots or English at all. It's called a palatalised **t** because it is essentially a **t** that has been dragged all the way back to your palate. Again there is more than one way of getting to this sound.

Before we get started though a quick note. The way this sound is exactly made varies a bit from dialect to dialect. But it's definitely not the same as a certain English sound you might be thinking of. So go with these exercises to get a good feel for the Gaelic palatalised **t** and be aware you may hear slightly different things from native speakers.

Method 1: The easiest way of correctly producing this sound is to take an English word beginning with **y**, for example *yeast* [jiːst]. Say it a few times and pay close attention to where and how your tongue is approaching the roof of your palate. You will notice that first of all you use the body of your tongue while the tip is pointing down and touching your lower teeth. Your tongue approaches your palate, well back from your alveolar ridge.

In the next step you need to prefix a **t** to the word yeast. When you say this combined form, make sure that you make the **t** in the same position as the **y**. Do not move your tongue forward or point it upwards for the normal position for English **t**. The result should be a sound vaguely similar to the English [ʧ] sound (as in *cheese* [ʧiːz]) but made with the body of your tongue against your palate.

Method 2: You can also get there by taking an English [t] and simply saying further back in your mouth at your palate instead of its usual place at your alveolar ridge. Again your tongue needs to point down and touch your lower teeth. Some people also find it helpful to think of this sound as a t that is being squeezed against the palate.

Method 3: If everything else fails, get a bit of rice paper and stick it on your tongue as shown in the picture. If you can't get rice paper, a fragment of a potato crisp (your favourite flavour, though not thick/crinkle cut) will work too though not quite as well.

 Now start by saying **y** (as in **y**east). The rice paper should stick to the roof of your mouth. Leave your tongue in that position and without moving it, say a t at that very spot in your mouth. Again, your tongue needs to point down and touch your lower teeth. The result will be a perfect [tʲ]. If the rice paper doesn't stick to the roof of your mouth, say a t but instead of using the tip of your tongue as you're used to, only use the bit of your tongue the paper is on. The result will also be a perfect [tʲ].

English speakers tend to produce the [ʧ] sound (as in *cheese* [ʧiːz]) and round their lips at the same time. Also the tip of your tongue points upwards. In Gaelic you should never round your lips for the [tʲ] sound or point your tongue upwards. Initially you're best off grinning slightly while saying [tʲ] which will keep your lips from rounding.

✎ Exercise 49.

Say the following words and nonsense syllables out loud:

tʲu	tʲu:
tʲi:	tʲɛ
tʲɯ:	tʲiəm
tʲe	tʲe:

Progress Report
→15%

p pj	b bj	t tʲ	d dʲ	k kʲ	g gʲ
m mj	ŋg ŋʲgʲ	N Nʲ n	L Lʲ l	R r rʲ	f fj
v vj	s ʃ	x ç	ɣ ɟ j	h hj	

T sounds are common and important, so we can add lots of new words:

Gaelic	Meaning	Gaelic	Meaning
tɔl	a desire	tʲuh	thick
tanə	thin	tʲe:	a female
tu:m	dip!	tʲelə	a lime
tul	a flood	tʲi:	a purpose

2.3.5   D sounds

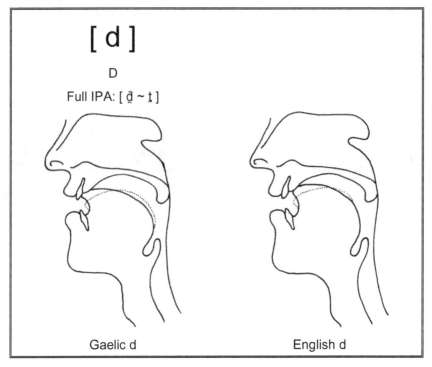

[d]

D

Full IPA: [d̪ ~ t̪]

Gaelic d   English d

This is our second dental sound and it also does not occur in Scots or English. There are different ways of getting to the correct pronunciation of it. What I told you about [t̪] also applies, so what you'll hear may vary a bit, but go with the exercises for now.

You will remember from the chapter on voicing (2.3.1) that voiced means that your vocal chords are vibrating. For Gaelic **d** there is no vibration and your tongue has to touch the base of your upper teeth. Scots/English **d** and Gaelic **d** are similar but not the same. For the Scots/English **d** your vocal chords are vibrating, so it's a voiced sound and your tongue touches your gum ridge to make the **d**, not your teeth.

Method 1: There is one environment in which very similar sounds occurs in English - in combination with **s**: *start* [sdaːrt], *step* [sdɛp], *stone* [sdoːn]. Start by saying one of these words even though it's not 'natural for English', make your tongue touch your teeth for the **s** and the **t**. Then gradually drop all other sounds until you are left only with the [d].

sdart ⇒	sda ⇒	sd ⇒	d
sdɛp ⇒	sdɛ ⇒	sd ⇒	d
sdoːn ⇒	sdo ⇒	sd ⇒	d

Method 2: The other way of getting there is by constricting your throat so no air can pass through. Hold your Adam's apple with your hand so you can feel the constriction. Then, without releasing the constriction say **d** (with your tongue touching your teeth though). The result will be [d]. Some people find it helpful to imagine that their throat is 'missing' and to produce this [d] with their lips only.

Method 3: There is one place where exactly this **d** sound occurs in English but it depends on your variety of English. In these varieties, the **d** before **th** in words like *hundredth* [hʌndrəd̪θ], *width* [wɪd̪θ], *breadth* [brɛd̪θ] is voiceless, unaspirated and dental. If you pronounce these words with the tongue touching your teeth for the **d** then all you need to do is drop off all other sounds in a word like *width* until you are just left with the hard [d] sound.

You will know that you're making the right sound if you hold one hand on your throat and the other in front of your mouth and can feel neither vibration in your throat (for the **d**) nor a puff of air.

To a native speaker of English, this [d] will sound like something halfway between an **d** and a **t** - which it is, so that's what you are aiming for. This may sound like nit-picking but having a voiceless and dental [d] is vital to Gaelic pronunciation and another clear giveaway of bad pronunciation.

✎ Exercise 50.

Say the following words and nonsense syllables out loud:

da	adə
ad	aːd
bɔd	mɔːd
fuːd	eːd

❋ ❋ ❋ ❋ ❋ ❋ ❋ ❋

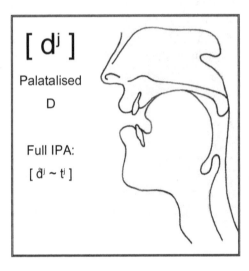

[dʲ]

Palatalised

D

Full IPA:

[dʲ ~ tʲ]

Again, Scots and English sounds are no help here. There are two ways of getting to this sound.

You may have noticed that this is yet another sound which is devoiced in Gaelic when the closest sound in Scots and English is voiced. In fact, Gaelic doesn't have any of the voiced stops you get in Scots and English (**b**, **d** and **g**). In Gaelic these are all devoiced.

Method 1: The easiest way of correctly producing this sound is to take a [tʲ] and get rid of the aspiration (the puff of air). Hold your hand in front of your mouth and say [tʲ]. You will feel a strong puff of air. Now try this again and again until you can say this sound, just without the puff of air.

As with [b], if you're having problems getting rid of the puff of air start by constricting your throat so no air can pass through. Hold your Adam's apple with your hand so you can feel the constriction. Then, without releasing the constriction say [tʲ]. The result will be [dʲ]. Some people find it helpful to imagine that their throat is 'missing' and to produce this [dʲ] with their tongue and palate only.

Method 2: You can also go back to the rice paper. Get a bit and stick it on your tongue as shown in the picture.

Now start by saying **y** (as in *yeast* [jiːst]). Hopefully the rice paper will stick to the roof of your mouth. Leave your tongue in that position and without moving it, say a [d] (the voiceless **d** but your tongue doesn't touch your teeth for this one) at that very spot in your mouth. For this sound too, the tip of your tongue is pointing down and touching your lower teeth. The result will be a perfect [dʲ]. If the rice paper doesn't stick to the roof of your mouth, say a [d] but instead of using the tip of your tongue as you're used to, only use the bit of your tongue the paper is on. The result will also be a perfect [dʲ].

The result in both cases will be a sound vaguely similar to the English [dʒ] sound (as in *juice* [dʒuːs]) but made with the blade of your tongue against your palate. English speakers tend to round their lips at the same time and point their tongue upwards. In Gaelic you should never round your lips for the [dʲ] sound or point your tongue up. Initially you're best off grinning slightly while saying [dʲ] which will keep your lips from rounding.

✎ **Exercise 51.**

Say the following words and nonsense syllables out loud:

dʲɔ	dʲɔ:
dʲi:dʲ	dʲu:dʲ
madʲə	adʲ
dʲe	dʲe:

Progress Report

→20%

p pj	b bj	t tʲ	d dʲ	k kʲ	g gʲ
m mj	ŋg ŋʲgʲ	N Nʲ n	L Lʲ l	R r rʲ	f fj
v vj	s ʃ	x ç	ɣ ɟ j	h hj	

Here are some examples involving the new sounds:

Gaelic	Meaning	Gaelic	Meaning
du:n	a fortress	dʲɔ:	breath
dad	anything	dʲu:dʲ	shy
fa:d	a peat	kudʲ	some
fu:dər	powder	madʲə	piece of wood

2.3.6   K sounds

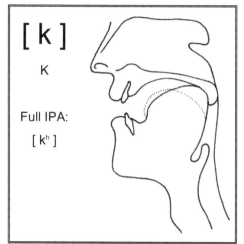

[k]

K

Full IPA:

[kʰ]

Good news. The last seven sounds we looked at were all new but you can relax a little for this one because it is very straightforward.

It is the same [k] you get in Scots *ca* [kaː], *cadger* [kadʒər], *connach* [kɔnəx] and *ken* [ken] and in English words like *cat* [kæt], *cow* [kau] and *custard* [kʌstəd].

Even though you already know this sound well and won't have any trouble making it, say the examples again though and pay very close attention to how this sound is formed. You will notice that the root of your tongue touches the top of your mouth somewhere 'at the back'. That place is called your velum. It's important for you to remember this position in your mouth because you will need this for a few other sounds later on which don't exist in English but use this location.

✎ Exercise 52.

Say the following words and nonsense syllables out loud:

ku	kuː
ko	koː
kau	kaum
kamə	komə

❋ ❋ ❋ ❋ ❋ ❋ ❋ ❋

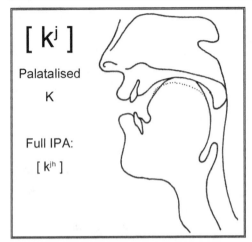

[kʲ]

Palatalised

K

Full IPA:

[kʲʰ]

Another sound which doesn't exist in Scots and English. It is a [k] that you make in the middle of your mouth at your palate instead of the back of your mouth at your velum. There's a variety of ways which will get you there.

Method 1: The easiest way of producing this sound is to take an English word beginning with **y**, for example *yeast* [jiːst]. Say it a few times and pay close attention to where and how your tongue is approaching the roof of your palate. You will notice that you use the body of your tongue to approach your palate while the tip of your tongue is pointing down and touching your lower teeth.

In the next step you need to prefix a **k** to the word yeast. When you say this combined form, make sure that you make the **k** roughly in the same position as the **y**. Do not move your tongue backward for the normal position for the **k** sound or curve it upwards.

Method 2: You can also get there by taking a [k] and simply saying further forward in your mouth at your palate instead of its usual place at the back. Again your tongue needs to point down and touch your lower teeth. Some people also find it helpful to think of this sound as a **k** that is being squeezed against the palate.

Method 3: Get a bit of rice paper and stick it on your tongue as shown in the picture.

Now start by saying **y** (as in *yeast* [ji:st]). Hopefully the rice paper will stick to the roof of your mouth. Leave your tongue in that position and without moving it, say a **k** at that very spot in your mouth. Again your tongue needs to point down and touch your lower teeth. The result will be a perfect [kʲ]. If the rice paper doesn't stick to the roof of your mouth, say a **k** but instead of using the back of your tongue as you're used to, only use the bit of your tongue the paper is on. The result will also be a perfect [kʲ].

The result should be a sound vaguely similar to the English [kj] sound (as in **c**ute [**kj**u:t]) but with the crucial difference that in Gaelic [kʲ] is one sound whereas English [kj] consists of two sounds, a [k] closely followed by a [j]. That means that for Gaelic your tongue goes upwards, touches the roof of your mouth, makes the [kʲ] and comes down again. In English, your tongue goes up at the back to make the [k], then slides forward to make the [j] and then comes down again.

So, if your tongue is sliding around for this sound, you're not doing it quite right.

✎ Exercise 53.

Say the following words and nonsense syllables out loud:

kʲe	kʲe:
kʲi	kʲɛ:
kʲa	kʲa:
kʲɔ	kʲɔ:

Progress Report

→26%

p pj	b bj	t tʲ	d dʲ	k kʲ	g gʲ
m mj	ŋg ŋʲgʲ	N Nʲ n	L Lʲ l	R r rʲ	f fj
v vj	s ʃ	x ç	ɣ ɟ j		h hj

Here are some examples for you with the new sounds:

Gaelic	Meaning	Gaelic	Meaning
kaːr	a car	kʲuːl	of music
kuː	a dog	kʲi.ə	a quay
koː	who?	kʲiad	a hundred
kaman	a shinty stick	kʲeːm	a step

2.3.7   G sounds

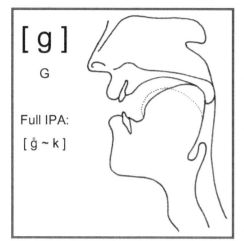

[g]

G

Full IPA:

[g̊ ~ k]

Normally Scots and English **g** is a voiced sound. And again, in Gaelic it's hard and voiceless. And there is again one place where precisely this sound shows up in English so it's not too bad.

You probably feel like putting me on fast forward when I point out yet again that voiced means that your vocal chords are vibrating.   If that is the case, well done to you! It means you have remembered what voicing is all about and, as I keep saying, it's important in Gaelic.

Method 1: The one environment in which this sounds occurs in Scots and English is in combination with **s**. Scots has it in words like *skiddle* [sgɪdlʸ], *skate* [sge:t], *scaud* [sgɑd] and *skoosh* [sgu:ʃ] and Standard English in *skunk* [sgʌŋk], *skin* [sgɪn] and *sky* [sgaɪ]. Start by saying one of these words and gradually dropping all other sounds until you are left only with the [g].

sge:t ⇒	sge: ⇒	sg ⇒	**g**
sgɪn ⇒	sgɪ ⇒	sg ⇒	**g**
sgaɪ ⇒	sga ⇒	sg ⇒	**g**

Method 2: The other way of getting there is by constricting your throat so no air can pass through. Hold your Adam's apple with your hand so you can feel the constriction. Then, without releasing the constriction say **g**. The result will be a nice hard [g]. Some people find it helpful to imagine that their throat is 'missing' and to produce this [g] with their lips only.

You will know that you're making the right sound if you hold one hand on your throat and the other in front of your mouth and can feel neither vibration in your throat (for the **g**) nor a puff of air.

To a native speaker of English, this [g] will sound like something halfway between a **g** and a **k** - which it is, so that's what you are aiming for. Having a voiceless [g] is vital to Gaelic pronunciation and another clear giveaway of bad pronunciation because getting this wrong, along with [d] and [b] will make your Gaelic sound unnaturally soft to native speakers.

If you have ever heard someone speak English with a heavy Brazilian accent, you'll have an idea of how soft your Gaelic would sound to a Gael.

✎ **Exercise 54.**

Say the following words and nonsense syllables out loud:

gu	gu:g
agə	bagə
ɯg	ɯ:g
mug	mugə

❆ ❆ ❆ ❆ ❆ ❆ ❆ ❆

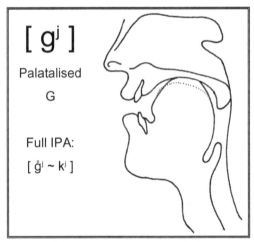

[gʲ]

Palatalised

G

Full IPA:

[g̊ʲ ~ kʲ]

Another sound which doesn't occur in Scots or English. There are two good ways of getting to this sound.

Method 1: The easiest way of making this sound is to take a [kʲ] and get rid of the aspiration (the puff of air). Hold a piece of paper in front of your mouth and say [kʲ]. The paper will move from the puff of air. Now try this again and again until you can say it without a puff of air moving the paper.

As with [b] and [d], if you're having problems getting rid of the puff of air start by constricting your throat so no air can pass through. Hold your Adam's apple with your hand so you can feel the constriction. Then, without releasing the constriction say [kʲ]. The result will be [gʲ]. Some people find it helpful to imagine that their throat is 'missing' and to produce this [gʲ] with their tongue and palate only.

Method 2: You can also go back to the rice paper. Get a bit and stick it on your tongue as shown in the picture.

Now start by saying **y** (as in *yeast* [jiːst]). Hopefully the rice paper will stick to the roof of your mouth. Leave your tongue in that position and without moving it, say a hard Gaelic [g] at that very spot in your mouth. Again your tongue needs to point down and touch your lower teeth. The result will be a perfect [gʲ]. If the rice paper doesn't stick to the roof of your mouth, say a [g] but instead of using the back of your tongue as you normally do for [k], only use the bit of your tongue the paper is on. The result will also be a perfect [gʲ].

In both cases the sound will be vaguely similar to the English [gj] you get in words like *angular* [æŋgjʊlə] but with the crucial difference that in Gaelic [gʲ] is one hard sound whereas English [gj] is soft and two sounds, a [g] followed by a [j]. So for Gaelic your tongue goes up, touches the roof of your mouth, makes the [gʲ] and comes down again. In English, your tongue goes up at the back to make the [g], then slides forward to make the [j] and then comes down. So this is another case where if your tongue is sliding around for this sound, you're not doing it quite right yet.

✎ **Exercise 55.**

Say the following words and nonsense syllables out loud:

gʲe	gʲeː
gʲɔ	gʲɔː
igʲə	bigʲə
ɛgʲ	ɛgʲə

Progress Report

→31%

p pⁱ	b bⁱ	t tʲ	d dʲ	k kʲ	g gʲ

m mʲ	ŋg ŋʲgʲ	N Nʲ n	L Lʲ l	R r rʲ	f fʲ

v vʲ	s ʃ	x ç	ɣ ʝ j	h hʲ

Here are a few examples which use the new sounds:

Gaelic	Meaning	Gaelic	Meaning
gɔrɔm	blue	gʲilə	whiteness
bagə	a bag	gʲin	none (of things)
gob	a beak	bugʲə	softness
gog gog	cluck cluck!	bigʲəd	smallness

2.4   The nasals and How to make a linguist drool

As the name 'nasals' suggests, this has indeed something to do with your nose. The big thing about (most) nasal consonants is that air doesn't pass through your mouth. Instead, it comes out through your nose. Try saying mmmm or nnnn and you will notice the air coming through your nose while your lips are closed. This also gives sounds a nasal quality which will be important later on.

We'll come to the bit about making a linguist drool in a moment.

2.4.1   M sounds

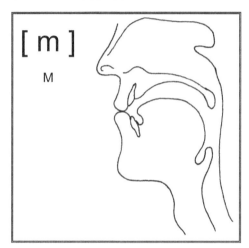

This sound is quite straightforward for Scots and English speakers.

It is exactly the same [m] sound that you get in Scots *man* [man], *mercat* [mɛrkət] and *muckle* [mʌklˠ].

In Standard English, you get it in words like *man* [mæn] or *month* [mʌnθ].

🖎 **Exercise 56.**

Say the following words and nonsense syllables out loud.

ma	ma:
aum	amə
kaum	kamə
me	mi:

❋❋❋❋❋❋❋

| [mj]

MJ | This sound also occurs in both languages. It's simply an [m] followed by a [j] (as we had with [pj] and [bj] previously). |

Scots has it in *meuggle* [mjuglʲ], *mew* [mju:], *mutuum* [mjutjuʌm] and *mure* [mju:r] and in Standard English *Munich* [mjunɪç], *music* [mju:sɪk] and *mule* [mju:l].

✎ Exercise 57.

Say the following words out loud:

      Munich [**mj**unɪç]   music [**mj**u:zɪk]   mule [**mj**u:l]

Now repeat the first part of every word:

      [**mj**u]   [**mj**u:]   [**mj**u:]

Now repeat only the [mj] sound:

      [**mj**]   [**mj**]   [**mj**]

✎ Exercise 58.

Say the following words and nonsense syllables out loud:

mju	mju:
mja	mjau
mjɔ	mjɔ:
mjo	mjɔ:

Progress Report

→31%

p pj	b bj	t tʲ	d dʲ	k kʲ	g gʲ
m mj	ŋg ŋʲgʲ	N Nʲ n	L Lʲ l	R r rʲ	f fj
v vj	s ʃ	x ç	ɣ ʝ j		h hj

Here are a few examples which use the new sounds:

Gaelic	Meaning	Gaelic	Meaning
madʲə	a stick	miad	size
mugə	a mug	nam	in my
tɔum	a hillock	mɔːd	an assembly
tʲiːm	time	mjuːg	whey

2.4.2   NG sounds

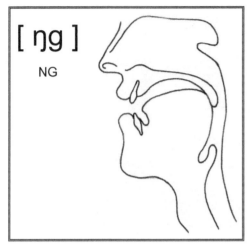

[ŋg]

NG

This sound (well, technically it's two sounds) also occurs in Standard English but not Scots.

It is found in words like *singer* [sɪŋgə], *finger* [fɪŋgə] and *linger* [lɪŋgə].

Note that only the *ng* found in the middle of English words is the same as in Gaelic. English **ng** has a different, much weaker pronunciation at the <u>end</u> of words like *sing* [sɪŋ] or *ring* [rɪŋ] in many of its varieties.

In Gaelic this **ng** sound is 'strong' in all positions in the sense that there is a rather audible [g] sound in it. So you get a nice and strong [ŋg] both in the middle and at the end of words. You don't have to worry about the beginning of words as this sound doesn't show up in that position.

🖎 **Exercise 59.**

Say the following words and nonsense syllables out loud:

ɔuŋg	uːŋg
uŋgə	aŋgə
ɛŋgə	aŋgɪdʲ
ɔŋgəs	eŋg

✳ ✳ ✳ ✳ ✳ ✳ ✳ ✳

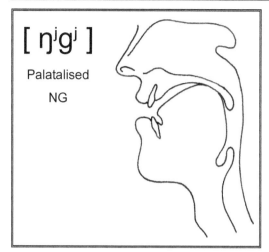

[ŋʲgʲ]

Palatalised
NG

On the other hand, this combination doesn't occur in either Scots or English.

There are a variety of ways which will get you there.

Method 1: Start with [ŋg] and simply make it further forward in your mouth at your palate instead of its usual place at the back. Some people also find it helpful to think of this sound as a [ŋg] that is being squeezed against the palate. Saying this particular sound between two [i] vowels makes it easier to say too. Since [ŋg] never occurs without a vowel somewhere next to it in Gaelic anyway, [iŋʲgʲɪ] is perfectly ok for practising on.

Method 2: There's always the rice paper! As before, stick a bit on your tongue as shown in the picture.

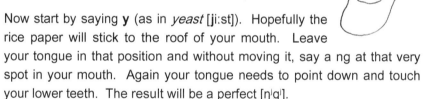

Now start by saying **y** (as in *yeast* [jiːst]). Hopefully the rice paper will stick to the roof of your mouth. Leave your tongue in that position and without moving it, say a ng at that very spot in your mouth. Again your tongue needs to point down and touch your lower teeth. The result will be a perfect [ŋʲgʲ].

Once again, if the rice paper doesn't stick to the roof of your mouth, say a **ng** but instead of using the back of your tongue as you're used to, only use the bit of your tongue the paper is on. The result will also be a perfect [ŋʲgʲ]. Again saying this particular sound between to [i] vowels makes it easier to say too, especially since it never occurs on its own in Gaelic anyway: [iŋʲgʲə]

✎ Exercise 60.

Say the following words and nonsense syllables out loud:

aiŋʲgʲɪ	uŋʲgʲə
eiŋʲgʲə	iŋʲgʲə

On the whole, this is a rather rare sound. Gaelic and Irish have this sound but there aren't many words which have [ŋg] per se. You will most commonly meet it in Irish is as the result of something called *urú* or 'eclipsis'. When this happens, a **g** sound at the beginning of a word turns into a **ng**. Something similar can happen in Gaelic too when a word like *nan* is followed by a palatal **g** sound but more about that later (in section 4.16.1).

For most people this will be a new letter too so here's an opportunity to practice. Note that this letter has a leg that goes below the line of text:

This symbol, by the way, is called *engma*. It started out life as a phonetic symbol and only had a lowercase version initially. But some languages which had had no writing system up until recently started using it as a 'normal' letter. In Europe the Sámi (which we'll meet again later) use it and it's also common in African alphabets.

Amusingly, they capitalise it differently. In Sámi, the capital letter is Ŋ, just a larger version of the small ŋ. So on a calendar you might find CUOŊOSMÁNNU (literally 'snow surface month') for FEBRUARY. In African writing systems, it's normally a capital **N** with a long leg: **Ꞑ**.

And no, just writing **ng** would not be easier. In the African language Wolof for example *Ŋeer* means 'to evaporate' but *Ngeer* is the psychedelic Sabara plant. And please don't ask me why I know this!

Progress Report					

p pj   **b bj**   **t tˡ**   **d dʲ**   **k kʲ**   **g gʲ**

➜**41%**

m mj   **ŋg ŋʲgʲ**   N Nʲ n   L Lʲ l   R r rʲ   f fj

v vj   s ʃ   x ç   ɣ ȷ j   h hj

Here are some examples involving the new sounds:

Gaelic	Meaning	Gaelic	Meaning
tˡɛŋgə	a tongue	kwiŋʲgʲ	a yoke
tuŋgə	Tong	ɛŋʲgʲɪ	wicked
uŋgə	an ingot	aʃlɪŋʲgʲ	a dream
pɔuŋg	a note	beiŋʲgʲ	a bench

2.4.3   N sounds

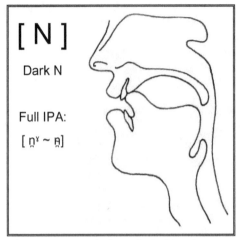

[N]

Dark N

Full IPA:

[n̪ˠ ~ n̪]

Now things are getting really interesting. This group of sounds, the **n**, **l** and **r** sounds, are real shibboleths for learners.

This is an interesting word by the way; if you have a Bible lying around, check out *Britheamhan* (if you have a Gaelic Bible) or Judges 12:5-6. Fortunately for learners Gaels are not quite as unforgiving about pronunciation but it's important to get these sounds right nonetheless!

The first **n** sound is the so called dark **n**. The full IPA symbol is somewhat cumbersome to read and write so I have borrowed the symbol used by most people who study Celtic languages for this sound - a capital [N]. It also helps people remember this sound as a 'thick' or 'dark' **n**.

Method 1: You make this sound by putting your mouth into an 'n position' but with the tip of your tongue touching the base of your upper teeth and the back of your tongue lowered. You're basically touching your teeth and making a trough shaped tongue. The result is a very dark and hollow sounding **n**.

Method 2: If you have problems making this hollow sound, find some small strawberries (or raspberries - anything of that sort of size that you're happy to put into your mouth), pop one or two in your mouth and hold them between your tongue and your palate. Now place the tip of your tongue against your teeth again and say an **n**. You will have no choice but to produce a hollow [N]. Say it a few times - don't forget to make it dental - to get used to the new 'mouth configuration' and then try it without the berries.

Method 3: English does have dental n sounds in certain combinations but English speakers don't lower the back of the tongue so it doesn't sound hollow. Dental [n̪] in English occurs when you get an [n] before [ð] or [θ] for example in words like *tenth* [tɛn̪θ], *plinth* [plɪn̪θ] or *month* [mʌn̪θ]. You can use this dental n sound as a starting point and then lower the back of your tongue at the same time. Put another raspberry in your mouth and start with the English word *tenth*. The berry will force you to say [tɛN̪θ] while touching your teeth and lowering the back of your tongue. Then drop off the extra sounds in *tenth* until you're left with the [N] only.

മലയാളം

Now this is how you make a linguist drool if you meet one at a party. It doesn't matter how much they've had to drink, they'll quickly sober up. Simply tell them that you speak (or are learning) a language which has 'three l, three n and three r phonemes' – 9 altogether. Be prepared for questions! And if you really want to wow them, tell them that there used to be a fourth l (which still exists in Harris Gaelic, by the way) and a fourth n in Old Irish.

On this occasion Gaelic does not only appear extravagant, it actually is. It is quite common for languages to have one of each but there are few languages indeed which have such a rich repertoire of them. Spanish and Yiddish which are both rich in l, n and r sounds only have 5 altogether and the only language which comes even close is a language called Malayalam (spot the palindrome!) from Kerala Province in India which has 3 n sounds, 3 l sounds and 2 r sounds. So it's actually something you can be proud of in an odd sort of way.

✎ Exercise 61.

Say the following words and nonsense syllables out loud:

Na	Na:
aNə	auN
ɔuN	Nɔ:
Nu:	Nɯ:

❋ ❋ ❋ ❋ ❋ ❋ ❋ ❋

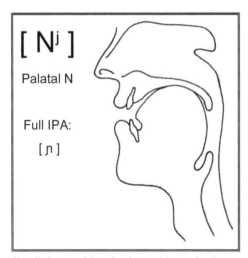

[Nʲ]

Palatal N

Full IPA:

[ɲ]

The second n sound doesn't occur in English either. It is transcribed as [ɲ] in full IPA but for the same reason as explained above, I have used [Nʲ] for this sound because it helps people remember that this is an **n** sound and palatal.

There are three ways of getting to this sound.

Method 1: The easiest way of making this sound is to take an English word beginning with **y**. Let's use *yeast* [jiːst] again. Say it a few times and pay close attention to where and how your tongue is approaching the roof of your palate. You will notice that you use the body of your tongue to approach your palate while the tip of your tongue is pointing down and touching your lower teeth.

In the next step you need to prefix an **n** to the word yeast. When you say this combined form make sure that you make the **n** in the same position as the **y**. Do not move your tongue forward or curve it upwards for the 'normal' position for the n sound. The result will be [Nʲ].

Method 2: You can also get there by taking an English [n] and simply saying further backward in your mouth at your palate instead of its usual place at the gum ridge using the body of your tongue rather than the tip or blade. Again, your tongue needs to point down and touch your lower teeth. Some people also find it helpful to think of this sound as an **n** that is being squeezed against the palate.

Method 3: If everything else fails, get a bit of rice paper and stick it on your tongue as shown in the picture. You should know the procedure by now!

Now start by saying **y** (as in *yeast* [ji:st]). Hopefully the rice paper will stick to the roof of your mouth. Leave your tongue in that position and without moving it, say an **n** at that very spot in your mouth. Again, your tongue needs to point down and touch your lower teeth. The result will be a perfect [Nʲ]. If the rice paper doesn't stick to the roof of your mouth, say an **n** but instead of using the tip of your tongue as you're used to in English, only use the bit of your tongue the paper is on. The result will also be a perfect [Nʲ]. Do it a few times until you get used to the feel of it.

The result should be a sound vaguely similar to the English [nj] sound (as in *new* [nju:]) but with the crucial difference that in Gaelic [Nʲ] is one sound whereas English [nj] consists of two sounds, an [n] closely followed by a [j]. Also, for the English [nj] your tongue points upwards rather than down. That means that for Gaelic your tongue goes upwards, touches the roof of your mouth, makes the [Nʲ] and comes down again. In English, your tongue goes up at the back to make the [n], then slides forward to make the [j] and then comes down again. So, if your tongue is sliding around for this sound and/or pointing up, you're not doing it quite right.

A lot of learners find it very hard to distinguish this [Nʲ] sound from the weak [n] which they're familiar with from English (see the next page). Again you shouldn't worry too much if you really can't hear the difference, context will usually give you enough clues to get the meaning right but make sure you say [Nʲ] in all the right places and no one will ever know you're struggling to hear this sound.

🔊 **Exercise 62.**

Say the following words and nonsense syllables out loud:

Nʲi	Nʲi:
aiNʲ	beiNʲ
eNʲə	aNʲə
ɯ:Nʲ	Nʲɔ:

❋ ❋ ❋ ❋ ❋ ❋ ❋ ❋

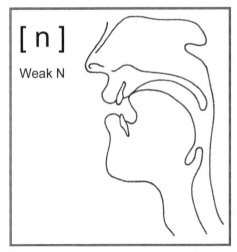

[n]

Weak N

The last **n** sound is quite straightforward as it occurs in all three languages.

You get it in Scots words like *neibour* [nibər], *cuning* [kʌnɪŋ] and *nakit* [nekɪt] and in Standard English too, for example in *night* [naɪt], *net* [nɛt] and *kin* [kɪn].

It is made by placing the tip of your tongue against your gum ridge and making an n sound.

So your tongue goes nowhere near your teeth or your palate for this sound.

A really 'boring' sort of **n** from a Gaelic point of view, hence the name 'weak N'. If your native language isn't Scots or English but has just one **n** sound, it's probably this one.

✎ **Exercise 63.**

Say the following words and nonsense syllables out loud:

anə	inə
ɯːn	iːn
ɔnə	mən
bɛn	gʲin

Keep up the good work, you've almost passed the half way mark!

Progress Report					
p pj	b bj	t tʲ	d dʲ	k kʲ	g gʲ
		→49%			
m mj	ŋg ŋʲgʲ	N Nʲ n	L Lʲ l	R r rʲ	f fj
v vj	s ʃ	x ç	ɣ ʝ j		h hj

Here are some examples involving the new sounds:

Gaelic	Meaning	Gaelic	Meaning
Naːbɪ	a neighbour	Nʲɛːv	heaven
Nɯːv	holy	kʲiːNʲ	heads
guNə	a gun	panə	a pan
Nʲed	a nest	kanə	a can

2.5   The liquids

Sadly this chapter does not involve an introduction to Islay malts. Instead, 'liquids' is the name that linguists have given to l and r sounds (because they share many similarities). I won't burden you with the details, it's just a convenient label (especially for linguists). Except as a heading, this word isn't vital to what we are doing here so you don't have to worry about the word itself.

2.5.1   L sounds

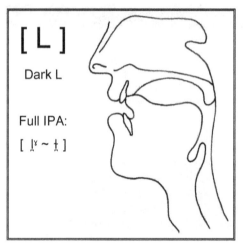

[L]

Dark L

Full IPA:

[l̴ˠ ~ ɫ]

Again, because the full IPA symbol is also difficult to make out and write, I've borrowed another symbol used by Celticists for this sound - a capital [L]. It will also help you remember that this sound is a 'thick L' or 'dark L'.

Method 1: You make this sound by putting your mouth into an 'l position' but with the tip of your tongue touching the base of your upper teeth and the back of your tongue lowered. You're basically touching your teeth and making a trough shaped tongue. The result is a very dark and hollow sounding l.

Method 2: If you have problems making this hollow sound, find some more small strawberries, pop one or two in your mouth and hold them between your tongue and your palate. Now place the tip of your tongue against your teeth again and say an l. You will have no choice but to produce a hollow [L]. Say it a few times - don't forget to make it dental - to get used to the new 'mouth configuration' and then try it without the berries.

Method 3: Some varieties of Scots and English also have a dark l in certain combinations but these usually aren't dental, meaning you don't touch your teeth with the tongue. Dark l in English occurs when you get an l after certain vowels at the end of a word for example in words like *sell* [sɛlˠ], *hill* [hɪlˠ], *kill* [kɪlˠ]. If you have this dark l, all you have to do is make sure you're tongue touches your teeth at the same time and you're there.

Method 4: English also has dental l sounds in certain environments but unfortunately these don't have the back of the tongue lowered to give you the hollow quality. Dental [l̪] in English occurs when you get an l before [ð] or [θ], for example in words like *health* [hɛl̪θ], *wealth* [wɛl̪θ], *stealth* [sdɛl̪θ]. You can start with this dental l and then lower the back of your tongue (you can use the trick with the berries) which will also give you [L].

✎ Exercise 64.

Say the following words and nonsense syllables out loud:

La	La:
aLə	baLə
ɔLə	faLə
ɯːL	Lɔum

פֿיש געפֿילטע?

In case you're into faking accents, this dark l really adds to a fake Yiddish accent, it's one of those sounds in those languages which give them this 'dark' flavour. Try saying words like *lokshn* or *gefilte fish* with dark l and you'll notice the difference!

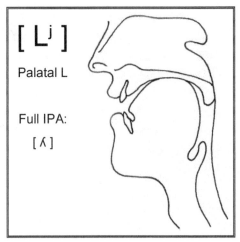

[Lʲ]

Palatal L

Full IPA:

[ʎ]

This I sound doesn't occur in Scots or English either. Not really surprising considering the unusually large number of n, l and r sounds in Gaelic!

The full IPA symbol for this sound is [ʎ], another symbol linguists nicked from the Greek alphabet. So for the same reason as before, I have used the Celticist symbol [Lʲ] for this sound because it helps people remember that this is an I sound and palatal. This time there are three ways of getting to this sound.

Method 1: The easiest way of correctly producing this sound is again to start with *yeast* [jiːst]. Say it a few times and again pay close attention to where and how your tongue is approaching the roof of your palate. You will notice that you use the body of your tongue to approach your palate while the tip of your tongue is pointing down and touching your lower teeth.

In the next step you need to prefix an I to the word yeast. When you say this combined form, make sure that you make the n in the same position as the y. Do not move your tongue forward or curve it upwards for the 'normal' position of an English I sound. The result will be [Lʲ].

Method 2: You can also get there by taking an English [l] and simply saying further backward in your mouth at your palate instead of its usual place at the gum ridge using the body of your tongue rather than the tip or blade. Again, your tongue needs to point down and touch your lower teeth. Some people also find it helpful to think of this sound as an I that is being squeezed against the palate.

Method 3: If everything else fails, get some more rice paper and stick it on your tongue as shown in the picture. You know the procedure by now!

Now start by saying **y** (as in *yeast* [ji:st]). Hopefully the rice paper will stick to the roof of your mouth. Leave your tongue in that position and without moving it, say an I at that very spot in your mouth. Again, your tongue needs to point down and touch your lower teeth. The result will be a perfect [Lʲ]. If the rice paper doesn't stick to the roof of your mouth, say an I but instead of using the tip of your tongue as you're used to in English, only use the bit of your tongue the paper is on. The result will also be a perfect [Lʲ]. Do it a few times until you get used to the feel of it.

This sound is vaguely similar to the English [lj] sound (as in *lure* [lju:r]) but with the crucial difference that in Gaelic [Lʲ] is <u>one sound</u> whereas English [lj] consists of two sounds, an [l] closely followed by a [j]. Also, for the English [lj] your tongue points upwards rather than down. That means that for Gaelic your tongue goes upwards, touches the roof of your mouth, makes the [Lʲ] and comes down again. In English, your tongue goes up at the back to make the [l], then slides forward to make the [j] and then comes down again.

So, if your tongue is sliding around for this sound and/or pointing up, you're not doing it quite right and you need to practice some more!

✎ Exercise 65.

Say the following words and nonsense syllables out loud:

Lʲi	Lʲi:
iLʲə	gʲiLʲə
e:Lʲ	fe:Lʲ
uLʲɪ	a:Lʲ

Not that you bought this book to improve your Spanish or Latvian but in case you're studying another European language the chances are that it will have a palatal [Lʲ]. Except for Germanic languages where this sound is rare, the [Lʲ] sound is very common throughout Europe.

❊ ❊ ❊ ❊ ❊ ❊ ❊ ❊

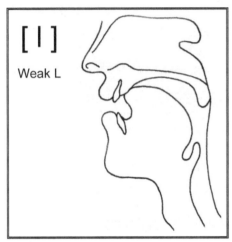

[l]

Weak L

At last a friendly face. The third l sound, the weak [l], is quite straightforward as it occurs in at the beginning of Scots words like *glaik* [glek], *leid* [lid], *link* [lɪŋk] and *licht* [lɪçt] and Standard English words, for example *long* [lɒŋ], *land* [lænd] and *lag* [læg].

It is produced by placing the tip of your tongue against your gum ridge and making an l sound. No funny business for a change!

✎ **Exercise 66.**

Say the following words and nonsense syllables out loud:

elə	alɪ
leʃ	blɛ
ka:l	ɯ:l
gʲilə	gle:

Progress Report

p pj	b bj	t tʲ	d dʲ	k kʲ	g gʲ
		→57%			

m mj	ŋg ŋʲgʲ	N Nʲ n	L Lʲ l	R r rʲ	f fj
v vj	s ʃ	x ç	ɣ ɹ j	h hj	

You're doing well! You're now well past the half way mark and there's a bit of good news. Of the remaining consonants, only three groups are what you might call weird. The others are pretty straightforward. Also, you will have a feel by now for the kind of things that are important for sounds in Gaelic, things like knowing where your palate is. So what's left will be a lot easier. Here are examples with the three l sounds:

Gaelic	Meaning	Gaelic	Meaning
Lag	weak	Lʲebɪ	a bed
ɔLə	oil	gʲiLʲə	a boy
faLav	leaving	gʲilə	whiteness
Lʲɛn	follow!	balə	a town

Ok, time for a breather. The next few pages are purely for fun.

You probably know that there are language families and that Gaelic is a Celtic language, that English and German are Germanic languages and that French, Spanish and Italian are Romance languages.

But you may not have been fully aware of how exactly these are related. So just for curiosity's sake I have given you the linguistic history of the word for the number 5, starting with the common ancestor [penkʷe] in a language called Indo-European thousands of years ago, down most of the branches of the family tree through time to the modern words for five in various languages.

You may discover some relatives you didn't know you had, like Albanian or Kashmiri! To make life easier for you and because you're becoming an expert at reading phonetic symbols, all the words are in the phonetic writing. That way you don't have to deal with over a dozen alphabets and hundreds of spelling rules.

The † symbol (called the 'dagger') means a language or family is extinct. The Hittite (or Hittie) languages for example were a group of Indo-European languages spoken in central and southern Turkey which had died out by the 1st century BC mainly due to the influx of Greek settlers after the conquests of Alexander the Great. If you've been to Turkey on a holiday, you may have actually run into them. Ḫattuša, the ancient capital of the Hittites near modern-day Boğazkale is an UNESCO World Heritage Site today. Allow me to digress?

The Hittites fought the Egyptians for the control of the Eastern Mediterranean for decades. Eventually they agreed the world's first major documented peace treaty in 1258 BC between King Ḫattušili and Pharaoh Ri'mīsisu (Ramses in shoddy spelling). The treaty lasted but when their capital Ḫattuša burnt down in 1180 BC, the Hittites pretty much vanished from history.

Ok, digression over.

We know very little about some of these languages which is why some examples are missing. Pictish for example is not documented well at all. The few linguistic clues we do have about Pictish, such as place names and personal names point strongly to it having been a Brythonic language. For example, Gaelic words like *preas* or *monadh* have no known roots in Old Irish but clear cognates in modern and ancient Brythonic - *pres* 'brushwood' and *monid* 'mountain'. So we can assume with some certainty that their word for five would have been similar to the Brythonic word for five but we're not entirely sure what it looked like.

Oh, and before you ask - Basque is not supposed to be on this tree. All current research points towards the Basques being the last of those ethnic groups that inhabited Europe long before the Indo-Europeans showed up. All other groups, such as the Etruscans or Iberians, were eventually assimilated by Indo-European languages. Except for the Basques who stubbornly kept on doing what they're best at - being Basque. As a result, although the language has borrowed many words, especially from Latin, Spanish and French, it is unrelated to any of those languages on the family tree. In fact, it's even more mind-blowing. It's what linguists call a 'language isolate', meaning that to date no one has found a proven link between Basque and any other language on the planet, dead or alive (except for Aquitanian, which was a precursor of Basque. Old Basque if you like). And believe you me, people have tried. But to this day, it remains an enigma. So while our Indo-Europeans would have counted *oinos, duō, treies, kʷetuer, penkʷe*, someone snacking on a pintxo overlooking the site that one day would house the Guggenheim would have pointed out to them it's really *bada, biga, hirur, laur, bortz...*

But now for the family tree I promised.

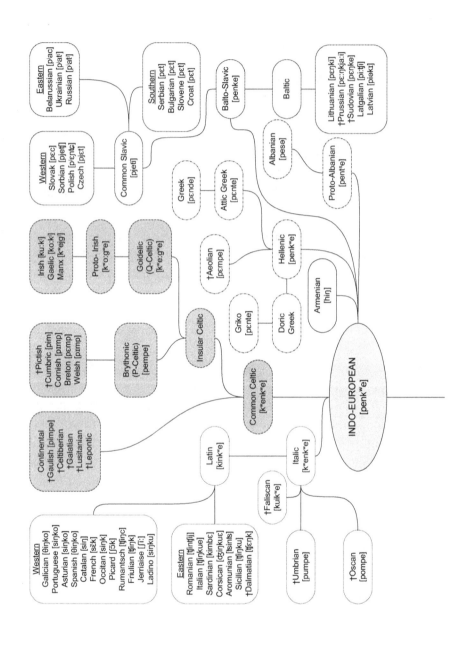

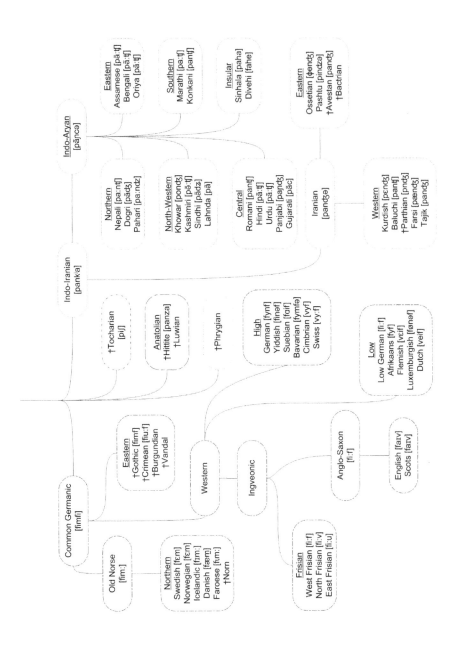

2.6   Taps and trills

Or in other words, r sounds. They are called taps and trills in linguist speak because some of them involve tapping something with your tongue while others are more like a trilling sound. While English dialects are rich in the sense that there are many kinds of r sounds, they are 'poor' in r sounds in the sense that each variety of English in general only has one r sound.

2.6.1   R sounds

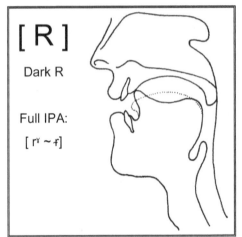

[R]

Dark R

Full IPA:

[rˠ ~ ɾ]

R sounds are a bit tricky too. The first r sound is transcribed as [rˠ] in full IPA, technically called a 'velarised trill', but again I have borrowed a symbol used by Celticists for this sound - a capital [R]. It also helps people remember this sound as a 'thick' or 'dark R'.

Speakers of Scottish English or Scots (or indeed any other language) who roll their r sounds (at the gum ridge, not at the back of the throat) can read straight on. Speakers of other varieties of English who do not have rolled r sounds should work through the next section on the [r] sound first.

Method 1: You make this sound by putting your mouth into an r position and lowering the back of your tongue. You're basically making a trough shaped tongue again as with [L] and [N]. The result is a very dark and hollow sounding [R]. Note that for this sound your tongue hits your gum ridge as is usual for the rolled r sounds. You do not have to hit your teeth for this sound.

Method 2: If you have problems making this hollow sound, find some raspberries, pop one or two in your mouth and hold them between your tongue and your palate. Now say an r. You will have no choice but to produce a hollow [R]. Say it a few times to get used to the new 'mouth configuration' and then try it without the berries.

A lot of languages, such as English and German, have a lot of variation in their r sounds. Think of the r sounds you get in Norfolk, Scotland, North of England, Wales, the US, India… This is not the case in Gaelic which is fairly restrictive in which variations of r sounds are acceptable This means that you have to pay close attention to producing the right r sounds and most importantly not to transfer the r patterns of your native language to Gaelic.

The reason is that Gaelic assigns different functions and places to its three r sounds whereas in English it doesn't really matter what sort of r sound you make. So as an English speaker you can roll it, tap it, curl your tongue, drop it… anything goes really. It's like being an only child - you can arrange your room any which way you want and can spread out across it. If you have to share the same room with 2 siblings, there will be quite clear boundaries of who hangs their posters where.

✎ **Exercise 67.**

Say the following words and nonsense syllables out loud:

Ra	Ra:
aRə	Ru:
a:R	kʲa:R
iRə	ʃiRəm

You may have guessed it already – having all these 'dark' sounds is also what gives Russian this 'thick' flavour to foreign ears. So maybe that makes Russian a logical choice for your next language!

❊ ❊ ❊ ❊ ❊ ❊ ❊ ❊

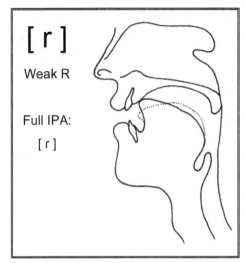

[r]

Weak R

Full IPA:

[ɾ]

Now this **r** sound doesn't pose a problem for speakers of Scots or Scottish English as it's the standard **r** sound for them. It occurs in words like *brak* [brak], *crowdie* [krʌudɪ] and *verra* [vɛrə].

If you're not a Scot, there's still a chance you may have this sound. Some American English dialects (and Scouse in Britain) turn a **t** between vowels into this tapped **r**. If you speak one of these dialects then words like *city* and *butter* will come out as if they were *ciry* and *burer*. This effect is the reason why you can see *get off* humorously spelled as *gerroff*.

In terms of what it sounds like, it's not dissimilar to the sound you hear children make when they're imitating electric drills or go 'brrrr!' when cold. Just a lot shorter.

But for the majority of English speakers getting this sound right will mean a bit of mouth acrobatics to begin with.

Method 1: For a lot of English speakers making r sounds involves curling the tip of the tongue backwards. For this **r** though you must not curl your tongue backwards. It is produced with the tip of your tongue pointing up (but not back!). Tap your gum ridge once or twice and the same time expel the air trapped behind your tongue. This will produce a sound which appears to be halfway between a **d** and an **r**. Which is the sound you want to be making.

Method 2: One environment which encourages this type of r even in English – and where it does in fact often occur in many varieties of English is after [θ]. Start with a word like *through* [θruː] or *thread* [θrɛd] and pay attention to what your tongue does for the [r]. It should be touching somewhere close to your teeth without really curling back. That's very close to the sound you're aiming for. Drop off all sounds except for the [θr] and repeat it many times to get used to the type of r sound, then say it on its own: [r].

Method 3: Start with the word *toddy* [tɒdɪ] and say it many times as quickly as possible without putting any emphasis on any word. It can help if you try and touch your teeth for the [t] sound. If you speed up enough, the result will be [tɒrɪ]. Once you get more of an [r] sound and less of a [d] sound, repeat it many times to get used to the new sound.

Method 4: If you speak Scouse or an American variety of English, start with a word like *butter* [bʌrə] or *city* [sɪrɪ] which instead of a [t] has an r sound in the middle. Repeat the word many times and focus on the [r] sound which should consist of a very quick tap near your gum ridge without your tongue curling backwards.

> If you jumped the [R] sound to do this
> section first, don't forget to go back!

I know that Gaelic r sounds are difficult, especially if you aren't used to rolling your r sounds but having those with the tongue curled back that you get in Southern English and many overseas varieties of English is like a red rag to a bull for native speakers!

✎ **Exercise 68.**

Say the following words and nonsense syllables out loud:

ara	arə
ɔrə	uːrə
mar	kur
rag	rɔːs

❀❀❀❀❀❀❀

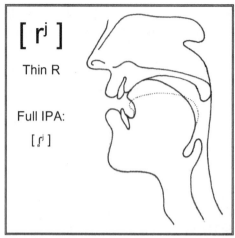

[rʲ]

Thin R

Full IPA:
[ɾʲ]

The last **r** sound is a little tricky too. Again there are a few ways you can get to this sound.

Method 1: For the previous [r] sound the tip of your tongue was touching your gum ridge, remember? For the [rʲ] sound you first of all have to use the tip and the blade of your tongue and have to touch the area between your teeth and the front bit of your palate.

Your tongue is either pointing forwards or slightly down. The result is a sound that sounds like a 'funny' **d** or **r** to a lot of people, which isn't a bad description.

Method 2: Got any rice paper left? Stick it on your tongue as shown in the picture, you'll need a slightly larger piece this time.

Now touch the area between your teeth and the front bit of your palate (the area just behind your gum ridge). The rice paper will stick to the roof of your mouth. Leave your tongue in that position and without moving it, say an **r** (or a **d**) at that very spot in your mouth. Remember that your tongue is either pointing forwards or slightly down. The result will be a perfect [rʲ]. If the rice paper doesn't stick to the roof of your mouth just keep your tongue right up there and say an r (or a **d**). The result will also be a perfect [rʲ]. Do it a few times until you get used to the feel of it.

From an English point of view this is a really weird sound but it's perfectly normal for Gaelic and extremely common so you can't avoid it I'm afraid.

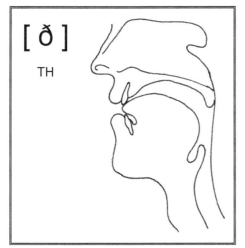

[ð]

TH

There's one more thing we need to mention. In a number of Hebridean dialects (parts of Lewis, Harris, the Uists and Benbecula) this sound has changed to a [ð]. This sound also occurs in Scots words like *thae* [ðe:] and *pouther* [pu:ðər] and in English in words like *the* [ðə] and *there* [ðɛə]. This sound is still considered a rather strong dialect feature in Gaelic, especially by mainlanders, so Hebridean speakers tend to be most familiar with it.

Try to stick with [rʲ] as it is a more neutral and widespread form but if you really cannot get your mouth around [rʲ], then go with [ð] instead. It's a better alternative than using [r] instead of [rʲ].

🖎 **Exercise 69.**

Say the following words and nonsense syllables out loud:

rʲi	rʲiʃ
u:rʲ	kurʲ
arʲə	a:rʲə
ɔrʲ	ɔrʲə

Progress Report					
p pj	b bj	t tʲ	d dʲ	k kʲ	g gʲ
				→65%	
m mj	ŋg ŋʲgʲ	N Nʲ n	L Lʲ l	R r rʲ	f fj
v vj	s ʃ	x ç	ɣ ʝ j		h hj

Here are some examples involving the new sounds:

Gaelic	Meaning	Gaelic	Meaning
Rag	stiff	aran	bread
Ra:v	an oar	rʲi	against
ba:R	top	kʲi:rʲ	a comb
marav	dead	mi:rʲən	pieces

2.7   The fricatives

This is another big group of sounds. Some of them occur in Scots, English and Gaelic but Gaelic has a considerable number of these sounds which don't exist in the other two. So because there will be many new ones, it will be helpful to understand a thing or two about what makes a fricative tick.

You may have already guessed that the word has something to do with friction. This is what lies at the heart of these sounds. You remember that when we looked at the plosives we learned that first of all your mouth shuts off the airflow and then pops open again. Fricatives are very similar to that except that your mouth does not close off the airflow completely. Instead, it leaves a narrow gap through which air literally

'hisses'. This hissing air creates the sound. For example, the word *pig* has a plosive made at your lips. Now, if you leave a little gap between your lips and try and say *pig*, what will actually come out is something that sounds almost like *fig*. Instead of a plosive, you made a fricative!

It's like the difference between popping a full balloon with a needle (⇒ it goes bang) and holding the neck of it and letting the air out of it (⇒ it squeals).

2.7.1   F Sounds

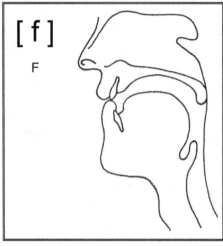

[f]

F

Not exactly free wheeling from here, but we're over the hill.

This sound for one exists in Scots, for example *fecht* [fɛçt], *feid* [fid], *gaff* [gaf] and *queff* [kwef] and Standard English words like *fat* [fæt], *fee* [fiː] and *fly* [flaɪ].

It is made by your upper teeth touching your bottom lip and squeezing air through the gap. Your vocal chords aren't vibrating for this sound, so it's voiceless.

✎ **Exercise 70.**

Say the following words and nonsense syllables out loud:

fa	faːn
afə	ɔfə
Lɔfə	af
ful	faLə

✻✻✻✻✻✻✻✻

[fj]

FJ

This sound also exists in Scots *fuggle* [fjuglˠ], *fugie* [fjudʒɪ], *feuch* [fjux], *feu* [fju:] and Standard English *few* [fju:], *feud* [fju:d] and *fume* [fju:m]. It is just an [f] followed by a [j] sound.

✎ **Exercise 71.**

Say the following words and nonsense syllables out loud:

fju:	fju:N
fjau	fjauL
fjɔ:	fja:
fjɔ:l	fjaN

Progress Report					
p pj	b bj	t tʲ	d dʲ	k kʲ	g gʲ
					➜70%
m mj	ŋg ŋʲgʲ	N Nʲ n	L Lʲ l	R r rʲ	f fj
v vj	s ʃ	x ç	ɣ ʝ j		h hj

Here are some examples involving the new sounds:

Gaelic	Meaning	Gaelic	Meaning
fɯ:Nʲ	inane	fju:N	fair
fe:Lʲ	a festival	fjaNag	a crow
dʲifər	a difference	fjɔ:rag	a squirrel
fi:rʲɪNʲ	truth	fjɔ:l	meat

2.7.2   V sounds

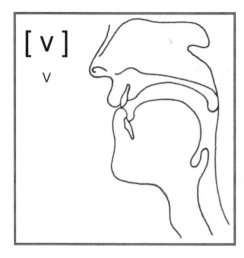

[v]

v

Another easy one. This sound occurs in Scots words like *vaig* [veg], *vane* [ven] and *pavie* [peːvɪ] and Standard English *veal* [viːl], *very* [vɛrɪ] and *vain* [veɪn].

It is made by your upper teeth touching your bottom lip and pressing air through the gap. At the same time your vocal chords are vibrating which give it the voicing.

✎ Exercise 72.

Say the following words and nonsense syllables out loud:

va	vaː
avɪ	vɔ
vo	voː
ava	kava

✿ ✿ ✿ ✿ ✿ ✿ ✿ ✿

[vj]

VJ

This sound is exactly what it looks like, a [v] followed by a [j].

It's not a very common sound in Scots or English but it does occur, for example in words like *view* [vju:] and *Vietnam* [vjɛt'næm].

🖎 **Exercise 73.**

Say the following words and nonsense syllables out loud:

vjau	vjauL
vjauN	vjɔ:
vjaLə	vja:
vju:gə	vja:R

Progress Report					
p pj	b bj	t tʲ	d dʲ	k kʲ	g gʲ
m mj	ŋg ŋʲgʲ	N Nʲ n	L Lʲ l	R r rʲ	f fj
→75%					
v vj	s ʃ	x ç	ɣ ʝ j		h hj

Here are some examples involving the new sounds:

Gaelic	Meaning	Gaelic	Meaning
mə va:hərʲ	my mother	rʲim vjɔ:	during my life
vɔ	from	da: vja:RN	two gaps
kɯ:v	gentle	da: vjauL	two clumps
baLav	deaf	mə vjauN	my young goat

2.7.3   S sounds

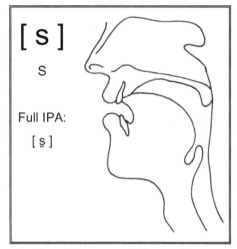

[s]

s

Full IPA:

[ş]

The Gaelic s sound is similar to English and Scots **s** with one crucial difference. In Scots and English the **s** is made by your tongue touching your gum ridge.

In Gaelic on the other hand you have to touch the base of your lower teeth for **s**.

In English and Scots **s** often turns into a soft, voiced sound when you modify a word by adding an ending, especially plural endings: *nostril* [nɒstrɪl] ~ *nose* [nəʊz], *house* [haʊs] ~ *houses* [haʊzɪz].

You must never do that for Gaelic as [s] always stays 'hard' [s] in Gaelic, no matter where in a word it shows up.

🖎 **Exercise 74.**

Say the following words and nonsense syllables out loud:

sa	sə
asə	kasə
ɔs	usə
agəs	isə

❋ ❋ ❋ ❋ ❋ ❋ ❋ ❋

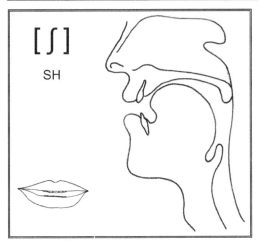

[ʃ]

SH

This sound is like the [ʃ] in Scots *sheltie* [ʃɛltɪ], *shake* [ʃek] and *rash* [raʃ] and Standard English *sheen* [ʃiːn], *ship* [ʃɪp] or *shine* [ʃaɪn].

Now say the word *shoe* [ʃuː]. Notice how your lips go very round for the [ʃ]? This is because your mouth is anticipating the [uː] for which you have to make your lips go round. This happens quite regularly in Scots and English.

In Gaelic, you should never say [ʃ] with lip rounding. In fact, in most cases you get somewhat spread lips so it's best to practice Gaelic [ʃ] while grinning slightly at the same time initially. It's a very friendly language somehow, all these sounds you have to grin for...

Also, for Gaelic [ʃ] your tongue is level or pointing towards your bottom teeth, not towards the roof of your mouth as it does in English. Try it. Say *shoe* and pay attention to where your tongue is pointing. Correct, it's pointing up. For Gaelic, down.

🖎 **Exercise 75.**

Say the following words and nonsense syllables out loud:

ʃi	ʃiː
iʃə	miʃə
ɔʃ	fɔʃ
ɯːʃ	Nʲiʃ

I'm sure you've seen this letter before. It's nothing but the old 'curly' s that you get in certain older typefaces when using italics.

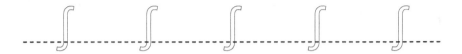

Progress Report					
p pʲ	b bʲ	t tʲ	d dʲ	k kʲ	g gʲ
m mʲ	ŋg ŋʲgʲ	N Nʲ n	L Lʲ l	R r rʲ	f fʲ
	→80%				
v vʲ	s ʃ	x ç	ɣ ʝ j		h hʲ

Here are some examples involving the new sounds:

Gaelic	Meaning	Gaelic	Meaning
sanəs	a sign	ʃiː	peace
suːNd	cheer	ʃeːməs	James
kasən	feet	boʃag	a handful
maːs	a buttock	kaːʃə	cheese

People who study Celtic languages often assume that everyone else also knows all about the history of the Celtic languages and people. Teaching Gaelic for many years has disabused me of this notion. People are generally very interested but, for the most part, the curriculum in Britain was not and is not particularly good on those points. So, a small crash course…

Whence did the Celts come from then? Good question. Based on a mixture of archaeological, historical and linguistic evidence we know that by the 5th century BC the Celtic branch of the Indo-European economic migrants had ended up settling in the area North of the Alps. They then began to branch out across Europe and it's round about this time they 'bump' into to the Romans and Greeks. The Romans call them the *galli* ('Gauls'). The Greeks on the other hand called them *κελτοί* (keltoi, 'Celts'), from where we get the modern word *Celt*.

The first traces of written Celtic languages are from the 6th century BC in a language called Lepontic in Northern Italy on the continent and from the 4th century onwards in the British Isles. Such as the famous Ogham inscriptions, like the one on the right telling you this slab was erected by the three sons of Maolan and Cuircthe.

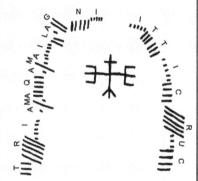

They occupied large swathes of Europe, from Galicia and the central areas of Spain to Gaul, Britain and Ireland, the North of Italy. Swathes of land along the Danube right to the Bosporus and, believe it or not, the kingdom of Galatia in central Turkey in the 3rd century BC! From sacking Delphi in Greece in the 3rd century and Rome in the 4th century, things went a bit pear-shaped for the Celts. Today, living Celtic languages and cultures are only found on the Atlantic fringe of Europe - Ireland, Scotland, the Isle of Man, Wales, Cornwall and Brittany and a few emigrant communities across the globe

2.8   The gutturals

I don't particularly like this word but I couldn't find anything better that's not overly technical. Anyway, the last section deals with all those fun 'throaty' and 'rasping' sounds. They are all fricatives but because this is a group of them that are sometimes a bit hard for learners, they get their own section.

2.8.1   The voiceless gutturals

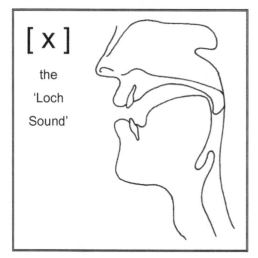

[x]

the

'Loch

Sound'

The first sound is quite easy for speakers of Scots and Scottish English. It is the same sound that occurs in Scottish English words borrowed from Gaelic like *loch* [lɔx] or *Kirkintilloch* [kɪrkɪnˈtɪlˠəx] and a lot of native Scots words, for example *hochle* [hoxlʲ], *lachter* [laxtər] and *peuch* [pjux]. Linguists call it the voiceless velar fricative.

The only thing to watch out for is that some Scots speakers make this sound a bit further back in their throat, effectively making the so called uvular[18] fricative [χ]. It's not the worst mistake you can make in Gaelic to have [χ] instead of [x]. If you want to make sure you're making the right sound, just follow the instructions below.

---

[18] Uvular means that it's made at your uvula, the dangly bit at the back of your throat you can see in the mirror if you stare deep into your mouth. In case you're wondering who came up with that word, that would be folks in the 14th century who wanted a fancy word and nicked the Latin word *ūvula* meaning 'little grape'.

Now for speakers of other English varieties the explanation needs to be a bit longer. Don't worry, anyone can learn to make this sound. Remember when we asked you to pay attention to what your mouth does when you make a [k] (section 2.3.6) and the basic idea behind fricatives (see 2.7)? This is where that comes in handy.

The only difference between [k] and [x] is that for [k] your mouth first blocks the airflow with your tongue at the back of the mouth. It then bursts this blockage open to make the [k] sound – correct, [k] is a plosive.

For [x], your mouth does exactly the same thing except that it never produces a complete blockage. Instead, a small gap is left at the back of your mouth (between your tongue and your velum) through which air can squeeze. The air squeezing through this gap produces friction which gives us our fricative [x].

Method 1: Say [aka] while paying close attention to the production of the [k]. Now say the same syllable but don't close off your airstream completely. You'll have the right sound when you can keep it going for a few seconds: [axxxa].

Method 2: Put your mouth into the right position for making a [k] but don't say it just yet. Now really tense up all the muscles in your mouth, neck and chest. Then squeeze some air through the [k] position. You will hear a slightly odd hissing sound. Now all you need to do is relax a little bit and you'll have a [x]. Finish it off by adding a vowel: [xaː]. Do this exercise over and over until you get used to making a sound in that position. Then just aim for the [x] sound without starting with a [k] and you will have cracked it!

✎ **Exercise 76.**

Say the following words and nonsense syllables out loud:

ax	ɔx
axə	uxg
xuː	xa
xaːx	axg

❋ ❋ ❋ ❋ ❋ ❋ ❋ ❋

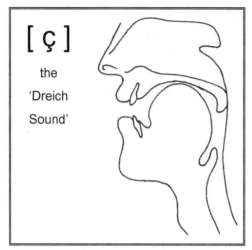

[ç]

the

'Dreich

Sound'

Have you noticed how most sounds in Gaelic come in twos? Usually you will get a 'normal' sound and then a similar but palatal one. For example [N] ~ [Nʲ] or [k] ~ [kʲ].

Well, this sound is the palatal counterpart to [x] and it doesn't exist in English.

You do get it in Scots where it appears as a variant of [x] near front vowels, for example *nicht* [nɪçt], *bricht* [brɪçt] and *dreich* [drɪç]. Because it occurs in the commonly known Scots word *dreich*, we'll call it that. It's a lot easier for most of my students to say *dreich* than to say 'voiceless palatal fricative'!

For people who didn't grow up with dreich weather, there are various ways of getting to this sound.

Method 1: If you have mastered [x], the only thing you have to change is that [ç] is made a lot further forward in your mouth (at your palate as opposed to your velum). Rice paper anyone? Stick it on your tongue as shown in the picture.

You know the drill by now, start by saying y and the rice paper will stick to the roof of your mouth. Leave your tongue in that position - touching your palate only very lightly - and without moving it hiss air through the gap. Again, the tip of your tongue is pointing down and touching your lower teeth. The result will be a perfect [ç]. If the rice paper doesn't stick to the roof of your mouth it doesn't matter. Just keep your tongue right up there and push air through. Do it a few times until you get used to the feel of it.

Method 2: Say [axa]. Now replace the [a] vowels with [i] vowels. The [i] vowels are made at the same place in your mouth as the [ç] so if you start with the [i] and stay in the same place when you aim for the [x], they will practically drag it forward in your mouth and you end up with [içi]. Same kind of friction, only further forward in your mouth.

Method 3: The [hj] sound which occurs in English words like *huge* [hju:dʒ] or *humid* [hju:mɪd] is not too far away from the [ç] sound. In fact, some English speakers have *huge* [çu:dʒ] rather than [hju:dʒ] etc. So if you have just the one 'rasping' sound with a lot of friction at the beginning of words like *huge* and *humid*, problem solved. Otherwise start off with a word like *huge* [hju:dʒ] and then try to exaggerate the articulation. In other words, produce more friction by narrowing the gap between your tongue and your palate. The result should be a lovely palatal [ç] sound.

✎ **Exercise 77.**

Say the following words and nonsense syllables out loud:

çi:	iç
içɪ	eç
fiçə	gliç
çɔ:	çu:

If you did French at school you will know this letter. It's just a **c** with a little hook underneath and goes by the name of cedilla[19]. It doesn't have to be a fancy hook, even a little straight line will do. If you want to, you can practice it a few times here:

---

[19] From *ceda,* the old Spanish name for the letter **z**, plus the diminutive ending *-illa,* so 'little **z**'. It's called little **z** because it's a modified form of the cursive form of this letter, the ȝ, originally used by the Visigoths in Spain.

I'm sure that you've noticed by now that Irish, Gaelic and Manx have a lot in common. In fact, Irish and Gaelic were so close to each other for a long time that they shared a single common written standard called Common Gaelic or Classical Gaelic. Gaelic was in fact Europe's first standardised language and was used well into the 17th century for writing anything from texts on law and medical treatises (Irish physicians were extremely sought after at one point!) to flippant comments in monastic documents.

If you compare the modern languages, you can still see many things they have in common and the way they split. Sometimes it feels like they sat down at a table at some point and shared the language 50-50, Irish taking the fancy grammar (Irish has more tenses, more endings…) and Gaelic the fancy sounds (Irish vowels for example are generally a lot more boring). The most beautiful example of this is the word for 'not' in Irish and Gaelic.

In Old Irish the word was nícon. When the (spoken) languages eventually split into Irish, Scottish and Manx Gaelic, they shared the word equally, the Irish taking the first half, the Scottish and Manx Gaels the second:

nícon

ní   chan

Progress Report						
p pj	b bj	t tʲ	d dʲ	k kʲ		g gʲ
m mj	ŋg ŋʲgʲ	N Nʲ n	L Lʲ l	R r rʲ		f fj
		→85%				
v vj	s ʃ	x ç		ɣ ɟ j		h hj

Here are some examples involving the new sounds:

Gaelic	Meaning	Gaelic	Meaning
xa Nʲel mi	I am not	çi: ʃiNʲ	we will see
mə xas	my foot	mə çauN	my head
Luxag	a mouse	fiçəd	twenty
εx	a horse	eç	horses

If all the Continental Celtic languages are extinct, where does that leave Breton?

If you remember the family tree of Indo-European languages, that might give you a clue because Breton is listed as an Insular Celtic language.

What happened was that Brittany was re-settled by Celts from Southern Britain between the 5th and 9th century AD. This occurred in the wake of the Roman withdrawal from Britain and the Anglo-Saxon invasion in the Southeast of (modern-day) England. A bit like a game of musical chairs where the Anglo-Saxons push in from the right and the Britons to the far left get pushed out.

That's why we today have a Celtic language spoken on the continent in spite of it being 'insular' in terms of its origin.

2.8.2   The voiced gutturals

[ɣ]

the

'*Dha* Sound'

This sound doesn't exist in either Scots or English but there are several ways of getting the right sound without too much trouble. Officially it's called the voiced velar fricative but, since that is a right mouthful, best call it the *dha* sound.

Method 1: If you have mastered [x] already then all you have to do is to voice it. Say [axa] and keep the [x] going for a bit. If you put your hand on your throat you will notice that there isn't any vibration as this sound is voiceless. Now 'make the sound soft' by adding the voicing and you will have a perfect [aɣa]. Again place your hands on your throat to check that you get vibration throughout the [aɣa] syllable.

Method 2: You can take a nice, voiced [g] (as in English *aghast*). The [g] and [ɣ] sounds are made in the same place. The only difference is in the degree of closure (remember the balloon thing?) When you say [aga] your mouth blocks off the airstream for the [g] and then suddenly bursts open again to make the [g]. The only difference with [ɣ] is that there is no closure, only a constriction which causes the air to squeeze through a narrow gap. This turbulence produces the [ɣ] sound. Start with saying [aga]. Now say it again without closing off the airflow fully and you get [aɣa].

This sound seems to be one of those most disliked by Gaelic learners and unfortunately for learners, it's very very common in Gaelic. The temptation is always great to 'replace' this with a sound that seems to be 'close enough' to the ears of someone who's not a native speaker.

The problem is that replacing it not only makes your Gaelic really hard to understand, it can also change the meaning of a lot of words quite dramatically. So I strongly recommend you practice this sound a lot until you can get it right. Pick a simple word which has the [ɣ] sound, for example [ɣa] 'to him' and practice it so much that you start dreaming about it. Then, whenever you might be a little unsure about the [ɣ] sound in a different word, go back to [ɣa] to remind you how the sound works and then go back to your new word.

✎ **Exercise 78.**

Say the following words and nonsense syllables out loud:

ɣa	mɔɣ
aɣəs	ɣu
əɣ	əɣə
ɣɯːl	ɣauL

Ok, we're down to the last two strange symbols. This letter is a slight variation of the Greek letter gamma which linguists picked because the Greek gamma in modern Greek is pronounced just like that. Note that this symbol is long and goes below the line of text, unlike the vowel symbol we had earlier. I've given you the vowel symbol once below for comparison:

Vowel	Consonant	Consonant	Consonant	Consonant

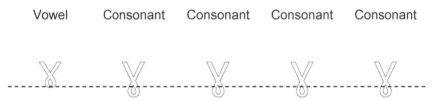

❋❋❋❋❋❋❋❋

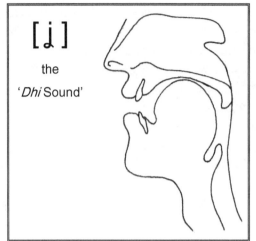

[ʝ]

the

'*Dhi* Sound'

This is the palatal counterpart to [ɣ] and because they form a nice contrasting pair, we'll call this one the *dhi* sound rather than the voiced palatal fricative.

It doesn't exist in Scots or English. There are two ways in which you can get to this sound.

Method 1: If you have mastered the [ɣ] sound, all you need to do is to shift it forward to your palate. It's the same process as going from [x] to [ç]. Start by saying [ɣa]. Now say [ʝi]. You will notice that even if you try to say [ɣi], the [i] practically drags the consonant forward to the [ʝ] position.

Method 2: The other way is by starting with its English 'close cousin', the [j] sound which occurs in words like *yes* [jɛs]. This sound is very similar to the one we're aiming for, the only difference being that to say [j], there is a fairly large gap through which the air passes between your tongue and your palate. To move from [j] to [ʝ], all you need to do is 'tighten up' to produce a narrower gap. Start with [ji] and then narrow the gap to get to [ʝi].

The last four sounds we looked at, [x] [ç] [ɣ] and [ʝ], unfortunately do not have any convenient names, mostly because they just don't occur in English. Apart from the technical names, which are a real mouthful, the best solution seems to be to call them after two commonly known Scots words which use this sound, *loch* and *dreich* and in the case of [ɣ] and [ʝ] after two very common and simple Gaelic words which have this sound, *dha* [ɣa] 'to him' and *dhi* [ʝi] 'to her'. If you can think of any better names, do let me know please!

✎ Exercise 79.

Say the following words and nonsense syllables out loud:

ɟi	ɟi:
ɟiəm	ɟɔ:
ɟɔ:Lə	ɟɔx
ɟe	ɟiən

This is the last odd looking letter. It's a **j** with a little curly finish:

❋ ❋ ❋ ❋ ❋ ❋ ❋ ❋

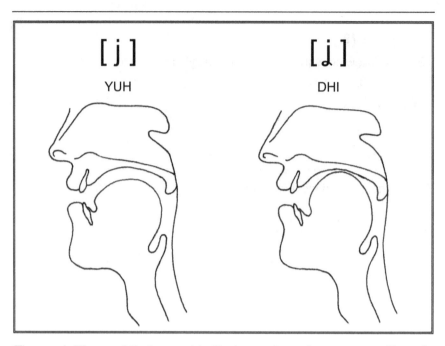

[j]   [ɟ]

YUH   DHI

The weak [j] sound that we get in Scots words such as *yammer* [jamər], *yaird* [jɛrd], *yestreen* [jɛstrin] and *yonder* [jondər] and English words like *yes* [jɛs], *you* [juː], *yellow* [jɛləʊ] also shows up in Gaelic.

If you compare the two pictures you can see that for the strong [ɟ] sound your tongue has much more to do while it's just 'flopping about' for the weak [j] sound. We will find out later (in section 4.6) when exactly you get [ɟ] and when you get [j].

🖎 **Exercise 80.**

Say the following words and nonsense syllables out loud:

ijə	ja
ajə	fɔj
Luɰj	ju
juː	jaL

Progress Report					
p pʲ	b bʲ	t tʲ	d dʲ	k kʲ	g gʲ
m mʲ	ng nʲgʲ	N Nʲ n	L Lʲ l	R r rʲ	f fʲ
				→93%	
v vʲ	s ʃ	x ç	ɣ ʝ j		h hʲ

Here are some examples involving the new sounds:

Gaelic	Meaning	Gaelic	Meaning
ɣu:Nʲ mi	I closed	ə ʝi:lə	to Islay
ɣa:g mi	I left	ə ʝi:	lacking
Lɣɣ	a law	xaj mi	I went
ʝiəm	off me	juxɪrʲ	a key

Here's another interesting fact for you. Did you know that the [ʝ], [Nʲ] and [Lʲ] sounds are the reason a number of words borrowed by Scots and English and a number of place-names have a totally unexpected **z**? Words like Dalziel, Enzie, MacKenzie and capercailzie.

What happened was that in the old days, there was a special letter called 'yogh' which was used to write a **y** sound. So when people came across words like *Dail Ghil* [dalʲʝil], *An Éinne* [ə Nʲe:Nʲə], *MacCoinnich* [maxˈkɣNʲɪç] and *capal-coille* [kahbəLˈkɣLʲə], the best way they could think of spelling these was using an **n** or **l** and a yogh, so you got *Dalȝiel, Enȝie, MacKenȝie* and *capercailȝie*. So far so good.

The problem was that this letter was never common even in its heyday, plus it also looked similar to a handwritten variant of the letter **z**, the *ȝ*. So soon people who weren't so familiar with these Scottish words began to think that the ȝ was actually a ȝ and started using a **z** in printed material instead. And thus the Dalziel, Enzie, MacKenzie and capercailzie spellings were born. Which in turn affected the way people pronounced these words in many cases.

2.8.3   H sounds

This sound is easy for Scots and English speakers. It is the same sound you get in Scots *hoot* [hut], *hous* [hus], *hither* [hiðər] and *hame* [hem] and Standard English words like *house* [haʊs], *home* [həʊm] and *hut* [hʌt].

✎ Exercise 81.

Say the following words and nonsense syllables out loud:

ha	ha:
hug	hɔum
hɛrə	ho:
hu:	he:

[hj]

HJ

This sound occurs in Scots *heuch* [hjux] and *heuk* [hjuk] and Standard English words like *huge* [hju:dʒ], *humid* [hju:mɪd] and *human* [hju:mən].

For some English speakers the [hj] sound has changed to [ç] (we talked about this in section 2.8). If that is the case for you, then ignore the English examples and simply follow a [h] sound with a [j] sound. This, incidentally, is also true for some Gaelic dialects where [hj] has become [ç].

✎ **Exercise 82.**

Say the following words and nonsense syllables out loud:

hjɔ	hjɔ:
hju	hju:l
hjɔ	hjɔ:
hju:R	hjɔ:mə

★★★100%★★★					
p pj	b bj	t tʲ	d dʲ	k kʲ	g gʲ
m mj	ŋg ŋʲgʲ	N Nʲ n	L Lʲ l	R r rʲ	f fj
v vj	s ʃ	x ç	ɣ ʝ j		h hj

That's it, you've done them all! There are some more exercises to come but now you have learned how to make all the sounds that you need for speaking really good Gaelic. Well done. For now, here are some examples involving the new sounds:

Gaelic	Meaning	Gaelic	Meaning
hog mi	I lifted	hjauL mi	I showed
ha mi	I am	hjɔ:L ɛ	he sailed
he:n	self	mə hjɔ:mər	my room
huərʲ ɛ	he got	rɔ hjauN	too tight

3.   More exercises

✎ Exercise 83.

In this exercise you will hear a short sentence which has words that sound very similar and only have one small difference. These are called minimal pairs. For example, the only difference between [sabɪdʲ] 'a fight' and [saːbɪdʲ] 'a Sabbath' is in the length of the vowel. Confusing them could be tricky and lead to all sorts of unforeseen consequences!

Each set of exercises focuses on hearing the difference between similar but different sounds. Don't worry about how the sentences are constructed at the moment, just accept them as they are.

- Listen to the two sentences on the DVD.

- Say the two sentences out loud yourself and pay special attention to the pair of similar words.

Set 01

	i	iː
01	va ʃil auN	va ʃiːl auN
	there was a drizzle	there were seeds
02	xuNɪgʲ ɛ ʃinə	xuNɪgʲ ɛ ʃiːnə
	he saw a teat	he saw Sìne

Set 02

	a	aː
01	ʃɛ sabɪdʲ ə vauN	ʃɛ saːbɪdʲ ə vauN
	it was a fight	it was a sabbath
02	xaiLʲ i kas	xaiLʲ i kaːs
	she lost a leg	she lost a case

Set 03

uː	ɯː
01 çaNɪç mi uːrʲ	çaNɪç mi ɯːrʲ
I bought soil	I bought a satire
02 ha duːr	ha dɯːr
they are obstinate!	they are expensive!

Set 04

p/pj	b/bj
01 va pian ɔrɔm	va bian ɔrɔm
I was in pain	there was a hide on me
02 Lɔrɔg i paxg	Lɔrɔg i baxg
she found a pack	she found a rowlock
03 ʃɔ dah nəm pjauN	ʃɔ dah nəm bjauN
this is the colour of the pens	this is the colour of the hills

Set 05

t	d
01 ʃɛ tɔxər ə vauN	ʃɛ dɔxər ə vauN
it was a dowry	it was an injury
02 ʃoN tuʃaL kʲaːR	ʃoN duʃaL kʲaːR
this is the wrong case	this is the wrong flute

Set 06

tʲ	dʲ
01 Lɔrɔg ɛ tʲeːd	Lɔrɔg ɛ dʲeːd
he found a string	he found a tooth
02 tʲeç a gLasəxu	dʲeç a gLasəxu
flee from Glasgow!	ten from Glasgow

Set 07

k	g
01	
ʃɛ kauL ə vauN	ʃɛ gauL ə vauN
it was a loss	it was a non-Gael
02	
ha kas auN	ha gas auN
there is a leg	there is gas

Set 08

k	kʲ
01	
ha kʲiad ka:RN auN	ha kʲiad kʲa:RN auN
there are a hundred cairns	there are a hundred areas
02	
haxɪrʲ mi ɛrʲ kaLag	haxɪrʲ mi ɛrʲ kʲaLag
I came across a bristle	I came across deceit

Set 09

kʲ	gʲ
01	
ʃɛ dɯNʲə kʲiar a hauN	ʃɛ dɯNʲə gʲiar a hauN
he's a swarthy man	he's a sharp man
02	
xuəLə mi kʲe:m	xuəLə mi gʲe:m
I heard a step	I heard a bellow

Set 10

g	gʲ
01	
ha i gaL	ha i gʲaL
she is crying	she is white
02	
rʲiNʲ ɛ mu:g	rʲiNʲ ɛ mu:gʲ
he sniffed	he grimaced

Set 11

L	Lʲ
01 çaNɪç mi LauN	çaNɪç mi LʲauN
I bought an enclosure	I bought ale
02 va Laːv saLəx	va Laːv saLʲəx
his hand was dirty	his hand was greasy

Set 12

Lʲ	l
01 Lʲɤɣ əNʲ dʲej	lɤɣ əNʲ dʲej
melt the ice!	the ice melted
02 Laj ɛ na Lʲebɪ	Laj ɛ na lebɪ
he lay in her bed	he lay in his bed

Set 13

N	Nʲ
01 xuNɪgʲ mi bɔNag	xuNɪgʲ mi bɔNʲag
I saw a slipper	I saw a droplet
02 prʲiːʃ ə vaNə	prʲiːʃ ə vaNʲə
the price of the band	the price of milk

Set 14

Nʲ	n
01 ha Nʲesgɪdʲ pianal	ha nesgɪdʲ pianal
her boil is painful	his boil is painful
02 ha Nʲed agəm	ha ned agəm
I have a nest	I have his nest

Set 15

N	n
01 **xa Nʲel ʃin na Naːdər** that's not in her nature	**xa Nʲel ʃin na naːdər** that's not in his nature
02 **ha Nɯjan tʲiːNʲ** her baby is ill	**ha nɯjan tʲiːNʲ** his baby is ill

Set 16

R	r
01 **ha kaːR ɛrʲ də ɣrɯim** there's dandruff on your back	**ha kaːr ɛrʲ də ɣrɯim** there's a car on your back
02 **çiː mi sgɔːR** I can see a cliff	**çiː mi sgɔːr** I can see a score

Set 17

r	rʲ
01 **xa bə tɤ ləm ə vaːr** I didn't like his bar	**xa bə tɤ ləm ə vaːrʲ** I didn't like his goal
02 **huərʲ ɛ aːrəx auN** he was raised there	**huərʲ ɛ aːrʲəx auN** he found a cattleman there

Set 18

s	ʃ
01 **rɤiNʲ əN tasəL fuəim** the donkey made a sound	**rɤiNʲ əN taʃəL fuəim** the axle made a sound
02 **xa Nɛçgʲ mi les** I can't see its benefit	**xa Nɛçgʲ mi leʃ** I can't see his thigh

Set 19

x	ç
01 ʃauL ɛrʲ ə xaːRN	ʃauL ɛrʲ ə çaːRN
look at the cairn!	look at the area!
02 dʲiən dʲaLav ə xuːbɪdʲ	dʲiən dʲaLav ə çuːbɪdʲ
draw a cuboid!	draw a pulpit!

Set 20

ɣ	ʝ
01 çaNɪç ɛ tʲeː ɣu	çaNɪç ɛ tʲeː ʝu
he bought a black one	he bought one of them
02 ʃɛ dʲoː ɣauL ə hauN	ʃɛ dʲoː ʝauL ə hauN
he's a decent Lowlander	it's a good bet

Set 21

f/fj	v/vj
01 ʃɔ fɛr ə faːj	ʃɔ fɛr ə vaːj
here's a man who paid	here's the man of his affection
02 xa tɤ leʃ ə figʲə	xa tɤ leʃ ə vigʲə
he doesn't like his pitcher	he doesn't like his pettiness
03 ha mi Reçgʲ mə fjauN	ha mi Reçgʲ mə vjauN
I'm selling my pens	I'm selling my mountains

PART 3

Phonology

or

How to put

all these sounds together

4.   Phonology or how to put all these sounds together

Well done! You've taken the first big step towards your *Blas na Gàidhlig*. You have learnt all the sounds that Gaelic has and how to make them - in other words, the phonetics of Gaelic. You have also learned a reliable way of how they can be written down. While this does not mean that you know how to build sentences, chat up  good looking Gaels and all that, it <u>does</u> mean that you can now pronounce <u>any</u> word that Gaelic might throw at you.   Quite an achievement, never underestimate it!

What we have to do now is look at Gaelic phonology.   That is, the way these sounds interact with each other and other issues to do with pronunciation such as where stress goes, what lenition is and when you get it and so on.

The following chapters are just as important as the previous ones, even more so perhaps.   So try to study them as well as you did the earlier ones.

4.1   A tiny bit of linguistic housekeeping

Before we can get started there is a small terminology issue which needs sorting out. Gaelic sounds can be grouped into two categories and because different people use different terms for these, I'm going to give you a quick summary of what I will be using and what you might see elsewhere and how they relate to each other. In this book, I'm going to use the following terms:

- Palatal(ised) when talking about palatal consonant sounds. In the transcription you can tell most palatal(ised) from the little [ʲ] after them: [dʲ tʲ gʲ kʲ Lʲ Nʲ rʲ] but there are few that are palatal(ised) without there being a [ʲ] to show you: [ʃ ʝ ç].

- Broad and Slender when talking about **letters** and the spelling. Much more on that later but broad letters are the vowel letters **a à á o ó ò u ù** and any consonant next to them (for example, in *aca, acair, tombaca* and *mac,* all the **c** letters are broad). The vowel letters **e é è i ì** and any consonant next to them are slender (for example, in *glic, mic, cir* and *muice,* all the **c** letters are slender).

So we have:

broad (*leathann*)	**slender**, narrow (*caol*)
velarised	**palatalised**
non-palatal	**palatal**

I won't be using the term velarised at all because in Gaelic, for the most part, that type of sound is rare (it's what produces the 'dark' sounds , for example [N], [L] and [R]).

Also, to jog your memory, remember that there in terms of their **pronunciation** (not the letters we use to write them normally), we split the vowels into two groups, front and back.   This, you will remember, depends on whether we make a sound at the front or at the back of our mouth:

Front		Back
i e ɛ	a	ɔ o u ɤ ɯ
iː eː ɛː		aː ɔː oː uː ɤː ɯː

Short [a] is sitting in the middle because it's slightly weird.   As we'll see later, Gaelic fluctuates between treating it as a front vowel or a back vowel because it sits right on the borderline between the two in terms of where we make the sound.

But enough of housekeeping, let's get stuck into the juicy bits.

4.2   The diphthongs and Why less is more

Don't worry, these aren't new sounds. So far we have only looked at individual vowels although some combinations have appeared in some exercises. But now it's time to look at these combinations, called diphthongs, in a structured way. 'Diphthong' is really nothing more than a fancy word for a sound where one vowel glides into another vowel. That's what this word literally means: a 'two sound'[20].

English has about 8 diphthongs, for example *dive* [daɪv]. In this example we start with an [a] vowel which then glides into the [ɪ] vowel. Other examples are: *loud* [laʊd], *sure* [ʃʊə], *mare* [mɛə]. Scots is poorer when it comes to diphthongs, only about 4, because it has retained more long vowels, some examples are *kye* [kaɪ], *bile* [bəil] and *powl* [pʌul].

When they don't glide into each other you get something called hiatus, which English doesn't do much but Gaelic has a lot of (see the next section) so the difference is important. For now, just focus on nicely running these vowel sounds together.

There are wild numbers flying around for how many diphthongs Gaelic has (anything up to 40). But to coin a phrase, 'you'll be fine with nine'. That may not always coincide exactly with what an individual native speaker might use but it is well within what they will consider acceptably good Gaelic.

The nine are:

ia	iə	uə	au	ɔu	ɣi	ɯi	ai	ei

An important point for later: from the Gaelic point of view, a diphthong counts as a long vowel. Which, since they consist of two short vowels 'glued' together, makes sense.

So, you will be fine with the above nine in terms of what you should pronounce to be understood. Just be aware that you may hear other diphthongs as well.

---

[20] From the Greek δίφθογγος 'díphthongos'.

Since they will usually be minor variations of the above nine, I will keep things simple and not bother you with all the possibilities, just the two most common ones: [au] is often [ɛu] and [ɔu] often [au].

✎ Exercise 84.

Repeat the following nonsense syllables:

ia	iav	ian	iam
iə	iəv	iən	iəm
uə	uəv	uən	uəm
ɣi	ɣiv	ɣin	ɣim
ɯi	ɯiv	ɯin	ɯim
au	auv	aun	aum
ɔu	ɔuv	ɔun	ɔum
ai	aiv	ain	aim
ei	eiv	ein	eim

4.3   Hiatus or How to yawn in Gaelic

The word hiatus comes from Latin and simply means 'gap'[21]. Which is really what it is. In the previous section we looked at how we run vowels together to make diphthongs.

What you can also do to two vowels when they come together is to keep them separate. The symbol used to show this in the Phonetic Alphabet is a full stop [.]. English doesn't do this much but there are some instances of it, mainly when certain prefixes meet a word beginning with a vowel, for example *co-op*, *re-entry*, *micro-organism* and *skiing*.

In Gaelic this happens a lot between all sorts of vowels in the middle of words.

✎ Exercise 85.

Repeat the following nonsense syllables:

ma.ə	pu.ə	a.ɪ
mo.ə	ni.ə	fo.ə
a.ə	ɯ.ə	Lʲi.ɪ

This is important because there are words in Gaelic which – save for hiatus – sound exactly the same or very similar.

Here's a list of the most common ones in Gaelic:

---

[21] You've probably met the term already in a common medical condition called 'hiatus hernia' (where part of your stomach sticks up through your diaphragm) which just translates as 'protrusion through a gap'. It's quite amusing in a way that all these fancy looking Latin and Greek words have really banal literal translation, don't you think?

Vowel/Diphthong		Hiatus	
bidh [biː]	will be	bithidh [bi.ɪ]	will be[22]
binn [biːNʲ]	sweet	bithinn [bi.ɪNʲ]	I would be
bruach [bruəx]	riverbank	bruthach [bru.əx]	slope
eòin [jɔːNʲ]	birds	Eoghainn [jɔ.ɪNʲ]	Ewen (gen.)
fiach [fiəx]	debt	fitheach [fi.əx]	raven
thuirt [huRʃdʲ]	said	thubhairt [hu.əRʃdʲ]	said
tinn [tʲiːNʲ]	ill	tighinn [tʲi.ɪNʲ]	coming

If you're musical, you can think of the words in the left column as having one beat and the ones in the right column as having two.

One pair you need to be very careful with, as someone (not me) once discovered when giving a talk to some very prim and proper Gaelic-speaking ladies. The topic was *boghadaireachd* [bo.ədɛrʲəxg] - archery. Unfortunately the person in question had not spent enough time on pronunciation and proceeded for quite some time to tell an increasingly silent audience how good she was at *bodaireachd* [bodɛrʲəxg], that her husband had introduced her to it, that she was now better at it then him and that they enjoyed doing it outdoors with other people…

Even though contrasting pairs like the above aren't very common, hiatus in general is. The most common way to spell hiatus is **th** between vowels but it can also be **bh**, **dh**, **gh** or **mh**. As a result the **th** (when it represents hiatus) isn't actually pronounced which can cause some confusion. But now you're in on the secret.

piuthar [pju.ər]	bhathar [va.ər]	motha [mo.ə]
fhathast [ha.əsd]	dùthaich [duː.ɪç]	siuthad [ʃu.əd]

---

[22] All the "long" forms of the irregular verbs like *bithidh ~ bidh, bhitheas ~ bhios* are so called emphatic forms used when a verb is emphasised, especially when used in answers.

The problem is that **th** can also represent [h]:

athair [ahərʲ]	màthair [ma:hərʲ]	gathan [gahan]
nathair [Nahɪrʲ]	cathair [kahɪrʲ]	bothan [bɔhan]

It's really tricky to tell which word has which as a result (without a degree in Old Irish - which isn't a realistic option for most people). But there are three reasons why, if you have to guess, you can get away with opting for hiatus:

- This [h] tends to be weak between vowels, more like a [ʰ]

- In fast speech this sound often ends up as hiatus anyway

- Not all dialects agree on which words have hiatus and some have gone a lot further, using hiatus even in words like *athair* [a.ɪrʲ]

The letter combinations **bh**, **dh**, **gh** and **mh** also frequently end up as hiatus between vowels:

bodhar [bo.ər]	ogha [o.ə]	gobha [go.ə]
odhar [o.ər]	comhairle [kõ.əRlə]	leabhar [Lʲo.ər]

In fact, they are hardly ever pronounced as actual consonants ([v], [ɣ] etc) between vowels. The only words that you're going to meet in a hurry where these are pronounced as [ɣ] between vowels are probably *laghail* [Lɣɣal] and *modhail* [moɣal].

Hiatus can't occur more than once in a word. When you add the [ən] ending onto a word which ends in [.ɪ], the **dh** (that was silent previously) is pronounced [j] as it is now located between vowels:

aghaidhean	taghaidhean	spreadhaidhean
[ɣ.ijən]	[tɣ.ɪjən]	[sbrʲɛ.ɪjən]

You meet this thing in all sorts of places - for example, there's a place on Islay called Oa (*An Obha* in Gaelic) and Scots has the word *oe* - from Gaelic *ogha*.

Incidentally, did you know that in Old Irish this hiatus thing was just spelled with two vowels, sticking the consonant in is a 'modern' idea: *athar* ⇐ ᴧeꝛ, *ogha* ⇐ ᴧue, *leotha* ⇐ Leu, *adha* ⇐ ᴧe, *motha* ⇐ moᴧ...

4.4   Nasal vowels

Ok, housekeeping. Nasal vowels aren't the same thing as nasalization, not in the Gaelic context anyway (the kind of thing that makes *an cù* sound like *an gù* we'll talk about in 4.16.1).

To produce a nasal vowel, you say the vowel with your velum lowered. Or in less linguistic terms, you speak through your nose while saying the vowel. If you hold your hand up to your nose while saying a nasal vowel, you can actually feel some of the air coming out.

A really good trick for making nasal vowels is to tilt your head back and say a vowel. In that position it's almost impossible to make vowels which aren't nasal. So you can get used to saying nasal vowels with your head in that position if you have difficulties with them.

The question of which vowels are nasal in Gaelic is a tricky one though. Dialects vary considerably as to which vowels are nasalized and which aren't and there isn't much of a consensus emerging in Standard Gaelic either so far.

The good news is that in spite of linguists arguing over the details, nasalization is noticeable but not highly important in Gaelic. Especially younger speakers more and more seem to be doing away with "unexpected" cases of nasalization. What that means is that Gaelic speakers often have very audibly nasal vowels but that in most cases, it doesn't change the meaning whether you have a nasal vowel or not.

Why bother with explanations then? Well, for one thing you will hear very nasal vowels from some native speakers and with no explanation this might be a little confusing.

In Gaelic these nasal vowels mainly occur in stressed syllables (see 4.12.1) in the following cases:

- after the nasal consonants **m-, mh-, n-**

- before the nasal consonants **-m, -mh, -n, -nn, -ng**

- always near a disappeared nasal (where the **-m, -mh, -n, -nn, -ng** isn't pronounced anymore and has only left behind a nasal quality)

Let's look at some examples:

After **m-**, **mh-**, **n-**		
màthair [mã:hərʲ]	mhill [vĩːLʲ]	naoidh [Nũ̃j]
Before **-m**, **-mh**, **-n**, **-nn**, **-ng**		
am [ãũm]	tàmh [tã:v]	aon [ũ̃:n]
fàinne [fã:Nʲə]	ceann [kʲãũN]	being [bẽĩŋʲgʲ]
Near Disappeared Nasal		
Amhlaidh [ãũLɪ]	innse [ĩ:ʃə]	còmhnard [kõ:nəRd]

As a rule of thumb this will do fine. As I said, it's erratic. For example, *mór* [moːr] never has a nasal vowel, even if it shows up as *mhór* however *faicinn* [fɛ̃çgʲɪNʲ], which doesn't even have a nasal in the stressed syllable, has a nasal [ɛ̃].

Theoretically nasalization occasionally does mark a difference in meaning, for example in the pair *cha bhi* [xa viː] 'will not be' and *cha mhi* [xa vĩː] 'I am not'. In practice it doesn't matter much because context will generally give you a clue to the intended meaning. In this case it's syntax: *cha bhi mi ann* 'I won't be there' vs *cha mhi a bhios ann* 'it won't be me who will be there'. The only word I've come across so far which has vowels that must be nasal is *dhia* [ʝĩã] 'yuck' which needs the nasalization to distinguish it from *dhia* [ʝia] 'God!'. For that reason, it's sometimes even spelled *dhiamh*.

So, watch out for it but don't lose any sleep over it.

4.5   Lenition

Ever wondered why it's [fɛsgar **m**ah] for 'good afternoon' but [madɪNʲ **v**ah] for 'good morning' and [gle: **v**a] on bottles of Glayva? Or why Gaels will tell you that Mhàiri is pronounced [**v**aːrʲɪ], not [**m**aːrʲɪ]? And that Hamish is really someone called *Seumas*? A thing called 'lenition' is behind all of this.

Lenition is one of the most obvious and important sound changes in Gaelic. It is extremely common and understanding it is vital to good Gaelic. It has many different functions in the language and there are many examples of spoken Gaelic where only the presence or absence of lenition will be the key to understanding a sentence.

Here are a few examples which will help you appreciate how it affects the pronunciation and the importance of getting it right. Don't worry about how it actually works at this stage, this is just to give you an idea of what the potential damage of getting it wrong is:

[ə maxg]	her son	⇔	[ə vaxg]	his son
[buəl ɛ]	hit him!	⇔	[vuəl ɛ]	he hit
[na Lʲebɪ]	in her bed	⇔	[na lebɪ]	in his bed
[ga kaːNʲəɣ]	criticising her	⇔	[ga xaːNʲəɣ]	criticising him

As you've probably already spotted, the kind of lenition you need to worry about only affects the first consonant of a word. So what then is lenition?

The word 'lenition' literally means 'softening' (from Latin *lenis*) which is appropriate because it describes the effect of a consonant getting softer.   That's actually what this effect is called in the Gaelic languages, in Gaelic it's *sèimheachadh* [ʃɛ:vəxəɣ] and in Irish *séimhiú* [ʃe:vu:], both meaning 'gentling'.   Welsh, Cornish and Breton also have lenition (where it's usually

called 'soft mutation').   In the following table, the first three columns show the examples on their own, as you would find them in a dictionary. The last column shows what happens when you put them together:

	the	woman/wife	small		the small woman
Gaelic	an	bean	beag	⇒	a' **bh**ean **bh**eag
Irish	an	bean	beag	⇒	an **bh**ean **bh**eag
Manx	yn	ben	beg	⇒	y **v**en **v**eg
Welsh	yn	**g**wraig	bach	⇒	y **w**raig **f**ach
Cornish	an	**g**wreg	byhan	⇒	an **w**reg **v**yhan
Breton	an	**g**wreg	bihan	⇒	ar **w**reg **v**ihan

Incidentally, some people refer to lenition as 'aspiration', especially in older books.   Aspiration is something different altogether if you remember.   It's that puff of air you get after a consonant such as [p] or [k]. But strictly speaking, lenition does not involve any puffs of air so try to stick to the term lenition or *sèimheachadh*.

Various things can cause lenition in Gaelic.   While this will take us into the realms of grammar, we will look at this in the next chapter because it's important and because there are few comprehensive lists that tell you where you get lenition.

A general pointer before we look at the sound changes themselves:

> A lenited sound will **generally** be made in broadly the same place
> in your mouth as the unlenited sound.
> Remember, you're basically weakening an existing sound!

Unlenited Sound	Lenited Sound	Example	
b	v	bLaː	⇒ gle: vLaː
bj	vj	bjɔː	⇒ gle: vjɔː
p	f	paldʲ	⇒ gle: faldʲ
pj	fj	pjaLagəx	⇒ gle: fjaLagəx
m	v	moːr	⇒ gle: voːr
mj	vj	mjauLdə	⇒ gle: vjauLdə
f	-	fuər	⇒ gle: uər
fj	j	fjuːN	⇒ gle: juːN
d	ɣ	dɔnə	⇒ gle: ɣɔnə
dʲ	ʝ	dʲɛrɛg	⇒ gle: ʝɛrɛg
t	h	tanə	⇒ gle: hanə
tʲ	h	tʲiːNʲ	⇒ gle: hiːNʲ
	hj	tʲauN	⇒ gle: hjauN
g	ɣ	gɔrɔm	⇒ gle: ɣɔrɔm
gʲ	ʝ	gʲiar	⇒ gle: ʝiar
k	x	kas	⇒ gle: xas
kʲ	ç	kʲaːR	⇒ gle: çaːR
Lʲ	l	Lʲeʃgʲ	⇒ gle: leʃgʲ
N	n	Nɯːv	⇒ gle: nɯːv
Nʲ	n	NʲiaLəx	⇒ gle: niaLəx
R	r	Rag	⇒ gle: rag
s	h	sũːNdəx	⇒ gle: hũːNdəx
ʃ	h	ʃɛrɛv	⇒ gle: hɛrɛv
	hj	ʃɔːLdə	⇒ gle: hjɔːLdə

As you can see all Gaelic consonants except one can be lenited (unless you're aiming for Harris Gaelic, where [L] can also be lenited). In the normal writing system this is usually shown by inserting an h after the consonant. There are four sounds which are regularly lenited in spoken Gaelic but don't show this in the normal writing system: [Lʲ] [N] [Nʲ] and [R]. The one sound which really never lenites is [L].

Note also how two of the palatal sounds, [tʲ] and [ʃ] can lenite to two different sounds: [h] and [hj]. If [tʲ] or [ʃ] are followed by a front vowel, you get [h]. If [tʲ] or [ʃ] are followed by a back vowel, you get [hj] (there will be more on this in section 5.6.3. If you want to, you can read that section first then come back here). Let's look at a few more examples:

Slender Consonant + Front Vowel		Slender Consonant + Back Vowel	
tinn [tʲiːNʲ]	glé thinn [hiːNʲ]	teann [tʲauN]	glé theann [hjauN]
teth [tʲe]	glé theth [he]	tiugh [tʲu]	glé thiugh [hju]
tearc [tʲɛrg]	glé thearc [hɛrg]	teòma [tʲoːmə]	glé theòma [hjoːmə]
sìn [ʃiːn]	shìn [hiːn]	seall [ʃauL]	sheall [hjauL]
seas [ʃes]	sheas [hes]	siùil [ʃuːl]	shiùil [hjuːl]
sèimh [ʃɛːv]	glé shèimh [hɛːv]	seòl [ʃoːL]	sheòl [hjoːL]

The question of what happens when you have more than one consonant at the start of a word is dealt with in section 5.6.6.

✎ Exercise 86.

Listen carefully to the following words which have all been lenited by the word in front of them. Think about what the original sound must have been and write it down. Remember that in some cases there may be more than one possibility. Here's an example:

01 mə xas ⇒ kas	06	11	16
02	07	12	17
03	08	13	18
04	09	14	19
05	10	15	20

✎ Exercise 87.

This is a listening exercise that you can do irrespective of your level of Gaelic. In Gaelic, if a verb at the beginning of a sentence is lenited, it shows that something is in the past tense. If it isn't, then it usually means that the verb has a different function.

For example, [vuəl miʃə] means "I hit" but [buəl miʃə] means "hit ME!". So picking up on lenition is important. You will hear short sentences consisting of just a verb and the word [miʃə] (ME!). Decide which are lenited and therefore in the past and which are an order to do something. Don't worry about the meaning of the verbs if you have just started Gaelic, just make sure you hear which ones are lenited and which aren't.

	Lenited ⇒ Past	Unlenited ⇒ Order
01		
02		
03		
04		
05		
06		
07		
08		
09		
10		
11		
12		
13		
14		
15		
16		
17		
18		

4.5.1   Single lenition and jumping lenition

If you're just starting with Gaelic, this will be jumping the gun a little bit (because in many ways this is a grammar issue) but you'll eventually find this very useful.

Ok, rule of thumb: lenition is always caused by something, it doesn't just "show up". The main (apparent) exception are words which are always lenited (mainly for historical reasons), for example:

théid [he:dʲ]	chì [çiː]	gheibh [ʝev]
nì [niː]	shuas [huəs]	shìos [hiəs]
fhathast [ha.əsd]	thugam [hugəm]	thalla [haLə]
Bhaltos [vaLdəs]	dhachaidh [ɣaxɪ]	fhéin [he:n]

Except for place-names, these are not numerous at all. Which means that in the vast majority of cases, there's something causing the lenition; most commonly a particular word or a grammatical context:

glé [gleː] ⇒ glé mhath [gle: vah]	
dà [da:] ⇒ dà chù [da: xu:]	lenition caused by word
mo [mə] ⇒ mo thaigh [mə hɤj]	
do [də] ⇒ cha do dhùin [xa də ɣu:Nʲ]	
dhùin [ɣu:Nʲ]	
caileag mhór [kalag vo:r]	lenition caused by grammatical context
móran thaighean [mo:ran hɛhən]	

To make things easier, I'm giving you a list of most words or types of words that cause lenition in Gaelic, grouped according to their behaviour. If you're just starting with Gaelic, don't worry about labels like definite article and genitive plural, you'll meet them as you progress. But when you do come across these, you can always come back to check how exactly lenition behaves.

As I said above, they're grouped into incidents of Single Lenition and Jumping Lenition - I'll explain after the table what these terms mean.

Single Lenition (which only affects the next word)	
▪ possessives and all derived forms	
mo, do, a[23]	mo **ch**at beag geal, a **th**aigh mór
'gam, 'gad, 'ga	'gam **bh**ualadh, 'gad **fh**aicinn
'nam, 'nad, 'na	'nam **sh**easamh, 'nad **dh**ùisg
'am, 'ad	'am **dh**éidh, 'ad **bh**alach
▪ certain prepositions	
a[24]*, bho, de, do, fo, mu, ro, tro*	bho **ch**at beag geal
air[25]	air **bh**ior mór, air **mh**àl mór
ar[26]	ar **fh**ichead
▪ certain words	
aon, dà, a' chiad	dà **bh**òrd beag buidhe
glé, ro, gun[27]*, chan, bu*	gun **bh**òrd beag buidhe
	bu **bh**òrd beag buidhe
▪ certain prefixes	
deagh, droch, dearbh, prìomh,	deagh **bh**òrd beag buidhe
mór, beò, ath, leth, àrd, so-,	leth **bh**òrd beag buidhe
do, mì-, co-, sìor-, ioma-,	sìor **fh**às mór
seann, ban-, etc	seann **bh**òrd beag buidhe
▪ the infinitive particle *a*	bu toil leam cat a **bh**ualadh
▪ the relative particle *a*	a **bh**uaileas, a **dh**ùineas

---

[23] Meaning 'his'.

[24] These are the short forms of *de* and *do*.

[25] Only in what are called 'stative expressions', expressions that describe a state, not an action (from the Gaelic point of view of course).

[26] This is, incidentally, short for *thar* 'over' and not a form of *air* 'on' and pronounced [ər]. There are some people today who pronounce it [ɛrʲ] but that's caused by people mistakenly spelling it *air*.

[27] Meaning 'without'.

▪ past tense and conditional	
with *do* dropped	**bhuail, dhùin, sheinn**
with *do/dh'/do dh'/na*[28]	cha do **bh**uail, dh'**fh**àg, na **sh**einn
conditional	**bh**uailinn, **dh**ùininn, **sh**einneadh
▪ comparative & superlative with **f-**	
as & nas	as **fh**aisge, nas **fh**aisge
▪ noun/noun determiner plus an indefinite plural noun	
common nouns	prìs **th**aighean beaga buidhe
móran, beagan, cus, torr...	móran[29] **th**aighean beaga buidhe

Jumping Lenition (affects all words in a group)

▪ vocative	
a	a **Dh**òmhnaill **mh**óir **bh**òidhich
▪ feminine nominative and prepositional nouns[30]	
	caileag **mh**ór **bh**òidheach
▪ the nominative definite article with a feminine noun	
a'	a' **ch**aileag **mh**ór **bh**òidheach
▪ the definite article after a preposition irrespective of gender	
bhon a'	bhon a' **bh**òrd **bh**eag **bh**uidhe
bhon a'	bhon a' **ch**aileag **mh**ór **bh**òidheach
▪ the genitive defininite article with a masculine noun	
noun + *a'*	dath a' **bh**ùird **bh**ig **bh**uidhe
▪ slenderisation of a masculine noun	
noun + masculine noun	dath bùird **bh**ig **bh**uidhe

---

[28] *Na* is a contracted form of *an do* used colloquially in various dialects in the Western Isles.

[29] Some speakers have blocked lenition after words like *móran;* see 4.5.4.

[30] In colloquial Gaelic, also in the genitive, for example *ad na caileig mhór bhòidheach, doras na h-eaglaise bheag...*

Now for the explanation I promised. Lenition in Gaelic behaves in two fundamentally different ways and being aware of that can solve some major headaches for you. When a word causes lenition <u>only</u> on the word immediately after it, we call that 'single lenition'.

dà chù mór geal   do chù mór geal

bho chù mór geal   aon chù mór geal

droch chù mór geal   'nad chù mór geal

cha bhuail mi   cha do bhuail mi

nas fhearr buileach   móran chasan fada

Most words which cause lenition in Gaelic belong to the above group. So most commonly, a word that causes lenition will cause it once, no matter how many words follow.

The other type is called 'jumping lenition'. Jumping lenition is good fun. When this happens, lenition will occur again and again until a new part of the sentence begins:

bhon chù mhór gheal

ron chù mhór gheal

air a' chrùn bheag bhuidhe

leis a' chrùn bheag bhuidhe

caileag mhór gheal

beinn mhór gheal

fir mhóra gheala

leis a' chrùn bheag bhuidhe

Now the fun bit begins. Both these can occur 'on top of each other':

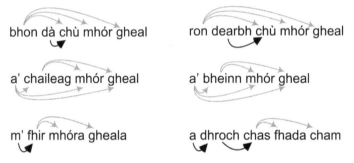

bhon dà chù mhór gheal

ron dearbh chù mhór gheal

a' chaileag mhór gheal

a' bheinn mhór gheal

m' fhir mhóra gheala

a dhroch chas fhada cham

As you can see, sometimes there are several things that cause lenition on the same word. In *bhon dà chù* for example, the *bhon* causes jumping lenition and lenites *cù* to *chù* but the word *dà* itself causes single lenition and also turns *cù* to *chù*. The outcome fortunately is the same, it's [xu:] in both cases. So what, you may be saying to yourself now but just hang on to that thought because it gets more interesting when we've looked at something called blocked lenition.

So when you come across lenition, just get into the habit for now of making yourself aware of what is leniting what. Because they can occur on top of each other and cancel out things like blocked lenition, which you will meet shortly, this will help you avoid headaches later. Try to avoid the somewhat mistaken learner rule of thumb 'when in doubt, lenite' that some people apply.

✎ Exercise 88.

Here are some short phrases that contain lenited words. Using the table on page 183, draw in the arrows (you may want to do this on a photocopy) to show which word is causing which lenition. Use different colours for Single Lenition and Jumping Lenition.

01 Seo mo chiad bhriogais fhada.

02 Thuit torr fhir bheaga gheala an-sin.

03 An do bhris e tro dhoras mór leis a' gheimhleag mhór ghobhlach?

04 Chuir mi d' fhìdheall shnog air ghleus dhut.

05 A Thormoid bhig bhìodaich, tha e ro dhaor!

06 Sin a' bhó bheag dhonn as fhaisge ort.

07 'S beag orm do dhroch chainnt shalach shàrachail.

08 Tha mo chéile airson sgoil mhór Ghàidhlig a thogail an-seo.

09 Chan fhaigh sinn deagh leabaidh bhog ron ath mhìos.

10 'S e gnìomh a dhearbhas mar a chanas a sheanair.

11 Cha mhi a chluinneas tu air a' bheinn mhór chas ghlas ud.

12 Sin a' cheist ghòrach as fhaide a thog e 'nam chlas a-riamh.

4.5.2   Why lenition?

This book isn't meant as a guide to the history of Gaelic but people ask this question so often that we will take a short trip to the past on this occasion.

Lenition is actually something very common in the languages of the world. Even English has it. You probably just never thought of it that way.

In general, lenition happens when you get a consonant stuck between two vowels. The consonant (which needs a lot of energy to make) tries to become more like the vowels (which take very little energy to make). So it changes to something slightly weaker. This can go on and on until the sound completely disappears over time. Like wedging an ice cube between two mugs of hot mulled wine…

For a [t] sound this might look something like this:

$$t \Rightarrow d \Rightarrow ð \Rightarrow h \Rightarrow nothing$$

For example, in Indo-European, the ancestor of most modern European languages, the word for 'mother' was

mātér

Note how the **t** was stuck between to vowels? Even worse, one of them was a long vowel. Now, take a piece of paper and write down the word for 'mother' in as many European and Indian languages (not Tamil) as you can think of: German, Scots, English, French, Italian, Spanish, Irish, Hindi…

Now let's look at what you got:

Mutter	mātā	mótina	madre	máthair
(German)	(Panjabi)	(Lithuanian)	(Italian)	(Irish)
mither	mata	māte	madre	màthair
(Scots)	(Gujarati)	(Latvian)	(Spanish)	(Gaelic)
mor	mor		mère	moir
(Norwegian)	(Pashtu)		(French)	[mɔːir]
				(Manx)

So what happened? Well, in some cases nothing much. We started with a [t] and we still have a [t]. In other cases, Scots for example, the [t] has become a [ð] - it has lenited (and voiced)! If you look at the other examples you will see that from [d] through to [h] every stage of lenition can be found in modern European languages.

The bottom row is interesting. It represents that 'last stage' as it were. In many cases, the old [t] has disappeared, in the case of French via Old French *medre* for example but either way, mission accomplished!

Now where does Gaelic fit into this? Well, the origin of lenition in Gaelic in most cases goes back to a consonant getting stuck between two vowels long, long, long ago. This isn't necessarily obvious in modern Gaelic so we have to learn when to lenite but that was the reason for it developing centuries ago.

Let's have a look at two examples ('the small man/woman'):

Common Celtic[31]
sindos wiros bekkos   ⇒ indah ferah bekkah
sindā benā bekkā   ⇒ indā bhenā bhekkā

So thousands of years ago, you had this **-ā** ending appearing with feminine nouns. That put the **b** between vowels and off lenition went. Masculine nouns were safe because the endings (both **-os** and the later **-ah**) ended in a consonant.

Because lenition now marked gender and case, the endings were really superfluous so people dropped them. And suddenly lenition wasn't a sound rule anymore in Gaelic but a grammatical rule. A few more sounds dropped off then and the spelling was tweaked and we get:

Old Irish	Common Gaelic	Scots Gaelic
ın ꝼeꝵ becc	⇒ ᴀn ꝼeᴀꝵ beᴀɤ	⇒ am fear beag
ın ḃen becc	⇒ ᴀn ḃeᴀn ḃeᴀɤ	⇒ a' bhean bheag

The dot is lenition, remember? And yes, that really happened. In fact, it still happens. If you go to Sardinia, you will find that people call a cat *gatu* [gatu]. But when they say 'the cat', they will say *su gatu* [su ɣatu]. Which is exactly what happened so long ago in the Celtic languages.

> This was an explanation about the historical origins of lenition. It may have started life as a simple sound rule thousands of years ago but it no longer operates in the modern language.
> This means you must **learn and remember** when to lenite.

That's it, no more on the history of lenition!

---

[31] These are all reconstructed forms, as we don't actually have written records. They were worked out by linguists who looked at the modern words and historical records and then worked out what the older forms must have looked like. A bit like forensic anthropology where you work out from a dead body how and when someone died.

4.5.3   Backformation, lenition and a hogshead

In spite of what you might be thinking of now, there is a serious link between the three words above. And you're about to find out just what that is. And you can relax a bit, this chapter is really here to give you an insight into how Gaelic ticks but not a lesson as such.

Have you ever noticed that languages can be a bit picky about what sounds or sound combinations you're allowed to have at the start of a word? English for example is quite happy with **ng** in the middle or at the end of a word (*ring, finger...*) but does not like it at the start of a word. Swahili on the other hand has no problem with that: *nguo* "cloth", *nguruwe* "pig", *ngariba* "professional circumciser"...

Gaelic in some ways is even pickier. It doesn't like fricatives at the beginning of a word unless something is in front of it causing lenition. As a result, when Gaelic comes across a new word with such a sound at the beginning, it automatically assumes that something has lenited this poor word and all you have to do to get to the basic word is to reverse the lenition. Over the centuries Gaelic has reshaped hundreds if not thousands of loanwords in this way to make them fit the language's idea of a 'proper word'.

Let's look at some words that were borrowed a long time ago:

haggis (Scots)	⇒ *taigeis* [tagʲɪʃ]
Hjaltlandi (Norse)	⇒ *Sealtainn* [ʃaLdɪNʲ]
hail (Scots)	⇒ *tadhal* [tɤ.əL]
hogshead (Scots)	⇒ *tocasaid* [tɔxgəsɪdʲ]
hǫll (Norse)	⇒ *talla* [taLə]
thrang (Scots)	⇒ *trang* [traŋg]
vaðill (Norse)	⇒ *fadhail* [fɤ.al]
vág (Norse)	⇒ *bàgh* [ba:ɣ]
vervain (Scots)	⇒ *bearbhain* [bɛrɛvɛNʲ]
võtum (Latin)	⇒ *bòid* [bɔ:dʲ]
wall (Scots)	⇒ *balla* [baLə]
warants (Old Norman French)	⇒ *barantas* [barəNdəs]
wheel (Scots)	⇒ *cuidheall* [kujəL]
whip (English)	⇒ *cuip* [kuçb]
wudacocc (Old English)	⇒ *budagoc* [budəgɔg]
yawl (English)	⇒ *geòla* [gʲɔ:Lə]
þormund (Norse)	⇒ *Tormod* [tɔrɔməd]
þrǽll (Norse)	⇒ *tràill* [tra:Lʲ]
þursa (Norse)	⇒ *tursa* [tuRsə]

So, as Gaelic doesn't generally like [w] [hw] [v] [θ] [h] and so on at the start, it turns them into the nearest equivalent unlenited sound that makes sense (from the Gaelic point of view of course):

[hw] ⇒ [k]	[w] ⇒ [b], [f]
[θ] ⇒ [t]	[j] ⇒ [gʲ]
[v] ⇒ [b], [u], [f]	[h] ⇒ [t]
[hj] ⇒ [ʃ]	

And so on. Words with [v] are interesting, some get reversed to [b] and some adjusted to [u] or [f], for example Norse *vík* to Gaelic *ùig*.

This applies to quite a few place-names too and can be good fun - find a bilingual map and look for places where the Gaelic name has t but the English name h:

Habost	⇒ *Tàbost*	Hasklete	⇒ *Tàcleit*
Haugh	⇒ *An Talchan*	Herbusta	⇒ *Tearbusta*
Holm (Inv)	⇒ *An Tuilm*	Holm (Lewis)	⇒ *Tolm*
Horgabost	⇒ *Torgabost*	Howmore	⇒ *An Togh Mór*
The How	⇒ *An Tobha*	Wiay	⇒ *Fuidheigh*

Sometimes only the place-name with the **t-** has survived and you have to go back to the Norse roots to see the h:

Tocamol	⇐ Haukaholmr
Tosabus	⇐ Húsa Bólstaðr
Tundal	⇐ Hundalr

Sometimes Gaels in different areas dealt with the same word differently. Here's a beautiful example: there's a place in Argyll called *An t-Òban* in Gaelic (anglicised as Oban) and a place in the Western Isles called *An t-Òb* (anglicised as Leverburgh). Both are masculine nouns grammatically speaking. Now there are signs welcoming people in both towns but one of the signs in Oban reads *Fàilte gun Òbain* whereas the one in the Western Isles says *Fàilte gun t-Òb*. The first is totally expected, the second very strange because according to grammar, we'd expect the **t-** to disappear. Normally this is explained as an 'exception' to inquisitive people by slightly confused locals. But something much more fascinating has happened here. Both words derive from the same Norse word *hóp* meaning a type of bay. But Gaels in different places dealt with the offending h in two different ways. In Argyll they decided to drop the h, so you got *òb* and ultimately *òban* 'a little bay'. In the Western Isles on the other hand the h was taken to be lenited t and promptly reconstructed as *tòb*. So both signs are perfectly grammatical and regular, except that it would make more sense to spell the second one *Fàilte gun Tòb*. Neat, isn't it?

So, ignoring instances of lenition, the only place where you regularly find [v] or [h] at the beginning of words is in Norse place names with **v** or **h** or very recent loanwords which haven't been gaelicised properly (yet):

Herað (Harris)	⇒ *Na Hearadh*
Hafn (Hann)	⇒ *Na Hann*
Haf (the Atlantic)	⇒ *Na Haf*
Vatnlausa (Valtos)	⇒ *Bhaltos*
Vatnsøy (Vatarsay)	⇒ *Bhatarsaigh*
video	⇒ *bhideo*

Place names are probably 'safer' from this than other words because in speech, they are very often used in the genitive or after a leniting preposition where [v] or [h] are ok. You're far more likely to hear *muinntir Bhaltois, Loch Bhaltois* or *a' dol a Bhaltois* than *Bhaltos* on its own. And of course in the case of **h** Gaelic often cheats and slaps a definite article in front of the word. So backforming these isn't a big priority.

The habit of doing this backformation thing (also called de-lenition) is so common that no words are safe. This is true in all modern Celtic languages - Breton for example turned Latin *fenestra* into *prenestr.* In Gaelic and Irish this still happens a lot when a word begins with a vowel because there is one consonant that disappears completely when lenited. Yes, the **f**. This is why in some dialects you get extra **f** sounds cropping up. You probably know *eagal* 'fear' but there are dialects where the speakers at some point assumed that *eagal* must have suffered lenition and, being good Gaels trying to speak properly, put the **f** back on and we have *feagal.* Very much like Eliza Doolittle stating that *in 'ertford, 'ereford and 'ampshire, 'urricanes 'ardly hever 'appen.*

In Gaelic, Irish and Manx this happened a lot over time:

Old Irish	Gaelic	Irish	Manx
áınne	fàinne	fáinne	fainey [fe:Nʲə]
uaċt	fuachd	fuacht	feayght [fi:əx]
allaſ	fallas	allas	ollish [ɑliʃ]
ecla	(f)eagal	eagla	aggle [a:ɣəl]

But this is something which is still active today so if you come across unexpected **f** sounds, you know what's happening!

Ok, another anecdote. Lenition over time can change the appearance of a word more dramatically than Hollywood makeup artists the appearance of ageing stars. The Gaelic word for sister, *piuthar* [pju.ər], is a stunning example of that. What would you say if I told you that the English word *sister*, the French word *sœur*, the Irish word *deirfiúr* and the Gaelic word *piuthar* have the same ancestor? Let's see if I can change your mind about what you just accused me of!

Go back about 5000 years and ask a local running around Europe[32] what they call their sister and the answer you'd probably get (assuming they didn't run you through) would be *swesōr*. Now let's follow this word in a few of the branches of the Indo-European family tree:

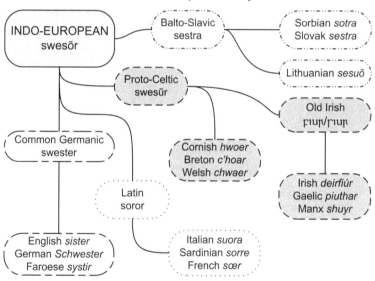

Ignoring that fascinating corner of Europe where the Basques have always lived. As I explained, they predate the arrival of the Indo-Europeans so their language is totally unrelated; they'd tell you that a woman's sister was **anizba* and a man's sister *arreba*.

Latin and Germanic are fairly obvious. As most, they took the original word, added a **t** and lost various bits of it. Something fascinating happened on the way to Old Irish ſiuſ[33] though. Because in the days before Old Irish the words for 'my', 'your' and 'his' already caused lenition, this turned *swesūr* into *hwehūr*. But as the **hw** never sat well with the Gael, it was soon turned into an **f**. The other branches of Celtic mostly just simplified the word. Anyway, by the time we arrive at Old Irish, unlenited 'our/your/their sister' was aſ ſiuſ, faſ ſiuſ, a ſiuſ and lenited 'my/your/his sister' was mo ſiuſ, do ſiuſ, a ſiuſ! Yes, slightly confusing.

Ok, we're almost there now. In Irish, some meaning changes take place and the word *siúr* comes to mean 'kinswoman' and to distinguish their kinswomen from their sisters, they stick *deirbh* 'true' (Gaelic *dearbh*) in front, so we eventually get modern Irish *deirfiúr*. So your sister in Irish is technically your 'true sister'.

What about Gaelic then? Well, with the application of only a moderate amount of whisky, Gaels decided that because everyone knows that **f** is nothing but lenited **p**, they unlenited the ſiuſ to piuſ, added the hiatus and hey presto, we have *piuthar*.

And because you're probably shaking your head now - other languages do things like that too. When the French for example borrowed Germanic words with **w-** in the 11th century, they slapped a **g** in front because they didn't like **w-** at the beginning. So **werra* 'war' became *guerre*, **wespa* 'wasp' became *guêpe*, **wimpil* 'pennant' became *guimpe* and so on.

---

[33] The ſ is a small **s** and the ſ is a small **r**.

Also in this group is the word *gaule* 'a Gaul'. Allow me to expand? The ancient Germanic tribes had the word **walχaz* which meant 'foreigner' and 'Romanised person'. In Old High German, this word had evolved into **walah*, which the Old French borrowed as *waulle* and then slapped the **g-** onto, turning it into *gaule*. Old English turned **walχaz* into *walesc*, which in turn gave rise to *Welsh*. As Romanised Germanic tribesmen were rare in Britain that era, in Old English it was used to refer to a Brythonic-speaking person - as they were the "main type of foreigner" from the Anglo-Saxon point of view as they invaded Britain.

4.5.4   When not to lenite

Have you ever wondered why it is that you have a *sgian-dubh* when all grammar books tell you it should be *sgian dhubh* because *sgian* is feminine? Or why you have lenition in *Dùn Bheagan* but not in *Dùn Dèagh*? Well, the mystery is about to be solved!

We already had a look at the different places in your mouth where Gaelic sounds are made. Accordingly, we can put the consonant sounds of Gaelic into three major groups:

Group 1 - Labial Sounds

written with the letters **b p m f**

Group 2 - Dental Sounds

written with the letters **d n t l s**

Group 3 - Velar Sounds

written with the letters **c g**

So what about them? Well, apart from the rules which tell you when you get lenition, there was another (simple) rule in old Gaelic which said that:

> If you get a sound at the end of a word which is in the same sound group as the first sound of the next word, do not lenite where lenition would normally apply

For example, grammar says you should lenite adjectives after a feminine noun. But *sgian-dubh* was not lenited in the old language because the last sound in *sgian* was in the same sound group as the first sound in *dubh*, they were both dental.

Modern linguists call these groups "homo-organic consonants". Much more interesting though, in Middle Irish these are called *consuinne ghaoil* or "kindred consonants". In modern Gaelic we'd say *consain ghaoil.* And yes, people did study Irish grammar and phonology that far back. Blocked lenition was known to them as *cadad consuinne* or "consonant hardening". The word *cadad* does not survive in Scottish Gaelic but you could call the process *cruadhachadh chonsan,* which would be a nice continuation of a very old name for them, don't you think?

But I digress. Here are more examples which show how this works:

Lenition Allowed	Lenition Blocked
Dùn Bheagan (Group 2+1)	Dùn Dèagh (Group 2+2)
Camshron (Group 1+2)	Caimbeul (Group 1+1)
Cromdhail (Group 1+2)	Cromba[34] (Group 1+1)
MacDhòmhnaill (Group 3+2)	MacGriogair (Group 3+3)
MacMhata (Group 3+1)	MacCaluim (Group 3+3)
air an fhearann (Group 2+1)	air an duilleag (Group 2+2)
air a' chù (Group 2[35]+3)	air an taigh (Group 2+2)
air a' ghad (Group 2+3)	air an leabaidh (Group 2+2)

Now, in Modern Gaelic this rule isn't as active anymore so we definitely say *ad dhonn*, not **ad donn*. This means that if you're talking about a special knife that goes with Highland dress, you talk about your *sgian-dubh* because this has become a fixed term in the language but if you talk about any old black knife, you talk about a *sgian dhubh*.

[34] *crom + bàigh*
[35] Even though the n is not present either in the spelling or the pronunciation, the language still behaves as if it still was there

Special Frozen Forms[36]	'Normal' Instances
sgian-dubh	sgian dhubh, sgian dhonn...
leth-taobh	leth-fhacal, leth-cheud...
aimbeart	aimhreit, aimhleas...
Caimbeul	cam-bhileach, cam-bheulach...

"But I've seen *NicGhriogair* or *MacIlleEathain* written!" Or worse, *Mac 'IllEathain*... I'm sure you have but technically both spellings are wrong. Or at least unhelpful. The issue with **c** + **c** or **c** + **g** in surnames is that first of all lenition is blocked. But because the sounds are so similar, the first **c** just doesn't get pronounced. This is not lenition but simply your mouth refusing to say the same thing twice in a row. So instead of pronouncing *NicGriogair* as with [çgʲ] + [g] you get [Nʲiç'gʲrʲigər] and instead of *MacGilleEathain* with [xg] + [gʲ] you get [maxgʲi'LʲɛhɪNʲ].

So absolutely no need for the **h** or dropping the **g** in surnames! It's just as much a spelling mistake as 'backround' is a common mis-spelling of 'background'.[37]

Here's a list of where this rule still applies:

After	Blocked	Not Blocked
Definite Article		
Nominative	an tunnag, an deoch, an lèine, an norrag...	an fheòrag...
Prepositional	air an drochaid, aig an taigh, san dùn...	san chàr...

---

[36] A frozen form is a form which only exists in very few set expressions. For example in English *waxing* (in the sense of 'growing') can only be used to describe the moon but not plants, children etc even though it could be used in such a way a long time ago.

[37] Google it if you don't believe me!

Genitive	deoch an dorais, dath an taighe…	dath an fheòir…
Chan + Future	cha[38] dèan, cha tòisich, cha nigh, cha dùin…	chan fhill…
+ Pronouns	cha tu, cha tusa, cha sinn, cha sinne	cha mhi…
Certain Words a' chiad	a' chiad turas, a' chiad sabhal…	a' chiad chas…
aon	aon turas, aon sabhal, aon taigh, aon neach…	aon ghath ..
bu[39]	bu tana, bu dona, bu salach…	bu mhi…
gun 'without'	gun salann, gun tuigse, gun drama…	gun chù…
seann[40]	seann duine, seann taigh, seann sluagh…	seann bhròg…
Genealogy	NicGriogair, MacCriomain, Caimbeul…	Camshron…

---

[38] Even though the -n has disappeared in pronunciation, its "echo" still prevents lenition. It's a bit like buried ruins in a field, you can't see the walls anymore but the wheat doesn't grow as well over the buried walls so you can "see the walls" from the air.

[39] *Bu* was *budh* a long time ago. In modern Gaelic **dh** is not a dental but used to be a dental [ð] and Gaelic still treats it as a dental.

[40] In old forms this can apply to *ath* (plus a dental), *droch* and *deagh* (plus **c** or **g**) as well, for example *ath turas*.

	Clann Dòmhnaill, Clann Raghnaill...	Clann Chamshroin...
	Sìol Tormaid, Sìol Diarmaid[41]...	Sìol Chaluim...
Place-names	Dùn Dèagh, Cromba[42], Innis Tuathail...	Dùn Bheagan...
Frozen forms	sgian-dubh, linn deug, mo nighean donn, ...	sgian dhubh...

The list above lists most categories where you're likely to encounter this phenomenon. It's probably impossible to give a fully exhaustive list but the important thing is that you are now aware of why this happens in the cases you're most likely to encounter.

And in case you have come across things like *cha thog* and *cha sheas*, that's mostly a Lewis thing. In parts of Lewis this rule is breaking down a bit with *cha* and *bu* (except with the irregular verbs so even in those areas *cha dàinig* is still unlenited). Which is neither good nor bad, it just is. Be aware of it but I wouldn't exactly recommend doing it yourself unless you're deliberately aiming for Lewis Gaelic.

Of course, very occasionally you will also encounter very conservative native speakers who still use forms such as *ad donn, mòran daoine* or *sgian salach* (as opposed to the more common *ad dhonn, mòran dhaoine* and *sgian shalach*). As it's increasingly rare, I wouldn't recommend you go for this very conservative pattern though.

In other cases, the rule has been in the process of breaking down for a while. For example, *àrd* and *làn* used to follow this rule (hence *àrd-doras, làn-dèanta, làn-dùbhlan...*) but even Dwelly lists a lot of lenited forms such as *àrd-shagart, làn-shoilleir* and *làn-thoilichte*.

---

[41] *Sìol* is moving towards lenition in all circumstances though.

[42] *Crom* 'crooked' + *bàigh* 'bay'.

So, there is single, jumping and blocked lenition to bear in mind when it comes to lenition. This can lead to quite complex effects. Let's start with something fairly straightforward, cases of single, jumping and blocked lenition happening one after the other:

air a' bhòrd mhór dubh   mo sheann chearc mhór dhubh

In the above, the *a'* (⇐ *an*) cannot lenite *dubh* because of the blocked lenition rule, so the lenition stops at *mhór*. The words *mo* and *seann* cause straightforward single lenition and after a feminine noun, we do not need to worry about blocked lenition so *cearc* lenites both adjectives.

But how about cases such as the following:

meud a' bhùird mhóir dhuibh   aois an dùin mhoir dhuibh

Although we have cases of blocked lenition in both cases, all adjectives still end up lenited because there are two separate instances of jumping lenition going on. The *a'* (⇐ *an*) again manages to lenite *bùird* and *móir* but cannot do anything to the *duibh* because of blocked lenition. However, because the slenderisation of *bòrd* to *bùird* also causes jumping lenition (the type that cannot be blocked), *duibh* is lenited to *dhuibh*. Similarly, in the second case an is blocked from leniting both *dùin* and *duibh* but because of the lenition caused by the slenderisation of *dùn* to *dùin, duibh* is lenited to *dhuibh*. I think 'cool!' covers it.

So you always need to make sure you've considered all possible cases of single, jumping and blocked lenition.

The following point is unrelated to the blocking rule. Although you can lenite virtually any Gaelic word (including the numbers, by the way) there are some words that resist lenition:

Possessives	ro **mo** chù, <u>tro **do**</u> dhoras, <u>bho **do**</u> thaigh…
Certain Words	<u>ro **gach**</u> doras, <u>anns **gach**</u> taigh…[43]
	cha **bu** mhi, cha **bu** diùid, cha **bu** mhór…
	<u>mar **s**inne</u>, <u>mar **s**ibhse</u>, <u>bu **s**inne</u>, <u>bu **s**ibhse</u>…
Demonstratives	<u>bho **seo**</u> a-mach, <u>tro **siud**,</u> <u>bu **sin**</u> am fear,
	air a' bhòrd **seo**…

Something vaguely reminiscent of this happens with the pronoun *thu* in certain settings. It's not the same thing but I'm listing it here because you then have all the instances of expected lenition not happening in one place.

is	is tu, is tusa
bu	bu tu, bu tusa
Future Relative	ciamar a bhios tu, mar a dh'òlas tu…
Conditional	bhiodh tu, a dh'òladh tu…

---

[43] Also *a h-uile* (which is short for *gach uile*): *dhan a h-uile cù*…

✎ Exercise 89.

Look at the following word combinations. The first word always lenites according to the grammar rules. Then decide whether the Blocked Lenition Rule can apply in this case and if yes, mark those groups where it is blocked. Here's an example:

aon + taigh   • *aon* normally lenites

           • *aon* is a word where the -n could block lenition

           • -n is in Group 2, t- in Group 2

              ⇒ Lenition is blocked ⇒ *aon taigh*

air an + cù   • *air an* normally lenites

           • *air an* is a combination where the -n could block lenition

           • -n is in Group 2, c- in Group 3

              ⇒ Lenition is not blocked ⇒ *air a' chù*

01 mo + ceann	14 bu + toil
02 dà + cas	15 gun + cliù
03 gun + dealbh	16 cha + mol
04 aon + taigh	17 a' chiad + duilleag
05 leis an + luchag	18 dath an + taighe
06 bhon + dùn	19 mo + tòn
07 sa + càr	20 cha do + tog
08 aon + màs	21 cha + tog
09 seann + dùthaich	22 aon + nead
10 a' chiad + cas	23 bu + diùid
11 bu + mór	24 mo + leabaidh
12 bhon + bó	25 seann + duine
13 cha + dùin	26 dath an + fir

❧ Exercise 90.

Because lenition is so common, here's another exercise for you. It combines all the things you've just learned about single and jumping lenition and blocked lenition. If you've just started doing Gaelic and aren't sure about the grammar yet, use the tables in the previous chapter. If you've 'done some Gaelic', try it without the lists, then go back and check if you've missed anything before checking the key.

Below are some sentences but lenition has not been marked. Mark all instances of lenition as you did in Exercise 87. Also mark blocked lenition by putting a double strikethrough through the arrows like this:

01 Nach do bhris do chlann bheag ghòrach aon d_oras?

02 Cha d_o b_ìd na coin t_ana d_onna ud mo c_at.

03 Bha móran d_aoine sa b_aile b_eag s_àmhach ud.

04 Ciamar a l_eughas mi sin gun s_olas 'nam s_eòmar b_eag?

05 Cha p_òs a' b_ean b_eag g_rinn sin do s_eann b_ràthair.

06 A M_àiri b_eag, tha thu 'gam s_ìor s_àrachadh le do b_eachdan.

07 An do t_uit am prìomh m_inistear air a' b_rat s_leamhnach seo?

08 Tha a d_eagh c_aman ris an d_oras t_rom g_orm.

09 Chan f_aca mi briseadh an d_orais t_ruim g_uirm.

10 Cha t_usa am fear a tha glé g_lé t_oilichte leis a' c_at m_ór d_ubh.

11 Cha m_ise an t_é a tha toilichte leis an d_roch c_o-dhùnadh seo.

12 B_uail dà p_eilear tron b_alla t_iugh b_uidhe fo m_o p_iuthar.

4.6   Initial [j] and [ɟ]

If you remember chapter 2.8, there was some confusing comment about [j] and [ɟ] and a promise about 'later'. Well, 'later' is now!

The strong [ɟ] only shows up in Gaelic as the result of lenited slender **d** or **g** at the beginning of a word. This means that everywhere else (in the middle or at the end of words) you only ever get [j]:

mo dheoch [mə ɟɔx]	chaidh [xaj]
dhìol [ɟiəL]	buidhe [bujə]
mo ghearan [mə ɟɛran]	laigh [Laj]
gheall [ɟauL]	cuidheall [kujəL]

So what's the catch? The catch is that you can also get [j] at the beginning of a word if it's not the result of slender **dh** or **gh**. This sometimes happens to words which begin with **e** or **i** followed by **a**, **o** or **u**[44]. So words like *eala* [jaLə] have a weak [j] at the beginning, not a strong [ɟ].

But then which words actually have this [j] since there are words like *eaglais* [egLɪʃ] which don't have it? The two easy cases are **eò** and **iu**. When a word begins with **eò** or **iu**, a [j] is always stuck on the front: *eòlas* [jɔːLəs], *eòrna* [jɔːRNə], *iuchair* [juxɪrʲ], *iùl* [juːL] etc.

---

[44] The *eu* group doesn't count as it's seen as a special combination which used to be spelled *éa*.

But when it begins with **ea** or **io** it's a bit more tricky. Words that begin in **ea** and are followed by [L] or [R] have the [j], all others do not. Words that begin in **io**, followed by an [L] or [N] plus another consonant have the [j], the others don't:

eaglais [egLɪʃ]		iomradh [imirəɣ]
earbsa [ɛrɛbsə]		iris [irʲɪʃ]
	vs	
eala [jaLə]		iolaire [juLɪrʲə]
earrach [jaRəx]		ionnsaich [jũːNsɪç]

You will find more detailed rules in the Guide and the most common ones in the wordlist at the end of the book. The only usable rules of thumb here are these two:

- if you have **ea** at the beginning of a word and it is pronounced [a], you get the extra sound, resulting in [ja].

- words where **io** is pronounced [u] or [uː] also get the extra sound, resulting in [ju] or [juː].

✎ Exercise 91.

All the following words either have a [j̠] or a [j] sound at the beginning. Double underline the words which have the strong [j̠] sound and underline the ones which have the weak [j] sound.

eala	dhìth	earrach	iuchair
dhìol	dhìom	a dh'fhios	cidhe
guidhe	a dh'Ìle	ghin	dh'ith
iùil	eòrna	ghearr	a ghiomach
dhiùlt	ghéill	Eòlaigearraidh	ghiùlain

4.7   Slenderisation or How to lose a vowel

If you remember, slenderisation is just another word for palatalisation. What this means is that sometimes in Gaelic a sound which wasn't palatal before is palatalised.

This can happen for a number of reasons, generally either to do with grammatical 'things' happening or phonological reasons (certain sounds bumping into each other):

blas [bLas] 'accent'	⇒	blais [bLaʃ] 'of an accent'
òg [ɔːg] 'young'	⇒	òig [ɔːgʲ] 'young' (genitive)
aol [ɯːL] 'lime'	⇒	aoil [ɯːl] 'of lime'

This effect can also spread and affect adjacent sounds. This is actually more common than the plain palatalisation which we just looked at:

balach [baLəx] 'boy'	⇒	balaich [baLɪç] 'boys'
ceòl [kʲɔːL] 'music'	⇒	ciùil [kʲuːl] 'of music'
geall [gʲauL] 'a bet'	⇒	gill [gʲiːLʲ] 'of a bet'

You can also have the reverse in which case it's called de-palatalisation:

cuir [kurʲ] 'put!'	⇒	cur [kur] 'putting'
màthair [maːhərʲ] 'mother'	⇒	màthar [maːhər] 'of a mother'
athair [ahərʲ] 'father'	⇒	athar [ahər] 'of a father'

Palatalisation is a really important feature of Gaelic. It happens a lot. And often it is the only clue to a difference in meaning as you've just seen.

This is one of those things in Gaelic which can be very difficult to hear for a learner, especially if there is background noise. But as I explained, as long as you make the right sounds when speaking yourself, you'll be fine on the whole.

It's not as crazy a concept as you might think. Languages often use some modification of a sound in a word to show a difference in meaning or use. English occasionally still uses a vowel change to indicate plural in some words: *mouse* ⇒ *mice*, *goose* ⇒ *geese* and even has a few cases of palatalisation itself. English has more recent examples too of course. Consider words like *stupid,* which can come out as [ʃtʃuːpɪd] (think Del Boy!) - with the entire group at the beginning palatalised because of the [j] sound that used to be before the **u** (in [stjuːpɪd]). You probably just never thought of it that way. And pairs like *Indian* and *Injun* or *idiot* and *eejit.*

If you think that is strange, in Sámi[45] you have to shorten a consonant in length to show the genitive case. So, for example, you would get *áhčči* 'the father' turning into *áhči* 'of the father'. As you can see, Gaelic and English are a lot less exotic compared to some other languages.

Back to Gaelic though. You've no doubt heard the phrase *no man is an island?* Well, you could apply that to sounds too and say *no sound is an island.* They don't stand alone, they sit next to each other and - almost like siblings - squabble. They fight for prominence, they vie for your brain's computing power and argue over the muscles of your mouth. Before you turn the page because this may sound obtuse - consider a word like *cóig* for a moment. You've probably come across it. Now, if you have, I want you to count the number of vowels you can <u>hear</u> in the pronunciation of *cóig*. Chances are, you're not entirely sure. If we look at the phonetics of it, we see that it's just one (long) vowel: [koːgʲ]. But you may have wondered for a moment about the 'bit' between the [oː] and the [gʲ] and might have even been tempted to put an [i] or [j] sound there.

---

[45] Sámi (or rather Sámegiella) is a language spoken from Central Scandinavia all the way to the Kola Peninsula by the Sámi (formerly called Lapps).

Hm, try not to. What's going on here is that these two sounds are made in different parts of your mouth. The [oː] towards the back and the [gʲ] in the middle. 'So what, that's all of 3 inches?' you might think but for our mouths that's considered a long way. So what happens is that you can hear a little bit of a 'transition sound' (called a 'glide') between the [oː] and the [gʲ] which to non-Gaelic ears might sound like an extra vowel.

The important point is that when you think you're hearing those tiny traces of sounds that aren't there in the phonetics, don't worry about them and don't try to consciously make them. If the phonetic spelling tells you that you have an [oː] followed by a [gʲ], aim for those sounds and your mouth will do the rest as they are just by-products of your tongue moving around. Anything else will throw you off target.

So... what has all this got to do with losing a vowel? If you want to know, take a peek at section 5.6.14 and come back here once you've read it.

✎ Exercise 92.

The following pairs all show a change in palatalness. Sometimes it also affects the vowel but don't worry about that for now. Listen to the recording and repeat the pairs. Although training yourself to hear the difference is important too, focus on getting the pronunciation right first.

01	duːn	duːNʲ	12	uːr	uːrʲ
02	Rɔːs	Rɔːʃ	13	kaːL	kaːl
03	kauL	kaiLʲ	14	baːs	baːʃ
04	krõxg	krũçgʲ	15	ɛx	eç
05	mɔːd	mɔːdʲ	16	ɔːL	ɔːl
06	ʃɔːL	ʃuːl	17	Luːɣ	Luj
07	kahd	kɛhdʲ	18	kaːx	kaːç
08	sLuəɣ	sLuəj	19	kalag	kalɛgʲ
09	maxg	miçgʲ	20	fɛr	firʲ
10	baːn	baːNʲ	21	maːhərʲ	maːhər
11	Lag	Lagʲ	22	kuNəRʃd	kuNəRʃdʲ

✎ Exercise 93.

Now let's try this exercise the other way round. The following pairs also involve a change in palatalness. But I've left a gap where the palatal sounds should be in the second column. Look at the words in the first column and work out what the palatal counterparts are and fill them in. Again, sometimes the vowels are affected too but I've given you all the vowel changes.

01	kLauN	kLɰNʲə	12	ma:L	ma:__
02	baLax	baLɪ__	13	puhdan	puhdɛ__
03	marag	marɛ__	14	kur	ku__
04	bɔxg	bɰ__	15	mɔnəɣ	mɔn__
05	frɰ:x	frɰ:__	16	kas	ka__ə
06	aran	arɛ__	17	ɛRəN	ɛRɪ__
07	sLahd	sLɛh__ə	18	brɔ:g	brɔ:__ə
08	kʲɔ:L	kʲu:__	19	bauL	bɰi__
09	ba:ɣ	ba:__	20	karax	karɪ__
10	kʲauN	kʲi:__	21	ahər	ahə__
11	mo:r	mo:__	22	fad	fa__

4.7.1   When to palatalise or Is *doras na h-eaglaise mhór* wrong?

An interesting question on several levels. Let's deal with the easy stuff first. Since it's a sound change that indicates that a word has a different function or meaning in relation to its basic function or meaning, you will most commonly come across this in words that are able to do that. In Gaelic that means verbs, nouns and adjectives. Words like *agus* or *ciamar* are static, so we don't have to worry about slenderisation. There are some of these little words that undergo palatalisation in some positions but as we'll meet those shortly anyway (in 4.9), I'm ignoring those for now.

Verbs are relatively easy. For the most part, verbs don't palatalise (which is why you have spelling variations of endings that verbs can take). Instead, the last consonant of a very stays the same, no matter what you stick on the end:

Root	Derived Forms	
mol [mɔL]	mholainn [vɔLɪNʲ]	a mholas [ə vɔLəs]
croch [krɔx]	chrochamaid [xrɔxəmɪdʲ]	crochaidh [krɔxɪ]
leugh [Lʲeːv]	leughaibh [Lʲeːvɪv]	leughar [Lʲeːvər]
buail [buəl]	bhuailinn [vuəlɪNʲ]	a bhuaileas [ə vuələs]
dùin [duːNʲ]	dhùineamaid [ɣuːNʲəmɪdʲ]	dùinidh [duːNʲɪ]
cuir [kurʲ]	cuiribh [kurʲɪv]	cuirear [kurʲər]

The only common change in terms of palatalness in verbs is actually away from being palatal:

Root	Verbal Noun
dùin [duːNʲ]	dùnadh [duːnəɣ]
buail [buəl]	bualadh [buəLəɣ[
loisg [Lɔʃgʲ]	losgadh [Lɔsgəɣ]
teagaisg [tʲegɪʃgʲ]	teagasg [tʲegəsg]

Adjectives are a bit more predictable. Ignoring irregular ones, most adjectives palatalise their final consonant when they change to the comparative/superlative form:

Root	Comparative/Superlative
dearg [dʲɛrɛg]	deirge [dʲerʲegʲə]
bog [bog]	buige [bugʲə]
òg [ɔːg]	òige [ɔːgʲə]
luath [Luə]	luaithe [Luəjə]

Slenderisation of adjectives is also involved when they follow a noun but more on that shortly.

Nouns now are the difficult customers. For starters we have to distinguish two different ways of dealing with nouns. There is the *seann nòs*, the old way, of declining a noun in Gaelic and the *nòs ùr*, the new way. The conservative model (the 'old way') is what you will be most familiar with as a learner as it features in most grammar books. As a native speaker, you're probably more at home with the progressive model (the 'new way') of doing nouns.

Giving you the full paradigm would take us too far into the realms of grammar. In general, slenderisation occurs:

- as a result of the leniting article

- following feminine nouns in most grammatical cases

- following a slenderised masculine noun

- after a plural noun in an indefinite noun phrase (eg *dath chat...*)

The main difference between the conservative and the progressive model lies in the treatment of feminine nouns in the prepositional case and the genitive case where the progressive system no longer slenderises and has extended lenition to all adjectives after singular feminine nouns:

Conservative	Progressive
air duilleig mhóir	air duilleag mhór
ris an t-slait mhóir	ris an t-slat mhór
dath na duilleige móire	dath na duilleig(e) mhór
dath na slaite móire	dath na slait(e) mhór

If you want a more detailed explanation of the case system, you'll find lots of information on the Akerbeltz website.

Incidentally, 'progressive' and 'conservative' are not personal judgements. In this context they're linguistic terms that simply distinguish an older model and a more recent model of doing something.

Secondly, neither of them is right or wrong. They're both right and wrong but that's the wrong question to ask anyway. The more important point is, when is the *seann nòs* right and when is the *nòs ùr* right, which brings us back to the question of style of speech and register which we met in the Section VII of the Introduction. All living languages change and Gaelic is no exception. But that means that with time there will be things that go out of fashion. First they'll feel formal, then overly formal and at some point so old-fashioned that people will stop using it.

In Old English for example it was perfectly normal that you could take out one *bōc* or lots of *bēċ* from the library but if you walked in today and asked for some beek, they'd probably ask you "some big what?" Or if you were practising your verbs you'd be *ic mōt, þū mōst, hē/hit/hēo mōt, wē/gē/hīe mōton.* But how strange would it be for you to say *I mote, thou most, he/she/it mote, we/you/they moten* instead of *I/you/he/she/it/we/you/they must*? At best, you'll find something like *so mote it be* in a fantasy novel and if you *listen to the wireless*, you're either very old or trying to be funny.

In comparison to English, Gaelic is extremely under-researched so it's hard to say precisely how old or widespread the new system is. But even if you look at older publications and recordings, you will find signs of it. For example in the 1878 translation[46] of Queen Victoria's Leaves from the Journal of Our Life in the Highlands, we find constructions like *aig culthàobh clóich mhor*, rather than *cloiche móire*. Or in an 1896 edition of the magazine Mac-Talla, we have *aig bun craoibh mhór dharaich* rather than *aig bun craoibhe móire daraiche*.

---

[46] A poor translation as translations go but all the more interesting because it's less sanitized than others.

4.8   Pre-aspiration or Remembering CTP

This is another interesting feature Gaelic has but fortunately a fairly simple one. CTP just stands for the 3 letters that this involves but feel free to come up with your own readings to help you remember this, from clutch-the-pearls to coal-to-power, it's all good if it helps your memory!

We have already met aspiration, the puff of air that follows sounds like **c**, **t** and **p** in both English and Gaelic. Now the curious thing about Gaelic is that it does something rather more interesting to **c**, **t** and **p** elsewhere. When you get **c**, **t** or **p** in the middle or at the end of a word, the puff of air shows up in front of the consonant, rather than after. Hence the name 'pre-aspiration'.

Now, the degree of pre-aspiration Gaelic speakers use and the exact quality of it varies from dialect to dialect. For some, it is very weak, for others, it is very strong. But every living dialect has it and on the whole, it's getting stronger.

We'll aim for the middle ground and go for the most common type of pre-aspiration across dialects. This means that it will be very strong before **c** and moderate before **t** and **p**. Very strong before **c** means that the 'puff' will come out as a [x] or [ç] (depending on broad and slender). Moderate means that it will be only a [h]. Pre-aspiration tends to be:

- strongest after a short vowel
- weak after a long vowel or diphthongs
- weak in unstressed syllables (see section 4.12.1).

Here are some examples:

Broad **c t p**		Slender **c t p**	
mac [maxg]	goc [gɔxg]	mic [miçgʲ]	bric [brʲiçgʲ]
muc [muxg]	aca [axgə]	lic [Lʲiçgʲ]	muice [muçgʲə]
cat [kahd]	put [puhd]	ite [ihdʲə]	lite [Lʲihdʲə]
at [ahd]	bàta [ba:hdə]	croit [krɔhdʲ]	peiteag [pehdʲag]
cupa [kuhbə]	sop [sɔhb]	drip [drihb]	cipean [kʲihban]
cop [kɔhb]	apa [ahbə]	clip [klihb]	pàipear [pɛ:hbɛr]

Remember, the puff of air moves to the front so the symbol in the phonetic spelling has to adjust too. If you wrote [hp], that would mean two puffs, one in front and one after but Gaelic doesn't do that, so we write it [hb] in this book.

When in doubt over how strong it needs to be, make it stronger rather than weaker. If you happen to struggle with this when reading Gaelic, get a piece of paper and put a **ch** in front of every word with **c**, **t** and **p** that you want to practice and then say it several times. For example:

Broad **c t p**		Slender **c t p**	
mac ⇒ machc	goc ⇒ gochc	mic ⇒ michc	bric ⇒ brichc
cat ⇒ cacht	put ⇒ pucht	ite ⇒ ichte	lite ⇒ lichte
cupa ⇒ cuchpa	sop ⇒ sochp	drip ⇒ drichp	cipean ⇒ cichpean

That should give you the right amount of puffing. Actually Gaels sometimes confuse their spellings like this, the word for a pit for example is *sloc* but you sometimes see it written as *slochd* because the pre-aspiration is so strong. These mis-spellings are old and have been cropping up for a few centuries, a testimony to the age and strength of pre-aspiration in Scots Gaelic. So the spelling aside, there is no difference in pronunciation between pairs with **-c** and **-chd** in most dialects:

boc [bɔxg]	bochd [bɔxg]	tac [taxg]	tachd [taxg]

Pre-aspiration is relatively rare amongst the world's languages and strangely enough occurs most commonly in language around the Northern Arctic – Inuit languages, Icelandic, Sámi, some Norwegian dialects, Scottish Gaelic (but not Irish)… The curious thing is that most of these languages aren't related to each other genetically yet they share this very distinctive feature. Maybe it's the cold or the long winters?

Here are a few examples, in case you have some friends fresh in from the Arctic:

Icelandic	Faroese	Northern Sámi
sakka, þekkja, mættir, koppar, happ	lýkka, gakk, koppur, óhapp	áhkáš, behtolaš, bahčit, čeahpát

Or, perfect excuse for an Arctic holiday, all these pre-aspirated sounds, don't you think? You can start by checking out Sámi pre-aspirated

sounds at the *Beaivváš Sámi Teáhter* (a Theatre company which, amongst other things, stages MacBeth in Sámi), then visit the Faroe Islands for some *skólpasúpan*[47] and more pre-aspirates, take a boat to Iceland and quiz some natives while relaxing at the famous natural hot spring baths in Grindavík (don't get the book wet!). Then round it all off and try *mattak* (google it!) on a visit to Greenland. What do you think?

---

[47] A traditional soup made from, err… parts of winter lambs.

4.9   The jumping consonants

Now 'jumping consonants' is something you get in most languages. It's the peculiar effect when a consonant at the end of one word jumps to the next word if it begins with a vowel. It's what makes Diagon Alley work as a pun in Harry Potter, or the 'four candles' joke in The Two Ronnies.

This boils down to the fact that it's easier for your mouth to have a vowel at the end of a word rather than a consonant (if the next word begins with a vowel that is).

Here are some more examples from English (where this is sometimes called 'juncture'):

nuncle	⇐ comes from *an uncle*
nickname	⇐ from Middle English *an ekename*
your ear	sounds just like *your rear* or even *urea*

Because this happens quite a lot, there are even cases where people hypercorrect. This means that they look at a word, think that it has the "wrong" pronunciation and change it. The adder is a lovely example of such hypercorrection - the word actually comes from Old English *nǣddre* (compare also the German word *Natter,* which still has the **n**) but people at some point dropped it because they thought it shouldn't be there in 'proper speech'.

Gaelic does that too but as always, with a twist. We need to distinguish three different groups. They don't have names as such, so I've just labelled them A, B and C.

Let's look at the simple case first. In this group, the largest, sounds 'jump' and behave along similar lines as they do in English. All you have to do for this to happen is to run your Gaelic together nicely and not to make pauses where you shouldn't (see also 4.11).

GROUP A

This group contains:

- most words (nouns, adjectives, verbs and so on)

- most forms of the possessive pronouns (except the forms with *a* 'his' as this disappears completely before a vowel):

m' ad [mad]	'gam iarraidh [ga miəRɪ]
d' ad [dad]	'gad iarraidh [ga diəRɪ]
ad [ad]	'ga iarraidh [ga iəRɪ]
a h-ad[48] [ə had]	'ga h-iarraidh [ga hiəRɪ]
ar n-ad [ər nad]	'gar n-iarraidh [gar niəRɪ]
ur n-ad [ər nad]	'gur n-iarraidh [gar niəRɪ]
an ad [ə nad]	'gan iarraidh [ga niəRɪ]

'nam ad [na mad]	'am ad [ə mad]
'nad ad [na dad]	'ad ad [ə dad]
'na ad [na ad]	
'na h-ad [na had]	
'nar n-ad [nar nad]	
'nur n-ad [nar nad]	
'nan ad [na nad]	

- the feminine genitive article *na h-*

---

[48] The **h-** and **n-** are historically part of the pronoun, so they qualify for 'jumping'. More on that later.

All you need now is some words that begin with a vowel:

aon uair	⇒ [ɯː nuərʲ]	lus uaine	⇒ [Lu suəNʲə]
gun ùbhlan	⇒ [gə nuːLən]	àrd ìre	⇒ [aːR diːrʲə]
m' athair	⇒ [mahərʲ]	d' ubhal	⇒ [du.əL]
a h-athair	⇒ [ə hahərʲ]	ar n-athair	⇒ [ər nahərʲ]
ur n-im	⇒ [ər niːm]	an ad	⇒ [ə nad]
'gam ithe	⇒ [ga miçə]	'gad ithe	⇒ [ga diçə]
'ga h-ithe	⇒ [ga hiçə]	'gar n-ithe	⇒ [gar niçə]
'gur n-ithe	⇒ [gar nɪçə]	'gan ithe	⇒ [ga nɪçə]
'nam aran	⇒ [na maran]	'nad aran	⇒ [na daran]
'na h-aran	⇒ [na haran]	'nan aran	⇒ [na naran]
na h-oidhche	⇒ [nə hɣ̃jçə]	na h-Alba	⇒ [na haLabə]

GROUP B

The second group is a lot smaller. In this group, the sound jumps and adjusts for slenderness. This means that if it hits the front vowels [i] [e] or [ɛ] it slenderises, if it hits any other vowel it doesn't change. Words which do that are:

- *ag* [əg] ⇒ [ə g] or [ə gʲ]

- *is* (verb)[49] ⇒ [ə s] or [ə ʃ], including *mas* ⇒ [mə s] or [mə ʃ]

- *nas* (comparative) and *as* (superlative) – before slender **fh**

Here are some examples:

Broad		Slender	
ag amas	⇒ [ə **g**aməs]	ag iarraidh	⇒ [ə **gʲ**iəRɪ]
ag òl	⇒ [ə **g**ɔːL]	ag ithe	⇒ [ə **gʲ**içə]
ag ullachadh	⇒ [ə **g**uLəxəɣ]	ag éirigh	⇒ [ə **gʲ**eːrʲɪ]
is toil	⇒ [ə **s**dɔl]	is fheudar	⇒ [ə **ʃ**eːdər]
's fhada	⇒ [**s**adə]	's diombach	⇒ [**ʃ**dʲũːmbəx]
's ann	⇒ [**s**auN]	's e	⇒ [**ʃ**ɛː]
's mathaid	⇒ [**s**mahɪdʲ]	's i	⇒ [**ʃ**iː]
as fhasa	⇒ [ə **s**asə]	as fhearr	⇒ [ə **ʃ**aːR]
nas fhaisge	⇒ [nə **s**aʃgʲə]	mas fhìor	⇒ [ma **ʃ**iər]

---

[49] Not *is* meaning "and"

GROUP C

The last group has the twist. First of all, it only affects **n** sounds at the end of words. Here the **n** sound does three things: it jumps, it adjusts for slenderness and it strengthens. So the outcome is either a [N] or a [Nʲ]!

No, I'm not kidding. I'm sure you know the word *nuair* [Nuərʲ]. Well, it has the strong [N] because it's actually a contraction of *an uair* [ə Nuərʲ]! In fact, the habit of doing this is so strong that it spills into Hebridean English where you hear people pronounce things like *I was in Eòlaigearraidh* as [ɪ NʲɔːLɪgʲəRɪ] with a strong palatal [Nʲ] latched onto *Eòlaigearraidh!*

Fortunately there aren't many words which do this:

- all forms of the definite article that have an audible **n**, including the prepositions: *an* [ən], *nan* [nən], *bhon* [vɔn], *bhon an* [vɔnən], *ann an* [aNən], *anns an* [ãũNsən], *san* [sən], *chun* [xun], *chun an* [xunən]…

  Note that the prepositions do something funny. If you use only the preposition with the fused article, the **n** does the jumping and strengthening bit. If it is followed by a free article, the first **n** remains weak, and only the second does the jumping and strengthening: *dhan eaglais* [ɣa NʲegLɪʃ] vs *dhan an eaglais* [ɣanə NʲegLɪʃ]

- *gun* [gən] 'that'

- *nan* [nan] 'if'

- *chan* [xan] 'no(t)'

- *an* [ən] question particle

- *far an* [far ən] dependency particle

[n] ⇒ [N]		[n] ⇒ [Nʲ]	
an t-aran	⇒ [əN taran]	an t-iasg	⇒ [əNʲ tʲiasg]
an olann	⇒ [ə NɔLəN]	an iuchair	⇒ [ə Nʲuxərʲ]
nan òg	⇒ [nə Nɔ:g]	nan each	⇒ [nə Nʲɛx]
san ùir	⇒ [sə Nu:rʲ]	san eòrna	⇒ [sə Nʲɔ:RNə]
fon aran	⇒ [fɔ Naran]	fon eala	⇒ [fɔ NʲɛLə]
fon an aran	⇒ [fɔn ə Naran]	fon an eala	⇒ [fɔn ə NʲɛLə]
gun aisig e	⇒ [gə Naʃɪgʲ ɛ]	gun éist e	⇒ [gə Nʲe:ʃdʲ ɛ]
gun òl e	⇒ [gə Nɔ:L ɛ]	gun ith e	⇒ [gə Nʲiç ɛ]
nan òladh e	⇒ [nə Nɔ:Ləɣ ɛ]	nan itheadh e	⇒ [nə Nʲiçəɣ ɛ]
chan ann	⇒ [xa NauN]	chan eil	⇒ [xa Nʲel]
an ann?	⇒ [ə NauN]	an e?	⇒ [ə Nʲɛ:]

When you lenite **f**, it disappears completely. So you're left with a word that has a vowel at the beginning, which means if the lenition is caused by something containing *an,* the same thing happens here too:

[n] ⇒ [N]		
fàradh [fa:rəɣ]	⇒ air an fhàradh	[ɛrʲ ə Na:rəɣ]
faoileag [fɯ:lag]	⇒ ron fhaoileag	[rɔ Nɯ:lag]
fùdar [fu:dər]	⇒ dath an fhùdair	[dah ə Nu:dərʲ]
foillsich [fɣiLʲʃɪç]	⇒ chan fhoillsich	[xa NɣiLʲʃɪç]
[n] ⇒ [Nʲ]		
feòil [fjɔ:l]	⇒ san fheòil	[sə Nʲɔ:l]
féis [fe:ʃ]	⇒ air an fhéis	[ɛrʲ ə Nʲe:ʃ]
fitheach [fi.əx]	⇒ dath an fhithich	[dah ə Nʲi.ɪç]
fill [fi:Lʲ]	⇒ chan fhill	[xa Nʲi:Lʲ]

It also strengthens [fl][50] to [L], and [fr] and [frʲ] to [R] when the **f** is lenited away in these combinations:

[fl] ⇒ [L]		
fleasgach [flesgəx]	⇒ anns an fhleasgach	[as ə Lʲesgəx]
fliodh [flɤɣ]	⇒ an fhliodh	[ə Lʲɤɣ]
fliuch [flux]	⇒ chan fhliuch	[xa Lʲux]
[fr]/[frʲ] ⇒ [R]		
fras [fras]	⇒ anns an fhras	[as ə Ras]
fraoch [frɯːx]	⇒ san fhraoch	[sə Rɯːx]
fròg [frɔːg]	⇒ an fhròg	[ə Rɔːg]
frìth [frʲiː]	⇒ an fhrìth	[ə Riː]
freagair [frʲegɪrʲ]	⇒ chan fhreagair	[xa Regɪrʲ]
frithealaich [frʲihəLɪç]	⇒ chan fhrithealaich	[xa RihəLɪç]

In spite of their similar written appearance, words like *'nan uallach* 'in their load' and *nan uallach* 'of the loads' are pronounced differently. Here are some contrasting examples:

an oidhche	⇒ [ə Nɤ̃jçə]	the night
an oidhche	⇒ [ə nɤ̃jçə]	their night
nan iasg	⇒ [nə Nʲiəsg]	of the fish
'nan iasg	⇒ [na niəsg]	in their fish
nan uallach	⇒ [nə NuəLəx]	of the loads
'nan uallach	⇒ [na nuəLəx]	in their load

Wonderful stuff, isn't it? But whatever you think of these jumping consonants, this is something you really have to learn to listen out for. The reason simply being that between lenition and these jumping and sometimes strengthening consonants, we get 'phantom words'.

---

[50] Broad **fl** is already always [fL], so you don't have to worry about it.

A phantom word is something that looks (or sounds) like a word but is just the product of several other things happening. Take the following example:

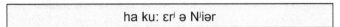

ha ku: ɛrʲ ə Nʲiər

Now if you hear someone say this, as a native speaker of anything but a Celtic language, you will assume five words: [ha], [ku:], [ɛrʲ], [ə] and [Nʲiər]. The first three words aren't too bad, it's quite obviously *tha cù air* 'is dog on'. But at first sight the other two look like we have *a* and *niar*. You rack your brains, you run for Dwelly's, you browse the Faclair Beag[51] only to find that the only entry like that is 'an old fashioned word for not'. You might then figure that the [Nʲ] actually goes with the *air an*, which is of course correct. Hm, *air an iar* 'on the West'? Possible of course but not likely, ever seen 'a dog on the West'? It's only when you add lenition to the equation that we get a bit closer. The solution of course is *air an fheur*. That's what a phantom word is and unfortunately Gaelic is full of them.

So whenever you hear a noun with [N] or [Nʲ] at the beginning, you must always consider that this is either a word that originally began with a vowel - or if lenition is involved, with an **f**.

---

[51]   www.faclair.com

Oh, and while we're on the topic - this jumping habit is also the reason why Gaelic has these seemingly strange, hyphenated single letters (like **h-** or **n-**) at the beginning of some words. These "stray" letters are not actually part of the noun but historically part of whatever is going in front of the noun (usually the definite article or a possessive pronoun). These sounds have just been jumping forward so much for so long that the spelling has followed suit. Here's what happened to the possessives in Gaelic and Irish for example:

	my	your	his	her	our	your	their
Indo-European	mei	tū	esja	esjā**s**	nsaro**n**	svaro**n**	esjo**n**
a lot of time passes							
Old Irish	mo	do	a	a **h-**	ar **n-**	far **n-**	a **n-**
not quite as much time passes							
Irish	mo	do	a	a **h-**	ar **n-**	bhur **n-**	a **n-**
Gaelic	mo	do	a	a **h-**	ar **n-**	ur **n-**	an

A couple of interesting points. The Indo-European words are also the ancestors of the English possessives, which is why they look so similar (remembering that it used to go 'my, thy, his, her...').

Secondly, if you remember what we said about why we lenite (see section 4.5.2), it clearly shows why in modern Gaelic *mo, do* and *a* (his) lenite whereas the others don't - they are the ones that started life out with a vowel at the end, all the others ended in consonants.

And thirdly, it's the reason why **h-** and **n-** are written with lowercase letters. Since the Gaelic writing tradition looks on them as word endings that are slightly lost, it would be strangE tO capitalisE theM. Hence you get things like *Pàrlamaid na **h**-Alba* and *ar **n**-Athair a tha air Nèamh* in Gaelic or *Dún na **n**Gall* and *Poblacht na **h**Éireann* in Irish.

🖎 Exercise 94.

In this exercise you must join up two parts of a sentence. Don't worry too much about understanding all the grammar in these short sentences. The important thing is that you realise what happens at the juncture between these two parts. If a word causes lenition, it's marked with an asterisk (star) but remember there's such a thing as blocked lenition too (4.5.4). Here's an example of how it works:

ha kuː sən* + faŋg	ha kuː sə Naŋg

ha kuː sən* + kaːr	(càr)
ha ən* + fjaNag ʃɔ moːr	(feannag)
ha kuː auNs ən* + tɤj	(taigh)
ha kuː ɛgʲ ən* + fɛr	(fear)
ha kuː ɛrʲ ən* + fiar	(feur)
ha ən* + kalag ʃɔ moːr	(caileag)
ha ən* + bɛn ʃɔ moːr	(bean)
ha kuː ɛgʲ ən* + ad	(ad)
ha kuː ɛrʲ ən* + elan	(eilean)
ha ərn + ahərʲ ə'ʃɔ	(athair)
ha kuː ɛgʲ ən* + ɯNʲag	(uinneag)
ha ən* + fiːdʲag ʃɔ moːr	(fìdeag)
ha ən* + fjɔːrag ʃɔ moːr	(feòrag)
ha ərn + aran mah	(aran)
ha elan sən* + ɛr	(ear)

This is really important so when you've done this exercise, I recommend you look up some more words in the Wordlist at the back of this book which begin with a vowel or **f** and practise some more. Use the same sentences as above - it's not about the grammar - and practice until you can do this without thinking. It will not only help you sound more Gaelic, it will also help you understand Gaelic a lot better.

🐦 Exercise 95.

This exercise works best if you already know a little Gaelic but even if not, you can try it.   Listen to the following short sentences and pay special attention to the part where the [ən]* joins up with a noun.   Try and figure out what the words are.   If you don't know the words, don't worry but try and write down what you think the original word could have been.   Write down every possible option you can think of.   Even if they're words that don't exist.   Here's an example:

va kahd εgʲ ə NʲeːLʲ   ⇒ [NʲeːLʲ] Néill or [eːLʲ] éill or [feːLʲ] féill

You can either use the phonetic symbols or just the normal spelling if you already know some Gaelic.   Then check the key for the solution and listen again.

01.
02.
03.
04.
05.
06.
07.
08.
09.
10.

✎ Exercise 96.

This exercise is on phantom words. I know we haven't looked at how to read and write Gaelic yet so you may wish to leave this particular exercise until after you have done those chapters and then come back to this exercise. If you already have some Gaelic under your belt you can do this exercise now.

Most of the following short phrases contain a phantom word each that is the result of either a jumping consonant or a jumping consonant plus lenition. Decide what the original word is likely to be and look them up in your dictionary. If you can't find the word, think again about other possibilities for what might be the first sound. Don't worry too much about the grammar going on in the phrases.

01. ha i sə Nʲiəxgər	16. ha mux gauN
02. dah ə Nɯːl	17. ha kuː ɛrʲ ə NʲɛrəN voːr
03. ha baNʲə sə Nuː	18. ʃɔ dobɪrʲ
04. ha diax moːr	19. ʃiː meːdal
05. ha fɛr sə Nʲɛr	20. ha u ɛrʲ ə Nʲelan
06. ha faLd ɛrʲ NʲiaL	21. higʲ ɛ sə Nʲuxər
07. kurʲ ɯʃɡʲə ɛrʲ ə Nuːdər	22. ha i gə neːʃ
08. ʃɔ dah	23. ha kLax ɛrʲ ə Nahərʲ
09. leʃ ə NʲɛRʃd ʃɔ	24. vɔ Nɣdʲə
10. eːʃdʲ rʲiʃ ə Naram	25. ha gah sə Nʲɔːl
11. huərʲ mi maːrəx	26. hɔrʲ ʃɔ ɣa Nʲɛx
12. ɪs dɔnə ə NuəLʲ	27. ha boː ɛrʲ ə Nʲiar
13. gav danal	28. ha Nad ɛgʲ ə NʲeːLʲ
14. ha ʃɔ gə neːfəxg	29. ha dad əˈʃɔ
15. ɛrʲ ə NanəRʃd	30. leʃ ə Nɯːvər ʃɔ

4.10   Retroflex consonants or Hebridean Tongue Yoga

Retroflex simply means that the tip of your tongue curls backwards while making a consonant. These sounds are more commonly associated with languages from the Indian subcontinent (which is why many people who want to mimic an Indian accent simply curl their tongue back for **t**, **d**, **s**, **r**, **l** and **n**) or American English (the American **r** sound!) but they also make an appearance in Gaelic in a vaguely confusing way.

In the consonant groups **rt**, **rd** and **rn**, the **r** is often retroflex anyway because of the way our mouth works. So words like *ceart, àrd* and *càrn* come out like this (the little tail indicates a retroflex sound):

[kʲaɹʂd]	[aːɹd]	[kaːɹɳ]

What can happen in colloquial speech is that the **r** sound [ɹ] gets dropped altogether. So words like *ceart, àrd* and *càrn* come out as:

[kʲaʂd]	[aːd]	[kaːɳ]

For the native speaker the retroflex sounds left are enough of a clue that 'an **r** used to be there' so they know which word someone is saying.

One word where you have most likely already come across this is *coimhearsnachd*. Listening to native speakers say this word one gets the impression that there is a [ʃ] sound. But actually all we have is a retroflex s: [kõjərʂɳəxg]. This also happens in the English of many Hebrideans, for example *first* [fəɽʂd].

You should be aware of this but since it's not 'compulsory' in speaking there's no need to kill yourself in trying to make retroflex sounds in the early stages of learning Gaelic.

And no, Gaels aren't mental, just in case that thought crossed your mind. A lot of languages which have these sounds with a curved back tongue acquired them when they 'lost' some r sounds. In Faroese for example combinations like **rs** never have the **r** sound. Instead you get an **s** with a curved back tongue so for example the word for March - which is *Mars* - comes out as [maş].

4.11   How to string words together

This is an extremely important chapter. If you were to read just one of the remaining chapters, I'd recommend you read this one.

One of the main mistakes people make when learning a language is to have pauses in the wrong places. To some degree this is to be expected. After all, the learner isn't entirely familiar with the new language and the ways in which sounds interact in this language. But Gaelic learners seem to have a particular problem getting over this initial difficulty.

This doesn't only make it more difficult for them to make sentences in Gaelic but it can also lead to Gaelic which is very difficult to understand for native speakers or even fluent learners. For that reason I can't stress enough how important this section is.

The title of an amusing little book by Lynne Truss humorously illustrates what a pause in the wrong place can do to meaning (bearing in mind that many commas indicate small pauses in speaking or changes of intonation). Its title is "Eats, shoots and leaves", based on the following old panda joke - which exists in various guises:

A panda walks into a café, sits down and orders a sandwich. He eats the sandwich, pulls out a gun and shoots the waiter.

As the panda stands up to go, the manager shouts, "Hey! Where do you think you're going? You just killed our waiter and you haven't even paid for your sandwich!"

The panda yells back, "Hey man, I'm a panda! Look it up!"

The manager checks the dictionary and finds the following badly punctuated entry: "Panda, a mammal from Asia with distinct black and white stripes. Eats, shoots and leaves."

There are many more examples I could give you but this will do to illustrate the point.

Fortunately it's not difficult from a technical point. To begin with, grab a piece of paper and a pen because I want you to write something down. Close this book for a moment and write a very brief definition of what a word is (in spoken language that is). That is, set down a rule that can be used to chop up a sentence into words. Now take 2 or 3 minutes to think about it and write down your answer.

Right. Chances are that you have a puzzled look on your face. And that your rule contains a *sometimes, usually* or *but not always.* Or, if you put down *something that has a meaning* – what about a word like *and* or *a*? *Something that's between two spaces* is also a common one. But think about it, spaces between words are a very recent introduction and some languages like Japanese still don't.

It was in fact a trick question. It's actually extremely difficult to find such a definition. Linguists have tried for decades, if not centuries, to find a rule that can be consistently applied across languages and have failed. They're still looking for an answer…

Thing is, unless you're listening to Victor Borge's Phonetic Punctuation, when we say something it just comes out as one long string of sounds.

Few pauses, no full stops, spaces, exclamation marks… just think of the last time you overheard someone speaking in a language you don't speak. Could you have said where the word breaks were?

It turns out that the best we can do in terms of a definition is to say that it's something speakers of a language can identify at a gut level without being able to give a good reason. In an English (written) text this gut feeling has been conventionalised by putting spaces in between what we think of as separate words. But it's not always clear… if *I* is a word and *am* is a word, then how many words is *I'm*?

And it's no surprise that since the definition of a word is based on gut feelings that different languages have different ideas. How many words in the sentence "you smashed them with your foot"?

Well "6 of course" you'll probably think. Thing is, not every language will agree with you on that one:

German (8)	du hast sie mit deinem Fuß kaputt gemacht
English (6)	you smashed them with your foot
Basque (3)	oinez puskatu zenituzten
Siksika[52] (1)	kitsíípoksskihpiaaw

How does that help you with your Gaelic? Well, there are two main points here:

- All languages run their words together

- Just because something is considered a single word in English, the same doesn't have to be true for Gaelic or any other language.

The conclusion of point one is easy - you may initially have lots of pauses in your Gaelic because you're struggling with lots of things at the same time. But you must try as soon as possible to start running your Gaelic together.

It may make life easier for other learners in your class to have long pauses in your Gaelic. Long pauses mean they don't have to worry about unpicking all the sounds that you have just run together. But in the long run you're heading for a brick wall. You'll hit that wall when you listen to native speakers or fluent learners who run their Gaelic together naturally. Even though you might know all the words and the grammar and in theory would understand them if they (unnaturally) spaced out everything, chances are you'll understand very little.

The second point is a bit more philosophical but nonetheless important. When you learn a language you naturally tend to view it from the point of view of your native language. It helps to make yourself aware of that every now and then because seeing the new language from the point of view of your native language isn't always helpful. This is one such occasion!

---

[52] A native American language from Alberta that used to be called Blackfoot.

In the case of Gaelic this tends to be English. English tends to have lots of 'little words' which it considers separate units. In Gaelic the units tend to be larger. There's quite a bit of evidence for this. For example, we find phrases like the one below in the Book of Deer[53]:

ᚪᚱᛁᛗᚩᚱᛗᚫᚱ

In modern Gaelic we would write that as *air a' mhorair* 'on the lord'. Whoever wrote that passage in the Book of Deer seems to have thought of *air a' mhorair* as one unit, not three. And yes, there are spaces between words in the Book of Deer, just in case you were wondering. Just not between chunks like ᚪᚱᛁᛗᚩᚱᛗᚫᚱ.

Even more compelling, in chapter 4.5.2 you found out where lenition comes from. The phenomenon is very common throughout the languages of the world as you'll remember. The weird thing is that the Celtic languages don't only do lenition in the middle of a word but apparently across words. Apparently? Well, if you think of *air* + *a'* + *mhorair* as three separate units, it's weird (ask a linguist). But if you think of it as one unit, it all makes a lot more sense – *aira'mhorair* [ɛrʲə'vɔrərʲ] – because that's the way it comes out.

That was a long explanation - my apologies and thanks for bearing with me. Let's look at some practical advice now because it's all very well just saying that you need to run your Gaelic together.

---

[53] A 12th century manuscript from the monastery of Old Deer in Aberdeenshire which has one of the earliest examples of written Scots Gaelic (up until then most people wrote in Common Gaelic which was essentially a standardised form of Middle Irish).

In general, phrases (in the linguistic sense) run together. That is, units that logically and structurally go together, for example:

noun + adjective	{cù mór}, {cat beag}, {cas fhliuch}…
article + noun	{an cù}, {a' chas}, {an t-sròin}…
article + noun + adjective	{an cù mór}, {a' chas fhliuch}…
article + nouns	{dath nan cat}, {taigh nan daoine}…
number + noun	{dà chù}, {trì cait}, {dà chas}…
possessive + noun	{mo chù}, {do chat}, {a cas}…
prepostion + noun	{air a' chù}, {bhon chat}…
particle + adjective	{ro mhór}, {glé bheag}, {as lugha}…
particle + verb	{chan eil}, {nach e}, {gun ith}…

The same applies to a learner's best friend, the *ag* in front of a verbal noun:

ag + verbal nouns	{ag iarraidh}, {a' ceannach}, {ag òl}…

The list isn't complete but you'll get the idea I think.

One very helpful way of thinking about this is that if two or more words are in a leniting relationship, they're one unit. Or in other words, something that causes lenition and everything it lenites is one unit.

{air a' chù bheag bhrèagha}	{mo mhàthair bheag dhubh}
{a cheannaicheas}	{gun mhàthair}
{'gam iarraidh}	{'nad shuidhe}
{cha bhuail}	{dà chù}
{a Mhàiri!}	{ro mhór}

You need to think about these as categories – sometimes a word from a category will lenite but another won't. Some words have blocked lenition (see 4.5.4) but if they're in the same category, the same thing applies. For example, *aon* and *dà* lenite but the other numbers don't but because they're "all numbers", they all get treated as a unit:

{aon chù}	{trì coin}
{dà chat}	{cóig cait}
{air a' bhalach}	{air an taigh}
{cha cheannaich}	{cha déid}

Another good clue are conjunctions, they usually introduce a new chunk:

{agus}	{is}
{ach}	{oir}
{a chionn 's}	{ged}

Now what was that about pauses? Well, apart from issues surrounding word stress and sentence stress (see the next chapters) understanding where the breaks between these 'logical chunks' are will help you make your Gaelic flow better. Let's start with a couple of English examples. Read the sentences out loud and make a longish pause after each curly bracket:

{a cute} {little kitten fell} {down the} {stairs today but} {wasn't hurt}
{when I} {left the} {hall I saw a} {dog coming round} {the corner}
{I was} {walking when} {I saw snow} {falling up} {on the moor}

Now, did that flow well? Not really. And in the second and third example you're actually being confusing to a listener because {a dog coming round} means something else than {dog coming round the corner}. And while {snow falling} {up on the moor} is old hat, {snow} {falling up} {on the moor} is probably headlines. So in English the 'logical breaks' would be here:

> {a cute little kitten} {fell down the stairs} {today} {but} {wasn't hurt}
>
> {when} {I left the hall} {I saw} {a dog} {coming round the corner}
>
> {I was walking} {when I saw} {snow falling} {up on the moor}

Runs much better, doesn't it? The same applies to Gaelic broadly speaking.

In order to make it flow and come out in a way someone else will have a much better chance of following what you're saying, you need to 'break up' your sentences in the right places. Fortunately this isn't rocket science but it does involve some getting used to and a bit of extra work for the learner. When you're doing exercises, think about what goes together and practise saying those chunks together to build your sentence. And if you have to make a pause when speaking because you need to remember a word or how to deal with grammar, try to make a pause where it would be 'natural' rather than right in the middle.

> {tha} {cù mór dubh} {aig piuthar mo mhàthar} {is} {tha e} {glé thinn}
>
> {bhiodh e} {a' dol ann} {ged nach robh iad} {anns an taigh mhór}

✎ Exercise 97.

This exercise will help you become more aware of the way things are grouped together in a sentence. Look at the sentences below (you'll probably know the story) and think about where you could put pauses without making them sound 'broken up' or 'unnatural'. I've taken out most of the punctuation as it would give you clues.

01.	I came forward cautiously and giving ear as I came heard some one rattling with dishes and a little dry eager cough that came in fits but there was no sound of speech and not a dog barked.
02.	The door as well as I could see it in the dim light was a great piece of wood all studded with nails and I lifted my hand with a faint heart under my jacket and knocked once.
03.	Then I stood and waited.
04.	The house had fallen into a dead silence a whole minute passed away and nothing stirred but the bats overhead.
05.	I knocked again and hearkened again.
06.	By this time my ears had grown so accustomed to the quiet that I could hear the ticking of the clock inside as it slowly counted out the seconds but whoever was in that house kept deadly still and must have held his breath.
07.	I was in two minds whether to run away but anger got the upper hand and I began instead to rain kicks and buffets on the door and to shout out aloud for Mr Balfour.
08.	I was in full career when I heard the cough right overhead and jumping back and looking up beheld a man's head in a tall nightcap and the bell mouth of a blunderbuss at one of the first-storey windows.

✎ Exercise 98.

Take an English magazine or newspaper and select an article which has reasonably long and complex sentences. Read it out loud and imagine you're reading it to an audience. Make a vertical line in all the places where you think a 3 second pause would be acceptable between the chunks. Think about why you would put the pauses where you put them. If you're thinking "well, because this goes with that of course", you're on the right track.

✎ Exercise 99.

Take a Gaelic text. Go through it and mark the places where you think 3 second pauses would be acceptable with vertical lines. The chunks that make sense in an English sentence will broadly speaking be similar in a Gaelic sentence. Then read the text out loud, making the pauses where you placed your lines and run everything between the vertical lines together. Repeat this several times over and say the bits between your vertical lines faster each time, running all words together smoothly.

4.12   Stress and intonation in Gaelic

And no, I don't mean the fact that learning a language is quite a bit of work. Stress is about where you put the emphasis when speaking. That can be a question of where it goes in an individual word, in a phrase or where the emphasis ends up in a sentence. And crucially, where you don't put it in Gaelic.

Intonation you can think of as the 'melody' of a sentence, where it rises and falls and so on.

Unlike some other aspects of Gaelic, thankfully this is a fairly straightforward issue. But it's very important nevertheless as it differs quite a bit from what you might be used to.

4.12.1 Word stress

This is about where stress goes in individual words. We'll start by looking at what happens in English but first we need to take a quick detour and look at what a syllable actually is.

First of all, syllables are a concept primarily based on the pronunciation of a word, not the way it's written. For example, the spelling in *Leicestershire* suggests way more syllables (about five) than the spoken word actually contains (just three).

The most practical way for you to split a word into syllables is like this:

- there are open syllables. These consist of a vowel on it's own or one or more consonants plus a vowel, for example:

  $\overset{\text{V}}{[\text{a}]}{}^{54}, \overset{\text{V}}{[\text{u}]}, \overset{\text{C V}}{[\text{pa}]}, \overset{\text{C V}}{[\text{ku}]}, \overset{\text{C V}}{[\text{t}^\text{j}\text{a}]}, \overset{\text{C V}}{[\text{ʃɔ}]}, \overset{\text{C C V}}{[\text{tra}]}, \overset{\text{C C V}}{[\text{krɔ̃}]}\ldots$

- there are closed syllables. These consist of either:
  - a vowel (group) and one or more consonants
  - one or more consonants, a vowel and one or more consonants

  For example:

  $\overset{\text{V C}}{[\text{ak}]}, \overset{\text{V C}}{[\text{eʃ}]}, \overset{\text{V V C}}{[\text{ɣiLʲ]}} \overset{\text{C V C}}{[\text{pag}]}, \overset{\text{C V C}}{[\text{mɔL}]}, \overset{\text{C V C}}{[\text{bir}]}, \overset{\text{C V V C}}{[\text{kʲauN}]}, \overset{\text{C V C C C}}{[\text{maRʃd}]}, \overset{\text{C V C C}}{[\text{ka:RN}]}\ldots$

- for our purposes, a consonant on its own cannot be a syllable and needs to join the next group. So in syllable terms you get:

  $\text{'s e} \Rightarrow \overset{\text{C V}}{[\text{ʃɛ:}]}, \text{'s toil} \Rightarrow \overset{\text{C C V C}}{[\text{sdɔl}]}, \text{'s ann} \Rightarrow \overset{\text{C V V C}}{[\text{sauN}]},$

---

[54] C stands for any consonant, V for any vowel. You'll see in a moment why that's a convenient way of summarising them.

So when you try to split a Gaelic word into its syllables, you must split the sounds into the above units. The preferred unit is an open CV (consonant + vowel) syllable, so when you have a choice, split a word so you get the maximum number of CV units:

[bən|ta:h|də]	not	[bən|ta:hd|ə]
[bjauN|dən]	not	[bjau|Ndən]
[kʲiə|Lə|xəɣ]	not	[kʲiəL|əx|əɣ]
[Lʲɛh|bə|Nən]	not	[Lʲɛhb|ə|Nən]

This also means trying to split up as many of the consonant groups as possible. Of course, if you get groups at the beginning or end of the word, you can't split them up as there are no vowels to pair them with:

[ka:R|Nəɣ]	but	[ka:RN]
[sdrɔ:Nʲ|dʲən]	but	[sdrɔ:Nʲ]
[kʲaRʃ|dɪç]	but	[kʲaRʃd]
[brʲɛx|gə|xəɣ]	but	[brʲɛxg]

This may or may not involve 'breaking up' parts of a word which from a logical point of view go together: *ca/ma/nachd* (which is *cam* + *an* + *achd*), *uai/rea/dai/rean* (which is *uair* + *eadair* + *ean*)…

Remember that occasionally you get 'extra' sounds in Gaelic that are in the pronunciation but not the spelling. As we are working off the pronunciation when counting syllables, these of course count as sounds:

putag	[puh|dag]	freiceadan	[frʲeç|gʲə|dan]
ceartaich	[kʲaRʃ|dɪç]	sròn	[sdrɔ:n]
Alba	[a|La|bə]	arm	[a|ram]

Ok, I think you get the idea so back to word stress.

Now, in English (and Scots) word stress is very unpredictable. For most words, as a learner of English you have to learn where the stress goes. The spelling doesn't show you at all:

Sometimes you even get pairs where the meaning changes:

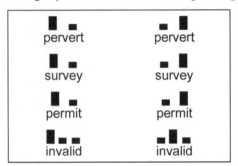

Now take a deep breath - and smile, because Gaelic is very neat and tidy when it comes to stress. The basic rule is that you're only allowed one stress per word at the most and by default this goes on the first syllable of a word no matter how many syllables the word has or how many endings you have stuck on:

1 Syllable	2 Syllables	3+ Syllables
cas [kas]	bàta [ba:hdə]	camanachd [kamanəxg]
sìth [ʃiː]	beanntan [bjauNdən]	leabhraichean [Lʲɔːrɪçən]
lag [Lag]	ceannard [kʲaNəRd]	dìochuimhneachadh [dʲiəxənəxəɣ]

Since it is so predictable, it's not normally indicated in either the phonetic writing or the normal Gaelic writing system.

As you probably guessed from the last comment, there are cases when stress isn't where you might expect it to be. The good news is that the spelling is generally very clear about indicating this. In the phonetic writing this is shown by putting the stress symbol ['] before the stressed syllable.

Now, there are four ways in which Gaelic shows you that stress isn't where you'd expect it.

- With capital letters (one or two usually) in the middle of a word:

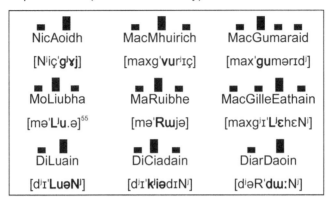

This is especially important with surnames as there is a difference between *mac Phàdraig* 'a son of a man called Patrick' and *MacPhàdraig* 'MacPatrick':

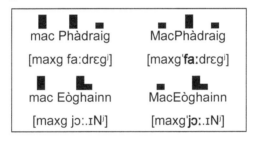

---

55 As in *Crois MoLiubha* "Crossmyloof", a place in Glasgow meaning the Cross of St Malieu.

While we're on the topic, just watch out for the difference in the way Irish and Gaelic handle surnames. Both use capital letters to indicate that stress is 'somewhere else' but in Gaelic you write them as one word, in Irish you write them separately:

Gaelic	Irish
MacAonghais	Mac Aonghais
MacColla	Mac Colla
MacGilleDhuibh	Mac Giolla Dhuibh
MacRaghnaill	Mac Raghnaill
MacShuibhne	Mac Shuibhne

- By writing two nouns separately but with two capital letters and no definite article between them (mostly place names and clan names):

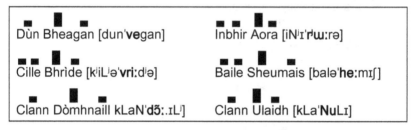

Dùn Bheagan [dun'vegan]   Inbhir Aora [iNʲɪ'ɾʷɯːrə]

Cille Bhrìde [kʲiLʲə'vriːdʲə]   Baile Sheumais [balə'heːmɪʃ]

Clann Dòmhnaill kLaN'dõ̃ː.ɪLʲ]   Clann Ulaidh [kLa'NuLɪ]

This in turn means that mis-spellings like the following suggest the wrong stress placement, theoretically resulting in the wrong pronunciation:

Mis-spelling	suggests	but actually is
Inbhirnis	[iNʲɪɾʲnɪʃ]	[iNʲɪɾʲ'niʃ]
Portrigh	[pɔRʃdri]	[pɔRʃ'driː]

- By using a hyphen[56]:

an-diugh [əNʲˈdʲu]   a-mhàin [əˈva:Nʲ]   a-nuas [əˈNuəs]

a-réir [əˈRe:rʲ]   taigh-beag [təˈbeg]   an-uiridh [əˈNurʲɪ]

- By having a marked long vowel in a single word outside the first syllable. This applies mostly to a small handful of loanwords and some names:

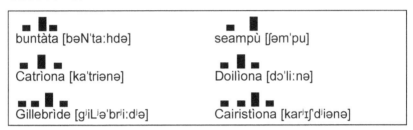

buntàta [bəNˈta:hdə]   seampù [ʃəmˈpu]

Catrìona [kaˈtriənə]   Doilìona [dɔˈli:nə]

Gillebrìde [gʲiLʲəˈbrʲi:dʲə]   Cairistìona [karʲɪʃdʲiənə]

The bad news is that we have something of a Catch 22 situation. Not everyone knows that the hyphen shows that stress is 'somewhere you're not expecting it' and (perhaps also due to the influence of English hyphen use) people have started putting hyphens into words where you don't necessarily need one. This is especially true with a lot of the prefixes (like *deagh, droch, àrd* etc). For example:

Common spelling	suggests	but actually is
àrd-ìre	[a:Rdirʲə] or [aRdˈi:rʲe]	[a:Rd i:rʲə]
droch-bheachd	[drɔxvəxg] or [drɔxˈvɛxg]	[drɔx vɛxg]
bileag-fiosrachaidh	[bilagfisrəxɪ] or [bilagˈfisrəxɪ]	[bilag fisrəxɪ]
cruth-tìre	[kruhtʲirʲə] or [krəˈtʲi:rə]	[kruh tʲi:rʲə]

So when you see a hyphenated word, bear in mind that it might be a 'modern' spelling where someone has misunderstood the hyphenation principle in Gaelic.

---

[56] This does not include the hyphens in **h-** or **n-**.

✎ Exercise 100.

Listen to the recording and underline the syllable or word which bears the stress.

01	a-mhàin	[əva:Nʲ]	02	dùinte	[du:Nʲdʲə]
03	bruidhinn	[bri.ɪNʲ]	04	dìomhair	[dʲiəvɪrʲ]
05	amannan	[aməNən]	06	eagalach	[egəLəx]
07	casan	[kasən]	08	móran	[mo:ran]
09	MacAoidh	[maxgɯj]	10	a-steach	[əʃdʲɛx]
11	taighean	[tɛhən]	12	Dùn Barra	[dunbaRə]
13	ciallachadh	[kʲiaLəxəɣ]	14	cabadaich	[kabədɪç]
15	an-diugh	[əNʲdʲu]	16	mearachd	[mɛrəxg]
17	balaich	[baLɪç]	18	caistealan	[kaʃdʲəLən]
19	athraichean	[arɪçən]	20	lus	[Lus]

✎ Exercise 101.

Look at the following words and underline the syllable or word which bears the stress.

01	DihAoine	dʲɪhɯ:Nʲə	02	taigh-òsta	təjo:sdə
03	leabhraichean	Lʲo:rɪçən	04	cunbhalach	kunuvəLəx
05	NicGilleRuaidh	NiçgʲiLʲəruəj	06	agamsa	agəmsə
07	atharraich	ahəRɪç	08	a-null	əNu:L
09	an-uiridh	əNurʲɪ	10	dèanamh	dʲiənəv
11	Dùn Bheagan	dunvegan	12	caileagan	kalagən
13	craobhan	krɯ:vən	14	Inbhir Theòrsa	ɪNʲɪrʲhjo:Rsə
15	beanntan	bjauNdən	16	a-nuas	əNuəs
17	margaideachd	maragɪdʲəxg	18	tìr-mór	tʲirʲmo:r
19	buntàta	bəNda:hdə	20	freagarrach	frʲegəRəx

4.12.2 Unstressed words

Now, having introduced you to the concept of word stress I must emphasise something else. Not all words do or even can carry stress. The words which tend not to get stress are so called function words. These are words which are purely functional, they are needed to make a sentence but don't have any meaning as such. Normally in a sentence the only words which carry stress is the other group which is called content words. Content words are words which have a 'meaning' of their own rather than just a function. As a rule of thumb, if you can kick it, act it out or draw a picture of it easily, it's a content word. Content words also include adjectives by the way. Here are a few examples from English which should make the difference clear:

Content Word	Function Word
wildebeest	the
running	a
seventeen	not
chunky	if
brown	with
introduced	of

Function words tend to be very short and rarely have more than one syllable in Gaelic. Broadly speaking - unless you're told otherwise - assume that what is a function word in English is also going to be a function word in Gaelic.

4.12.3 Compounds and stress

In the previous section we talked about the hyphen being used to indicate that stress isn't where you expect it. This use of the hyphen is not only very common in adverbs but also the so-called compound nouns.

In terms of stress and what happens to it with compounds, English and Gaelic aren't too dissimilar so we'll look at what English does first.

What happens in compounding is that you take two words, each with their own stress and meaning and join them up. The first result is a change in meaning, the second (usually) is that one of the stresses disappears. Let's look at some examples:

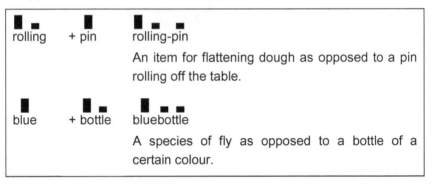

rolling   + pin   rolling-pin

An item for flattening dough as opposed to a pin rolling off the table.

blue   + bottle   bluebottle

A species of fly as opposed to a bottle of a certain colour.

You get the idea. In English we usually write words together if they form a new compound but sometimes we also use a hyphen. And sometimes you're just left guessing.

Because of the *caol ri caol* spelling rule (see chapter 5.20) Gaelic tends not to write words together as much. It prefers to use the hyphen if writing together would break the *caol ri caol* rule. So when you see a hyphen between two Gaelic words in most cases this is there to tell you that you don't have stress where normally expected.

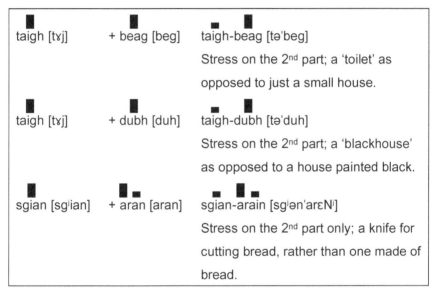

■	■	■ ■
taigh [tɤj]	+ beag [beg]	taigh-beag [təˈbeg]
		Stress on the 2nd part; a 'toilet' as opposed to just a small house.
■	■	■ ■
taigh [tɤj]	+ dubh [duh]	taigh-dubh [təˈduh]
		Stress on the 2nd part; a 'blackhouse' as opposed to a house painted black.
■	■ ■	■ ■ ■
sgian [sgʲian]	+ aran [aran]	sgian-arain [sgʲənˈarɛNʲ]
		Stress on the 2nd part only; a knife for cutting bread, rather than one made of bread.

Generally in such compounds the stress will end up on the distinguishing word. For example, there are many kinds of house but if we're talking about a blackhouse, a *taigh-dubh*, the important part is *dubh* which therefore takes the stress.

If the stress ends up on the first syllable, two words are either written together if that doesn't break the *caol ri caol* rule (sometimes even then) or hyphenated.

Gaelic dislikes writing words together unless they have <u>really</u> fused together, so words are hyphenated more often than *caol ri caol* rule requires.   The following examples all show a shortening of the unstressed vowel, indicating full fusion:

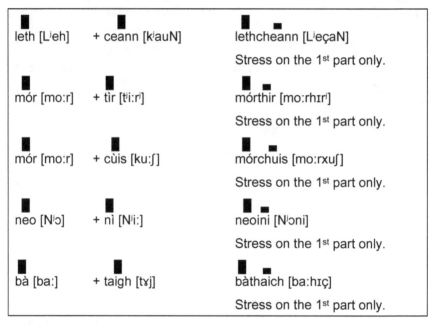

leth [Lʲeh]   + ceann [kʲauN]   lethcheann [LʲeçaN]

Stress on the 1st part only.

mór [moːr]   + tìr [tʲiːrʲ]   mórthir [moːrhɪrʲ]

Stress on the 1st part only.

mór [moːr]   + cùis [kuːʃ]   mórchuis [moːrxuʃ]

Stress on the 1st part only.

neo [Nʲɔ]   + nì [Nʲiː]   neoini [Nʲɔni]

Stress on the 1st part only.

bà [baː]   + taigh [tɤj]   bàthaich [baːhɪç]

Stress on the 1st part only.

We'll see in the next section how this works in detail.

✎ Exercise 102.

Sort the following word pairs according to how many stresses they have (one or two). Think about how that affects the meaning and say each pair out loud a few times.

	One stress	Two stresses
a red shank, a redshank		
free climbing, freeclimbing		
livestock, live stock		
a redneck, a red neck		
a stonefish, a stone fish		
a stag party, a stagparty		
a blackhead, a black head		
a blackbird, a black bird		
a running joke, a running joke		
the goldenrod, the golden rod		
a green finch, a greenfinch		

4.12.4 Unstressed vowels

This is another important topic because if you understand how Gaelic deals with unstressed vowels, it will make your life a lot easier.

As we have seen in the previous sections, Gaelic has a strong tendency to put all the stress on the first syllable of a word. By the same definition, all other syllables in the same word must be unstressed. In other words, Gaelic blows all its powder on the first syllable and has nothing left for the rest of the word.

As a result there are strong restrictions on which vowels can show up in unstressed syllables. As a rule of thumb, unstressed vowels are boring:

- Long vowels or diphthongs are never allowed in unstressed syllables (though on occasion they show up in compounds)

- Of the short vowels only [a] [ə] [ɪ] occur regularly

- [ɛ] generally only occurs when certain endings are slenderised; for example the diminutive endings **-ag** [ag] ⇒ **-eig(e)** [ɛgʲ(ə)] and **-an** [an] ⇒ **-ain** [ɛNʲ])

This means that when you are faced with an unfamiliar (written) word, almost all unstressed vowels are either going to be [ə] or [ɪ]. Generally the letters **i** and **ai** are pronounced [ɪ], the letters **a**, **ea**, **e** and **o** are pronounced [ə]:

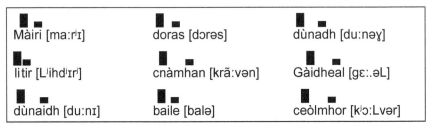

Màiri [maːrʲɪ]   doras [dɔrəs]   dùnadh [duːnəɣ]

litir [Lʲihdʲɪrʲ]   cnàmhan [krãːvən]   Gàidheal [gɛː.əL]

dùnaidh [duːnɪ]   baile [balə]   ceòlmhor [kʲɔːLvər]

The only problematic one is [a]. It is the one sound which is hard to predict in Gaelic. There are certain endings which always have [a] (see 4.12.5) but, beyond that, it has to be learned which words have [a] and not [ə].

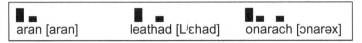

aran [aran]   leathad [Lʲɛhad]   onarach [ɔnarəx]

The good news is that [a] in unstressed syllables is fairly rare (those special endings in 4.12.5 aside) so when in doubt always go for [ə] rather than [a]. Chances are that you will be right and even if not, it's not one of the worst mistakes you can make in Gaelic.

This habit of reducing unstressed vowels permeates Gaelic. It also occurs when two words fuse together, for example in compounds or place names.

Here the general rule is that

- a long vowel or diphthong gets reduced to a short vowel[57]

- a short vowel is reduced to a schwa.

Basically it gets 'taken down a notch':

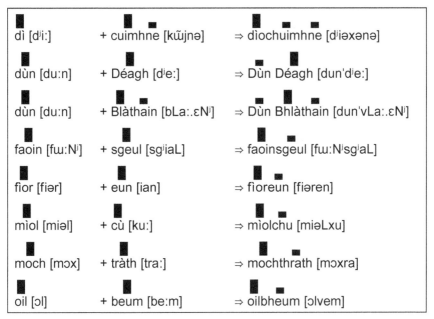

dì [dʲiː]   + cuimhne [kũ̃jnə]   ⇒ dìochuimhne [dʲiəxənə]

dùn [duːn]   + Déagh [dʲeː]   ⇒ Dùn Déagh [dunˈdʲeː]

dùn [duːn]   + Blàthain [bLaː.ɛNʲ]   ⇒ Dùn Bhlàthain [dunˈvLaː.ɛNʲ]

faoin [fɯːNʲ]   + sgeul [sgʲiaL]   ⇒ faoinsgeul [fɯːNʲsgʲaL]

fìor [fiər]   + eun [ian]   ⇒ fìoreun [fiəren]

mìol [miəl]   + cù [kuː]   ⇒ mìolchu [miəLxu]

moch [mɔx]   + tràth [traː]   ⇒ mochthrath [mɔxra]

oil [ɔl]   + beum [beːm]   ⇒ oilbheum [ɔlvem]

---

[57] Usually via something called a half-long vowel, which is exactly what the name suggests, shorter than a long one but longer than a short one.

It's not easy but if you think about it, it's not so different from what English and other languages do. For example, what do you call the service Catholics have in church? *Mass,* correct. With a nice clear [a] (or [æ] depending on your variety of English but a nice, strong, clear vowel anyway). And what do you call that holiday where kids expect too many presents these days? Correct, *Christmas,* where the [a] has been taken down to a weak [ə]. You probably just never thought of it that way. And it's not just Christmas of course. To mariners, a mainsail is a [meinsᵊl] and a halyard is a [hæljəd], even though a sail is a [seɪl] and a yard is a [yɑːrd].

Even though the above examples might suggest otherwise, lenition itself is not a reliable indicator of stress shift as there are various prefixes which do or do not cause stress shift.

As a very general rule, you will get stress shift when you have a noun-noun or noun-adjective compound.

So where does the stress go? Well, as we said before, it normally ends up on the distinguishing word, that is the word that gives the new meaning to the compound. Take the English word *bread-knife* for example. There are many kinds of knife but you mean those meant for cutting bread. So *bread* is the distinguishing word. Or *whitewash*. There are many kinds of wash but whitewash refers only to those which make white, so *white* is the distinguishing word.

■ **█** ■ sgian-arain [sgʲənˈarɛNʲ]	Stress on the 'bread' part because of all the knives in the universe, you mean those designed for cutting bread.
█ ■ ■ leabhar-lann [Lʲɔ.ərLaN]	Stress on the 'book' part because of all the places where you could store things, you mean those for books.

When you get a 'real' prefix the picture is much muddier. Some prefixes tend to cause forward stress (that is, send the stress to the second word), some tend to draw the stress to themselves and some (even though they may lenite) tend to leave equal stress on both words. And some do either, depending on? Good question! The prefix *neo-* for example sometimes draws onto the first part and sometimes onto the second part :

neo-chiontach [NʲɔçəNdəx]   neo-éifeachdach [Nʲɔ'eːfəxgəx]

Note that even though these words aren't fused together in writing, the vowels in such prefixes can still end up being shortened or reduced if the word has only one stress left.

To add to the problem, words which have prefixes and are very common tend to fuse together over time. Which means that wherever the stress was, it'll be on the first syllable in the end. Take the prefix *ban-* for denoting a female 'something'. For starters, even though the spelling suggests the pronunciation *[ban] it generally comes out as [baN] or [baNə]. In some words it's 'attached' loosely and you get stress on both words:

bana-bhuidseach [baNə vudʲʃəx]

In other words, however, this has fused tightly with the noun, so tight in fact that you can get vowel lengthening (see 5.6.2) or just a reduction of everything not in the first syllable, depending on which way the prefix *ban-* swung:

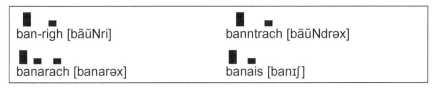

ban-righ [bãũNri]   banntrach [bãũNdrəx]

banarach [banarəx]   banais [banɪʃ]

The effect prefixes have on stress is very much a changing thing in Gaelic. The best guidance I can give you is as follows. Unless written as one fused word, the following prefixes tend to put equal stress on both prefix and noun:

Equal Stress	
ana- [ana]	ao- [ɯː]
ath- [ah]	deagh- [dʲoː]
deann- [dʲauN]	droch- [drɔx]
eu- [eː]	fìor- [fiər]
fo- [fɔ]	sàr- [saːr]
seann- [ʃauN]	sìor [ʃiər]

If there is no space or hyphen between a word and its prefix, you can generally assume that it's a totally fused word and just follows the normal rules of stress (that is, on the first syllable):

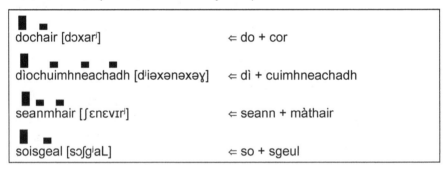

dochair [dɔxarʲ]   ⇐ do + cor

dìochuimhneachadh [dʲiəxənəxəɣ]   ⇐ dì + cuimhneachadh

seanmhair [ʃɛnɛvɪrʲ]   ⇐ seann + màthair

soisgeal [sɔʃɡʲaL]   ⇐ so + sgeul

So, if there is a hyphen you should:

- Check whether the word is in the wordlist at the end of this book (where stress is indicated).

- Check with a native speaker.

- Check with a dictionary that has a reliable IPA pronunciation guide.

- Bearing in mind the danger of modern mis-spellings, make an educated guess. Find the distinguishing word (the 'important' word) and put the stress on it. You will have a good chance of being right.

✎ Exercise 103.

Look at the following words and underline the part that you think has the stress. Then tick the box to indicate your reason for marking this syllable rather than any other. Don't worry about pronouncing the words in this exercise, the important thing here is to find the stressed syllable.

	'normal' word, stress on first syllable	hyphen, stress on the 'important' word	capital letters, stress on the 'important' word	exception
01 cuimhneachadh				
02 an-diugh				
03 MacGumaraid				
04 buntàta				
05 DiSathairne				
06 taigh-dhealbh				
07 a-null				
08 Dùn Dèagh				
09 grad-shealladh				
10 a-réir				
11 DiCiadain				
12 NicGilleMhìcheil				
13 clàraichte				
14 an-uiridh				
15 drannd-eun				
16 puinnseanachadh				
17 NicAoidh				
18 cnoc-faire				
19 ban-tighearna				
20 Inbhir Nis				

✎ Exercise 104.

Decide whether the underlined vowels are stressed (and therefore potentially 'interesting') or unstressed (and therefore expected to be 'boring'). Don't worry about pronouncing the words in this exercise, the important thing here is to find the stressed vowels.

	1st vowel	2nd vowel	3rd vowel	4th vowel
01 còisirean				
02 amannan				
03 an-diugh				
04 ball-coise				
05 càraichean				
06 cuideachadh				
07 MacDhòmhnaill				
08 fuaradairean				
09 inntinniche				
10 mac Dhòmhaill				
11 deasachaidhean				
12 DiarDaoin				
13 oillteachadh				
14 caolachadh				
15 cothroman				

✎ Exercise 105.

Each of the following words has an underlined vowel. From the three vowels given for each word, chose the one you think is the most likely candidate for the underlined vowel and make a brief note why you think that vowel is the most likely. At this stage you may or may not be familiar with aspects of the Gaelic spelling system but even if you know nothing about it you will be able to succeed in this exercise by making educated choices and guesses.

01 bothan	ia	ɔ	ə
02 cìsean	ə	o	eː
03 pàganaich	aː	ə	uː
04 maoineachadh	a	ɪ	ɯː
05 aran	ɛː	ɛ	a
06 adhbrannan	ə	eː	ɤː
07 toileachadh	ə	e	ɛ
08 taigh-tasgaidh	iː	ɔ	ɪ
09 muinntireas	ɪ	ɯi	ə
10 muladach	ai	a	ə
11 sgrìobhadair	iː	ɪ	oː
12 freagarrachadh	ɛ	ə	au
13 clachan	ɔu	a	ɪ
14 buannachadh	a	u	uə
15 ime	ɪ	i	e

✎ Exercise 106.

The following words are all compound nouns where two words have fused together closely.   Bearing in mind what you learned about compound nouns, underline the word in the following examples which you think is the important word that will receive the stress. For example, in *sgian-dubh* the second part is the important half and will get most of the stress.   Feel free to use a dictionary if you're not sure about the meanings, this is not a vocabulary test.

01 taigh-dhealbh	07 mór-thìr	13 glaine-fìona
02 taigh-dubh	08 brat-ùrlair	14 dealbh-chluich
03 sgian-arain	09 meanbh-chuileag	15 àrd-sgoil
04 uisge-beatha	10 taigh-mór	16 cas-bheart
05 mór-chùiseach	11 sgoil-àraich	17 taigh-tasgaidh
06 bun-sgoil	12 coileach-dubh	18 slat-iasgaich

Of these 18 examples, mark all those that you think would take on a very different meaning if you simply stressed both words equally. Think about why that is the case.

4.12.5 Exceptions and special endings

Earlier we talked about the problem of identifying clear [a] in unstressed syllables.   Fortunately there are certain endings which always have either clear or unstressed vowels. If you remember these, a lot of your [a] ~ [ə] headaches will go away!

Plural endings in Gaelic have <u>only</u> unstressed vowels:

-(a)ichean [ɪçən]	-(a)ich [ɪç]
leabhraichean [Lʲɔːrɪçən]	balaich [baLɪç]
litrichean [Lʲihdrɪçən]	aithrisich [arˈɪʃɪç]
-(e)an [ən]	-(a)idhean [ɪjən]
taighean [tɛhən]	molaidhean [mɔLɪjən]
comasan [koməsən]	céilidhean [kʲeːlɪjən]
-tan [dən]	-tean [dʲən]
beanntan [bjauNdən]	sgoiltean [sgɔldʲən]
lìontan [LʲiəNdən]	ceistean [kʲeʃdʲən]
-(e)annan [əNən]	-(e)achan [əxən]
uaireannan [uərʲəNən]	déileachan [dʲeːləxən]
deochannan [dʲɔxəNən]	ballachan [baLəxən]

Some other very common endings (as long as they are unstressed, that is, and are words of more than one syllable) also always have weak vowels:

-(a)ich [ɪç]	-(a)inn [ɪNʲ]
caraich [karɪç]	rachainn [raxɪNʲ]
cuidich [kudʲɪç]	mholainn [vɔLɪNʲ]
-(e)achadh [əxəɣ]	-(a)idh [ɪ]
aithneachadh [aNʲəxəɣ]	cuideachaidh [kudʲəxɪ]
abachadh [abəxəɣ]	buailidh [buəlɪ]
-(e)adh [əɣ]	-(e)ann [əN]
dhùineadh [ɣuːNʲəɣ]	buidheann [bujəN]
dùnadh [duːnəɣ]	caorann [kɯːrəN]
-(a)ig [ɪgʲ]	-(a)igeadh [ɪgʲəɣ]
dùraig [duːrɪgʲ]	bodraigeadh [bɔdrɪgʲəɣ]
aisig [aʃɪgʲ]	fàilligeadh [faːLʲɪgʲəɣ]

The -(a)igh ending requires an extra explanation. If this ending appears in a common noun or a verb, it behaves like -(a)idh:

dachaigh [daxɪ]	éirigh [eːrʲɪ]
ìomhaigh [iəvɪ]	aiseirigh [aʃerʲɪ]
ionnsaigh [jũːNsɪ]	ùrnaigh [uːRNɪ]

If, however, if -aigh occurs in a place-name or personal name in an unstressed syllable, it is generally pronounced [aj]:

Steòrnabhaigh [ʃdʲɔːRNəvaj]	Bhatarsaigh [vahdərsaj]
Rònaigh [Rɔːnaj]	Beàrnaraigh [bjaːRNəraj]
MacAmhlaigh [maxˈgãũLaj]	Fhionnlaigh! [jũːNLaj]

The few endings which normally have the clear vowels are:

-ail [al]	-eid [adʲ]	-eil [al]
beòthail [bjɔ:.al]	aiseid [aʃadʲ]	càirdeil [ka:Rdʲal]
fearail [fɛral]	rifeid [Rifadʲ]	pròiseil [prɔ:ʃal]

The **-aid** ending is a little tricky. Depending on the dialect, it can show up with just about any short Gaelic vowel there is [ɪ ɛ æ a ɑ ɔ ə]. Of these, [æ], [ɑ] and [ɔ] are rather marked[58] dialect features.

On that basis, I recommend you go for [ɪ], [ɛ] or [ə] in this ending. I'm using [ə] throughout as it is a common vowel in unstressed syllables and unspecific, so most native speakers will accept it easily enough. It also avoids the problem that even within a particular dialect, this ending can have different pronunciations. Whichever you choose, try and be consistent about it.

Clear [a] also appears in the following two endings:

-(e)ag [ag]	-(e)an [an]
marag [marag]	lochan [Lɔxan]
feòrag [fjɔ:rag]	balachan [baLəxan]

Note that in the normal spelling there is an ambiguity. The **-(e)an** ending has two functions, it can either be a plural ending [ən] or the diminutive[59] ending [an]. So when speaking, you must make sure you don't mix the two up. It can be ambiguous, for example if you come across the place name *Lochan nan Cnàmh* on a map.

---

[58] Meaning they are "less widespread" than the others.

[59] Making something small and cute, like the **-y** or **-ie** ending in English mummy, daddy, doggie…

This could either be a place called 'Little Loch of the Bones' or 'The Lochs of the Bones'. You either have to ask a local for the pronunciation to decide or look at the features on the map. If it's lots of lochs, it is probably *lochan* [Lɔxən], if there is only one small one, it's probably *lochan* [Lɔxan].

Two of these special endings also behave slightly unexpectedly when they slenderise. In both cases the vowel changes to [ɛ] and in the case of -(e)an, the n becomes palatal. This tends to be the case for all words which in their basic form (the form they're listed under in dictionaries) end in -(e)an and -(e)ag, irrespective of whether they're obvious diminutives or not. Remember, we're talking about the basic form here, not plurals!

-ag [ag] ⇒ -aig [ɛgʲ]	-eag [ag] ⇒ -eig [ɛgʲ]
marag [marag] ⇒ maraig [marɛgʲ]	caileag [kalag] ⇒ caileig [kalɛgʲ]
gealag [gʲaLag] ⇒ gealaig [gʲaLɛgʲ]	bileag [bilag] ⇒ bileig [bilɛgʲ]

-an [an] ⇒ -ain [ɛNʲ]	-ean [an] ⇒ -ein [ɛNʲ]
lochan [Lɔxan] ⇒ lochain [LɔxɛNʲ]	cuilean [kulan] ⇒ cuilein [kulɛNʲ]
aran [aran] ⇒ arain [arɛNʲ]	cipean [kʲihban] ⇒ cipein [kʲihbɛNʲ]

One more thing. The word *aiseag* is an exception. The -eag in *aiseag* is not the diminutive ending (which is also the reason it's gramatically masculine, not feminine). By coincidence, the word has simply ended up looking like it has the -eag ending. The pronunciation is [aʃəg], with a schwa, not a clear [ag].

✎ Exercise 107.

The following words have been part transcribed into IPA except for the vowels in the unstressed syllables.

- Insert the vowels you expect.

- Then listen to the recordings and decide whether you think you picked the right one.

- Check the Key to make sure you got the right vowels

- Listen to the recordings again.

01. dùnadh	duːn__ɣ		02. aran	ar__n
03. urras	uR__s		04. togail	tog__l
05. cothrom	kɔR__m		06. sitig	ʃihdʲ_gʲ
07. móran	moːr__n		08. caileag	kal__g
09. cailleach	kaLʲ__x		10. toman	tom__n
11. leabhar	Lʲɔ.__r		12. Donnchadh	doNox__ɣ
13. cupa	kuhb__		14. craobhan	krɯːv__n
15. balaich	baL__ç		16. beagan	beg__n
17. càise	kaːʃ__		18. dìochuimhnich	dʲiəx__n__ç
19. boireann	bɔrʲ__N		20. boireannach	bɔrʲ__N__x
21. corra	kɔR__		22. tunnag	tuN__g
23. sgoile	sgɔl__		24. sgoiltean	sgɔldʲ__n
25. sgileil	sgʲil__l		26. ceannard	kʲauN__Rd
27. dèanamh	dʲian__v		28. éiridh	eːrʲ__
29. aiseag	aʃ__g		30. litir	Lʲihdʲ__rʲ
31. bochdainn	bɔxg__Nʲ		32. beinne	beNʲ__
33. peantadh	pɛnd__ɣ		34. càirdeil	kaːRdʲ__l
35. ceartas	kʲaRʃd__s		36. dhùineas	ɣuːNʲ__s
37. cinnteach	kʲiːNʲdʲ__x		38. dùinidh	duːNʲ__
39. rachainn	rax__Nʲ		40. bhathar	va.__r

4.12.6 Sentence intonation

The details of Gaelic sentence intonation are under-researched. But on the bright side, with a few good pointers about what to listen out for, unlike other pronunciation issues this should be something you can 'listen into'. Unlike other aspects of Gaelic, this is for once a fairly straight-forward thing even though it works differently compared to English.

We'll actually start by having another look at English. Read this sentence out loud:

I have a son in Edinburgh

What did you do with your voice? Unless you're Australian, you went down with your voice towards the end. Now the good news is that's pretty much the same thing Gaelic does. In any statement or negated (when denying something) sentence, whatever you must make sure that overall your voice ends up lower compared to your starting point:

ha maxg agəm aNəN dunˈeːdⁱəN

Now, how many different ways do you have to turn the above sentence into a question in English? Oversimplifying, two. You could either change your sentence structure and opt for *do I have a son in Edinburgh?* Or you could go up with your voice at the end of the sentence

I have a son in Edinburgh?

Going up at the end of a sentence is a very common way of turning a sentence into a question in Western European languages. The catch being…? Correct, Gaelic doesn't.

Gaelic has preserved an old sentence intonation pattern (that's what you call what you do with your voice in a sentence). What you get is an overall fall in all sentences. Regardless of whether it's a statement, denial or a question. It's actually not as daft as it sounds. English **wh** question[60] sentences also have a fall, for example in a sentence like:

Who has a son in Edinburgh?

Anyway, English aside, that's really the main secret to Gaelic sentence intonation. Whatever you do at the beginning or in the middle of your sentence, make sure that you end up lower than you started. This doesn't mean that you can't go up at all in a Gaelic sentence, it just means that overall you have to go down. So what you get is:

ha maxg agəm aNəN dun'e:dʲəN

xa Nʲel maxg agəm aNəN dun'e:dʲəN

ə vel maxg agəm aNəN dun'e:dʲəN

nax el maxg agəm aNəN dun'e:dʲəN

---

[60] Questions that begin with **wh**: **wh**o, **wh**en, **wh**ich, **wh**y, **wh**ence…

One thing you should definitely avoid is using a rising intonation to turn a Gaelic statement into a question. It will sound as novel to native Gaelic speakers as the kind of intonation you get on Australian soaps sounds to the rest of the English-speaking world.

What you do instead is to use the question words (*a/an/am/nach*) to make a questions. Yes, I'm oversimplifying quite considerably. But as rough guidelines, these will put you on the right track. It's also one of those things that are fairly easy to pick up on by listening and copying the overall intonation. We probably find it easier to deal with a new melody than a new tongue position…

✎ Exercise 108.

In the following sentences the first one is always a statement, followed by the two possible question forms and the negation. Listen carefully to each group of four, then repeat and pay special attention to the falling intonation. If you're just starting Gaelic, don't worry about the meaning too much. The most important thing is that you understand that Gaelic uses the same pattern for statements, questions and denials.

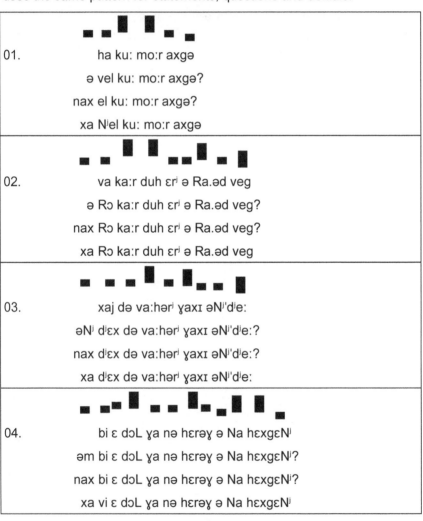

01.

ha ku: moːr axgə

ə vel ku: moːr axgə?

nax el ku: moːr axgə?

xa Nʲel ku: moːr axgə

02.

va kaːr duh ɛrʲ ə Ra.əd veg

ə Rɔ kaːr duh ɛrʲ ə Ra.əd veg?

nax Rɔ kaːr duh ɛrʲ ə Ra.əd veg?

xa Rɔ kaːr duh ɛrʲ ə Ra.əd veg

03.

xaj də vaːhərʲ ɣaxɪ əNʲ'dʲeː

əNʲ dʲɛx də vaːhərʲ ɣaxɪ əNʲ'dʲeː?

nax dʲɛx də vaːhərʲ ɣaxɪ əNʲ'dʲeː?

xa dʲɛx də vaːhərʲ ɣaxɪ əNʲ'dʲeː

04.

bi ɛ dɔL ɣa nə hɛrəɣ ə Na hɛxgɛNʲ

əm bi ɛ dɔL ɣa nə hɛrəɣ ə Na hɛxgɛNʲ?

nax bi ɛ dɔL ɣa nə hɛrəɣ ə Na hɛxgɛNʲ?

xa vi ɛ dɔL ɣa nə hɛrəɣ ə Na hɛxgɛNʲ

The second part of this exercise is similar to the first part but with a slightly different visual format because there are people who find it more intuitive than the first one. It doesn't matter which one you prefer, they both 'work'.

Again, listen carefully to each group of four, then repeat and pay special attention to the same, falling intonation in all cases. Don't worry about the meaning too much.

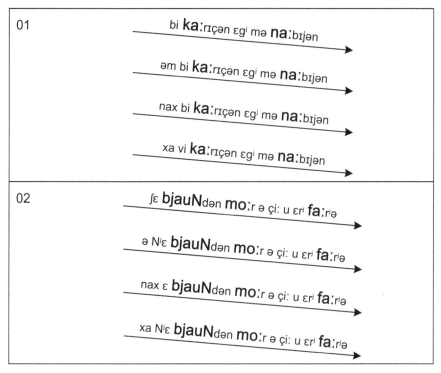

4.12.7 Stressing words

Because Gaelic has this thing about stress only falling on the first syllable of a word and having an overall fall in a sentence, this has certain repercussions.

In English, we can put emphasis pretty much on any part of a sentence by using our voice. We can also turn a statement into a question by using our voice:

> You live in Govan.
>
> You live IN Govan?
>
> YOU live in Govan?
>
> You LIVE in Govan?
>
> You live in GOvan?
>
> You live in GoVAN[61]?

Each of these sentences has a somewhat different meaning and the only difference is one of emphasis.

While you can use your voice to a certain degree in Gaelic, try not to overdo this. Instead of using voice, Gaelic prefers to use the following instead:

- fronting
- emphatic pronouns (*mise* [miʃə], *thusa* [usə]…)
- emphatic suffixes (*-sa* [sə], *-se* [ʃə]…)

---

[61] Seriously, this is a humorous local pronunciation.

You can find descriptions of how these work in most good course books, so the following example is just to demonstrate how Gaelic would deal with the same (question) statements:

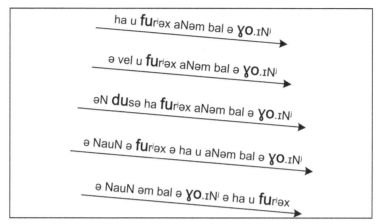

So, as you can see, Gaelic on the whole prefers to stick endings on words or shift the word order around rather than doing fancy things with intonation.

There are certain groups of words which never receive stress. Fortunately they're relatively easy to tell. Nouns, numbers, verbs and adjectives can all have stress (the so called content words). That means that most other words are unstressed.

This is especially true of these little function words (remember, words which have a grammatical function but no 'content'). The fact that you may be able to stress their counterparts in an English sentence is irrelevant, this is Gaelic we're talking! Here's a list of the most common ones:

a [ə] & na [na]	relative particles (that, who, which...)
an cat a dh'fhalbh [əŋ kahd ə ɣaLav]	an taigh a thog iad [əN tɤj ə hog ad]
na nì mi [na ni: mi]	na chuala mi [na xuəLə mi]

gun [gən]	conjunction 'that' (all forms)
gun robh e [gə Rɔ ɛ]	gum faic i [gu fɛçgʲ i]
gun do dh'fhàg e [gəN də ɣa:g ɛ]	gun dèanadh e [gəNʲ dʲianəɣ ɛ]

an [ən]	question particle (all forms)
an robh e? [ə Rɔ ɛ]	an tusa mo mhac? [əN dusə mə vaxg]
am bi e? [əm bi ɛ]	a bheil e? [ə vel ɛ]

an [əN⁽ʲ⁾]	definite article (all forms)
an neach mór [ə Nʲɛx mo:r]	na daoine beaga [nə duɯ:Nʲə begə]
Poblachd na h-Éireann [pɔbLəxg nə he:rʲəN]	dath nan cat [dah nəŋ kahd]

chan [xaN⁽ʲ⁾]	negation (all forms)	
	chan eil e [xa Nʲel ɛ] cha mhi [xa vĩ]	cha tog e [xa tog ɛ] chan atharraich e [xa NahəRɪç ɛ]
nach [nax]	**negative question particle**	
	nach robh e? [nax Rɔ ɛ] nach bi e? [nax bi ɛ]	nach i se do bhean? [nax iʃə də vɛn] nach eil e? [nax el ɛ]
do [də]	**past tense marker**	
	an do dh'fhàg e? [əN də ɣaːg ɛ] cha do rinn e. [xa də rɤiNʲ ɛ]	nach do ràinig e? [nax də raːnɪgʲ ɛ] an do cheannaich e? [əN də çaNɪç ɛ]
mo [mə] etc	**possessive pronouns**	
	mo chù [mə xuː] do chat [də xahd]	ar n-athair [ər nahɪrʲ] a thaigh [ə hɤj]

There are some which can be both stressed or unstressed depending upon the sentence:

ged a [gad ə]	although
ged a dh'fhàg iad [gad ə ɣaːg ad]	ged a théid i [gad ə heːdʲ i]
ged a dhùisg e [gad ə ɣuːʃgʲ ɛ]	ged a rachainn [gad ə raxɪNʲ]

gun [gən]	without
gun taigh [gən tɤj]	gun cheann [gən çauN]
gun bhuannachadh [gən vuəNəxəɣ]	gun fhìrinn [gə niːrʲɪNʲ]

na(s) [na]	than
nas motha na esan [nəs mo.ə na esən]	nas àirde na mise [nə saːRdʲə na miʃə]
na b' àille na sinne [nə baːLʲə na ʃiNʲə]	na bu lugha na ise [nə bə Luɣə na iʃə]

na [na]	not (negative imperative particle)
na dèan seo! [na dʲian ʃɔ]	na bean rium! [na bɛn rʲəm]
na bi cho gòrach! [na bi xɔ gɔːrəx]	na abair sin! [na abɪrʲ ʃin]

agus [agəs]	and
▪ ▮ ▮▪ ▮▪ mo chat agus mise [mə xahd agəs miʃə]	▮▪ ▪ ▮ Agus an taigh! [agəs əN tɣj]
▮▪▮▪▮▪ càise agus aran [kaːʃ agəs aran]	▮▪▮▪ ▮▪ Calum agus Màiri [kaLəm agəs maːrʲɪ]

far [far]	off
▮▪ ▮ far a' bhùird [far ə vuːRdʲ]	▮▪ ▮▪ far na sràide [far nə sdraːdʲə]
▮▪ ▮▪ far an rathaid [far ə Ra.ədʲ]	▮▪▮▪ far an taighe [far əN tɛhə]

Prepositions are an odd group, they can receive (some) stress, add an emphatic ending or be fronted:

▮ ▪ ▪ ▮ ▪ ▮
Chaidh mi ann leis a' chù
[xaj mi auN leʃ ə xuː]

▮ ▪▪▮▪ ▪ ▪▪
'S ann leis a' chù a chaidh mi ann
[sauN leʃ ə xuː xaj mi auN]

▮ ▪▪ ▮ ▪
Chaidh mi ann leis-san
[xaj mi auN leʃsən]

It often depends on the function and position of a preposition whether it is or is not stressed. As a rule of thumb you can assume that if the preposition introduces an object, it won't take stress. If the preposition "stands by itself", it's likely to be stressed:

Preposition by itself	Preposition + Object
tha e ris	tha e ris a' ghrian
tha e air	tha e air a' mhullach
chuala mi mu dhéidhinn	chuala mi mu dhéidhinn nan con
tha seo air a shon	tha seo air a shon fhéin

And the last point. As you saw above, *chaidh* didn't get a stress in the middle of the sentence. It's usually the case that only verbs at the front of a sentence regularly receive stress but not verbs that come after some relative particle in the middle of a sentence:

Stress possible	Stress unlikely
Bha…	… a bha…
Bhitheadh…	… a bhiodh…
Cha bhi…	… nach robh…
Chuala…	… far an cuala…
Théid…	… a théid…

So. In a nutshell the message is, don't overuse your voice to stress words in Gaelic. Use fronting or emphatic endings. And avoid putting stress on those little words, it messes the whole flow of a sentence up.

4.13   Colloquial speech and disappearing sounds

This is another very important chapter, especially for understanding spoken Gaelic.

When we speak 'normally' we don't pronounce every word carefully and on its own - no matter what language we're speaking. Contractions abound and sounds are lost left right and centre. Here are a few examples of what can happen in colloquial Scots/English:

we are	⇒ we're	it is	⇒ it's
what's up?	⇒ whassup?	what are you	⇒ wotcha
going to	⇒ gonnae	do you	⇒ d' ye
isn't it?	⇒ innit?	is that	⇒ 's tha'

Gaelic is no exception. A lot of sounds that you see in written Gaelic just aren't there in the spoken language. Sounds are dropped, words are run together, shortened... a lot of things can happen. I know that as a learner it is easy to succumb to the temptation of wanting to pronounce every last letter you see in a written sentence. Perhaps this is a phase every learner has to go through but if you want my advice - try your best not to. Every living language has conventions on what is appropriate in the spoken language and that includes conventions on running together words and dropping 'stuff'. The sooner you embrace that, the sooner your spoken Gaelic will improve and the easier it will be for native speakers to accept and understand your speech.

It's virtually impossible to collect a full list of all the sounds that get dropped in Gaelic and all the words that get contracted but I can give you some strong pointers. They will enable you to gradually pick up more nuances yourself.

The sound in most danger of dropping off is the schwa [ə], especially if next to another vowel or at the end of a phrase or sentence. However, other short vowels are by no means safe either. The general rule of thumb is:

> If two vowels meet (across two words) then the weaker one is dropped
> as long as it does not affect the meaning of the sentence.

Pretty much like that saying *deil tak the hinmost*. And we'll see in a moment why the bit about meaning is important but first some examples:

's e cat a tha ann	⇒ [ʃɛː kahd ə hauN]
an càr a bha agad	⇒ [əŋ kaːr ə vagəd]
bha a athair ann	⇒ [va ahərʲ auN]
an oidhche ud	⇒ [ə Nɣĩç əd]
tha e uaine	⇒ [ha uəNʲə]
tha i uaine	⇒ [ha i uəNʲə]

Notice something in the last pair? The more common **e** is frequently dropped but **i** isn't, even when it has vowels on either side. This is where the second part of the above rule kicks in. If we dropped both **e** and **i**, we would lose vital information because we couldn't be sure if we're talking about him or her. But because the convention is to keep the **i** and drop the **e**, the difference is still clear.

By the way, these are general principles. This means there is no need for you to swamp your written Gaelic with apostrophes to show all the sounds that drop off in the spoken language. There are a few well-established forms like *b' e* instead of *bu e* but unless you're trying to be deliberately colloquial, there is little point in writing things like *bh' agam r' a h-ithe 'n oichdh' ud*.

This might reflect the spoken language but no language on this planet has a 1-1 match between the spoken language and the written language. *D' ye really show evr'y soun' droppin' out 'n spoken English when ye 'rite?* It's just not helpful for someone trying to read what you've written even though we can cope with that well enough in spoken language.

That aside, there are so many different levels of 'slurred' speech - there's slow and careful, normal speed, fast speech, extremely fast... what speed do you pick?

Better to stick with something fairly legible and neutral like *bha agam ri a h-ithe an oidhche ud* and to adjust your speech to the style you want. The other style could be appropriate too, say if you're writing a Gaelic cartoon or joke collection. But probably not for an essay. As always, bear in mind the question of style. Think about how formal you would be writing the same piece in English. If you adjust your style of Gaelic along similar lines, you should be fine. This is all not so much about right or wrong in an absolute sense but about the question of when either is appropriate.

Another case in point are certain particles and prefixes which contain vowels in the written language that only show up under special circumstances in the spoken language. I'll only mention some of the most common groups. They show the principle nicely and you can then listen out for similar cases on your own.

The first case is *a'* [ə] and *ag* [əg] in front of verbal nouns. You probably already know that the **g** drops off in front of a consonant (except **r** sometimes, for example in *ag ràdh* [ə graː], *ag rùsgadh* [ə gruːsgəɣ]). But what also happens for every native speaker in normal speech is that the [ə] also disappears except if there is a consonant directly in front of it. Here are some examples:

Tha mi a' dol dhachaigh.	[ha mi dɔL ɣaxɪ]
Tha iad **a'** dol dhachaigh.	[had ə dɔL ɣaxɪ]
Tha Màiri a' dol dhachaigh.	[ha maːrʲɪ dɔL ɣaxɪ]
Tha Calum **a'** dol dhachaigh.	[ha kaLəm ə dɔL ɣaxɪ]
Bha an cù ag iarraidh cnàmh.	[va ŋ kuː gʲiəRɪ krãːv]
Bha na coin **ag** iarraidh cnàmh.	[va nə kɔNʲ ə gʲiəRɪ krãːv]

This always happens and having the [ə] in all environments is one of those clean giveaways of a not-so-good learner.

The -*adh* [əɣ] ending in the conditional also follows a similar pattern, the [ɣ] tends to disappear before another consonant:

mhola**dh** tu	[vɔLə du]
mhola**dh** e	[vɔLəɣ ɛ]
mhola**dh** i	[vɔLəɣ i]
mhola**dh** sinn[62]	[vɔLə ʃiNʲ]
mhola**dh** sibh	[vɔLə ʃɪv]
mhola**dh** iad	[vɔLəɣ ad]
mhola**dh** Ailean	[vɔLəɣ alan]
mhola**dh** Dùghlas	[vɔLə duːLəs]

Another case applies to adverbs which have initial *a*-. The rule is the same fortunately:

Tha mi **a**-muigh.	[ha mi muj]
Tha iad **a**-muigh.	[had ə'muj]
Thàinig Màiri **a**-steach.	[haːnɪgʲ maːrʲɪ ʃdʲɛx]
Thàinig Calum **a**-steach.	[haːnɪgʲ kaLəm ə'ʃdʲɛx]

So, [ə] is always in danger of disappearing or being disappeared. Especially at the end of a word, phrase or sentence. If you go along with this, it will make your Gaelic flow much better.

This 'dropping of same sounds' also happens with consonants. The general idea is that when they're too similar, the first sound loses out. English does this too - try and say *bad timing, tough fish* and *Rick Kennedy* at speed and watch the consonants drop like flies.

---

[62] A colloquial alternative to *mholamaid* used by some speakers.

This is fairly easy to get right, just make sure you don't make huge pauses between words and your mouth will deal with most of the rest.

[b] + [b]	òb beag ⇒ [ɔː beg]
	gob bodhar ⇒ [go bo.ər]
[d] + [d]/[t]	Bad Darach ⇒ [baˈdarəx]
	nead traoin ⇒ [Nʲe truːNʲ]
[dʲ] + [dʲ]/[tʲ]	caraid deònach ⇒ [karɪ dʲɔːnəx]
	bréid tiugh ⇒ [brʲeː tʲu]
[g] + [g]/[k]	nochd gun chadal ⇒ [Nɔx gən xadəL]
	aiseag cosgail ⇒ [aʃə kɔsgal]
[gʲ] + [gʲ]/[kʲ]	cóig giomaich ⇒ [koː gʲimɪç]
	Pàdraig ciar⇒ [paːdrɪ kʲiər]
[x] + [x]	Bruach Chluaidh ⇒ [bruəˈxLuaj]
	crìoch cham [krʲiə xaum]
[ç] + [ç]	balaich chiara ⇒ [baLɪ çiarə]
	comhartaich chiùin ⇒ [kõ.əRʃdɪ çuːNʲ]
[s]/[ʃ] + [s]/[ʃ]	nas sine ⇒ [nə ʃinə]
	fras salach ⇒ [fra saLəx]

Something similar also happens when the -te/-ta ending is used on words which end in two consonants. Here, as a rule of thumb, drop the middle consonant if otherwise you'd get a combination of sounds that you would have to work very hard to say:

cleachd [klɛxg] + -te	cleachdte [klɛxdʲə]
craic [krɛçgʲ] + -te	craicte [krɛçdʲə]
glac [gLaxg] + -te	glacte [gLaxdʲə]
rùisg [Ruːʃgʲ] + -te	rùisgte [Ruːʃdʲə]
srac [sdraxg] + -te	sracte [sdraxdʲə]
stamp [sdaumb] + -ta	stampta [sdaumdə]

Another big thing that happens in colloquial Gaelic is that the -nn-
nasalises away before another dental consonant or r on a regular basis
and all you're left with is a very nasal vowel:

annta [ãũNdə]	[ãũdə]
cinnteach [kʲĩːNʲdʲəx]	[kʲĩːdʲəx]
connspaid [kõũNsbɪdʲ]	[kõũsbɪdʲ]
cunnradh [kũːNrəɣ]	[kũːrəɣ]
cunntadh [kũːNdəɣ]	[kũːdəɣ]
innleachd [ĩːNʲLʲəxg]	[ĩːLʲəxg]
ionnlaid [jũːNLɪdʲ]	[jũːLɪdʲ]
ionnsaigh [jũːNsɪ]	[jũːsɪ]
muinntir [mũĩNʲdʲɪrʲ]	[mũĩdʲɪrʲ]
sunntach [sũːNdəx]	[sũːdəx]

More fun… if you remember, lenition is blocked in certain cases. In the
case of *an*, *nan*, *chan* etc this affects **dental** sounds: **d**, **n**, **t**, and **l**. But
because Gaelic doesn't like 'too much of the same' it drops the **n** in front
of **n** and **l**. This is not shown in the spelling but is common practice in
spoken Gaelic. You'll notice that the following examples are a lot easier
to say if you do:

an làmh	⇒ [ə Laːv]	air an latha	⇒ [ɛrʲ ə La.ə]
an leabaidh	⇒ [ə Lʲebɪ]	air an lìn	⇒ [ɛrʲ ə Lʲiːn]
an norrag	⇒ [ə NoRag]	air an nead	⇒ [ɛrʲ ə Nʲed]
an nighneag	⇒ [ə Nʲiːnag]	air an neach	⇒ [ɛrʲ ə Nʲɛx]

Although not a dental, initial [R] also follows the same pattern in the vast
majority of dialects. In the case of *chan*, this is even shown in the
spellling:

chan robh	⇒ [xa Rɔ]	gun robh	⇒ [gə Rɔ]
an ruig e?	⇒ [ə Rɯgʲ ɛ]	an rùisg thu?	⇒ [ə Ruːʃgʲ u]
an rionnag	⇒ [ə RuNag]	air an rùd	⇒ [ɛrʲ ə Ruːd]

If you have a map of Scotland, pull up the Western Isles sheet and look for a place marked *Clachan-a-Luib*[63] on English maps. In Gaelic, this is *Clachan an Lùib*, so the **n** is there in writing but not when it's said!

The same effect is, of course, what causes many of the changes to the **n** of the Gaelic definite article, especially from *an* to *a'* (before a consonant). For the sake of clarity, here's a full list of how the article changes before nouns, depending on what sound comes next.

I have included the Irish counterparts because Irish preserves the older spelling convention (in this instance) but, as you can see, follows the same patterns in pronunciation:

Vowels & f			
Gaelic		**Irish**	
an aiste	[ə Naʃdʲə]	an aiste	[ə Næʃtʲə]
an òige	[ə Nɔːgʲə]	an óige	[ə Noːgʲə]
an uair	[ə Nuərʲ]	an uair	[ə Nuərʲ]
an fhàinne	[ə NaːNʲə]	an fháinne	[ə NɑːNʲə]
an iris	[ə Nʲirʲɪʃ]	an iris	[ə Nʲirʲəʃ]
an éisteachd	[ə Nʲeːʃdʲəxg]	an éisteacht	[ə Nʲeːʃtʲəxt]
an fhéill	[ə NʲeːLʲ]	an fhéile	[ə Nʲeːlə]

---

[63] Near Carinish on the West side of North Uist.

Labials (b p m f)			
Gaelic		Irish	
am ball	[ə(m) bauL]	an ball	[ə(m) bɑ:L]
am bealach	[ə(m) bjaLəx]	an bealach	[ə(m) bʲæ:Ləx]
am pàiste	[ə(m) pa:ʃdʲə]	an páiste	[ə(m) pɑːʃtʲə]
am peann	[ə(m) pjauN]	an peann	[ə(m) pʲɑ:N]
am moladh	[ə mɔLəɣ]	an moladh	[ə mɔLə]
am meall	[ə mjauL]	an meall	[ə mʲɑ:L]
am facal	[ə(m) faxgəL]	an focal	[ə(m) fokəL]
am feall	[ə fjauL]	an feall	[ə fʲɑ:L]

c & g			
Gaelic		Irish	
an còta	[əŋ kɔ:hdə]	an cóta	[əŋ ko:tə]
an ceann	[əŋʲ kʲauN]	an ceann	[əŋʲ kʲɑ:N]
an gall	[əŋ gauL]	an gall	[əŋ gɑ:L]
an gearan	[əŋʲ gʲɛran]	an gearán	[əŋʲ gʲurɑ:n]

Other consonants			
Gaelic		Irish	
an doras	[əN dɔrəs]	an doras	[ə(N) dɔrəs]
an deoch	[əNʲ dʲɔx]	an deoch	[ə(Nʲ) dʲox]
an toradh	[əN tɔrəɣ]	an toradh	[ə(N) torə]
an teanga	[əNʲ tʲɛŋgə]	an teanga	[ə(Nʲ) tæːŋgə]
an loch	[ə Lɔx]	an loch	[ə Lɔx]
an leanabh	[ə Lʲɛnav]	an leanbh	[ə LʲɑNəv]
an nàire	[ə Naːrʲə]	an náire	[ə Nɑːrʲə]
an nead	[ə Nʲed]	an nead	[ə Nʲɑd]
an raineach	[ə RaNʲəx]	an raithneach	[ə rɑNʲəx]
an rìgh	[ə Riː]	an rí	[ə riː]
an sagart	[ə sagəRʃd]	an sagart	[ə sɑgərt]
an siùcar	[ə ʃuːxgər]	an siúcra	[ə ʃuːkrə]

Another thing that happens is that lenition goes into 'overdrive' and lenites a number of words in ways most textbooks don't mention. Leniting more sounds probably makes it easier to speak faster as they generally require less energy. Just what you needed, Gaels speaking even faster. But that's what happens so best be prepared for it. Here are a few examples, you will get a more complete list shortly:

Careful/Formal Speech	Colloquial Speech
'gam [gam]	'gham [ɣam]
agus [agəs]	[aɣəs]
agam [agəm]	a'm [əm]
agad[64] [agəd]	[ajəd] & a'd [əd]
gu [guʲ]/[gɔ]	[gəʲ]/[ɣɔ]
do [də]	dha [ɣa] & a [ə]
de [dʲɛ]	[də], [ʝɛ] & a [ə]

Ok, *do* and *de* require some more explaining. For most Gaelic speakers, especially but not exclusively in the Hebrides, these two have fallen together under the pronunciation [də] in spoken Gaelic. This goes back a long time - even Dwelly more than a century ago included a minor rant about the "pernicious practice of confounding *do* and *de*" in his dictionary.

Whenever it arose and for whatever reason, [də] is firmly entrenched in native Gaelic. You have to rely on context to decide if the intended meaning is *to* or *of* and in the majority of cases, that's easily done:

---

[64] Only affects *agam* & *agad* but not the other forms of *aig*.

[bagə də hjuːxgər]	unlikely to mean "a bag to sugar", hence "a bag of sugar"
[na vauN də ɣɯːNʲə]	unlikely to mean "what was present to people", hence "what was present of people"
[hɔrʲ də vaːrʲɪ ɛ]	unlikely to mean "give it of Màiri", hence "give it to Màiri"
[haːnə mi də ɣuːgʲ]	unlikely to mean "I came of Uig", hence, "I came to Uig"

As a learner this also works, as long as you remind yourself that *de* is translated as *of* but in a partitive sense, not in the sense of *from a place.*

This of course also allows the reduction of *do* and *de* to [ə], as context still provides sufficient clues to the meaning. Reducing *do* and *de* to [ə] is not exclusively Hebridean and is recorded as far South as Arran.

So why is your teacher saying [dɔ] and [dʲɛ] then? They are probably hyper-correcting themselves. That means they look at the way it's written and figure it ought to be pronounced [dɔ] and [dʲɛ], whatever they normally say when they're not consciously thinking about it.

The form *dha* [ɣa] is becoming more widespread in place of *do,* most likely because it does not lenite or add **dh'** to words beginning with a vowel.[65] And a note on the two derived forms *don* and *den.* Historically they probably were [dɔNⁱ⁾] and [dʲɛNⁱ⁾] but in spoken Gaelic they are almost never pronounced that way. They usually show up as *dhan* [ɣaNⁱ⁾] and *dhen* [ʝɛNⁱ⁾ and, funnily enough, here you do get the distinction between *dhan* and *dhen* although it is not uncommon either for speakers to reduce both to [ɣaNⁱ⁾].

Now, it's not lenition as we know it but between vowels, broad **ng** 'lenites' to [ɣ̃] or 'nasalizes' away. As a rule of thumb, expect weird stuff to happen around **ng**, wherever it is in the word.

---

[65] Linguists call this an avoidance strategy. This happens in languages when a particular thing is suddenly perceived as odd or cumbersome.

aingeal [ãɲʲgʲaL]	[ãĵãL]
ceangal [kʲɛ̃ŋgəL]	[kʲɛ̃.ə̃L]
daingeann [daɲʲgʲəN]	[dã̃ĵə̃N]
meangan [mɛŋgən]	[mɛ̃ɣ̃ə̃n]
teanga [tʲɛŋgə]	[tʲɛ̃ɣ̃ə̃]

So Coylumbridge is called that because the **ng** in the original Gaelic name *Drochaid na Cuingleum* was nasalized away, so it came out as [drɔxɪdʲ nə kũĩləm].

This habit of simplifying complicated groups of sounds is of course something that is not restricted to Gaelic. Most languages do this kind of thing. English for example likes to simplify final **-ng** and **-nd**, so you end up with pronunciations like *singin'* and *blin'* rather than *singing* and *blind*.

So, don't be afraid to drop certain sounds from a word if you find out that Gaelic speakers don't pronounce them. And on this occasion the best advice really is to listen to native speakers talk to each other or some recordings of Gaelic songs and listen out for the things that they drop off.

4.14   Short and long forms

English has this concept of short and long forms too so no long explanations are needed. There are words in both languages which have short forms which are used when using a colloquial style and/or when you speak quickly. Apart from the things we talked about in the previous section what you get in Gaelic is a general 'shortening' of words:

- Function words in particular have short forms.

- Final [ə] is often dropped in <u>any</u> position

- Some final consonants tend to get dropped

- An **r** before a dental often results in a retroflex group (see 4.10)

- difficult (from the native speaker point of view) consonants groups are often reduced

Here's a list of the more common ones, sorted according to type. Note that not all short forms have written forms:

Careful Speech	Short Forms	
Verbs		
tha [haː]		[ha], [h]
a bheil [ə vel]	bheil	[vel]
chan eil [xa Nʲel]	'n eil	[Nʲel]
gu bheil [gə vel]	g' eil	[gel]
bha [vaː]		[va], [v]
an robh [əN Rɔ]		[ə Rɔ], [Rɔ]
bithidh [bi.ɪ]	bidh	[bi]
bhitheas [vi.əs]	bhios	[viəs], [vəs]
bhithinn [vi.ɪNʲ]	bhinn	[viNʲ]
bhitheadh [vi.əɣ]	bhiodh	[vjɤɣ] [vəɣ]
bhitheamaid [vi.əmɪdʲ]	bhiomaid	[vimɪdʲ]
chì [çiː]		[çi]
chunnaic [xuNɪgʲ]	chunna	[xuNə]
faighinn [fajɪNʲ]		[faiNʲ]
thàinig [haːnɪgʲ]	thàna	[haːnə]
tighinn [tʲi.ɪNʲ]		[tʲiNʲ]
ràinig [raːnɪgʲ]	ràna	[raːnə]
nì [niː]		[ni]
dèan [dʲian]		[dʲɛn]
rinn [rɤiNʲ]		[rəNʲ]
théid [he.ɪdʲ], [heːdʲ]		[hedʲ]
thubhairt [hu.əRʃdʲ]	thuirt	[huRʃdʲ]

Careful Speech	Short Forms	
Pronouns & Nouns		
mi [miː]		[mi]
mise [miʃə]	mis'	[miʃ]
thu [uː]		[u]
thusa [usə]	thus'	[us]
e [ɛː]		[ɛ], [a], [ə]
i [iː]		[i] [ɪ]
ise [iʃə]	is'	[iʃ]
sinn [ʃiːNʲ]		[ʃiNʲ]
sibh [ʃiv]		[ʃɪv] [ʃu]
sibhse [ʃiːvʃə]	sibhs'	[ʃiːʃə] [ʃɪvʃ]
iad [iəd]		[ad]
iadsan [iədsən]		[adsən], [aːsən]
coltach [kɔLdəx]		[kɔLəx]
té [tʲeː]		[tʲe]
té eile [tʲeː elə]	téile	[tʲeːlə]
smaointinn [smɯːNʲdʲɪNʲ]	smaoint'	[smɯːNʲdʲ]
tuigsinn[66] [tɯgʲʃɪNʲ]	tuigs'	[tɯgʲʃ]
urrainn [uRɪNʲ]	urra	[uRə]

---

[66] And other verbal nouns that end in *-tinn* or *-sinn*.

Careful Speech	Short Forms			
Prepositions				
agam [agəm]	a'm		[əm]	
agad [agəd]	a'd		[əd]	
agad-sa [agədsə]			[agəsə]	
againn [agɪNʲ]			[aNʲ]	
'gam [gam]	[gəm]		[ɣəm]	
'gad [gad]	[gəd]		[ɣəd]	
'ga [gaː]	[ga]	[gə]	[ɣa]	[ɣə]
'ga h- [gaː h]	[ga h]	[gə h]	[ɣa h]	[ɣə h]
'gar n- [gaːr n]	[gar n]	[gər n]	[ɣar n]	[ɣər n]
'gur n- [gaːr n]	[gar n]	[gər n]	[ɣar n]	[ɣər n]
'gan [gaː n]	[ga n]	[gə n]	[ɣa n]	[ɣə n]
air [ɛrʲ]			[ərʲ]	
ort-sa [ɔRʃdsə]			[ɔRʃə]	
ann [auN]			[aN]	
innte [ĩːNʲdʲə]			[ĩNʲdʲə]	
'nam	[nam]	[nəm]	'am [əm]	
'nad	[nad]	[nəd]	'ad [əd]	
'na [naː]	[na]		[nə]	
'na h- [naː h]	[na h]		[nə h]	
'nar n- [naːr n]	[nar n]		[nər n]	
'nur n- [naːr n]	[nar n]		[nər n]	
'nan [naː n]	[na n]		[nə n]	
de [dʲɛ]/[də]	dhe, a		[ʝɛ], [ə]	
dhìot [ʝiəhd]			[ʝihd]	
dhiubh [ʝuː] ~ [ʝiəv]			[ʝəv]	
leam [lɔum] ~ [luːm]			[ləm] ~ [lum]	
leibh [lɣiv]			[ləv]	

leotha [lɔ.ə]	leo	[lɔ]
do [də]	dha, a	[ɣa], [ə]
dhomh-sa [ɣõːsə]		dhomh [ɣõ]
dhut-sa [ɣuhdsə]		[ɣusə]
dha [ɣaː]		[ɣa]
dhi [ʝiː]		[ʝi]
dhuinn [ɣɯiNʲ]		[ɣiNʲ]
dhuibh [ɣɯiv]		[ɣəv]
dhaibh [ɣaiv]		[ɣav]
gu [gu]/[gɔ]		[gə]/[ɣɔ]
mu [ma]		[mə]
rium [rʲɔum] ~ [rʲuːm]		[rʲəm] ~ [rʲum]
rinn [rɯiNʲ]		[riNʲ]

Careful Speech	Short Forms	
Numbers		
aon [ɯ̃ːn]		[ɯ̃]
deug [dʲiag]		[dʲig]
ceud [kʲiad]		[kʲid]
cóignear [koːgʲnər]		[koːgʲər]
seachdnar [ʃɛxgnər]		[ʃɛxgər]
ochdnar [ɔxgnər]		[ɔxgər]
Other Words		
an-dé [əNʲˈdʲeː]		[əˈNʲeː]
an-diugh [əNʲˈdʲu]		[əˈNʲu]
an do [əN də]	na	[nə]
ann an [auN əN⁽ʲ⁾]		[aNə N⁽ʲ⁾] [əNəN⁽ʲ⁾]
anns an [auNs əN⁽ʲ⁾]	anns an, san, sa	[asəN⁽ʲ⁾] [səN⁽ʲ⁾] [sə]
anns na [auNs nə]	sna	[snə]

an-raoir [əNˈRɣirʲ]	raoir	[əˈRɣirʲ] [Rɣirʲ]
an-seo [əNʲˈʃɔ]	a-seo, ana-sheo	[əˈʃɔ] [anəˈhjɔ]
an-sin [əNʲˈʃin]	a-sin, ana-shin	[əˈʃɪn] [anəˈhin]
an-siud [əNʲˈʃid]	a-siud, ana-shiud	[əˈʃɪd] [anəˈhid]
a-rithist [əˈrʲi.ɪʃdʲ]	a-rìs	[əˈrʲiːʃ]
ath bhliadhna [a vliəNə]		[afləN]
càite [kaːhdʲə]	càit, cà	[kaːdʲ] [kaː]
càite an do [kaːhdʲ əN də]	cà na	[kaː nə]
carson [kaRˈsɔn]	c'on	[kɔn]
co-dhiù [kəˈʤuː]		[kʲuː]
ged nach [gad nax]		[ga nax]
gun do [gəN də]	gun a	[gəN ə]
mar gun… [mar gən]		[magən]
nuair a [Nuərʲ ə]		[Nərʲ ə], [ərʲ ə]

A word of warning though. You can't just drop off sounds you don't like. For example, if you're struggling with the [ɣ] sound a bit, that doesn't mean you can just drop them all and blame it on colloquial speech. You can only do that to sounds that native speakers are happy to drop in spoken Gaelic.

4.15   Yet more exercises

Although one can definitely overdo it, there is a lot to be said for a certain amount of rote learning when you're learning a new language. It can certainly help you fix new sounds and structures in your brain. In a way, you're memorising a basic framework.

For exactly this reason the following batch of exercises will introduce you to a number of Gaelic basic phrases, rhymes, ditties, songs, riddles and suchlike. To make it easier for you, each piece will already be in phonetic transcription and of course there is a recording that you can listen to. You will also find a translation so you know what you're learning.

I will not explain the grammar or give you the 'normal' spelling of all these for a very good reason. These pieces are all there to help you fix the sounds of Gaelic in your head and get you to a stage where they will simply 'roll off your tongue'. This is not an exercise about understanding the past conditional tense and the vocative plural. There is no harm in trying to figure how it roughly fits together but, on the whole, you should focus on getting the sounds and the rhythm right and memorising them. And you might pick up a thing or two to teach to your (grand)children if they are going to a Gaelic school, how cool would that be?

It is up to you how many you memorise but undoubtedly the more you do, the quicker the sounds will begin to be 'just right'.

✎ Exercise 109.

In the following sentences all words have been written in full. Look at the sentences and cross out the sounds that you're expecting not to be there when the sentence is spoken. For example: *Bha a chù a bhàsaich an-uraidh ás an àite ud.* Then listen to the recordings and see if you managed to work out all the dropped vowels.

01 Tha a athair ás an Òban agus tha iad a' dol ann a-nochd.

02 Bha uinneagan na h-eaglaise àrd briste on oidhche ud.

03 Cha bhi e toilichte idir 's tu a' bualadh a òrdag cho cruaidh.

04 Is urrainn dhut maille a chur air le bhith a' cur seo an-sin.

05 Leum e a-mach air an uinneag agus chan fhaca e an cù.

06 Thàinig i an-seo an-diugh is chan fhalbh i gu DiSathairne.

07 Thig an-seo is chì thu a' bhó as motha a chunnaic thu a-riamh!

08 A Ailig, am faca e an trod a bha eatarra an-seo dà bhliadhna air ais?

09 Bu àbhaist dhomh a dhol ann ach sguir mi dheth dà latha air ais.

10 Dé an dath a tha air na cait bheaga a fhuair thu an-raoir?

✎ Exercise 110.

This exercise brings together a lot of the things you have studied so far.
It consists of sentences, each of which drills a particular sound or group
of sounds. They have been put together not for their meaning but to drill
sounds. It's a type of exercise used by trainee actors in drama school
for pretty much the same purpose.

Listen to the pronunciation and then repeat the sentence yourself several
times. Try and learn individual ones off by heart and practice them
through the day, then move on to another one.

[b]	bi baLəx brɔːnəx aNəm bɔhan bujə
[t]	tɯgʲɪ N tahərʲ tuːrəx taNəsg tanə
[tʲ]	tʲilɪgʲ tʲeʃdʲənəs tʲiəvɪ tʲirəm ɛrʲ tʲenə tʲe
[d]	duːNʲɪ N dɯNʲə dɔuN dɔrəs aNəN dunʲdɔ̃ːɪLʲ
[dʲ]	xa dʲeːdʲ dʲiəgɛrʲə dʲuːdʲ dʲes ɛrʲ dʲuːra
[kʲ]	kʲaNɪçɪ kʲɛhəRNəx kʲiəLəx kʲɛːçgʲ ɛrʲ kʲɛhb kʲiənal
[g]	gɤdʲɪ s gLanɪ gɔrɪ gruəməx gugə gagəx
[gʲ]	gʲuːLɪNʲɪ gʲiLʲə gʲiar gʲuɪʃ nə gʲaLɛgʲə gʲilə
[N]	Nɔxgɪ Naːbɪ Naːrʲəx aNə Naːhdʲɪçən Nɯːvə dɯːNan
[Nʲ]	Nʲiɪ Nʲiːan ə NʲɛrɪNʲ Nʲihən ɛgʲ ə NʲeːLʲ
[L]	Laj Lɯːxan Laːdʲɪrʲ Luːvər sə Lagan Lurəx Laːa
[Lʲ]	Lʲɛnɪ kaLʲəx nə kɤLʲə rʲi gʲiLʲə Lʲeʃgʲ trɔ NʲeːLʲ
[R]	Reːbɪ Rɤ̃ːəL Rɔːməx Radan Rag Riəvəx ɛrʲ Ra.əd Reː
[r] [rʲ]	xurʲ mə riːvɪNʲ riəvəx kʲiːrʲ jɛrɛg ɛrʲ ɔrʲ əN dɔrɪʃ
[x]	xa xan ə xuːRʃdʲ nax Rɔ xas xrɔum xɔ bɔxg
[ç]	çiː çeːl i çuːNs gə vel ə çaːRNag çuːNʲ gleː çɔːəx
[ɣ]	ɣLan ə ɣauNsɛrʲ mɔɣal ə ɣaː ɣɯːLag ɣɔrɔm ɣɯiNʲ
[ɟ] [j]	ɟuːLɛNʲ mə jɛrɛgəN gleː ɟuːdʲ da: jeːdʲag jiar gu jaLə

❧ Exercise 111.

This rhyme simply lists the names of the five fingers in Gaelic. Most of them have more than one name depending on whom you ask, so I've given you the lot - take your pick! The *Fionnlagh/Màiri* and *Mac/Nic* pairs are gender specific, ie *Fionnlagh Fada* is a boy's middle finger and *Màiri Fhada* a girl's.

		fjũ:NLəɣ fadə ~ maːrʲɪ adə	maxg ə Nabə	Luːdag veg
ɔːRdag	kɔLɔgag			
	baLavag	əŋ guNə fadə	maxg əN tradɪç ~ Nʲiçgʲ əN tradɪç	Luːdag veg ə Nɛrʲɛgʲɪdʲ
	tɔLɔgag	kʲaNə'fed		kɣihdʲag
	sgʲaLabag	gʲiLʲə fadə		pLɯːsgag

✎ Exercise 112.

Another good starter - the sounds that the animals make in Gaelic. Yes, of course the animals say different things in Gaelic. In English frogs go 'ribbit' but in Greek they go 'vrekekeks kouaks kouaks' and in Gaelic... well, you'll see. Have fun!

the chicken	the crow	the bee
gog gog gag gaːg	gɔːrag gɔːrag	fɛrəman farəman
the frog	the whale	the cow
krãːg krãːg	xuʃɪlˈiː xuʃɪlˈɔː	mõː mõː
the dog	the donkey	the goat
af af	hĩ hõ hõ	megʲ megʲ
the sheep	the goose	the snake
mɛ̃ mɛ̃	Raːxg Raːxg	faʃː
the cat	the swan	the duck
mjãũ mjãũ	gulag gulag	vãːg vãːg
the cockerel	the cuckoo	the horse
gog ə ɣujə ɣɯjə	gug guːg	uiɔ hõ
the dove/pigeon	the owl	the pig
duːRd duːRd	ʃuˈxuː ʃuˈxuː	grõsd grõsd

Because you may have trouble finding the normal spelling for these in any dictionary, you will find it (just this once) at the end of the solutions to the exercises.

✎ Exercise 113.

This is another good way of practising your new sounds. They don't always make an awful lot of sense but then, do they in any language?

---

abɪrʲ maxg ə Nabə gən də xab ə ɣobəɣ

say son of the abbot without pursing your lips

əm faxgə dum baxgəx nɔm faxgə du ə vaxg

xa Naxgə mim baxgəx ɪs xa Naxgə mi vaxg

ax nəm fɛçgʲɪNʲsə m baxgəx nɔ nəm fɛçgʲɪNʲsə vaxg

xa vagrɪNʲ ɛrʲ ə vaxgəx ɪs xa vagrɪNʲ ɛrʲ ə vaxg

did you see the cripple or did you see his son?

I didn't see the cripple and I didn't see his son,

but if I saw the cripple or if I saw his son,

I wouldn't threaten the cripple and I wouldn't threaten his son.

---

barɪLʲ əm brɣiNʲ barɪLʲ ɪs barɪLʲ balʲalɛNʲ

a barrel in a barrel and the barrel of Balallan

---

xa ro Lɯːɣ Ruəɣ Luə rʲiəv ɪs xa ro Lɯːɣ Luə rʲiəv Ravər

a brown calf was never swift and a swift calf was never fat

---

jiç dav duh u av ɛrʲ Nʲɛːv

a black ox ate a raw egg in heaven

---

ged ə vɔLə du ə mɔL xa Naːs ə mɔL mɔLəx

even should you praise the shingle beach the shingle beach won't grow hairy

---

juLɪrʲən ɛrʲ juLɪNʲ juLɪrʲ irʲəN ɪs juLɪrʲ vorʲəN

eagles on a stackyard, a male eagle and a female eagle

---

ihdʲən nə kʲirʲçgʲə brʲihgʲə aNə Lʲihdʲə mə hɛnavər

the feathers of the speckled hen in my grandmother's porridge

maʃ i da: hi ba: hi ba:hɪ mɪʃ i maʃ i ma: hi

if it's your kiln, extinguish it; I'll extinguish it if it's my kiln

RɔLag ɪs bLɔj RɔLɛgʲ agəs RɔLag La:n

a small roll and a bit of a small roll and a whole small roll

tri: uərʲən gəN ə ɣɔL imirəL tʲimiçəL imilag mɛna xulɛgʲ

three times around a midge's bellybutton without going astray

✎ Exercise 114.

The first one is a simple rhyme along the lines of *one two buckle my shoe* and really good for learning the numbers up to twelve.

ə huː n ə ɣaː kʲimar ə haː	one two, how are
ə triː ə kʲehɪrʲ brɔːgən Lʲɛhɪrʲ	three four, shoes of leather
ə koːgʲ ə ʃia uʃgʲə s fiə	five six, water and calm
ə ʃɛxg ə hɔxg ɪs mi ha bɔxg	seven eight and I'm not well
ə Nɣj ə dʲeç fɛçgʲ nə heç	nine ten, look at the horses
ə huːn dʲiag ə ɣaː jiag	eleven twelve,
brɔːgən gən faːjəɣ	unpaid shoes

The second one is a counting-out rhyme. Traditionally the person counting out would point at the feet of people with a stick or tap them but pointing with your fingers works just as well!

Lɣ.ər pɔxgan	forked bag
Larə pɔxgan	lara-bag
pɔxgan ʃehbɪNʲ	half-pint bag
ʃehbɪNʲ ʃoːnadʲ	Janet's half-pint
daː viar vi.an	two middle fingers
miar ĩçgʲi.aNʲ	Maclain's finger
duː.əL gLas	grey Dugald
ə legʲ as	who let go
ə çauN sə xuːLan	of his head and his gut
bɔnadʲ ə'max	cap out
sdɔxg ə'ʃdʲɛx	stump in

This little piggy...

ʃɔ Nʲ tʲe: vrʲiʃ ə savəL	this is the one who broke into the barn
ʃɔ Nʲ tʲe: ɣɤdʲ əm ba:R	this is the one who stole the crops
ʃɔ Nʲ tʲe: hes ə gavərg	this is the one who was on the lookout
ʃɔ Nʲ tʲe: rɯh ɛrʲ faLav	this is the one who ran away
ɪs ʃɔ Nʲ tʲe: veg ə be:dər ʝi	and this is the little one who had to pay
fa:jəɣ ɛrʲ fad	for it all

The following rhymes test how much breath you have. Some count up so the target is to get as high up as possible until you run out of breath. In the other variation you set a target by starting high and counting down.

ha:nɪgʲ kaLʲəx a Lɔx'abər	an old woman came from Lochaber
ə ʝiəRɪ sgadan a Lɔx'vrɯ:Nʲ	seeking herring from Loch Broom
xa də ʝiəR i ɛrʲ sgʲiLʲɪNʲ	she didn't want for it a penny
ax na xū:Ndəɣ i gə nanal	but what she could count without drawing breath
sgʲidər sgadan ə hɯ:n	jellyfish herring one
sgʲidər sgadan ə ɣa:	jellyfish herring two
sgʲidər sgadan ə tri:	jellyfish herring three
sgʲidər sgadan ə kʲehɪrʲ	jellyfish herring four
sgʲidər sgadan ə ko:gʲ	jellyfish herring five
sgʲidər sgadan ə ʃia	jellyfish herring six
sgʲidər sgadan ə ʃɛxg	jellyfish herring seven
sgʲidər sgadan ə hɔxg	jellyfish herring eight
sgʲidər sgadan ə Nɣj	jellyfish herring nine
sgʲidər sgadan ə dʲeç	jellyfish herring ten
sgʲidər sgadan ə hɯn dʲiag	jellyfish herring eleven
sgʲidər sgadan ə ɣa: ʝiag	jellyfish herring twelve
sgʲidər sgadan ə tri: dʲiag	jellyfish herring thirteen
...	...

This one is excellent for practising your puff of air before **c**:

dʲeç bɔçgʲəNən dʲeç krɛçgʲəNən	ten goat-skins ten hides
Nɯj bɔçgʲəNən Nɯj krɛçgʲəNən	nine goat-skins nine hides
ɔxg bɔçgʲəNən ɔxg krɛçgʲəNən	eight goat-skins eight hides
ʃɛxg bɔçgʲəNən ʃɛxg krɛçgʲəNən	seven goat-skins seven hides
ʃia bɔçgʲəNən ʃia krɛçgʲəNən	six goat-skins six hides
koːgʲ bɔçgʲəNən koːgʲ krɛçgʲəNən	five goat-skins five hides
kʲehɪrʲ bɔçgʲəNən kʲehɪrʲ krɛçgʲəNən	four goat-skins four hides
triː bɔçgʲəNən triː krɛçgʲəNən	three goat-skins three hides
daː vɔçgʲəN daː xrɛçgʲəN	two goat-skins two hides
bɔçgʲəN ɪs krɛçgʲəN	one goat-skin one hide
kurʲ ʃɛxəd mar ʃin ɛ	pass it like that

ə çɛrg ɣu nə Nʲiməɣ duh	black hen of the many blacks
ko viəd u rug u Nʲdʲu	how many eggs did you lay today
u ɣõ heːn su ɣuhd heːn	one egg for me and one egg for you
su rʲi rɣiNʲ edərɪNʲ	and one egg to share between us
suh əN dɯNʲə vɔxg	and the egg of the poor man
daː u ɣõ heːn sdaː ɣuhd heːn	two eggs for me and two eggs for you
triː ɯjən ɣõ heːn striː ɯjən ɣuhd heːn	three eggs for me and three eggs for you
…	…

This one is actually a little game. You stand behind a sitting person and (gently!) knock on their head with your fingers and say the rhyme. The sitting person the has to guess how many fingers you were knocking on their head with.

ɯːn ɛrʲ buçgʲan	one on a little buck
ɣaː ɛrʲ buçgʲan	two on a little buck
madʲə ʃu.al	walking stick
kuːL əN duːRNʲ	back of the hand
kʲɛrg veg	little chicken
riəvəx vaːn	brindles and white
rug əN tu	who laid the egg
ɛrʲ əN sbaːR	on the beam
brʲiʃɪ ɛ mə	it'll break before
Rɯgʲ ɛ Laːr	it'll hit the floor
kuːNd rɔ̃.əd s	count before
as də ʝeː	and after you
ko viad ɣː.ərg	how many horns
ə hɛrʲ ə vɔxg	are on the buck?

4.16   A bit more on dialects

As you progress with your Gaelic, you will meet Gaelic speakers who speak different dialects. The differences between the surviving modern Gaelic dialects aren't huge but can still be confusing to the learner. For that reason, you are being presented with a middle-ground form of Gaelic in this course.

As a learner of English the same will happen to you, you will meet native English speakers (and even teachers) in and out of the classroom who have different accents. But that doesn't mean you have to always speak exactly like the person you're speaking to as long as you know that your own pronunciation is good.

Be honest, last time you travelled south of the border, did you suddenly lapse into Broad Yorkshire, Geordie, Scouse or Cockney? Not really. And neither should you feel compelled to switch back and forth between dozens of Gaelic dialects when all you're wanting is milk in your coffee.

That doesn't mean dialects are bad, nothing of the sort. But as a learner you have the freedom to use a more or less Standard Pronunciation and don't have to do all dialects just because your Tuesday night teacher happens to speak a different Gaelic dialect than your Saturday morning teacher.

But it is necessary to mention a few of the more puzzling things some dialects do because you may have some trouble understanding what's going on otherwise.

The main problem is something called eclipsis, which appears in some dialects and can greatly distort the shape of spoken words. The other points are just some general pointers as to what you can expect.

4.16.1 Eclipsis or Why am I married to *an nuine agam?*

This effect is often called nasalization because it is caused by a nasal. It affects consonants and can actually be more of a 'voicing thing' than nasalization in the sense we met earlier (see 4.4). I'm using the term eclipsis, which is slightly less common in Scottish Gaelic linguistics but it has the advantage of keeping it separate from the other type of nasalization.

Before you lose patience with me, let me tell you that you're fortunate for two reasons. For one thing, if you run your Gaelic together smoothly, your mouth will do this to some degree anyway without you having to think about it. And secondly, Gaelic dialects like to disagree on what exactly happens or if it happens at all.

So why do you need to know what's going? Because it can distort the pronunciation of noun phrases considerably. So if you're not aware of it at all, this can throw you a bit.

This happens with many of those little grammatical words ('particles') which end in **-n**:

- all forms of the definite article which end in a nasal: *an, nan, nam.* This includes all prepositions which end in a nasal (the remnant of the definite article): *dhan, dhen, chun, leis an...*

- the conjunction *gun/gum* 'that'

What happens is that **n** and **m** are very soft, voiced sounds (see 2.4). Although Gaelic doesn't have any voiced stops as such, being near **n** or **m** can cause them to become soft, to 'voice' as linguists call it. This can result in very breathy sounding stops or in some cases the complete loss of the original sounds. The following table has the recommended pronunciation in the left column, followed by examples of what can happen. The funny [ⁿ] symbol is a sound similar to the puff of air after **p**, **t** and **c**, only a lot more 'breathy'. You really don't have to worry about how to make it though.

Remember that Gaelic **b**, **d** and **g** are normally hard. All the hard sounds which have been 'softened' (voiced) are marked with a circumflex either underneath or above **ḇ**, **ḏ** and **ğ**.

Suggested	Outcome 2	Outcome 3	Outcome 4
am bùth	am bùth	am bùth	
[əm **bu**ː]	[əm **ḇu**ː]	[ə **mu**ː]	
am bearn	am bearn	am bearn	
[əm **bj**aːRN]	[əm **ḇj**aːRN]	[ə **mj**aːRN]	
an doras	an doras	an doras	
[əN **d**ɔrəs]	[əN **ḏ**ɔrəs]	[ə **N**ɔrəs]	
an deò	an deò	an deò	
[əNʲ **dʲ**ɔː]	[əNʲ **ḏʲ**ɔː]	[ə **Nʲ**ɔː]	
an guth	an guth	an guth	
[əŋ **g**uh]	[əŋ **ğ**uh]	[ə **ŋ**uh]	
an geall	an geall	an geall	
[əŋʲ **gʲ**auL]	[əŋʲ **ğʲ**auL]	[ə **ŋʲ**auL]	
am punnd	am punnd	am punnd	am punnd
[əm **pu**ːNd]	[əm **ḇu**ːNd]	[əm **ḇʰu**ːNd]	[əm **hu**ːNd]
am peann	am peann	am peann	am peann
[əm **pj**auN]	[əm **ḇj**auN]	[əm **ḇʰj**auN]	[ə **mj**auN]
an taigh	an taigh	an taigh	an taigh
[əN **t**ɤj]	[əN **ḏ**ɤj]	[əN **ḏʰ**ɤj]	[əN **h**ɤj]
an teas	an teas	an teas	an teas
[əNʲ **tʲ**es]	[əNʲ **ḏʲ**es]	[əNʲ **ḏʲʰ**es]	[əNʲ **h**es]
an cù	an cù	an cù	an cù
[əŋ **k**uː]	[əŋ **ğ**uː]	[əŋ **ğʰ**uː]	[əŋ **h**uː]
an ceann	an ceann	an ceann	an ceann
[əŋ **kʲ**auN]	[əŋʲ **ğʲ**auN]	[əŋʲ **ğʲʰ**auN]	[əŋʲ **hj**auN]

The reason I have not given you a map or a table that lists them according to area is that the pattern of eclipsis in Gaelic is, well, complicated. For example it is a common pattern for a speaker to be saying [əN ḍⁿɣj] and [əm ḅʰuːNd] but you may equally find people who mix and match and say [əN ḍⁿɣj] and [ə muːNd].

This is one of those things that make it tricky even for native speakers to understand each other. Lenition happens more or less the same way in every area but this nasalization doesn't so it also makes life confusing. For example, in certain dialects [dah nəm bjauN] could either be *dath nam beann* or *dath nam peann!* If you are aiming for a particular dialect, I suggest you find yourself a local native speaker, ask them to say the words in the above list (perhaps even record them) and use whatever they're saying as a model.

Oh and before you ask, this is not quite the same thing as the Irish *urú* thingy. In Irish, nasalization occurs with nasals which haven't been 'there' for a long time (for example, nine boats is *naoi mbád* because *naoi* used to have a final -n, just as English *nine* or German *neun* still have today.)

Irish		Indo-European
naoi mbád	[Niː maːd]	*newṇ
deich mbád	[dʲe maːd]	*dekṃ

In Gaelic this thing only ever happens if a nasal is currently present (compare *naoidh bàtaichean* where there is no eclipsis). And before you move on to the exercises, there's a place in Ross which shows this sound change in action. There's a place north of the Black Isle which on the map is Port an Righ. Looks very Gaelic, doesn't it? It is except it has nothing to do with kings, it's a sort-of phonetic approximation of the Gaelic name, which is *Port an Draoidh*, the Harbour of the Druid. What happened was that *Port an Draoidh* underwent nasalization, so [pɔRʃd əN drɣj] became [pɔRʃd ə Nrɣj] which our poor mapmaker must have mistaken for Port an Righ!

✎ Exercise 115.

Listen to the following short phrases and sentences and identify the nasalized sounds and work out what the underlying, most likely original sound was.

	Phrase	Sound	Original
01	va muː əˈʃɪn	m	m or b
02			
03			
04			
05			
06			
07			
08			
09			
10			
11			
12			
13			
14			
15			

4.16.2   Final devoicing or Why *a-muigh* sounds like *a-muich*

OK, this is another one of those things you just have to be aware of. When you listen to native Gaelic speakers you'll notice that sometimes they do funny things to the end of their words. For example, *a-muigh* comes out a bit as if it was *a-muich, naoidh* can sound like it was *naoich* and the ll in *call* can be somewhat reminiscent of the Welsh double ll.

Gaelic is one of those languages which have what linguists call final devoicing. That means that the last sound of a word can lose its voicing, so it goes from a sound where the chanter reed in your throat is vibrating to one where it isn't, making a soft sound a lot harder.

If you have ever heard a German speak English with a strong German accent, sounding very hard to your ears, final devoicing was one of the culprits. In German there is a rule that says every consonant at the end of a word has to be voiceless. So when Germans speak English with a strong accent, they make *bug* sound like *buck*, *bad* like *bat*, *nib* like *nip* and *dead* like *debt*.. English, as you can tell, is a language which definitely does not allow you to devoice final consonants. Excluding Hebridean English that is…

Fortunately this is not obligatory in Gaelic so as a learner you really don't have to try and train your tongue to do that. But you do have to be aware of the fact that when you listen to native Gaelic, some speakers will replace voiced consonants at the end of a word with a voiceless counterpart. Remember that **b**, **d** and **g** already are hard in Gaelic so they won't change at all. In a few cases the devoiced version has in fact become the standard pronunciation, for example in *ith*.

Here are a few examples you can listen to so you get a feel for what it sounds like:

[L] ⇒ [L̥[67]]	ball [bauL]	⇒ [bauL̥]
	call [kauL]	⇒ [kauL̥]
[Lʲ] ⇒ [L̥ʲ]	cill [kʲiːLʲ]	⇒ [kʲiːL̥ʲ]
	foill [fɤiLʲ]	⇒ [fɤiL̥ʲ]
[j] ⇒ [j̊]	a-muigh [əˈmuj]	⇒ [əˈmuj̊]
	naoidh [Nɯj]	⇒ [Nɯj̊]
[ɣ] ⇒ [ɣ̊]	moladh [mɔLəɣ]	⇒ [mɔLəɣ̊]
	lagh [Lɤɣ]	⇒ [Lɤɣ̊]

But, as I said, it's neither universal nor obligatory, so be aware of it and leave it at that.

---

[67] To make this, put your tongue into the position where you'd make a normal [L] and exhale sharply.

4.16.3   Other common changes

There are other things that change between dialects. The following lists are by no means a full picture of what dialects do. The idea is simply to make you aware of some of the other things you will encounter that might confuse you.

- **-(e)adh**
  The ending **-(e)adh** [əɣ] can appear as [əg] for example:

dùnadh [duːnəɣ]	[duːnəg]
dhèanadh [ʝianəɣ]	[ʝianəg]
marbhadh [maravəɣ]	[maravəg]

This - just in case cheating has crossed your mind - does not affect any of the other [ɣ] sounds, so *dhut* is still [ɣuhd]!

- **-(e)amh** and **-(a)ibh**
  In an unstressed syllable the endings **-(e)amh** [əv] and **-(a)ibh** [ɪv] often appear as [u] and [ɪ], for example:

ainneamh [aNʲəv]	[aNʲu]	
dèanamh [dʲianəv]	[dʲianu]	
claidheamh [kLajəv]	[kLaju]	
agaibh [agɪv]	[agu]	[agɪ]
cùlaibh [kuːLɪv]	[kuːLu]	
cuiribh! [kurʲɪv]	[kurʲu]	[kurʲɪ]

- Fricatives between vowels
  Between vowels, fricatives such as [v], [h] or [ɣ] can often turn into
  hiatus:

craobhan [krɯːvən]	[krɯː.ən]
eughach [eːvəx]	[eː.əx]
lugha [Lɯɣə]	[Lɯ.ə]
leathad [Lʲɛhəd]	[Lʲɛ.əd]
marbhadh [maravəɣ]	[mara.əɣ]
frithealaich [frʲihəLɪç]	[frʲi.əLɪç]

- [a(ː)] and [ɛ(ː)]
  In stressed syllables [a]/[aː] and [ɛ]/[ɛː] often alternate between
  dialects for example:

ainneamh [aNʲəv]	[ɛNʲu]
leantainn [LʲaNdɪNʲ]	[LʲɛNdɪNʲ]
anmoch [anamɔx]	[ɛnɛmɔx]
thairis [harʲɪʃ]	[hɛrʲɪʃ]
bainne [baNʲə]	[bɛNʲə]
na b' fhearr [nə bjaːR]	[nə bɛːR]
nas blàithe [nəs bLaːjə]	[nəs bLɛːhɔ]
ràithe [Raːjə]	[Rɛːhə]
cearr [kʲaːR]	[kʲɛːR]

- [u] and [ɯ]
  In stressed syllables [u] and [ɯ] often alternate between dialects in
  front of a palatal consonant (and sometimes even elsewhere) for
  example:

tuiteam [tuhdʲəm]	[tɯhdʲəm]
uile [ulə]	[ɯlə]
an-uiridh [əˈNurʲɪ]	[əˈNɯrʲɪ]

- Variant verbal noun endings
  The endings for verbal nouns sometimes change from dialect to dialect:

leantainn [LʲɛndɪNʲ], leantail [Lʲɛndal]

ruigsinn [RɯgʲʃɪNʲ], ruighinn [Ri.ɪNʲ]

eughachd [eːvəxg], eughach [eːvəx]

fantainn [fandɪNʲ], fantail [fandal], fanachd [fanəxg], fanail [fanal]

faireachdainn [farʲəxgɪNʲ], faireachadh [farʲəxəɣ]

innse [ĩːʃə], innseadh [ĩːʃəɣ]

If you come across such variants and are unsure which to use, google both verbal nouns separately and see how many results you get for each. Then use the more common one.

- Simplification of **ng**
  The **ng** sounds (especially the slender ones) are often reduced with great variation in the outcome (see also 4.13), for example:

farsaing [farsɪŋʲgʲ]	[faʂɪgʲ]	[faʂɪNʲ]
aisling [aʃlɪŋʲgʲ]	[aʃlɪgʲ]	
fulaing [fuLɪŋʲgʲ]	[fuLɪgʲ]	[fuLɪNʲ]
fulang [fuLəŋg]	[fuLəg]	
tarraing [taRɪŋʲgʲ]	[taRɪgʲ]	[taRɪNʲ]

Occasionally, the reduced forms are the only commonly heard pronunciations:

ingne/ionga (⇒ ìne)	[ĩːnə]
iongnadh (⇒ ìonadh)	[ĩə̃nəɣ]
tàir(r)ngidh[68]	[taːRNʲɪ]

---

[68] Future tense of *tarraing* "pull".

- Variation in **rt/rd** groups

  We've already dealt with the extra sound that must be inserted into **rt** groups (and optionally into **rd** groups). One other thing that needs explaining in this context is that depending on the area, there are variations in what people ultimately pronounce. Apart from the [Rʃd] pronunciation, pronunciations with [s] are also common, resulting in [Rsd]. Something slightly more exotic happens in a lot of Hebridean dialects where the [R] is deleted and the remaining consonants turning into retroflex consonants (see 4.10), resulting in [ʂɖ]:

ceart	[kʲaRʃd]	[kʲaRsd]	[kʲaʂɖ]
murt	[muRʃd]	[muRsd]	[muʂɖ]
bàrd	[ba:Rʃd]	[ba:Rsd]	[ba:ʂɖ]
òrdag	[ɔ:Rʃdag]	[ɔ:Rsdag]	[ɔ:ʂɖag]

  Related to this is the habit, in particular in some areas of the Hebrides, to suspend the broad/slender distinction in **rd/rt** groups, pronouncing them all as broad. Again, be aware of this but unless you're aiming for a specific dialects, don't feel compelled to do this yourself:

toirt	[tɔRʃdʲ]	[tɔRsd]
thuirt	[hu:Rʃdʲ]	[hu:Rsd]
cuairt	[kuəRʃdʲ]	[kuəRsd]
àirde	[a:Rdʲə]	[a:Rdə]

- [ɔ] in unstressed syllables

  Some dialects have [ɔ] instead of unstressed [a] or [ə] for example:

feumail [fe:mal]	[fe:mɔl]
eòlach [jɔ:Ləx]	[jɔ:Lɔx]
òirleach [ɔ:Rləx]	[ɔ:ɭɔx]

- Phantom endings

  In some dialects a 'phantom' ending **-(e)adh** is appearing (mostly) in feminine genitives. This does not seem to affect all nouns though and the pattern is unclear. Just be aware of it happening sometimes:

na cloiche [nə kLɔçə]	na cloicheadh [nə kLɔçəɣ]
na coise [nə kɔʃə]	na coiseadh [nə kɔʃəɣ]
na feòla [nə fjɔːLə]	na feòladh [nə fjɔːLəɣ]
na gaoithe [nə gɯjə]	na gaoitheadh [nə gɯjəɣ]
na làimhe [nə Laivə]	na làimheadh [nə Laivəɣ]
na h-oidhche [nə hɣ̃ĩçə]	na h-oidhcheadh [nə hɣ̃ĩçəɣ]
eile [elə]	eileadh [eləɣ]

If there's an adjective, this ending appears after the adjective, for example *na làimhe móireadh* [nə Laivə moːrʲəɣ].

A similar phantom ending occurs in some dialects in the prepostional case:

sa choille [sə xɣLʲə]	sa choillidh [sə xɣLʲɪ]
sa chiste [sə çiʃdʲə]	sa chistidh [sə çiʃdʲɪ]
sa bhùth [sə vuː]	sa bhùthaidh [sə vuːˌɪ]

- Changes to the possessive pronouns

  In Lewis, Harris, Wester Ross and East Sutherland some speakers have developed alternative forms for the words our and your. Even in these areas not everyone uses these but because they are so radically different, you need to be aware of these. The third person *an* [ən] 'their' is not affected:

Standard	Local variants
ar n-athair [ər nahɪrʲ]	ar h-athair [ər hahɪrʲ]
ar n-aran [ər naran]	ar h-aran [ər haran]
'gar n-iarraidh [gar niəRɪ]	'ghar h-iarraidh [ɣar hiəRɪ]
'nar n-aodainn [nar nɯ:dɪNʲ]	'nar h-aodainn [nar hɯ:dɪNʲ]
ur n-athair [ər nahɪrʲ]	ur h-athair [ər hahɪrʲ]
ur n-aran [ər naran]	ur h-aran [ər haran]
'gur n-iarraidh [gar niəRɪ]	'ghur h-iarraidh [ɣar hiəRɪ]
'nar n-aodainn [nar nɯ:dɪNʲ]	'nar h-aodainn [nar hɯ:dɪNʲ]

- Transposed **ml** and **mr**

  The sound combinations **ml** and **mr** are somewhat unstable. That means that depending on where you are, people often transpose the two sounds - or even drop one. So be aware that words like the following can show up 'the other way round' too:

Standard	Local variants
imleag [imilag]	[ilimag]
imlich [imilɪç]	[ilimɪç]
imrich [imirʲɪç]	[irʲimɪç]
iomradh [imirəɣ]	[iriməɣ]
iomrall [imirəL]	[iriməL]

Finally, here's a list of some very common words which often cause confusion to beginners because they have very different pronunciations from dialect to dialect. Going into the ins and outs of why these are so different would go a bit too far, so I won't.

	Standard	Variants		
coimhead	[kõjad]	[kɛ̃.ad]	[kõ.ad]	[kũ.ad]
esan	[esən]	[æʃən]	[aʃɪn]	
feadhainn	[fjɣɣɪNʲ]	[fjo.ɪNʲ]	[fo.ɪNʲ]	
foghar	[fo.ər]	[fɣvər]		
gabh	[gav]	[gɔ]	[ga]	
gabhail	[gahal]	[gɔ.al]	[gaval]	[gu.al]
gheibh	[ʝev]	[ʝo]		

4.17   The fine detail

If you look very very closely at the sounds of any language, you will find quite of lot of very fine variation going on. Not only between different speakers but even in the language of each individual speaker.

Although we could go 'into the next layer down' that would be taking things too far. It would end up with you feeling more like you're doing a PhD in Gaelic Phonology than following a guide to good Gaelic pronunciation. As it is, you have probably followed the most detailed learners' guide to the sounds of Gaelic you could possibly find.

Having come this far, you will have a very good grasp of Gaelic pronunciation; a good idea of how the sounds of Gaelic join together and interact with each other; and of the main 'weird' things that go on. That puts you right on so many points of Gaelic pronunciation that you will already have a good *Blas na Gàidhlig*.

This means that the remaining issues and finer details aren't that vital and that you may or may not pick up on them over time. However, you'll rarely be way off. It's like learning how to drive. Once you've passed your test, you may lack practice to some degree but you have all the skills required to get from A to B. With time, you will become more confident and experienced. You may never become a F1 driver and race in Monte Carlo but that's not vital for most drivers, is it? All you want to do is get to your destination safely without visiting A&E or racking up points on your licence.

PART 4

The Gaelic Writing System

or

The genius of the

ancient Irish monks

5.   The Gaelic writing system

Written Gaelic looks daunting to people who don't speak it with all its unfamiliar letter combinations. But it's actually relatively easy to learn how to read it. Compared to English or Japanese anyway.

/naɪtlɪ/

Unlike English, Gaelic really has a stunningly regular and efficient spelling system - once you get under its skin. There is very little about it that's superfluous, almost every letter that is there has a function, something to tell you about the pronunciation of the word. And that despite the fact that its basic outline was devised ages ago from the 6th century[69] onwards and has changed little since!

The reason Gaelic words sometimes appear to have many 'silent' letters to learners is because there's information in the spelling that they're just not picking up on. Take the word *teaghlach* for example. People often complain about the **gh** being a pain in the neck but actually it's vital. The **gh** tells you that the preceding vowel is [ɣː]. If you left it out and wrote it as *tealach*, the word would be pronounced [tʲaʟəx].

At best, you could tweak the spelling but on the whole the list of things in need of revision is short. Certainly shorter than in English with its spellings centuries out of date - or simply irregular: *knight, knife, rough, honour...* If anything, changes made in the last 50 years or so to the way Gaelic is written have made it messier, not better.

Still, it takes some getting used to and some of the spelling rules aren't that obvious at first sight and need spelling out (pardon the pun).

---

[69] Which is fairly impressive. Welsh also started in the 6th century but English, German and Church Slavonic weren't written down until the 8th and 9th century and even French had to wait until the 11th century!

5.1   A word about Manx Gaelic

And just the briefest comment on Manx Gaelic. A lot of people complain about the way Gaelic is written and often regret that it's not written like Manx Gaelic is. On the face of it, it seems like a good idea so let's take a look.

Manx Gaelic has a writing system based largely on English invented by a bishop in the 17th century and further "improved" by a variety of other people. This undoubtedly makes written Manx look more pronounceable to an English

speaker. But as always the devil is in the detail and Manx is pronounced very differently than it might seem to an English speaker. The result is a system that has been criticised widely over the centuries as being neither historic (i.e. breaking the orthographic closeness between Irish, Scottish Gaelic and Manx) nor phonetic (i.e. really bad at representing the actual sounds of the language).

Let's look at just a few examples:

Manx	looks like it's	but actually is
caggey 'war'	[kægɪ]	[kaːɣə]
faasaag 'beard'	[faːzɑːg]	[fəˈzɛːg]
bane 'white'	[beɪn]	[bɛːᵈn]
çhibbyrt 'fountain'	[tʃɪbərt]	[tʃuvərt]
mygeayrt 'around'	[mædʒɑːt]	[məˈgit]

Maybe it works for Manx but I'll leave you to decide whether we'd be better off spelling Scottish Gaelic like that (bearing in mind Scottish Gaelic has preserved a much more complex sound system than Manx) and whether it's really any easier…

But enough of that, let's start and take a look at one of the most fundamental principles in the Gaelic writing system.

5.2   Broad and slender

The medieval scribes who first wrote down Irish on paper (well, ok, vellum) had a problem. They had 21 letters in the Latin alphabet, some of which they didn't use, either because they represented sounds that Old Irish didn't have (such as **z** and **q**), because they were double (**c** ~ **k**) or didn't exist back in the 6th century (**j** and **v**). And yet they had roughly 50 sounds in the Old Irish language which needed writing.

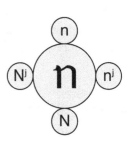

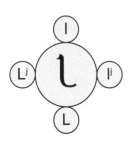

The solution was pure genius. They realised that Old Irish had about 40 consonants which fell broadly into two categories - palatal sounds and sounds which aren't palatal. So all they needed to do was find a consistent way of indicating these two qualities. Someone had a Eureka moment and the seed for the future *caol ri caol is leathann ri leathann*[70] rule was born.

What they had realised in their flash of genius was that in Old Irish the vowel sounds could be split into two groups - back and front:

Front	Back
i [i] í [i:] e [e] é [e:]	u [u] ú [u:] o [o] ó [o:] a [a] á [a:]

They also realised that in a spoken word, if a consonant was surrounded by front vowels it tended to be palatalised and if it was surrounded by back vowels, it tended not to.

---

[70] *Slender with slender and broad with broad,* the "Prime Directive" of Gaelic and Irish spelling..

So all they had to do was to extend this rule slightly to:

> If a consonant is surrounded by **i** and/or **e** letters
> its pronunciation will be palatal(ised),
>
> If it is surrounded by **u** and/or **o** and/or **a** letters its
> pronunciation will not be palatal(ised).

They then also found a way of writing the 12 (!) **l**, **n** and **r** sounds of Old Irish using the letters **l**, **ll**, **n**, **nn**, **r** and **rr** in conjunction with the broad/slender rules and, a few other details aside, the Gaelic way of writing was born. A few adjustments aside to accommodate for changes in the modern language, the principles have stayed the same for over a thousand years!

> ıꝛın ċeċꞃᴀmᴀꝺ ƀⱡíᴀꝺᴀın   *anns a' cheathramh bhliadhna*

Not bad when you remember that in roughly the same period, English looked like this:

> þ̄ȳ fēorþan gēare   *in the fourth year*

Let's look at some examples of what these two groups actually refer to:

Broad			Slender	
Spelling	Sound		Spelling	Sound
ca	[ka]	⇔	cea	[kʲa]
cu	[ku]	⇔	ciu	[kʲu]
lo	[Lɔ]	⇔	leo	[Lʲɔ]
lu	[Lu]	⇔	liu	[Lʲu]
su	[su]	⇔	siu	[ʃu]
so	[sɔ]	⇔	seo	[ʃɔ]
ach	[ax]	⇔	aich	[aç]
dhu	[ɣu]	⇔	dhiu	[ʝu]

And so on. Remember the above are just examples, we'll need to know a few more things for reading normal Gaelic but this is the most important principle.

✎ Exercise 116.

Don't worry about the pronunciation or meaning of the words in the exercises in this section, they focus purely on the broad/slender distinction.

In the first exercise, underline all vowel letters that in Gaelic are considered slender (as you can see in the first example).

01 seachdain	11 fàilidhean	21 tànaiste	31 deifrich
02 cilltean	12 banais	22 isean	32 fighe
03 faoin	13 giobach	23 rùisgte	33 tèarainn
04 cìsean	14 eilean	24 geòidh	34 daoine
05 leabaidh	15 mìneachadh	25 eile	35 cnuic
06 Éireannach	16 leòman	26 leisgeadair	36 ròlaisteach
07 sònraichte	17 teagaisg	27 ùineachan	37 ciste
08 cruithneach	18 falmhaich	28 geamannan	38 aiseag
09 bochdainn	19 làthaireachd	29 caileige	39 urram
10 nighean	20 bràigh	30 ainmich	40 feòragan

Note that any vowel letter you didn't underline is therefore thought of as broad.

Now, for the next exercise, underline all consonant letters that are considered slender. Remember, you have to look at the vowel letters immediately next to the consonant letter in question to make that decision. If there are no vowel letters in front, look for the first vowel letter after (for example at the beginning of a word) and if there are none after, just look at the first vowel letter before the consonant letter (for example consonant letters at the end of a word). If there is a string of consonant letters, they will all be of the same quality, so look to the vowel letters nearest to the left or right end of your consonant letter group to make your decision.

01 seachdain	11 fàilidhean	21 tànaiste	31 deifrich
02 cilltean	12 banais	22 isean	32 fighe
03 faoin	13 giobach	23 rùisgte	33 tèarainn
04 cìsean	14 eilean	24 geòidh	34 daoine
05 leabaidh	15 mìneachadh	25 eile	35 cnuic
06 Éireannach	16 leòman	26 leisgeadair	36 ròlaisteach
07 sònraichte	17 teagaisg	27 ùineachan	37 ciste
08 cruithneach	18 falmhaich	28 geamannan	38 aiseag
09 bochdainn	19 làthaireachd	29 caileige	39 urram
10 nighean	20 bràigh	30 ainmich	40 feòragan

5.3   Utter madness or what?

Well, actually not. Many languages which use alphabets make use of neighbouring sounds to tell people how to pronounce a consonant. Not all are as consistent as Gaelic about this but that hardly makes the Gaelic way a bad one. Think of English:

Hard	Soft
gall, gas, guitar	gym, gin, gent
cot, car, cut	city, centre, cyborg
render, does, dough	soldier, deuce, dew

Of course English then goes and upsets the applecart with words like *gill* and *get*.

Many other languages do the same thing by the way: German, Spanish, Greek, French… And in actual fact, if you do an analysis of how many letters a language needs to 'encode' a hundred sounds, Gaelic doesn't fare that badly. Italian needs just over 100 letters for 100 sounds, English needs a little over 120 letters. Gaelic needs about 140 letters per 100 sounds which may strike you as excessive but only until you find out that French needs almost 150.

Yes, they could have used diacritics. Slovak for example uses a caron (the upside down circumflex) to distinguish its palatal sounds č, ď, ľ, ň, š, ť and ž[71] from its non-palatal sounds c, d, l, n, s, t and z. Latvian uses a cedilla to mark the palatal sounds ģ, ķ, ļ and ņ. But historically few writing systems were born with diacritics. Instead, it was frequently the case that a diacritic would evolve from a full letter over time. In Ancient Greek for example, one of the earliest European writing systems with  diacritics, the breathing signs on vowels (for example ἀ and ἁ) developed from the left and right half of the letter H respectively. So they needed H before they could even think about adapting it. The Germanic umlaut (the two dots on ä etc) is nothing but a worn down e.[72] And so on.

Either way, these early scribes came up with a very efficient, if somewhat letter intensive system. They just didn't use diacritics (at least not until much later when they introduced the deletion mark above ḟ and ṡ to show that they had been lenited). Look on the bright side, at least Gaelic is almost religiously strict about its spelling rules!

---

[71] The squiggle behind ď is a reduced form of the caron.

[72] Which is, incidentally, the reason why you sometimes see spellings like Muenchen instead of München when Germans have some reason to avoid using the letter with the diacritic.

5.4   How to break up long words

Here's a hint before we get really started. When you've established how a word is supposed to be pronounced and it looks like a real mouthful to say, split the word into syllables. Then say the individual syllables and repeat them a few times, then start putting them back together. For example, let's say you've established that *ceumannan* is pronounced [kʲeːmǝNǝn] but can't get your tongue around it straight away.

Start with [kʲeː], then [mǝ] and then [Nǝn]. Say them separately a few times until you get used to the syllables. When you're confident with saying the syllables, latch them together: [kʲeːma] and then [Nǝn]. The put it all together and you have [kʲeːmǝNǝn].

kʲeː: | mǝ | Nǝn	dʲiǝ | xǝ | nǝ | xǝɣ	fuǝm | nǝ | xǝɣ
ceumannan	dìochuimhneachadh	fuaimneachadh
kɔ̃. | ǝ | Rǝ | xɪ | jǝn	ʃdʲɔːR | nǝ | vaɣ	çuː | Nʲɪ | çɪNʲ
comharrachaidhean	Steòrnabhagh	chiùinichinn
ʃɛ | ra | mɔ | nǝ | xǝɣ	sbia | rǝ | dǝ | rʲǝxg	krɯ | Nʲǝ | xɪ | jǝn
searmonachadh	speuradaireachd	cruinneachaidhean

Works wonders, even with the notorious word *dìochuimhneachadh*. Just split them up and before you know it, these long words will be rolling off your tongue with a flourish!

5.5   Using rhyming words

As we mentioned in the previous chapter, the Guide to Reading Gaelic is accurate but somewhat time consuming until you grow more familiar with the most common rules. One thing you can do to increase the speed at which you can pronounce written words is to use rhymes.

Generally speaking if you see two Gaelic words which share the same ending, you can safely assume that the rhyming parts are pronounced the same way and you only need to worry about the 'unknown bit' at the front.

The only thing you need to bear in mind is that these rhyming syllables need to be in a similar position (in terms of whether they're stressed or unstressed). Or in other terms, as a rule of thumb, this only works with groups of words which have the same number of syllables.

ball [bauL] ⇒	call [kauL]	mall [mauL]
	gall [gauL]	dall [dauL]
balla [baLə] ⇒	calla [kaLə]	malla [maLə]
	galla [gaLə]	dalla [daLə]
seas [ʃes] ⇒	meas [mes]	cleas [kles]
	deas [dʲes]	eas [es]
oideas [ɤdʲəs] ⇒	amaideas [amɪdʲəs]	creideas [krʲedʲəs]
	aindeas [aiNʲdʲəs]	càirdeas [ka:Rdʲəs]
tuilleadh [tuLʲəɣ] ⇒	tilleadh [tʲiLʲəɣ]	milleadh [miLʲəɣ]
	géilleadh [gʲe:Lʲəɣ]	filleadh [fiLʲəɣ]

So every time you work out the pronunciation of a new word, see whether you can find some rhyming pairs for it.

✎ Exercise 117.

Find rhyming words for the following examples. Try and find as many as possible and remember to make sure they have the same number of syllables to be 'eligible'.

ceann [kʲauN]	fead [fed]	cama [kamə]
caorach [kɯːrəx]	beinn [beiNʲ]	feum [feːm]
gaol [gɯːL]	siùil [ʃuːl]	mac [maxg]
tinn [tʲiːNʲ]	mothachadh [mɔ.əxəɣ]	fichead [fiçəd]
fileanta [filəNdə]	cluinn [kLɯiNʲ]	sgeul [sgʲiaL]

There are of course many other such pairs and I cannot list them all. But here's a trick you can use to make your own exercises. Go to the website of the Sabhal Mór Ostaig (the Gaelic college on Skye) and follow the link for the Stòr-dàta Briathrachais. This is the online version of the printed Stòr-dàta dictionary. Say for example you're looking for Gaelic words that end in **-igeadh**. Choose something like the following options:

and then hit *Lorg.* This will give you a list of all the words in the Stòr-dàta that end with the ending **-igeadh**. Try to think of words yourself though for this exercise before you use the Stòr-dàta.

5.6   Other spelling issues

The basics aside, there are a few more issues that we need to look at when it comes to reading Gaelic words.

5.6.1   The helping vowel

Gaelic has something called a 'helping vowel' (you may also come across the slightly more arcane terms 'svarabhakti' and 'epenthesis'[73] which both describe the same thing). It's basically an extra vowel which gets inserted in certain circumstances to break up a group of two consonants (called a consonant cluster). Occasionally you get it in Scottish English too when **r**, **n**, **l** and **m** sounds bump into each other.

film ⇒ [fɪlʸɪm]   arm ⇒ [a:rəm]   worm ⇒ [wʌrəm]   world ⇒ [wʌrəlʸd]

Now, what does this look like in Gaelic? Here are a few examples:

Alba ⇒ [aLabə]	searbh ⇒ [ʃɛrɛv]	garbh ⇒ [garav]
dearg ⇒ [dʲɛrɛg]	gorm ⇒ [gɔrɔm]	arm ⇒ [aram]

A bit like a laxative for consonant groups really. Helps break up the clutter. Now, if you have already come across this and got some Gaelic under your belt, get some paper and write down all the words with such a helping vowel you can think of. Then try and see if you can spot any pattern, what sort of sounds crop up all the time in words with a helping vowel?

---

[73] Svarabhakti is a word from Sanskrit, a language from ancient India. They were, believe it or not, the first people to study grammar and phonology as far back as the 8th century BC! That's why a number of modern linguistic terms are Sanskrit rather than Greek or Latin because in some cases the ancient Indians were the first to describe and name the effect. Svarabhakti literally just means 'vowel part'; epenthesis is Greek and means 'insertion'.

Now, as you know, in Gaelic this doesn't happen every time two consonants meet. You will probably have noticed that almost all of the examples that you wrote down involve a single l, n or r. Well spotted!

This doesn't happen near every l, n or r either but Gaelic is (fortunately) very clear about when this happens:

- the consonants must be in a stressed syllable

- the consonant cluster must consist of l n r + b bh ch g gh m mh or m + l r s ch

- it will not occur after a long vowel or diphthong, for example in words like *miorbhailt* [miərvəldʲ], *miolchu* [miəLxu], *iarmailt* [iərməldʲ], *neulmhor* [NʲiaLvər].

  The main exception to this rule is *Aonghas* where the **ao** happens to be short [ɯ] rather than the expected long [ɯ:]

There are a few exceptions but these four rules cover most words which have helping vowels.

So what vowel gets inserted? Well… the extra vowel is usually an exact copy of the first and carries as much stress as the first. That's it. Quite simple, isn't it? Mind that is in the common standard, dialects disagree about the exact nature of what the second vowel looks like and how long it is exactly. Some get quite elaborate. What is an [ɛ-ɛ] group in the Western Isles is pronounced [ɛ-a] on the mainland and so on. There are so many different variations it's a bit mind blowing frankly. As a learner the best way forward is to accept whatever people are saying but stick to the rule that when you say it, you repeat the first vowel. It will produce good Gaelic without frying your brain.

Unless you think this is just too simple, in which case you need to bear the following in mind:

- after **io** the second vowel is closer to [ə]: *iomradh* [iməɾəɣ]...

- after **ui** the second vowel is closer to [i]: *duilgheas* [duɫijəs]...

Here's a list now with examples for the 'simple' system:

l +	n +	r +	Examples	
b			Alba [aLabə]	sgolbach [sgɔLɔbəx]
	b		cainb [kɛnɛb]	-
		b	borb [bɔrɔb]	buirbe [buɾʲuubə]
bh			balbh [baLav]	dealbh [dʲaLav]
	bh		inbhe [inivə]	cunbhalach [kunuvəLəx]
		bh	marbh [marav]	doirbh [dɤrʲɤv]
ch			seilcheag [ʃeleçag]	colchag [kɔLɔxag]
	ch		crannchur [kraNaxər]	seanchaidh [ʃɛnɛxɪ]
		ch	dorcha [dɔrɔxə]	Fearchair [fɛrɛxarʲ]
g			tilg [tʲilig ʲ]	balg [baLag]
	g		dearg [dʲɛrɛg]	airgead [ɛrʲɛgʲəd]
gh			duilgheas [duɫuujəs]	eilgheadh [elejəɣ]
	gh		Aonghas [uunuu.əs]	coingheall [kɔnɔjəL]
		gh	Fearghas [fɛrɛɣəs]	dorgh [dɔrɔɣ]
m			alman [aLamən]	calma [kaLamə]
	m		ainm [ɛnɛm]	anmoch [anaməx]
		m	arm [aram]	gorm [gɔrɔm]
mh			falmhaich [faLavɪç]	talmhainn [taLavɪNʲ]
	mh		seanmhair [ʃɛnɛvarʲ]	gainmheach [gɛnɛvəx]
		mh	mormhair [mɔrɔvarʲ]	A' Mhormhaich [ə vɔrɔvɪç]

Certain combinations of **m** with another consonant have the same effect:

m +			Examples	
l			imleag [imilag]	iomlan [imiLan]
	r		imrich [imir'ıç]	iomradh [imirəɣ]
		s	eirmse [er'emʃə]	cuimseach [kɯmɯʃəx]
		ch	timcheall [t'imiçəL]	imcheist [imiçeʃd']

Gaelic likes this helping vowel a lot so sometimes it crops up in unexpected places. The following are best learned just like that:

calpa[74] [kaLabə]	eanraich[75] [ɛnɛrıç]	fairrge [faRag'ə]
forfhais [fɔrɔhıʃ]	Glaschu [gLasəxu]	onfhadh [ɔnɔhəɣ]
ulfhart [uLuhəRʃd]		

Incidentally, this helping vowel has linguists puzzled in a number of ways (to do with syllable structure and stress and all that) but I'm just going to point out that although the helping vowel on the face of it seems to add another syllable, it does not 'count' as such. That's why the helping vowel does not count as an unstressed vowel even though when you look at the phonetic symbols, it's a vowel 'not in the first syllable'. For example you could count [kaLamə] as being [ka | La | mə] and say that according to the rule of thumb that only the first syllable of a word is usually stressed, the [La] should be unstressed. I'm just going to tell you it isn't. From the Gaelic point of view, in words like [kaLamə] only the syllables after the helping vowel (in this case [mə]) are unstressed. Languages can be funny things.

---

[74] This used to be *colbtha*.

[75] And this is just bad modern spelling for *eanbhruich*.

This helping vowel has been around for quite a while. Irish, and to a lesser extent Manx, have it too. It's not as strong as in Gaelic though, usually just showing up as a schwa:

Irish		Manx	
ainm	[æ:nʲəmʲ]	ennym	[enəm]
orm	[orəm]	orrym	[ɑrəm]
Carghas	[karəɣəs]	Kargys	[karəgəs]
dorcha	[dorəxə]	dorraghey	[dɑrɑɣə]

You can even sometimes find it in the English spellings of place-names:

Achtemarach	Ach t-Seamraig [ax tʲɛmɛrɛgʲ]
Banavie	Banbhaidh [banavɪ]
Berridale	Bearghdal [bɛrɛdəL]
Blairhullichan	Blàr Thulchain [bLar huLuxɛNʲ]
Conaglen	Conghleann [kɔnɔɣləN]
Kirivick	Cirbhig [kʲirʲɪvɪgʲ]
Lerags	Na Leargan [nə Lʲɛrɛgən]
Tullochgorum	Tulach Gorm [tuLəx gɔrɔm]

And not just in Scotland:

Bellaheen	Beilchín
Darrigal	Deargail
Killimorebologue	Cill Íomair Bholga
Lough Namurrig	Loch na Mairge
Orrery	Orbhraí

5.6.2   How to make a vowel stretch

Vowel lengthening, a fun topic. It will help you understand why a word like *ceann* has a diphthong in it and comes out as [kʲauN] and why a word like *ceannach* doesn't, meaning it comes out as [kʲaNəx]. Technically it's called 'compensatory lengthening'. That means that instead of making one sound long (the **nn**), you make another sound long (the vowel). In other words, you compensate.

English does that too, in a roundabout sort of way. For example, the English word for *night* was pronounced [nixt] around the 14th century (and still is in Scots). The [x] then slowly disappeared. As it disappeared, it caused the [i] to get longer, so the word became [niːt]. In came the Great Vowel Shift and [niːt] became the familiar [naɪt].

Something very similar happened in Gaelic and that's important because just like English, the Gaelic writing system is a few centuries 'behind' - in the same way that the *night* spelling is behind the [nait] pronunciation.

Anyway. Gaelic used to have long consonants which left the same kind of trace and those long consonants are **ll**, **nn**, **rr** and **m**[76]. So when you come across a word which has **ll**, **nn**, **rr** and **m** you must pay attention to what happens to the vowel in a stressed syllable.

> In a stressed syllable vowels lengthen (or turn into a diphthong)
> before **ll**, **nn**, **rr** and **m**

And just in case you're wondering. This isn't optional in Gaelic and it's not a modern 'mispronunciation' either. It has been around for a long time. So long in fact, that it has crept into the anglicised spelling of Scottish place-names every now and then. Here are a few examples:

Anan**caun**	Àth nan Ceann [aː nəŋ kʲauN]
Camusnag**aull**	Camas nan Gall [kaməs nəŋ gauL]
H**aunn**	Hann [hauN]

---

[76] Which used to be spelt **mm** but that spelling went out of fashion centuries ago.

Now, here is a table which shows you what happens when certain vowel letters come before **ll**, **nn**, **rr** and **m** in a stressed syllable and with no vowel immediately following the **ll**, **nn**, **rr** or **m**:

before ll	before nn	before m	before rr
a			
call [kauL]	gann [gauN]	cam [kaum]	barr [ba:R]
(e)ai			
caill [kaiLʲ]	cainnt [kãĩNʲdʲ]	maim [maim]	feairrd [fja:Rdʲ]
ea			
seall [ʃauL]	ceann [kʲauN]	dream [draum]	cearr [kʲa:R]
ei			
	beinn [beiNʲ]	greim [grʲeim]	
i			
cill [kʲi:Lʲ]	binn [bi:Nʲ]	im [i:m]	
io			
	fionn [fju:N]		sgiorr [sgʲu:R]
iu			
		rium [rʲu:m][77]	tiurr [tʲu:R]
o			
toll [tɔuL]	fonn [fɔuN]	tom [tɔum]	torr [tɔ:R]
oi			
goill [gɣiLʲ]	roinn [RɣiNʲ]	stoim [sdɣim]	
u			
a-null [əˈNu:L]	grunn [gru:N]	cum [ku:m]	sgurr [sgu:R]
ui			
tuill [tɯiLʲ]	cluinn [kLɯiNʲ]	druim [drɯim]	

---

[77] [rʲu:m] is the stressed form, the unstressed form is [rʲəm]

This also applies when the **ll**, **nn**, **rr** and **m** is followed by a consonant:

calltainn [kauLdɪNʲ]	beanntan [bjãũNdən]
ciurrte [kʲuːRdʲə]	Caimbeul [kãĩmbəL]

However if **ll**, **nn**, **rr** and **m** are followed by a vowel, we never get the long vowel or diphtong:

seall [ʃauL]	⇒	sealladh [ʃaLəɣ]
cam [kaum]	⇒	caman [kaman]
caill [kaiLʲ]	⇒	caillidh [kaLʲɪ]
beinn [beiNʲ]	⇒	beinne [beNʲə]
cill [kʲiːLʲ]	⇒	cille [kʲiLʲə]
tom [tɔum]	⇒	toman [toman]
cluinn [kLɯiNʲ]	⇒	cluinnidh [kLɯNʲɪ]

So we need to expand the rule by saying that:

> In a stressed syllable vowels lengthen (or diphthongise)
>
> before **ll**, **nn**, **rr** and **m**
>
> unless the **ll**, **nn**, **rr** and **m** is followed by a vowel

It's like Superman and Kryptonite. All these 'strong' consonants which do weird things to the vowel in front of them lose all their powers in the vicinity of a Kryptonite vowel directly behind them.

If you happen to find this at odds with the rules for lengthening in the Gaelic Orthographic Conventions[78] that's fine. Like a number of other things, they basically got this one wrong. If you took their Section 4.i seriously, a word like *cailleach* would end up with a long vowel to become [kaːLʲəx]. Which unfortunately it doesn't, not in any Gaelic dialect.

---

[78] A first attempt at standardising and explaining the spelling rules of Gaelic, first by the Scottish Examination Board and then the Scottish Qualifications Authority (SQA).

Speaking of dialects, I better mention that in some dialects (in particular Lewis) a long [iː] that was lengthened by a **ll**, **nn**, **rr** or **m** turns into [ɤi] or [ei] and that you often hear [ɛu] instead of [au]:

tinn [tʲiːNʲ]	⇒ [tʲɤiNʲ]
im [iːm]	⇒ [ɤim]
ceann [kʲauN]	⇒ [kʲɛuN]
beanntan [bjãũNdən]	⇒ [bɛ̃ũNdən]

Note that there are two two-letter words, *im* and *am*, which even in the traditional spelling systems often show up as *ìm* and *àm*. Presumably because they're so short and some people might argue there's an overlap between the definite article *am* [əm] and *am* [aum] 'time' otherwise.   Which isn't really a problem because they would never occupy the same syntactic spot in a sentence but hey. The important thing is that if you add endings that place a vowel right after the **m**, you must never write the grave as, following the rules above, they shorten, so you get: *ìm/im* [iːm]   ⇒ *ime* [imə], *am/àm* [aum] ⇒ *ama* [amə], *amannan* [aməNən] etc.

You may think that all this stuff about vowels which lengthen and shorten sounds a bit mad. Well, it isn't really. If you think about it for a moment, English actually has something similar going on, only the other way round. Anyone remember that 1960s BBC programme called Look and Read (with that ghost called Wordy who can only be called weird) which had this thing about the 'magic e' in English? You may be too young to remember! Anyway, there are a lot of words in English which start out with a short vowel but if you add this Magic e, the vowel changes: *mat* ⇒ *mate*, *sit* ⇒ *site*, *pet* ⇒ *Pete*, *cop* ⇒ *cope*... and so on. I know it's not 100% the same thing but it's very close.

Back to Gaelic.   There a few points which need to be mentioned because they could be confusing. And an exception: *ceannard*. This is [kʲauNəRd], as it is derived from *ceannphort,* not *ceann* plus *àrd.*

- Words with inherent diphthongs
  There are certain letter combinations which always represent a diphthong or long vowel, no matter what other sounds are nearby. These are **ia** [iə], **ua** [uə] and **eu** [e:]/[ia] and all two-vowel combinations where one has an accent mark: **ìo** [iə] and **èa** [iə]. They do not undergo the same lengthening/shortening process, so the pronunciation always stays the same irrespective of what comes after it:

ceum [kʲe:m]	⇒ ceumannan [kʲe:məNən]
ciall [kʲiəL]	⇒ ciallachadh [kʲiəLəxəɣ],
fìon [fiən]	⇒ fiona [fiənə]
buan [buən]	⇒ buannachd [buəNəxg]
iarr [iəR]	⇒ iarraidh [iəRɪ]

- Words with inherently long vowels
  That means that there are certain words which have long vowels or double vowels near **ll**, **nn**, **rr** and **m** which are always long/double, even if there is a vowel coming after. Here are some examples:

dràma [dra:ma]	⇒ dràmadaiche [dra:madɪçə]
féill [fe:Lʲ]	⇒ féille [fe:Lʲə]
géill [gʲe:Lʲ]	⇒ géilleadh [gʲe:Lʲəɣ]
dìnnear [dʲi:Nʲər]	dìlleachdan [dʲi:Lʲəxgan]
mìnich [mi:nɪç]	trìlleachan [tri:Lʲəxan]

- Other groups causing lengthening
  Vowels before **rd**, **rl** and **rn** are also affected in a similar way but generally only by lengthening (without breaking into diphthongs). Any **r** or **n** will strenghthen to [R] and/or [N⁽ʲ⁾]:

bòrd [bɔ:Rd]	còrd [kɔ:Rd]
càrn [ka:RN]	bùrn [bu:RN]

They're also not affected by shortening because they're always a 'consonant group' (even when a vowel follows):

bòrd [bɔːRd]	còrdadh [kɔːRdəɣ]
càrnadh [kaːRNəɣ]	bùrn [buːRN]
Càrlabhagh [kaːRLəvaɣ]	mèirleach [mɛːRləx]

And yes, that's the reason why in older texts you find spellings like *carn* and *ard,* as the accents over these vowels technically are surplus to requirements.

- Unstressed Syllables
  If the **ll**, **nn**, **rr** or **m** is in an unstressed syllable, nothing 'odd' ever happens as unstressed vowels in Gaelic are always short:

mholainn [vɔLɪNʲ]	aodann [ɯːdəN]
Dòmhnall [dõː.əL]	aithghearr [açəR]
tioram [tʲirəm]	balgam [baLagəm]

The definite articles *am* and *nam* are also always unstressed and never lengthen:

am bòrd [əm bɔːRd]	am bàta [əm baːhdə]
cù nam balach [kuː nəm baLəx]	taigh nam bàrd [tɤj nəm baːRd]

- Helping Vowel
  If there is a conflict between the rules for vowel lengthening and the rules for helping vowel (see 5.6.1), insertion of the helping vowel takes precedence. For example, one might be tempted to lengthen the **i** in *imrich* (because you have an **m** not followed by a vowel). But because the rule for the helping vowel also applies here, it takes precedence and we get *imrich* [imirʲɪç]. So the **m** is now followed by a vowel, the lengthening rule can no longer apply.

iomradh [imirəɣ]	iomrall [imirəL]
imleag [imilag]	iomlan [imiLan]

✎ Exercise 118.

Take a sheet of paper and mark out two columns like this:

Long Vowel/Diphthong	Short Vowel

Then, using the rules you just studied, sort the words below into either column depending on whether the vowel letter represents a long vowel/diphthong or a short vowel in pronunciation.   Also write down (using the phonetic symbols in square brackets) which vowel you are expecting. When you're finished, check your table against the key to the exercises. I've done you an example of what it should look like:

Long Vowel/Diphthong	Short Vowel
ball [au]	balla [a]
ballrachd [au]	

Words: call, calltainn, calla, calltach, bann, banna, bannta, lom, loma, lomnochd, lomadh, gleann, gleanntan, gleanna, gleannan, gleanntaibh, gleannach, gleanntail, caillte, caill, caillteach, chailleadh, sgoinn, sgoinneil, sgoinne, cum, cumail, cumadh, cumadail, cumte, im, ime, imeach, cunntadh, cunntas, polltach, pollan, pollag, poll, pollach, galla, gall, galltachd, gallta, tinneas, tinn, tinnead, cinn, cinnte, cinntinn, cinneadh, cinneas, bearr, bearrta, bearradh, bearradair, bearrtach, dearrs, dearrsadh, dearrsach, am, ama, amannan, cluinntinn, chluinneadh, cluinn, cluinntear, chluinninn, lunnach, lunn, lunna, fionnar, fionn, fionnlach, fionnadh, foille, foill, foillear, till, tilleadh, thillinn, tilltinn, geall, gealltainn, gealladh, gheall, geallta, gealltanas, cainnt, cainnte, cainntean, cainnteachd, sparr, sparrta, sparradh, sparran, greimeadh, greimich, greimir, greim, seinn, sheinn, seinne, seinneadair, torradh, torran, torranach, torr, pronntach, pronnadh, pronn, pronnadair, pronntail, pronnas

5.6.3   Front and back vowels

This is another extremely important concept in Gaelic. For one thing, this is where you get the brownie points which I promised you in section 1.4. I mentioned this already when we were looking at the vowel sounds.

But let's go over it again. Start by saying [i:]. Now say [ɔ:]. Then jump between the two and observe what your tongue is doing.

It's sliding back and forth (ok, your lips are moving too but that's not the crucial point here). I know we're not talking about vast distances but simply the relative position. So the [i:] sound is made towards the front of your mouth and the [ɔ:] sound towards the back of your mouth. In Gaelic [i(:)], [e(:)] and [ɛ(:)] are made at the front of the mouth and are called Front Vowels. The [ɔ(:)], [o(:)], [ɤ(:)], [u(:)] and [ɯ(:)] vowels are made further back and therefore are called the Back Vowels.

Try a few more combinations and pay attention to what your tongue is doing (make all the vowels long for better effect):

i: ⇒ ɔ:	e: ⇒ ɔ:	e: ⇒ a:	ɛ: ⇒ u:
ɛ: ⇒ ɯ:	i: ⇒ a:	e: ⇒ ɯ:	e: ⇒ ɤ:

These were all going from the front of your mouth to the back of your mouth. Now try it the other way round:

ɔ: ⇒ i:	ɔ: ⇒ e:	a: ⇒ e:	u: ⇒ ɛ:
ɯ: ⇒ ɛ:	a: ⇒ i:	ɯ: ⇒ e:	ɤ: ⇒ e:

You will see in a moment why knowing this is important.

Front of Mouth   Back of Mouth

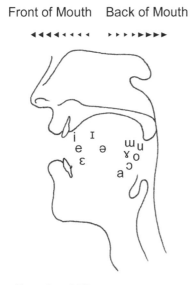

Now, we can safely ignore [ɪ] and [ə] for the purposes of this chapter. The [a] sounds need an explanation though. Irrespective of their narrow phonetic definition, long [aː] in Gaelic behaves as if it was a back vowel. Short [a] fluctuates between the two categories and is hard to predict with any accuracy.

✎ Exercise 119.

Decide whether the vowel in the following syllables is front or back. When looking at diphthongs, you have to decide whether both vowels in it are front or back or whether the first vowel is front followed by a back (for example [ia]) or back followed by front (for example [ai]).

		All Front	All Back	Front ⇒ Back	Back ⇒ Front
01	kuːL				
02	ʃɛː				
03	mil				
04	ʃia				
05	guh				
06	RɣiNʲ				
07	ʃiː				
08	aum				
09	Lɔh				
10	kʲed				

Why is this important at all? Well, there are some consonants in Gaelic which can show up with or without a [j] sound after them: [b] ~ [bj], [p] ~ [pj], [f] ~ [fj], [v] ~ [vj], [m] ~ [mj] and [h] ~ [hj]. Let's look at some examples:

bean [bɛn]	peant [pɛnd]	a Shìne [ə hiːnə]
⇕	⇕	⇕
beann [bjauN]	peann [pjauN]	a Sheòrais [ə hjɔːrɪʃ]
feur [fiar]	meig [megʲ]	glé bhinn [gleː viːNʲ]
⇕	⇕	⇕
feòir [fjɔːrʲ]	miùg [mjuːg]	glé bheò [gleː vjɔː]

It can't have anything to do with broad and slender as they are all slender according to the spelling, so what is happening?

What happens is that Gaelic used to have slender [pʲ] [bʲ] [fʲ] [vʲ] [mʲ] but lost them at some point in its history. Before front vowels no trace of that slenderness remains but in front of a back vowel, a trace of this slenderness has hung around - the [j]. That's all.

You must consider both the spelling and the sounds to get this right. The first step is to check if the [b] [p] [m] [f] [v] or [h] are marked as slender by the SPELLING. If yes, then you must consider the PRONUNCIATION of the following vowel sound.
If that is a back vowel, you will get the [j].

✎ Exercise 120.

All the words in this exercise begin with a consonant that is marked as slender by the spelling. By looking at the vowel immediately following the first consonant, decide whether you will get the [j] sound or not.

01 beanntan	[b_ãũNdən]	11 beagan	[b_egan]
02 fear	[f_ɛr]	12 bioran	[b_iran]
03 fiù	[f_uː]	13 thig	[h_igʲ]
04 bealach	[b_aLəx]	14 meall	[m_auL]
05 mearachd	[m_ɛrəxg]	15 fiadh	[f_iaɣ]
06 mèinn	[m_ɛːNʲ]	16 bìd	[b_iːdʲ]
07 a shiùcar	[ə h_uːxgər]	17 feòrag	[f_ɔːrag]
08 mo bheò	[mə v_ɔ]	18 Miùghalaigh	[m_uː.əLaj]
09 beantainn	[b_ɛndɪNʲ]	19 glé theann	[gleː h_auN]
10 feasgar	[f_esgər]	20 peacadh	[p_ɛxgəɣ]

The other reason why this is important is because it can help you anticipate another 'unexpected' change. In Gaelic the slender **n** (see 2.4.3) is sometimes pronounced [n] and sometimes [Nʲ] in an apparently unpredictable way.

Dialects treat this slightly differently but the general guideline is that [n] becomes [Nʲ] after a back vowel (including [aː] but not usually [a]).

[n]	[Nʲ]
bainis [banɪʃ]	bàine [baːNʲə]
gainmheach [gɛnɛvəx]	sròine [sdrɔːNʲə]
sine [ʃinə]	ùine [uːNʲə]

Note that some speakers extend this process to some of the long front vowels: *gréine* [grʲeːNʲə], *sineadh* [ʃiːNʲəɣ] but it's not necessary for you to do this.

✎ Exercise 121.

Based on the vowel in front of the single slender n in the following examples, decide if the n will be [n] or change to [Nʲ].

01 teine	[tʲe__ə]	11 gloine	[gLɤ__ə]
02 gin	[gʲi__]	12 raineach	[Ra__əx]
03 coin	[kɔ__]	13 mìnich	[mi:__ɪç]
04 céin	[kʲe:__]	14 cainb	[kɛ__ɛb]
05 cuin	[ku__]	15 mòine	[mɔ:__ə]
06 càineadh	[ka:__əɣ]	16 a bhuineas	[ə vu__əs]
07 DihAoine	[dʲɪ'hɯ:__ə]	17 duine	[dɯ__ə]
08 ainm	[ɛ__ɛm]	18 ciùineas	[kʲu:__əs]
09 fhéin	[he:__]	19 inis	[i__ɪʃ]
10 tuineach	[tɯ__əx]	20 caoineadh	[kɯ:__əɣ]

5.6.4   Intrusive sounds

That means, sounds which you must say but don't show up in the spelling as such. It's a bit like the extra **r** you sometimes get in English: *drawing ~ drawring, law and order ~ lawr and order* and so on. Or, even more bizarre, like the extra t that words like *against, amongst* and *amidst* picked up a few centuries back (these come from Middle English *aʒeins, amonges* and *amiddes*).

The helping vowel aside (see 5.6.1) there are two other situations in which Gaelic adds extra sounds. This affects two clusters: **rt** and **sr**.

When you get a Gaelic word which contains an **rt** group, Gaelic inserts a [ʃ] sound in between, so you get [Rʃd] and [Rʃdʲ]:

ceart [kʲaRʃd]	beartach [bjaRʃdəx]	mart [maRʃd]
DiMàirt [dʲɪ'ma:Rʃdʲ]	pàirt [pa:Rʃdʲ]	abairt [abəRʃdʲ]

You may also hear people inserting this [ʃ] in **rd** groups:

àrd [a:Rʃd]	DiarDaoin [dʲəRʃ'dɯ:Nʲ]	bòrd [bɔ:Rʃd]

In those dialects, this can also extend to combinations of a preposition plus a noun, for example *air do* [əRʃˈdə] or *air dòigh* [əRʃˈdɔːj].

But inserting [ʃ] in these groups is by no means universal so you don't have to do it unless you're aiming for a specific dialect that does that. However you decide to pronounce **rd**, be consistent about it!

When you get an **sr** group on the other hand, Gaelic inserts a [d], so you get [sdr]. This is pronounced in the same way as words which have **str**:

sròn [sdrɔːn]	srath [sdrah]	srann [sdrauN]
stràc [sdraːxg]	strìochd [sdriəxg]	strì [sdriː]

They behave differently though in spite of being pronounced the same way but more on that on page 358.

In Gaelic these extra sounds are never frowned upon like the extra **r** in *drawring*, they're normal, even necessary. Think of place-names like Strathclyde *(Srath Chluaidh)*, Stroanpatrick *(Sròn Phàdraig)* or Aultiphurst *(Allt a' Phuirt)*. These must have been around for quite a while to have ended up on maps.

5.6.5   Collapsing syllables

Part of this chapter takes us into the realms of grammar once more but because it involves sound changes, I have included it.

Some Gaelic words do funny things when you add endings, they can lose a syllable: *fosgail* ⇒ *fosgladh, cathair* ⇒ *cathrach* and so on.

This is another ancient thing in Gaelic. The technical term for it is syncope (Greek for 'cutting off'). It happens in English too but not quite with the same historical doggedness as in Gaelic. Think of lovely places like Worcestershire and Bournemouth where the spelling suggests more syllables than there actually are.

Old Irish had this wonderful rule that in words of more than two syllables, you delete ever second vowel to keep the word nice and short (Old Irish had a lot of potentially very long words). Take the world *samhail* for example. This was ᚱᴀmɩʟ in Old Irish. Adding the prefix co should have resulted in *cossᴀmɩʟ, but it didn't. Instead, Old Irish lost the second syllable by losing the ᴀ and you got coᚱmɩʟ, which is the root for the modern form *cosmhail*. Adding the negative prefix éc should have given us *éccossᴀmɩʟ you might think but again, what we got was écᚱᴀmɩʟ, the root of the word *eugsamhail*. And bits of this very ancient rule have survived into modern Gaelic and Irish.

So how does it work in modern Gaelic? Well, this loss of syllables doesn't affect all words today. It mainly affects verbs that have more than one syllable and end in a so-called liquid: **-l, -ll, -n, -nn, -ng, -r, -rr**.

There aren't that many of these but here are some examples:

Present	Future
ba**g**air [bagɪrʲ]	⇒ ba**g**raidh [bagrɪ]
brui**dh**inn [bri.ɪNʲ]	⇒ brui**dh**nidh [bri:nɪ]
fo**gh**ain [fo:.ɪNʲ]	⇒ fo**gh**naidh [fo:nɪ]
fo**sg**ail [fɔsgal]	⇒ fo**sg**laidh [fɔsgLɪ]
frea**g**air [frʲegɪrʲ]	⇒ frea**g**raidh [frʲegrɪ]
ta**ch**air [taxɪrʲ]	⇒ ta**ch**raidh [taxrɪ]
ta**g**air [tagɪrʲ]	⇒ ta**g**raidh [tagrɪ]
ta**rr**aing [taRɪŋʲgʲ]	⇒ tà**i**r**ng**idh [ta:RNʲɪ]

This also affects the other tenses and moods such as the future relative, the conditional or the imperative of these verbs, for example:

Future Relative	Conditional	Imperative
a bha**g**ras [ə vagrəs]	bha**g**radh [vagrəɣ]	ba**g**ram! [bagrəm]
a dh'fo**ghn**as [ə ɣo:nəs]	dh'fho**ghn**adh [ɣo:nəɣ]	fo**ghn**am! [fo:nəm]
a dh'fho**sg**las [ə ɣɔsgLəs]	dh'fho**sg**ladh [ɣɔsgLəɣ]	fo**sg**lam! [fɔsgLəm]
a fhrea**g**ras [ə rʲegrəs]	fhrea**g**radh [rʲegrəɣ]	frea**g**ram! [frʲegrəm]
a tha**chr**as [ə haxrəs]	tha**chr**adh [haxrəɣ]	ta**chr**am! [tachrəm]

The other group of words which does this are feminine nouns that end in -(a)ir. To form the genitive, they lose a syllable and add the ending -(e)ach. The same applies to the plural, which is always in -(a)ichean. Here are some common examples:

Nominative	Genitive	Plural
cathair [kahɪrʲ]	⇒ cathrach [karəx]	⇒ cathraichean [karɪçən]
iuchair [juxɪrʲ]	⇒ iuchrach [juxrəx]	⇒ iuchraichean [juxrɪçən]
litir [Lʲihdʲɪrʲ]	⇒ litreach [Lʲihdrəx]	⇒ litrichean [Lʲihdrɪçən]
nathair [Nahɪrʲ]	⇒ nathrach [Narəx]	⇒ nathrichean [Narɪçən]
obair [obɪrʲ]	⇒ obrach [obrəx]	⇒ obraichean [obrɪçən]
tobair [tobɪrʲ]	⇒ tobrach [tobrəx]	⇒ tobraichean [tobrɪçən]

By the way, don't confuse these words with (grammatically) masculine words like *clach/air, iasg/air, uair/eadair* or *cluich/eadair*. These are completely different as they are made up of a base word like *clach* 'stone' plus the ending -air (which means someone or something that does something, like -er in English kicker, runner, blower…). Words like *cathair* or *iuchair* on the other hand you can't chop apart into a meaning bit and an ending, which is a good way of identifying them.

Now before you get your 'yes but' in before me, there are indeed words which don't have the collapsing syllables anymore even though they would 'qualify'. Words like *màthair* (genitive *màthar* but plural *màthraichean*) or *piuthar* (genitive *peathar* but plural *peathraichean*). It would seem that Gaelic speakers are developing a bit of a dislike for this change and are slowly moving away from these forms. *Màthair* for example used to have *màthrach* as a genitive. This doesn't mean you can just ignore these forms but it can help you understand why there are some words which don't do this anymore.

✎ Exercise 122.

Decide if the following words have the agentive ending **-air** or **-adair** (marking someone or something doing something) or whether it's a word that cannot be split up in a sensible way.

	Ending marking an agent	Cannot be split
01 fuineadair		
02 seanmhair		
03 abair		
04 boghadair		
05 crùnair		
06 acair		
07 fuaradair		
08 reiceadair		
09 onair		
10 socair		
11 stiùireadair		
12 dìobair		
13 mair		
14 nigheadair		
15 frasair		

5.6.6   Consonant groups

That's when you have a group of two or more consonants, for example **cr**, **br**, **str**... They're also called clusters for the same reason. We've already looked at **sr** but I've included it here too so you get the complete picture. Most of them behave regularly, meaning they do exactly what you expect them to do but some do (apparently) odd things, so here's a list of the unexpected ones:

- **-chd**

   The **d** in this combination has changed into [g] to become more similar to the [x] in a process called 'assimilation'. All living languages do assimilation - it means that two sounds that are next to each other will sometimes affect the pronunciation of one or both. For example, in English it is very hard to hear the difference between *mountain goats* and *mounting goats* because the **-n** in mountain anticipates the **g-** in *goats.* It does so by becoming more like the **g-** and in the process turns into **-ng**. Bingo.

   But back to Gaelic. Only the broad form is common:

achd [axg]	beachd [bɛxg]	cleachd [klɛxg]
eughachd [eːvəxg]	barrachd [baRəxg]	cléireachd [kleːrʲəxg]

   While we're on the topic, note that nouns ending in **-chd** that only have one syllable are masculine, those with more than one syllable are feminine (grammatically speaking).

- **cn-**

   In words that begin with **cn**, the **n** has turned into a [r] and made the nearest vowel nasal. Note that the **c** here is always broad [k], even if the nearest vowel is slender; the **r** follows the normal broad and slender rules:

Broad		Slender	
cnoc [krɔ̃xg]	chnoc [xrɔ̃xg]	cnead [krʲẽd]	chnead [xrʲẽd]
cnag [krã̃g]	chnag [xrãg]	cneas [krʲẽs]	chneas [xrʲẽs]

- **dr-**

  The **d** and **dh** are always broad [d] and [ɣ], the **r** follows the normal broad and slender rules:

Broad		Slender	
dragh [drɣɣ]	dhragh [ɣrɣɣ]	dris [**drɪʃ**]	dhris [ɣrʲɪʃ]
drama [dramə]	dhrama [ɣramə]	dreach [**drɛx**]	dhreach [ɣrʲɛx]

- **gn-**

  At the beginning of a word, **gn** behaves similar to **cn-**, so the **n** turns into [r] and nasalises the nearest vowel. Again, the **g-** and **gh-** in this group are always broad:

Broad		Slender	
gnog [**grõg**]	ghnog [ɣrõg]	gnè [**grʲẽ:**]	ghnè [ɣrʲẽ:]
gnàth [**grã:**]	ghnàth [ɣrã:]	gnìomh [**grʲĩ͂ɵv**]	ghnìomh [ɣrʲĩ͂ɵv]

  Elsewhere **-gn(-)** is [gn] or [gʲn]:

Broad		Slender	
cagnadh	[kagnəɣ]	uaigneach	[uəgʲnəx]
deugnaich	[dʲiagnɪç]	cóignear	[ko:gʲnər]

- **-lc-** and **-rc-**

  This is an entertaining cluster. Due to its environment (I could go into details but they wouldn't really help you), **l** and **r** in this group are devoiced. In short, what you have to do is put your tongue in the normal position for **l** or **r** (following the normal rules on how to pronounce them) and then hiss air past your tongue. That's it.

Broad		Slender	
olc [ɔl̥g]	cearc [kʲɛr̥g]	cuilc [kul̥gʲ]	uircean [ur̥gʲan]
falcag [fal̥gag]	dearc [dʲɛr̥g]	sgailc [sgal̥gʲ]	àirc [a:r̥gʲ]

  Some dialects go a little overboard and actually insert a [x] or [ç] between these, for example [kʲɛr̥xg] or [kul̥çgʲ] but you don't have to go quite that far.

- **mn-**

  Again, the **n** turns into [r] and nasalises then nearest vowel. This combination is very rare and mostly occurs in forms of *bean:*

| mnà | [mrã:] | mhnà | [vrã:] |
| mnathan | [mrã.ən] | mhnathan | [vrã.ən] |

- **-nd-**

  In this group, the **n** changes to [N] or [Nʲ] depending on broad/slender, resulting in [Nd] or [Nʲdʲ]:

Broad		Slender	
buntainn	[buNdɪNʲ]	mòinteach	[mɔ:Nʲdʲəx]
buntàta	[bəN'da:hdə]	slàinte	[sLã:Nʲdʲə]
cionta	[kʲiNdə]	susbaint	[susbɪNʲdʲ]

- **sg-** (and **sc-**)

  The **s** is always broad, the **g** follows the normal broad and slender rules and the group cannot be lenited. Note that in very rare cases, some people still use the older **sc-** spelling. Fortunately that does not affect the pronunciation or behaviour.

Broad		Slender	
sgath [sgah]	sgurr [sgu:R]	sgìth [sgʲi:]	sgian [sgʲian]
sgoil [sgɔl]	Scarp [sgarb]	sgeul [sgʲiaL]	sgealb [sgʲaLab]

- **sl-** & **sn-**

  The **l** and **n** in these combinations at the beginning of a word always are strong [L], [Lʲ], [N] or [Nʲ] when not lenited. When lenited, you get weak [n] and [l]. In cases of broad **l** the strong [L] remains as Gaelic only has one broad **l** left (see section 5.6.8):

Broad		Slender	
sluig [sLɯgʲ]	shluig [Lɯgʲ]	slìob [ʃLʲiəb]	shlìob [liəb]
slàn [sLa:n]	shlàn [La:n]	slighe [ʃLʲi.ə]	shlighe [li.ə]
snàmh [sNa:v]	shnàmh [na:v]	snìomh [ʃNʲiəv]	shnìomh [niəv]
snog [sNog]	shnog [nog]	sneachd [ʃNʲɛxg]	shneachd [nɛxg]

In **sn**, when the **s** is lenited away by **an t-**, the pronunciation behaves as if it was a **tn** group:

Broad		Slender	
san t-snagan	[səN **trã**gan]	san t-sneachd	[səN **trẽ**xg]
san t-snuadh	[səN **trũə**ɣ]	san t-snèip	[səN **trẽ**:hb]

- **sp-**
  The **p** in this group behaves like a **b**; the **s** is always broad and the group cannot be lenited:

Broad		Slender	
spòrs [sbɔ:rs]	spàg [sba:g]	spéis [sbe:ʃ]	spiris [sbirʲɪʃ]

- **sr-** and **str-**
  Both these groups are pronounced the same way.

Broad		Slender	
sruth [sdruh]	shruth [ruh]	sreath [sdrɛh]	shreath [rɛh]
sròn [sdrɔ:n]	shròn [rɔ:n]	srian [sdrian]	shrian [rian]
stràc [sdra:xg]	-	strì [sdri:]	-
strùb [sdru:b]	-	striochd [sdriəxg]	-

Unfortunately **sr** and **str** behave differently when it comes to lenition. Words which are spelled **str** can't be lenited and words with **sr** can be lenited.   The problem is that untidy spelling habits have introduced the **str** spelling to a number of words which shouldn't have it and vice versa. This makes it really difficult for the learner to figure out which ones to lenite.   To help you along here's a list of the most common, unlenitable ones:

| stràbh | stràc | strì | striochd |
| strìopach | stròc | strùb | structar |

So even after a word that causes lenition, these would remain the same:

dà stràbh	dà stràc	dà strì	dà strìochd
dà strìopach	dà stròc	dà strùb	dà structar

So what to do with the other words which have **sr/str** if even dictionaries aren't always reliable references? Well, the vast majority of words which have unlenitable str are loanwords from Scots, Norse or English (*stràbh* ⇐ *straw, stràc* ⇐ *strake, strì* ⇐ *strìð, structar* ⇐ *structure, strìopach* ⇐ *strupe…*) so as a rule of thumb, if it looks like it's a word that has been borrowed from English or Scots, then it most likely has **str**, if it looks like something that's a native Gaelic word then it's most likely **sr**. Failing that, google the word in a leniting environment, for example "do strìochd" and "do shrìochd" (in quotation marks like that) and see which one gets more reliable-looking results.

- **st**
  After **s**, you get either [d] or [dʲ] and the group cannot be lenited. It occurs in the middle or at the end of words too:

Broad		Slender	
stuth [sduh]	stàth [sda:]	stiall [ʃdʲiaL]	stéidh [ʃdʲe:]
asta [asdə]	pòsta [pɔ:sdə]	aiste [aʃdʲə]	ceist [kʲeʃdʲ]

The older **sd** spelling behaves exactly the same way and has the same pronunciation: *òsta* [ɔ:sdə] vs *òsda* [ɔ:sdə].

- **tn-**
  This is a very rare combination on its own, occurring only in the word *tnùth* and derived forms. Again, the **n** turns into [r] and turns the nearest vowel nasal:

tnùth [**trũ:**]	tnùthail [**trũ:.al**]	tnùthmhor [**trũ:vər**]

Remember though that the **t-sn** group behaves in the same way, as discussed above under **sn**.

Elsewhere **-tn(-)** is [(h)dn] or [(h)dⁱn]:

Broad		Slender	
Greatna	[grʲɛhdnə]	taitneach	[tahdʲnəx]

This is a very rare combination which occurs only in a handful of words and in quite a few cases, the **t** is usually dropped (sometimes even in spelling). For example, *airtneal* is usually [aRNʲəL] and *claistneachd* is commonly *claisneachd* [kLaʃNʲəxg].

- **tr-**

    This group, irrespective of whether it is broad or slender is always [tr]. Unlike **sl**, **sn** and **sr** above (where the **sh** is "dropped"), when **tr** is lenited, the **t** becomes [h]:

Broad		Slender	
trom [**tr**ɔum]	throm [**hr**ɔum]	trì [**tr**i:]	thrì [**hr**ⁱi:]
tràth [**tr**a:]	thràth [**hr**a:]	tric [**tr**içgʲ]	thric [**hr**ⁱiçgʲ]

Note that many dialects transpose the lenited form and have [rhɔum], [rʲhiçg], [rha:] etc. If you listen carefully to native speakers, you may also notice a slightly "hissed" quality to the [r]. That is the result of something called de-voicing, so in those cases you get [r̥h] or [hr̥] (very similar to the Welsh **rh**).

If you want to copy that, start practising with words like *try* or *pry,* because in those positions English also has a devoiced [r̥]. Make sure you don't get vibration in your throat for the [hr̥] and you got it. This trick only works for people who roll their **r** sounds!

So, there you go, that's the complex consonant clusters of Gaelic explained. I should mention a couple of general points perhaps. You have probably noticed that in certain groups, Gaelic ignores the broad/slender distinction. That is the general pattern and the most straightforward pattern for you to follow as a learner. Just be aware that it's not universal - no surprises there. For example, in some areas slender **sg** is [ʃgʲ] and slender **tr** is [trʲ] but again, unless you live in a Gaelic-speaking area and are aiming for a particular local dialect, you can probably do without making life more difficult.

And as I mentioned before, these aren't bad pronunciations, they're the established, proper pronunciations of such consonant groups. Pull out your map of Scotland again and look for Colintraive, Kincraigie and Ceannacroc - in Gaelic these are *Caol an **t-Sn**àimh, Cionn **Chn**agaidh* and *Ceann nan **Cn**oc*.

5.6.7 *Ceud* or *Ciad?*

You either already have or soon will come across the **eu/ia** conundrum. Some **eu** words are pronounced with [e:] and some [ia].

To keep it short, this is down to a historic sound change where long [e:] sounds got 'broken' into [ia] sounds. It's a bit like Old English *hús* [hu:s] becoming *house* [haʊs].

Unfortunately not all [e:] sounds have changed to [ia] in modern Gaelic so we need to learn how to disentangle the spelling.

When you come across **eu** in Gaelic the rules of thumb are as follows:

- Normally **eu** is pronounced [ia]:

feur [fiar]	beul [biaL]	eun [ian]
leus [Lʲias]	seud [ʃiad]	meud [miad]

- If **eu** is followed by **m**, it is generally pronounced [e:]:

ceum [kʲe:m]	beum [be:m]	Seumas [ʃe:məs]
feum [fe:m]	geum [gʲe:m]	leum [Lʲe:m]

Now there are certain words (such as *ceus* [kʲe:s], *beus* [be:s], *treun* [tre:n]…) which seem to upset these rules. But on closer inspection most of these words are part of a loose group of 'high register' words. Meaning that they are words which don't appear often in everyday conversation and are restricted to fairly formal Gaelic. Posh words you might say. This presumably contributes to their more conservative pronunciation.

Languages are good at this kind of thing, preserving archaic bits of language if the setting is right. Think of English expressions that have been frozen in time: *our Father who art in heaven* (*who art* isn't really common anymore) or *la Reyne le veult* (a Norman French expression still used by the Westminster Parliament).

Now, not all dialects agree exactly on which **eu** gets broken into [ia] and which isn't. A few dialects break them all (even words like *Seumas* are pronounced [ʃiaməs]), some break most, some break fewer. Fortunately that means that with the above rules, your Gaelic is going to be acceptable to most native speakers. This is quite a famous feature in Gaelic called the 'breaking of long é', so on this occasion I'm giving you a map showing who's breaking how much in Scotland:

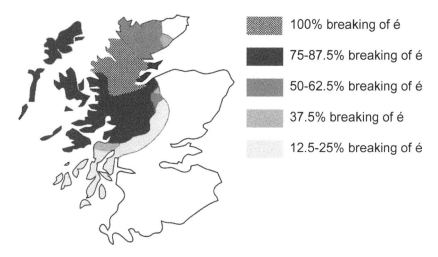

▨	100% breaking of é
▮	75-87.5% breaking of é
▮	50-62.5% breaking of é
▮	37.5% breaking of é
▮	12.5-25% breaking of é

It shows quite nicely the split into the so-called central and peripheral dialects (geographically speaking). This means that, for example, the peripheral dialects share many features with other peripheral dialects but that there are marked differences with any central dialect.

Ok, back to practical issues. Gaelic spelling isn't messy very often but sometimes it is. The **ia** group is one of these. In the vast majority of cases, **ia** is pronounced [iə]:

ciall [kʲiəL]	dias [dʲiəs]	fiach [fiəx]	srian [sdriən]
dia [dʲiə]	cliabh [kliəv]	fiadh [fiəɣ]	sgian [sgʲiən]

But occasionally you will get a word which has clear [ia] instead:

fiamh [fiav]	bian [bian]	fianais [fianɪʃ]	Iain [iaNʲ]
Niall [NʲiaL]	miadh [miaɣ]	pian [pian]	sia [ʃia]

There is, sadly, no hard and fast rule to tell the two apart. You will either have to look the word up or, when that isn't an option, go with [iə] as it is statistically more common. It is not the worst mispronunciation you could make, in the scheme of things and dialects, as usual, don't always agree either - *fiach* is [fiəx] in most places but [fiɑx] in Wester Ross for example.

So… that only leaves the solution of this chapter's title *Ceud or Ciad?* The answer is - both. Both words were pronounced and written the same even in Old Irish: céτ [kʲeːd]. The long [eː] in both words broke and eventually ended up being [iə] in modern Gaelic. While they sound exactly the same in the spoken language, for reasons of clarity in writing Gaels have adopted two different spellings: *ciad* [kʲiəd] 'first' vs *ceud* [kʲiəd] '100'.

5.6.8   The thing about l, n and r

Are you sitting comfortably? Just asking because it's story time again. *Fadó fadó* as the Irish say, long long ago, there was a language called Old Irish. And this language was incredibly rich because it had 4 different l sounds, 4 different n sounds and 4 different r sounds. Yep, that makes 12 altogether. Virtually unheard of. This is what it looked like:

L	Lʲ	N	Nʲ	R	R*[79]
lˠ[80]	l	nˠ	n	r	rʲ

Now over time this system was simplified… slightly. Ulster Irish hardly changed any of it and still has 11 of the original 12 sounds:

L	Lʲ	N	Nʲ	R	
lˠ	l	nˠ	n	r	rʲ

---

[79] There was a second strong R* but no one knows how exactly it was pronounced.

[80] These two, [lˠ] and [nˠ] are like [L] and [N] except that instead of touching your teeth, you touch your alveolar ridge.

Some dialects of Irish and Gaelic have swung to the other extreme and reduced the system vastly. In East Sutherland Gaelic for example, there are only six left:

L	Lʲ			R	
	l	nˠ	n		

Most other Gaelic dialects, certainly those with a significant number of speakers left today, have stuck with nine:

L	Lʲ	N	Nʲ	R	
	l		n	r	rʲ

And that's the system you have studied in this book and will be hearing from your Gaelic teachers in all likelihood. Unless they're from Harris, in which case they still have the [lˠ].

So why the trip into history? Because it has something to do with the way these are written. Here's a small maths problem for you: you have 3 letters - l n r - but you need to represent 4 l sounds, 4 n sounds and 4 r sounds with them. What to do?

Ok, smart idea, you say that there are broad and slender consonants in Gaelic, which is correct. That means if we can find a way of putting that into the spelling system, then we have a way of telling six of them (L lˠ N nˠ R r) apart from the other six (Lʲ l Nʲ n R* rʲ). Now what?

Now for a bit of ingenious thinking by some monks in a cold *scrīptōrium*. They also realised that Gaelic thinks of some of these as 'strong' sound (L N R Lʲ Nʲ R*) and some as 'weak' (lˠ l nˠ n r rʲ). Since the strong ones also had the tendency to be long, they had a Eureka moment and decided to write the strong ones with a double letter, so we got:

L	Lʲ	N	Nʲ	R	R*
broad ll	slender ll	broad nn	slender nn	broad rr	slender rr
lˠ	l	nˠ	n	r	rʲ
broad l	slender l	broad n	slender n	broad r	slender r

Neat, isn't it? So let's narrow it down to what we have today in modern Gaelic. What's interesting is that when the system was simplified, it didn't always go the same way:

L	Lʲ	N	Nʲ	R	
broad ll	slender ll	broad nn	slender nn	broad rr	slender rr
l		n		r	rʲ
broad l	slender l	broad n	slender n	broad r	slender r

So what does that mean for you reading (and writing) modern Gaelic?

- All l, n and r sounds at the beginning of a word are 'strong' [N], [Nʲ], [L], [Lʲ] or [R] (for r, please see the next bullet point):

Broad l n		Slender l n	
nàdar [Naːdər]	naosg [Nɯːsg]	nead [Nʲed]	Niall [NʲiaL]
nuair [Nuərʲ]	norrag [NɔRag]	neul [NʲiaL]	nigh [Nʲi]
lag [Lag]	lann [LauN]	leabaidh [Lʲebɪ]	liath [Lʲiə]
lus [Lus]	lòn [Lɔːn]	leas [Lʲes]	lìon [Lʲiən]

The only way you can get a weak l or n at the start of a word is by leniting it (for broad initial l, see below):

Broad n		Slender l n	
mo nàdar	[mə naːdər]	mo nead	[mə ned]
dà naosg	[da: nɯːsg]	dà neul	[da: niaL]
mo norrag	[mə nɔRag]	cha do nigh	[xa də ni]
		mo leabaidh	[mə lebɪ]
		glé liath	[gle: liə]
		a leas	[ə les]

The weak n in nì [niː] 'will do' is an exception. It is weak because the n simply wasn't always at the beginning of the word. It comes from Old Irish ᴅo ᵹní (the same root as the word gnìomh), hence the weak n. Note that this distinguishes it from nì 'a thing' which is [Nʲiː].

- There is no slender 'strong' r so all initial r letters and double rr anywhere else are always strong [R], irrespective of broad/slender:

Broad r-		"Slender" r-	
rag [Rag]	ruadh [Ruəɣ]	riadh [Riəɣ]	rian [Rian]
ròcas [Rɔːxgəs]	ròn [Rɔːn]	riochd [Rixg]	réidh [Reː]
giorra [gʲiRə]	orra [ɔRə]	rionnag [RuNag]	oirre [ɔRə]

The loss of the other strong r goes back so far that the spelling has caught up with the pronunciation in many cases:

Old Irish	Older Gaelic Spelling	Modern Spelling
ciɲɲiuꝺ ⇒		ciorram [kʲiRəm]
ꝝiɲɲe ⇒	girre ⇒	giorra [gʲiRə]
ɲiċ ⇒	rith ⇒	ruith [Ruj]
ɲicc- ⇒	rig ⇒	ruig [Ruɡʲ]

Again, the only way you can get a weak r at the start of a word is by leniting it:

Broad r		'Slender' r	
glé rag	[gle: rag]	fo rian	[fɔ rian]
dà ròcas	[da: rɔːxgəs]	glé réidh	[gle: re:]
glé ruadh	[gle: ruəɣ]	dà rionnag	[da: ruNag]

- There only is one broad l in Gaelic and it's always [L], no matter where in the word it is:

lag [Lag]	balla [baLə]	call [kauL]
lom [Lɔum]	mala [maLə]	càl [ka:L]
lùb [Lu:b]	balach [baLəx]	faiceall [fɛçɡʲəL]

It is also the only initial consonant in Gaelic which is never affected by lenition:

glé lag [gle: Lag]	glé lom [gle: Lɔum]	an do lùb [əN də Lu:b]
mo laogh [mə Lɯːɣ]	dà lus [da: Lus]	a lùbas [ə Lu:bəs]

- Because lenition is not shown in the normal writing system when it occurs, you must be extra careful in those cases where there is no obvious word causing lenition (like *glé* or *dà* for example). Verbs in the past tense or conditional for example:

Lenited l-	Lenited n-	Lenited r-
leig i [legʲ i]	nigh mi [ni mi]	reic mi [reçgʲ mi]
leudaich i [liadɪç i]	nàirich i [naːrʲɪç i]	ràinig i [raːnɪgʲ i]
leanamaid [lɛnəmɪdʲ]	nigheamaid [ni.əmɪdʲ]	ragamaid [ragəmɪdʲ]
lìonainn [liənɪNʲ]	nochdainn [nɔxgɪNʲ]	roinninn [rɤNʲɪNʲ]

- Exceptions, you ask? Sure… there is a tiny handful of (mostly) function words that for one reason or another have weak [l], [n], [r] or [rʲ] at the beginning of a word:

Weak initial l-	Weak initial n-	Weak initial r
le [le]	'nam ad [na mad]	ri [rʲi]
leam [lɔum]	'nad ad [na dad]	rium [rʲuːm]
leat [lahd]	'na ad [na ad]	riut [rʲuhd]
leis [leʃ]	'na h-ad [na had]	ris [rʲiʃ]
leatha [lɛ.ə]	'nar n-ad [nar nad]	rithe [rʲi.ə]
leinn [leiNʲ]	'nur n-ad [nar nad]	rinn [rʲiːNʲ]
leibh [leiv]	'nan ad [na nad]	ribh [rʲiːv]
leotha [lɔ.ə]	no/na [nɔ]/[na] 'or'	riutha [rʲu.ə]
	na(n) [nəN⁽ʲ⁾] 'the'	ro [rɔ] 'before' & 'too'
	na [na] 'do not!'	romham [rõ.əm]
	na(s) [nəs]	romhad [rõ.əd]
	na [nə] ⇐ an do	roimhe [rõjə]
	nach [nax]	roimhpe [rõihbə]
	na [na] relative part.	romhainn [rõ.ɪNʲ]
	nì [niː] future of *dèan*	romhaibh [rõ.ɪv]
		romhpa [rõhbə]
		ré [reː] 'during'

The preposition *ri* requires an extra explanation. In much of the Hebrides, in the forms of *ri* (except for *ri, ris* and *rithe*) the [rʲ] (or [ð] in Lewis) has been replaced with broad [r]. So you get:

rium [rɔum]	riut [ruhd]	ris [rʲiʃ]	rithe [rʲi.ə]
ruinn [ruiNʲ]	ruibh [ruiv]		riutha [ru.ə]

That is also the reason for the relatively recent *ruinn* and *ruibh* spellings which attempt to reflect to change to a broader **r** sound. And in case you wondered, I'm going to give you one more example that shows why an initial sound can be weak. The Old Irish ancestor of *rium* for example was ꞃꞁumm, with the **r** after the **f** and before an **i**, resulting in [rʲ]. Perfectly regular until the **f** was lenited away…

Remember that in spoken Gaelic the **a-** often gets dropped in adverbs, sometimes leaving a weak **l**, **n** or **r** at the beginning of a word:

(a-)nis [ə'niʃ]	(a-)réir [ə'rʲeːrʲ]	(a-)réiste [ə'rʲeːʃdʲə]
(a-)riamh [ə'rʲiəv]	(a-)rithist [ə'rʲi.ɪʃdʲ]	

Being an adverb is no guarantee though that the first sound after the **a-** will be weak:

(a-)nall [ə'NauL]	(a-)nìos [ə'Nʲiəs]	(a-)nochd [ə'Nɔxg]
(a-)nuas [ə'Nuəs]	(a-)null [ə'NuːL]	(a-)raoir [ə'Rɣirʲ]

- In the middle or at the end, you can get any l, n or r sound. The 'strong' sounds are written using double letters: ll, nn and rr. Check out the Guide for slender single n though because it tends to come out as [Nʲ] in certain environments today. Some examples:

Non-initial l & ll	Non-initial n & nn	Non-initial r & rr
caileag [kalag]	Sìne [ʃiːnə]	mìrean [mirʲən]
cuilean [kulan]	caoineadh [kɯːNʲəɣ]	sireadh [ʃirʲəɣ]
buil [bul]	cuin [kuNʲ]	cìr [kʲiːrʲ]
càil [kaːl]	sin [ʃin]	maoir [mɯːrʲ]
milleadh [miLʲəɣ]	cinnteach [kʲĩːNʲdʲəx]	's fheairrde [ʃaːRdʲə]
cailleach [kaLʲəx]	sinne [ʃiNʲə]	Nirribhidh [Nʲirɪvɪ]
till [tʲiːLʲ]	cinn [kʲiːNʲ]	Loch Sirr [Lɔx ʃiːR]
foill [fɤiLʲ]	roinn [RɤiNʲ]	Oirrinn [ɔRɪNʲ]
mala [maLə]	anail [anal]	aran [aran]
balach [baLəx]	anart [anəRʃd]	òran [ɔːran]
càl [kaːL]	bàn [baːn]	sàr [saːr]
ìosal [iəsəL]	can [kan]	càilear [kaːlər]
balla [baLə]	connadh [kɔNəɣ]	curran [kuRan]
ullamh [uLəv]	annas [aNəs]	sporran [sbɔRan]
call [kauL]	bann [bauN]	cearr [kʲaːR]
fìdheall [fiː.əL]	bonn [bouN]	torr [tɔːR]

You could argue that it would make sense to spell the above words *nnàdar, nnead, llag, lleabaidh, rrag* etc. On the other hand, since virtually all l, n and r sounds at the beginning of a word (unless affected by lenition) are strong, that would just be a waste of precious ink and vellum!

5.6.9   Other helpful hints

You've battled your way through the Guide, internalised helping vowels and have started dreaming of 'compensatory lengthening' but is there anything to make it any easier?

There are other general patterns to all these rules in the Guide which may not be completely obvious. So I'm going to list any other general patterns that can help you reduce the number of individual rules you have to learn. I'm not going to repeat patterns that we've talked about already so if you want to double-check the helping vowel for example, then go back to that section.

Allow me to start on a historical note (again). Old Irish had 5 simple vowels which could be long or short: [a] [e] [i] [o] and [u]. Gaelic has something much more complex as you're fully aware of by now. Gaelic became so much more complex because, over time, the vicinity of certain consonants changed the vowels near them. A bit like washing white bed linen with a red sock... you end up with a still red sock and pink linen.

So the thing with vowels in Gaelic is that we cannot look at the vowel letters on their own. In many cases we have to consider the consonant that comes after them too, before we can make a decision about the pronunciation.

In terms of the consonants, once you have understood the broad/slender concept of the Gaelic spelling system (see 5.2), consonants on the whole are relatively easy to figure out.

5.6.10 Unstressed vowels

There's a whole section on this (see 4.12.4) but this is such a useful hint I'll repeat it. For the most part, vowels in unstressed syllables are boring. They generally end up as [ə] or [ɪ]. So whenever in doubt about how to pronounce an unstressed vowel and you don't have time to figure it out, go for [ə].

5.6.11   How to tell apart the two short o sounds

In Gaelic the default reading for the letter **o** in a stressed syllable is [ɔ]. The round [o] routinely shows up if there is a **b**, **g** or **m** (plus a vowel) coming after it:

gob [gob]	obair [obɪrʲ]	ob [ob]	tobair [tobɪrʲ]
bog [bog]	gog [gog]	togail [togal]	thogras [hogrəs]
coma [komə]	cromag [kromag]	lomadh [Loməɣ]	droman [droman]

It will help if you memorise a set of three such as *gob, bog* and *coma,* then you can always refer back to them if you're unsure about a new word with **o** in it. This just applies to a short **o** on its own, not combinations like **io** or **eo** etc.

The round [o] also commonly appears if a short **o** (not **oi**) is followed by hiatus:

ogha [o.ə]	gnothach [grõ.əx]	motha [mo.ə]
todhar [to.ər]	bodhar [bo.ər]	foghainn [fo.ɪNʲ]

5.6.12   And how to tell apart the two short e sounds

This affects the **ea** letter combination in a stressed syllable. Generally this is [ɛ] in Gaelic. The [e] sound only occurs if followed by an **s**, **d** or **g**. One of my students coined the line Some Dogs Growl to help him remember the letters that cause an **ea** to be [e] rather than [ɛ]. The combination **ei** is also generally [e] rather than [ɛ]:

neas [Nʲes]	seas [ʃes]	leas [Lʲes]	freagair [frʲegɪrʲ]
nead [Nʲed]	cead [kʲed]	fead [fed]	beadaidh [bedɪ]
beag [beg]	creag [krʲeg]	seagal [ʃegəL]	eagach [egəx]
eilid [elɪdʲ]	creid [krʲedʲ]	ceist [kʲeʃdʲ]	breith [brʲeh]

Unless Vowel Lengthening intervenes of course in which case you get the [ei] diphthong.

5.6.13 Dealing with th

This is usually either [h], hiatus (see 4.3), [j] or silent. It is never ever the th you get in English words like thing or father.

As far as picking one of the above options, you can follow the following guidelines:

- At the end of a word, th is usually [h] after a short vowel and silent after a long vowel, for example:

After short vowel		After long vowel	
gath [gah]	math [mah]	blàth [bLaː]	bùth [buː]
crith [krʲih]	bleith [bleh]	sgòth [sgɔː]	dlùth [dLuː]
roth [Roh]	sruth [sdruh]	maoth [mɯː]	sìth [ʃiː]

If the word following a word ending in [h], the [h] often disappears (this also applies to words where the [h] is not written th but bh or gh for example):

gath mór [ga moːr]	roth mór [Rɔ moːr]	sruth fada [sdru fadə]
cruth math [kru mah]	ugh beag [u beg]	dubh mór [du moːr]

- In the middle of a word, broad th is almost always hiatus after a long vowel, for example:

blàthaich [bLaː.ɪç]	beòthaich [bjɔː.ɪç]	dùthaich [duː.ɪç]
sgòthach [sgɔː.əx]	sgìthich [sgʲiː.ɪç]	dìthich [dʲiː.ɪç]
làthach [Laː.əx]	gnàthaich [grãː.ɪç]	snàthaid [sNaː.ɪdʲ]

The main exceptions are *bàthaich* [baːhəç], *màthair* [maːhərʲ] and *bràthair* [braːhərʲ].

- After a long back vowel or diphthong, slender th is [j]:

ràitheach [Raːjəx]	làitheil [Laːjal]	fàitheam [faːjəm]
dlùithe [dLuːjə]	gaoithe [gɤjə]	luaithe [Luəjə]

Incidentally, at the end of an adjective **-th** today has the interesting habit of blocking case marking. This means that if you have an adjective like *sgìth* following a plural noun, no extra vowel is added. Or, in a case like *math,* no vowel is added in the plural and it is not slenderised in the genitive. Compare the following:

Ending in -th	Ending in something else
daoine math [duɯːNʲə ma]	daoine móra [duɯːNʲə moːrə]
balaich sgìth [baLɪç sgʲiː]	balaich bheaga [baLɪç vegə]
falt coin mhath [faLd koNʲ va]	falt coin ghil [faLd koNʲ ʝil]
cas eòin thràth [kas jɔːNʲ raː]	cas eòin dhuibh [kas jɔːNʲ ɣɯj]

5.6.14 Vowel mutations and Is the plural of moose meese?

This is technically speaking probably not a phonology issue but because it affects sounds and spelling in quite a radical way that often puzzles people, I'm going to explain a thing or two about it.

The issue in question is that of the occasionally radical changes to vowels you get when they move into the genitive or the plural. For example:

ceòl [kʲɔːL]	⇒ ciùil [kʲuːl]	cas [kas]	⇒ coise [kɔʃə]
seòl [ʃɔːL]	⇒ siùil [ʃuːl]	fras [fras]	⇒ froise [frɔʃə]
fear [fɛr]	⇒ fir [firʲ]	peann [pjauN]	⇒ pinn [piːNʲ]
each [ɛx]	⇒ eich [eç]	òrd [ɔːRd]	⇒ ùird [uːRdʲ]

And so on. The whole thing isn't dissimilar to what today are irregular plurals or verbs in English: *mouse ~ mice, goose ~ geese, eat ~ ate* and so on.

Most of these changes, both to the consonants and vowels, in both languages ultimately go back to a front vowel (generally [i]) that was stuck on at some point. It hung around for long enough to mess up the consonant and vowel in front of it and then disappeared. For example, in Germanic (the common ancestor to English, Dutch, German, Norwegian, Icelandic etc going back some 2500 years) the word for a mouse was *mūs*. If the one cute mouse invited its family to come round, you ended up with *mūsi* in your kitchen. So far so good.

Now the **-i** sets about wreaking havoc because your mouth being lazy, it can't be bothered shifting from way back for the [u:] to the front of your mouth to make the [i]... so the [u:] becomes an [i:] to please the ending. And because we've now got two things telling us its plural, the **-i** is now surplus to requirements and goes away leaving us with *mȳs*. Which later become *mice*.

Gaelic is just a tiny bit crazier when it comes to this. For example, going back to Q-Celtic (the common ancestor to Irish, Gaelic and Manx) the word for son was *macc* [mak] which in the genitive became *maqi* [maki]. By the time we hit Old Irish, this has become mᴀc [mak] and mᴀıcc [makʲ]. So the **-i** has already disappeared but before it did so, it palatalised the [k] to [kʲ]. But like the ripples in a lake when you throw a stone in, it wasn't quite done yet. Eventually the ripples reached the vowel and changed mᴀıcc [makʲ] to meıc [mekʲ] and then to mıc [mikʲ], which in modern Gaelic became *mic* [miçgʲ].

The only problem is that this isn't exactly regular and also to some degree undergoing change, so it's difficult to establish any sensible rules that you could use. Therefore you will have to learn these changes as part of the vocabulary. Just like learners of English have to learn that it's "one goose" but "two geese" but "one moose" and "two moose" (not meese).

One good pointer though. This only affects words that are one syllable long - which means that all words which have two syllables or more are 'regular'!

5.6.15 The 'old spelling' and the 'new spelling'

There are just a few of points which need to be addressed in terms of changes to the spelling that have been made in recent years because people couldn't leave well alone.

The first one is perhaps the most obvious one: abolishing the acute accent on **ó** and **é**. In the traditional spelling **ó** was used to differentiate the [oː] sound from **ò** [ɔː] and **é** [eː] from **è** [ɛː], for example:

Traditional		New
bó [boː]	⇒	bò [boː]
cóig [koːgʲ]	⇒	còig [koːgʲ]
dé [dʲeː]	⇒	dè [dʲeː]
séid [ʃeːdʲ]	⇒	sèid [ʃeːdʲ]

The traditional spelling used both accents because there is no other way of predicting when you get either sound. Of course changing the spelling hasn't affected the pronunciation of these sounds! Well, for native speakers anyway. Learners these days get this wrong quite a lot because few of the new books published use both accents.

Some argue that abolishing them has perhaps made it easier for native speakers to write Gaelic. An odd argument, as it was native speakers who came up with the system in the first place, I find. Either way, it has not made it any easier for learners to read or learn Gaelic. So when you come across a word in modern spelling with **è** or **ò**, you need to either check in an older dictionary (like Dwelly's) whether the traditional spelling was with **é** or **ó**, check a reliable pronunciation guide or consult a native speaker.

Long [e:] is fairly common in Gaelic so it's not practical to give you a list. However, the [ɛ:] pronunciation of the **è(i)** group (in the new spelling) is actually very rare, so as a rule of thumb, when you come across **è(i)** in the new spelling, assume it is [e:] except in the following words:

bèicear⁺ [bɛ:çgʲər]	gnè⁺ [grʲɛ̃:]	mèilich [mɛ:lɪç]
mèinn [mɛ:Nʲ]	mèirleach [mɛ:Rləx]	sèimh⁺ [ʃɛ̃:v]
sgèimh [sgʲɛ̃:v]	snèip [ʃNʲɛ:hb]	stèisean [sdɛ:ʃan]

Long **ó** is even less common. In fact, less than a dozen common words have compulsory **ó** across all dialects (they don't all agree on **ó** vs **ò**, for example *mòine* is [mo:Nʲə] in the Hebrides but [mɔ:Nʲə] on the mainland). So I suggest you always go for [ɔ:] except in the following words:

bó [bo:]	có [ko:]	cóig⁺ [ko:gʲ]
Eóghann⁺ [jo:əN]	fón⁺ [fo:n]	leóbag⁺ [Lʲo:bag]
mór⁺ [mo:r]	ó! [o:]	óbh óbh⁸¹ [o: vo:v]
Tómas⁺ [to:mas]		

Remember the words marked with ⁺ above have long [o:] in all derived forms as well. For example, *móran* [mo:ran], *mórachd* [mo:rəxg] etc all have long [o:].

The **o** in the **-oghn-** and **-obhl-** group is also pronounced [o:]. You will see words with those groups spelled with and without the accent. As the lengthening of the vowel to [o:] is caused by the dropped **gh**, technically the accent is not needed but either way, in those groups the vowel is also [o:]:

gŏbhlach [go:Ləx]	fŏghnaidh⁺ [fo:nɪ]	rŏghnach [Ro:nəx]

---

⁸¹ A long form of the exclamation *obh obh.*

The second point regards the use of **u** in unstressed syllables. As we mentioned in the chapter on unstressed vowels, it is difficult to tell whether the letter **a** is pronounced [a] or [ə] in an unstressed syllable. In the traditional spelling there was a tendency to use the letter **u** to represent the lazy [ə]. This was possible as the letter **u** almost never is pronounced [u] in an unstressed syllable:

Traditional	New
Calum [kaLəm]	⇒ Calum [kaLəm]
agus [agəs]	⇒ agus [agəs]
dorus [dɔrəs]	⇒ doras [dɔrəs]
nàdur [Na:dər]	⇒ nàdar [Na:dər]
solus [sɔLəs]	⇒ solas [sɔLəs]

Again not a problem from the native speaker's point of view but for a learner it would have been easier if [ə] was consistently represented by **u** in unstressed syllables. I'm mentioning this point because if you're not sure whether a certain word has [a] or [ə], you can check the spelling in an older dictionary and if it has **u**, then it will be pronounced [ə].

The third point is about the spelling of the irregular verbs. Traditionally a number of spellings have been used to write the dependant forms of them:

Var 1	Var 2	Var 3	Var 4	Var 5 (GOC)	Pronounced
d'thàinig	dàinig	d'tàinig	tàinig	tàinig	[da:nɪgʲ]
d'theach	deach	deach	deach	deach	[dʲɛx]
d'théid	déid	d'téid	téid	tèid	[dʲe:dʲ]
d'thuirt	duirt	d'tuirt	tuirt	tuirt	[du:Rʃdʲ]
d'thoir	doir	d'toir	toir	toir	[dɔrʲ]
d'thug	dug	d'tug	tug	tug	[dug]

Now, all these are pronounced the same way (see the last column) and given the pronunciation, Variant 2 would have been the one which most accurately represents the modern language and complies with the general conventions on how to pronounce written Gaelic.

For whatever reason, GOC has gone for those forms which are perhaps the most 'correct' from a historical perspective. Personally I would have worried more about people mispronouncing them because now we have historically accurate forms and loads of learners saying *[xa taːnɪgʲ] rarther than [xa dànɪgʲ].

Let's ignore the detailed discussion of the pros and cons of the different variations and focus on how to deal with the issue practically:

> When dealing with a spelling where irregular verbs have initial **t**,
> you must remember to pronounce them
> as if they were written with a **d** at the beginning.

As if life wasn't complicated enough, there are also new so-called phantom words (newly fused words) that break and muddle several rules all at once. They muddle the vowel lengthening rules and break the broad/slender spelling rule:

Traditional	New
le m' ogha [le mo.ə]	⇒ lem ogha [le mo.ə]
le d' ogha [le do.ə]	⇒ led ogha [le do.ə]
le ur cead [ler kʲed]	⇒ ler cead [ler kʲed]
do m' ogha [də mo.ə]	⇒ dom ogha [də mo.ə]
tro m' ad [trɔ mad]	⇒ trom ad [trɔ mad]
ri ar taigh [rʲir tɤj]	⇒ rir taigh [rʲir tɤj]

You must take great care when coming across these to pronounce them

- without long vowels
- with broad [d] and [r]

5.6.16 Exceptions

There are a few words which simply have unpredictable pronunciations for a number of reasons. Here are some of some common ones (excluding those already dealt with in other sections):

á+ [a]	a dh'aithghearr [ə ɣaçaR]
a **h**-uile[82] [a xulə]	**Ao**nghas+ [ɯnɯ.əs]
air neo [əR Nʲɔː]	**ban**righ(inn)+ [bãũNrɪ(Nʲ)]
bliadhna [bliəNə]	(gu) bràth [braːx]
calpa+ [kaLabə]	ceangal+ [kɛ̃.əL]
cothrom+ [kɔRəm]	deimhinn [dʲevɪNʲ]
eachdraidh+ [ɛxdrɪ]	eugh+ [eːv]
Gàidheal+ [gɛː.əL]	gaoith(e)+ [gɤj(ə)]
ged [gad]	ghille! [iLʲə]
inbhir+ [iNʲɪrʲ]	iarann+ [iəRəN]
innis+ [ĩːʃ]	iodhlann+ [juLəN]
ionnsaigh+ [jũːNsɪ]	meadhan+ [mi.an]
leugh+ [Lʲeːv]	muilnean/muilleann [muiLʲən]
muillear+ [muiLʲɛr]	oirnn+ [ɔːRNʲ]
pàipear+ [pɛːhbɛr]	Raghnall+ [Rɤ̃ː.əL]
ràinig+ [raːnɪgʲ]	thàinig [haːnɪgʲ]
tionndaidh+ [tʲũːNdaj]	toirsgian [tɔrɔʃɡʲən]
tu+ [du]	

Remember the + means that all derived forms are also irregular:

innis+ [ĩːʃ]	⇒ innse [ĩːʃə], innsidh [ĩːʃɪ], dh'innseas [ʝ̃ĩːʃəs]…
eugh+ [eːv]	⇒ eughachd [eːvəxɡ], dh'eugh [ʝeːv]…

---

[82] This is regular but the spelling is up the chute, it's short for *(g)ach uile*…

5.6.17   Loanwords, potatoes and the police

Now the issue of loanwords isn't exactly something a learner has to sort out but it is useful to be aware of a thing or two about it because loanwords are as common today as they were in the days of Kenneth MacAlpin.

To begin with, all living languages borrow words and/or concepts, Gaelic included. On the whole, that's not a problem for a language unless the borrowing gets a bit out of hand. It also depends on how the language doing the borrowing and the language being borrowed from work and whether they're at loggerheads over 'something'.

For example, English has borrowed thousands of words from languages all over the planet. On the whole, it's fairly easy for English to do that, it simply strips the loanword of anything non-English and Bob's your uncle. For example, when English borrowed the Cantonese word for fried noodles it replaced some sounds, ignored the high rising and low level tone and was happy with Chow Mein (which is pronounced rather differently in Cantonese).

The other way round isn't so easy because Cantonese is much more restrictive in terms of the sound combinations it has or allows. The word 'lift' (as in elevator) for example was a big problem. Cantonese doesn't allow two consonants one after the other, especially involving an [f]. In the end, the word was borrowed with what to Cantonese ears was a close match. So to this day it's called *līp* with a high level tone because all words in Cantonese need a tone. Not that the problems end there - because to date Cantonese people haven't decided on which character is best suited to write this word.

So each language brings its own set of "linguistic glasses" through which it sees foreign words which it is about to adopt. Including Gaelic. There are about 5 main filters in the set of glasses Gaelic wears:

- It doesn't like fricatives (except [s], [ʃ] and [f]) at the beginning of words. We already looked at that in section 4.5.3.

- It likes to palatalise consonants near front vowels.

- It likes to simplify or break up groups of consonants which are odd (from the Gaelic point of view of course!) and shortens words which are 'too long'.

- It's pretty insistent on initial stress and not having fancy vowels in unstressed syllables.

All in all, not a language to suffer loanwords too gladly. Here are a few examples of the words Gaelic has borrowed over the centuries and what it has done to them:

- *airgead* [ɛrʲɛgʲəd] from Latin *argentum* 'silver'. Gaelic has added a helping vowel but dropped the ending.

- *coinneal* [kɣNʲəL] from Latin *candela*. Gaelic has palatalised and also simplified the **nd** and dropped the ending.

- *pòg* [pɔːg] from Latin *pācem* (part of the 'kiss of peace' ritual in church). Gaelic has dropped the ending and changed the vowel a bit.

- *uinneag* [ɯNʲag] from Norse *vindauga* 'wind eye'. Gaelic has turned the offending initial **v** into a vowel, simplified the **nd** and changed the ending to something more Gaelic looking.

- *eilean* [elan] from Norse *eyland* 'island'. Gaelic has simplified both the first vowel and the ending.

- *àirneis* [aːRNʲɪʃ] from Old English *harnais* 'harness'. Gaelic dropped the offending **h**, lengthened the vowel before **rn** (which is a natural rule in Gaelic) and palatalised the **s** to [ʃ].

- *buidseach* [budʲʃəx] from English or Scots *witch*. Gaelic has strengthened the offending **w** into the next best thing, a [b] and added a native ending.

- *cuidheall* [kɯi.əL] from Scots *wheel*. Again Gaelic has strengthened the unacceptable **wh-** into a [k] and broken the long vowel with a hiatus. Since Scots has a dark **l** here, Gaelic has adjusted this into its own, dark and dental [L].

- *dotair* [dɔhdɛrʲ] from English or Scots *doctor*. The **-ct-** group isn't really acceptable in Gaelic so Gaelic has opted for replacing the **c** with pre-aspiration .

As you can see, Gaelic has been borrowing for a long time but generally made sure that any such words comply with the sound rules of Gaelic.

So why do you need to know this? Two reasons. On the one hand it's an aside to help you understand the way Gaelic works a little bit better.

And on the other hand it's a bit of a warning. Sometimes you are faced with a word for which there is no established Gaelic word around. If one decides to borrow a word from another language it's important to bear in mind how Gaelic works and how it treats sounds if you want to avoid coming up with Gaelic 'versions' which just sound totally weird from a Gaelic point of view. It's not always easy because native speakers have an innate but unconscious understanding of the language and its rules. Learners often have an incomplete understanding of how the language works. Added to that, there's the problem that all Gaelic speakers, natives and learners, are so fluent in and so used to English that all sorts of other factors can get in the way.

Here are some examples of what can happen:

- vitamin: *beothaman, beòthag, bhiotamain*. The first two are trying to avoid the **v** at the beginning and create a hybrid using the Gaelic word *beò*. The last barely adjusts at all except in terms of the spelling.

- hydrogen: *hidrigin, haidridean, hàidraidean*.   Here the basic disagreement is about whether to treat the **y** as a diphthong (because that's how it is pronounced in English) or whether to treat it like an [i] sound. The first option works better from the point of view of Gaelic sound rules but sounds odd to people who are familiar with the English word.   The other two sound less 'strange' but are problematic as it's difficult to write [ai] in Gaelic except before **ll, nn, rr** and **m**. The combination **ai** is usually [a] and **ài** usually [a:] or [ɛ:] but not [ai].   Then there is the soft **g** which has to become slender **d** in Gaelic.   So the last two either break the rules on how to pronounce written Gaelic or change the pronunciation.

The point is simply that it's a tricky business to get right and that one has to be careful with 'Gaelic versions' of English words that were made without too much thought given to the way Gaelic sounds work. It's all too easy to come up with something that looks like a good idea but creates headaches for the language on the whole. It's not just a case of 'so what?'

Being slightly more practical (from your point of view) this means that when we come to look at the detailed rules of how to read Gaelic, you need to bear in mind that some modern coinages and loanwords sometimes look and behave differently. Loanwords may have groups of sounds that don't normally exist in Gaelic and may not be fully "Gaelicised". For example, the word *lof* 'a loaf' is pronounced by native speakers with a weak **l** at the beginning - [lɔf] - without the expected strong [L] at the start of a word.

6.   The last word

So, you've reached the end of Blas na Gàidhlig... is that it then? Yep. Broadly speaking. There's always more detail that one could look at but you have now got a very firm foundation upon which to build your *Taigh na Gàidhlig*, figuratively speaking.

You have achieved a lot. You have taken the first and largest hurdle you will ever encounter in Gaelic. You've looked at all the sounds Gaelic can throw at you, you've learned how they fit together and how they interact and you've mastered the art of reading Gaelic. I know you still can't ask for a kebab in Gaelic or understand the Gaelic news but - and it's a large and important but - you have done an awful lot of real Gaelic and as you start to take the next steps you will see how much you have learned - not least when you meet native speakers who will comment favourably on your pronunciation - or other learners who have paid less attention to their pronunciation.

The rest will come with practice - lots of listening and speaking and time.

So as they say, *math da-rireabh*, well done indeed and never ever underestimate the importance of what you have achieved!

I.   Appendix I - The Wordlist

The Guide is Good... but it can take some time to get used to. So to make life easier for you I'm not only giving you the Guide but also a wordlist. Not just any old wordlist though. It contains most of the vocabulary that you will come across in the most common Gaelic courses around at the moment. It's not intended to be a dictionary but what it does is give you the phonetic spelling for all entries - including plural forms, genitives and so on. Here's a sample entry for *ceann*:

ceann   [kʲauN] *nm* head; *gen* & *pl* cinn [kʲiːNʲ] • ~-bhaile
                       [kʲaNəvalə] capital • ~-cropaig [kʲaNˈkrɔhbɛgʲ] stuffed
                       cod-head • ~ Locha [kʲaNˈLɔxə] Kinloch • ~ Loch Gilb
                       [kʲaNLɔxˈgʲilib] Lochgilphead • ~-suidhe [kʲauNˈsuɪjə]
                       president • ~-uidhe [kʲaNˈujə] destination

It tells you the pronunciation of the word, gives a basic meaning, lists genitives and plurals and their pronunciation and compounds that contain the word.

Please note that the irregular verbs are all listed at the end of the Wordlist on page 444 because they wouldn't fit in the list itself without it turning into utter chaos.

So you can rely on the Wordlist initially and bring out the guide only when you come across more advanced vocabulary that isn't in it. How's that for service?

By the way, there are no recordings for the wordlist itself though because that would get a bit unwieldy. If you're looking for a talking dictionary, try the Faclair Beag online which has an increasing number of sound files.

Abbreviations (with English examples where possible):

adj	adjective	*adv*	adverb
	• *cunning, sly*		• *cunningly, slyly*
coll	colloquial	*comp*	comparative
	• *gonna, ain't*		• *bigger, thinner*
conj	conjunction	*def prep*	definite preposition
	• *and, or*		• *on the*
dem	demonstrative	*emph*	emphatic
	• *this, that*		• *ME, HIM*
excl	exclamation	*gen*	genitive
	• *oh! wow!*		
hr	high register	*interr*	interrogative
	• *thy, quoth*		• *why? when?*
neg	negative	*nf*	feminine noun
	• *not, no*		
nm	masculine noun	*num*	numeral
			• *one, ten*
pl	plural	*pnf*	feminine proper noun
	• *cats, dogs*		
pnm	masculine proper noun	*prep*	preposition
			• *on, under*
pron	pronoun	*rel part*	relative particle
	• *me, you*		• *that, which*
short	short form	*v*	verb
	• *I'm, won't*		• *kick, eat*
vn	verbal noun	*voc*	vocative
	• *kicking, eating*		

AILM [alam]

a¹	[ə] *poss pron* his; lost before vowel: (a) athair [ahər^j]
a²	[ə] *poss pron* her; see a h-
a³	[ə] *rel part* that, who, which
a⁴	[ə] *prep* to; see do¹
á	[a] *prep* from; *def prep* ás an [asəN⁽ʲ⁾] *def prep pl* ás na [asnə] conjugated asam [asəm] asad [asəd] ás [as] aiste [aʃdʲə] asainn [asɪNʲ] asaibh [asɪv] asta [asdə] • ás aonais… [a suː:nɪʃ] without…
abairt	[abɪRʃdʲ] *nf* expression; *gen* ~e [abɪRʃdʲə] *pl* ~ean [abɪRʃdʲən]
abhainn	[ã.ɪNʲ] *nf* river; *gen* aibhne [ãĩnə] *pl* aibhnichean [ãĩnɪçən]
àbhaist	[aːvɪʃdʲ] *nf* habit, custom; *gen* ~e [aːvɪʃdʲə] *pl* ~ean [aːvɪʃdʲən] • mar as ~ [mar ə saːvɪʃdʲ] as usual
a-bhòin-dè	[ə voːNʲ dʲeː] *adv* the day before yesterday
a-bhòn-uiridh	[ə voː Nurʲɪ] *adv* the year before last
a-bhos	[əˈvɔs] *adv* over here
acair	[axgɪrʲ] *nf* anchor; *gen* acrach [axgrəx] *pl* acraichean [axgrɪçən]
acarsaid	[axgəRsadʲ] *nf* anchorage; *gen* ~e [axgəRsadʲə] *pl* ~ean [axgəRsadʲən]
ach	[ax] *conj* but
achadh	[axəɣ] *nm* field; *gen* achaidh [axɪ] *pl* achaidhean [axɪ.ən] • An t-~ Mór [əN taxə moːr] Achmore
a chionn	[ə çuːN] *conj* because
acras	[axgrəs] *nm* hunger; *gen* acrais [axgrɪʃ] • tha an t-~ orm [haN taxgrəs ɔrɔm] I am hungry
ad	[ad] *nf* hat; *gen* aide [adʲə] *pl* ~an [adən]
adag	[adag] *nf* haddock; *gen* adaige [adɛgʲə] *pl* ~an [adagən]
adhar	[a.ər] *nm* air; *gen* adhair [a.ɪrʲ]
adhbhar	[ɤːvər] *nm* reason; *gen* adhbhair [ɤːvɪrʲ] *pl* ~an [ɤːvərən]
Afraga	[afragə] *pnf* Africa; *gen* na h-Afraga [nə hafragə]
agh	[ɤɣ] *nf* heifer; *gen* aighe [ajə] *pl* aighean [ajən]
aghaidh	[ɤ.ɪ] nf face; *gen* ~e [ɤ.ɪ.ə] *pl* ~ean [ɤ.ɪ.ən] • an ~ [ə Nɤ.ɪ] *prep* against
a h-	[ə h] *poss pron* her; h- is lost before consonant: a h-athair [ə hahər^j] ⇨ a cù [ə kuː]

aig [ɛgʲ] *prep* at; *def prep* ~ an [ɛgʲ əNⁱⁱ⁾] conjugated agam [agəm] agad [agəd] aige [ɛgʲə] aice [ɛçgʲə] againn [agɪNʲ] agaibh [agɪv] aca [axgə]; with fused *poss pron* 'gam [gam] 'gad [gad] 'ga [ga] 'ga h- [ga h] 'gar n- [gar n] gur n- [gar n] 'gan [gan]

aighearach [ajərəx] *adj* lively; *comp* aighearaiche [ajərɪçə]

Ailean [alan] *pnm* Alan; *gen* Ailein [alɛNʲ] *voc* Ailein [alɛNʲ]

Ailig [alɪgʲ] *pnm* Alec

àill [a:Lʲ] *nf* desire • b' ~ leat? [baLʲəhd] pardon? • b' ~ leibh? [baLʲəv] pardon?

Aimeireaga [əˈmerʲəgə] *pn* America

aimsir [ɛmɛʃɪrʲ] *nf* weather; *gen* ~e [ɛmɛʃɪrʲə]

ainm [ɛnɛm] *nm* name; *pl* ~ean [ɛnɛmən] • ~m-baistidh [ɛnɛmˈbaʃdʲɪ] Christian name

ainmeil [ɛnɛmal] *adj* famous; *comp* ~e [ɛnɛmalə]

ainmich [ɛnɛmɪç] 1 *v* to mention 2 *vn & nm* ainmeachadh [ɛnɛməxəɣ] mentioning, mention; *gen* ainmeachaidh [ɛnɛməxɪ] *pl* ainmeachaidhean [ɛnɛməxɪ.ən]

ainneamh [aNʲəv] *adj* rare; *comp* ainneimhe [aNʲəvə]

air [ɛrʲ] *prep* on; *def prep* air an [ɛrʲ ə Nⁱⁱ⁾] *def prep pl* air na [ɛrʲ nə] conjugated orm [ɔrɔm] ort [ɔRʃd] air [ɛrʲ] oirre [ɔRə] oirnn [ɔ:RNʲ] oirbh [ɣrʲɣv] orra [ɔRə] • ~ beulaibh… [ɛrʲ biaLɪv] in front of… • ~ choireigin [ɛrʲ xɔrʲegʲɪn] or other • ~ cùlaibh… [ɛrʲ ku:Lɪv] behind… • ~ neò [ɛrʲ Nʲo:] alternatively • ~ sgàth [ɛrʲ sga:] for the sake of

airc [argʲ] *nf* distress; *gen* ~e [argʲə]

àirc [a:rgʲ] *nf* ark; *gen* ~e [a:rgʲə] *pl* ~ean [a:rgʲən]

àirde [a:Rdʲə] *nf* height • Àird Ghobhar [a:Rdʲ ɣo.ər] Ardgour • Àird nam Murchan [a:Rdʲ nə muruxən] Ardnamurchan

àireamh [a:rʲəv] *nf* number; *gen* àireimh [a:rʲəv] *pl* ~an [a:rʲəvən]

airgead [ɛrʲɛgʲəd] *nm* money; *gen* airgid [ɛrʲɛgʲɪdʲ]

airidh [arʲɪ] *adj* worthy; *comp* ~e [arʲɪ.ə]

airson [ɛRˈsɔn] *prep* for (the sake of)

Àisea, an ~ [ə Nɛ:ʃə] *pnf* Asia; *gen* na h-Àisea [nə hɛ:ʃə]

aiseag [aʃəg] *nm* ferry; *gen* aiseig [aʃɪgʲ] *pl* ~an [aʃəgən]

ait [ahdʲ] *adj* cheerful; *comp* ~e [ahdʲə]

àite [a:hdʲə] *nm* place; *pl* àitichean [a:hdʲɪçən] • ~-còmhnaidh [ahdʲəˈkõ:nɪ] place of residence • ~-obrach [ahdʲⁱobrəx] workplace

aithghearr   [açaR] *adj* sudden; *comp* ~a [açaRə] • a dh'~ [ə ɣaçaR] soon

aithne   [aNʲə] *nf* acquaintance • 's ~ dhomh… [saNʲə ɣõ] I am acquainted with… • chan ~ dhut… [xa NaNʲə ɣuhd] you don't know…

àithne   [a:Nʲə] *nf* command; *pl* àitheantan [a:jəNdən]

aithnich   [aNʲɪç] 1 *v* to recognise 2 *vn* & *nm* aithneachadh [aNʲəxəɣ] recognising; *gen* aithneachaidh [aNʲəxɪ]

àlainn   [a:LɪNʲ] *adj* beautiful; *comp* àille [a:Lʲə]

Alastair   [aLəsdɪrʲ] *pnm* Alistair

Alba   [aLabə] *pnf* Scotland; *gen* na h-~ [nə haLabə] • ~ Nuadh [aLabə nuəɣ] Nova Scotia

Albannach   [aLabəNəx] *nm* Scotsman; *gen* & *pl* Albannaich [aLabəNɪç]

allt   [auLd] *nm* burn; *gen* & *pl* uillt [uiLʲdʲ] • ~ a' Bhonnaich [aLdə'voNɪç] Bannockburn

àm   [aum] *nm* time; *gen* ama [amə] *pl* amannan [aməNən]

a-mach   [ə'max] *adv* out (movement)

amadan   [amədan] *nm* fool; *gen* & *pl* amadain [amədɛNʲ]

amar   [amər] *nm* basin; *gen* amair [amɪrʲ] *pl* ~an [amərən] • ~-snàimh [amər'sNa:v] swimming pool

a-màireach   [ə'ma:rʲəx] *adv* tomorrow

Ameireaga   see Aimeireaga

a-muigh   [ə'muj] *adv* outside (location)

an 1   [ən] *poss pron* their; before F B M P am [əm], before C G [əŋ]

an 2   [əNⁱ] see ann an

anabarrach   [anabaRəx] *adj* extremely

anail   [anal] *nf* breath; *gen* analach [anaLəx] *pl* ~ean [analən]

a-nall   [ə'nauL] *adv* over here (motion towards speaker)

anart   [anəRʃd] *nm* linen; *gen* anairt [anəRʃdʲ] *pl* anairtean [anəRsʃdʲən]

an-còmhnaidh   [əŋ'kõ:nɪ] always

an-dé   [əNʲⁱdʲe:] *adv* yesterday; *coll* [ə'Nʲe:]

an dèidh   [əNʲ dʲe:] *prep* after

an-diugh   [əNʲⁱdʲu] *adv* today; *coll* [ə'Nʲu]

an-dràsta   [əN'dra:sdə] *adv* now

an iar   [ə Nʲiər] *adj* western

a-nìos   [ə'Nʲiəs] *adv* up (motion towards speaker)

a-nis   [ə'niʃ] *adv* now

anmoch [anaməx] *adv* late; *comp* anmoiche [anaməçə]

ann an [aNəN⁽ʲ⁾] *prep* in; *short* an [əN⁽ʲ⁾] *def prep* anns an
[auNsəN⁽ʲ⁾] *short* [asəN⁽ʲ⁾] san [səN⁽ʲ⁾] & sa [sə] *def prep*
pl anns na [auNsnə] *short* sna [snə] conjugated annam
[aNəm] annad [aNəd] ann [auN] innte [ĩːNʲdʲə] annainn
[aNɪNʲ] annaibh [aNəv] annta [ãũNdə] conjugated with
poss pron 'nam [nam] 'nad [nad] 'na [na] 'na h- [na h]
'nar n- [nar n] 'nur n- [nar n] 'nan [nan]

Anna [aNə] *pnf* Ann

annasach [aNəsəx] *adj* unusual; *comp* annasaiche [aNəsɪçə]

a-nochd [əˈNɔxg] *adv* tonight

an-raoir [əˈRɣirʲ] *adv* last night

an-seo [əˈʃɔ] *adv* here (location)

an-sin [əˈʃin] *adv* there

an-siud [əˈʃid] *adv* over there

a-nuas [əˈNuəs] *adv* down (motion towards speaker)

an-uiridh [əˈNurʲɪ] *adv* last year

a-null [əˈNuːL] *adv* over there (motion away from speaker)

aodach [ɯːdəx] *nm* clothes; *gen* aodaich [ɯːdɪç]

aodann [ɯːdəN] *nm* face; *gen* & *pl* aodainn [ɯːdɪNʲ]

aoigheachd [ɣjəxg] *nf* hospitality

aois [ɯːʃ] *nf* age; *gen* ~e [ɯːʃə] *pl* ~ean [ɯːʃən]

aon [ɯ̃ːn] *num* one; *counting form* a h-~ [ə hɯ̃ːn] • ~ deug
[ɯ̃ːn dʲiag] 11

aonach [ɯːnəx] *nm* high lying heath; *gen* aonaich [ɯːnɪç] *pl*
aonaichean [ɯːnɪçən] • An t-~ Eagach [əN tɯːnəx egəx]
Aonach Eagach • An t-~ Mór [əN tɯːnəx moːr] Aonach
Mor

aonad [ɯːnəd] *nm* unit; *gen* aonaid [ɯːnɪdʲ] *pl* ~an [ɯːnədən]

aonaichte [ɯːnɪçdʲə] *adj* united

aonan [ɯːnan] *nm* one (person)

Aonghas [ɯnɯ.əs] *pnm* Angus; *gen* & *voc* Aonghais [ɯnɯ.ɪʃ]

aosta [ɯːsdə] *adj* aged

aotrom [ɯːdrəm] *adj* light; *comp* aotruime [ɯːdrəmə]

Apainn, an ~ [ə NahbɪNʲ] *pnf* Appin; *gen* na h-Apainne [nə hahbɪNʲə]

ar [ər] *poss pron* our; see ar n-

àraidh [aːrɪ] *adj* certain; *comp* ~e [aːrɪ.ə]

Arainn [arɪNʲ] *pnf* Arran

Arainneach [arɪNʲəx] a person from Arran; *gen* & *voc* & *pl* Arainnich
[arɪNʲɪç]

aran [aran] *nm* bread; *gen* arain [arɛNʲ] • ~-coirce [aranˈkɔrʲgʲə] oatcake

àras [aːrəs] *nm* dwelling; *gen* àrais [arɛNʲ] *pl* ~an [aːrəsən]

Àrasaig [aːrəsɛgʲ] *pnf* Arisaig

arbhar [aravər] *nm* corn; *gen* arbhair [aravɪrʲ]

Arcaibh [argəv] *pnf* Orkney • Na h-~ [nə hargəv] the Orkneys

àrd [aːRd] *adj* high; *pl* ~a [aːRdə] *comp* àirde [aːRdʲə]

àrd-sgoil [aːRdsgɔl] *nf* secondary school; *gen* ~e [aːRdsgɔlə] *pl* ~tean [aːRdsgɔldʲən]

a-riamh [əˈrʲiəv] *adv* ever

a-rithist [əˈrʲi.ɪʃdʲ] *adv* again

arm [aram] *nm* 1 weapon 2 army; *gen* & *pl* airm [ɛrʲɛm]

ar n- [ər n] *poss pron* our; n- is lost before consonant: ar n-athair [ər nahərʲ] ⇔ ar màthair [ər maːhərʲ]

arsa [aRsə] *v hr* says, said

Asainte [asɪNʲdʲə] *pnf* Assynt

ás déidh [as dʲeː] *prep* after

a-staigh [əˈsdɤj] *adv* inside (location)

astar [asdər] *nm* distance; *gen* astair [asdɪrʲ] *pl* ~an [asdərən]

a-steach [əˈʃdʲɛx] *adv* inside (motion)

Astràilia [asˈdraːlja] *nf* Australia

Astràilianach [asˈdraːljanəx] *nm* Australian; *gen* & *pl* Astràilianaich [asˈdraːljanɪç]

ath [ah] *adj* next

àth [aː] *nm* ford; *pl* ~an [aː.ən]

athair [ahərʲ] *nm* father; *gen* athar [ahər] *pl* athraichean [arɪçən]

Athall [ahəL] *pnf* Atholl; *gen* Athaill [ahɪLʲ]

atharraich [ahəRɪç] 1 *v* to change 2 *vn* & *nm* atharrachadh [ahəRəxəɣ] change, changing; *gen* atharrachaidh [ahəRəxɪ] *pl* atharrachaidhean [ahəRəxɪ.ən]

BEITH [beh]

bac [baxg] *nm* hollow; *gen* baic [baçgʲ] *pl* ~an [baxgən]

baga [bagə] *nm* bag; *pl* ~ichean [bagɪçən]

bàgh [baːɣ] *nm* bay; *gen* bàigh [baːj] *pl* ~an [baːɣən] • ~ a' Chaisteil [baɣəˈxaʃdʲal] Castlebay • ~ a Tuath [baɣəˈtuə] Northbay

Bàideanach [baːdʲənəx] *pn* Badenoch; *gen* Bhàideanach [vaːdʲənəx]

baile [balə] *nm* town; *pl* bailtean [baldʲən] • ~ a' Chnuic [balə xn̪ũçgʲ] Balchrick • ~ Àirneach [bal'a:RNʲəx] Balerno • ~ Àtha Cliath [bala'kliəh] Dublin • ~ Dubhthaich [balə'ɣuhɪç] Tain

bainne [baNʲə] *nm* milk

baisteadh [baʃdʲəɣ] *nm* baptism; *gen* baistidh [baʃdʲɪ] *pl* baistidhean [baʃdʲɪ.ən]

baisteach [baʃdʲəx] *nm* baptist *comp* baistiche [baʃdʲɪçə]

balach [baLəx] *nm* boy; *gen* & *pl* balaich [baLɪç]

balgam [baLagəm] *nm* mouthful; *gen* balgaim [baLagəm] *pl* ~an [baLagəmən]

balgan [baLagan] *nm* small bag; *gen* & *pl* balgain [baLagɛNʲ] • ~- buachair [baLagɛNʲ'buəxɪrʲ] mushroom

ball [bauL] *nm* member, ball; *gen* & *pl* buill [buiLʲ] • ~-coise [baL'kɔʃə] football

balla [baLə] *nm* wall; *pl* ~chan [baLəxən]

bàn [ba:n] *adj* white (hair or fur); *pl* ~a [ba:nə] *comp* bàine [ba:Nʲə]

ban(a)- [ban(a)] *pref* female; the form ban- before an unlenited consonant or a vowel is usually [bãũN]; bana- is usually pronounced [bana]:
ban-dia [bãũN dʲiə] goddess • ban-ogha [bãũN o.ə] granddaughter • banrigh [bãũNrɪ] queen ban-tigheama [bãũN tʲi.əRNə] lady
Bana-Bharrach [bana'vaRəx] a woman from Barra • bana-charaid [bana xarɪdʲ] female friend • Bana-Leòdhasach [bana'Lɔ:.əsəx] a woman from Lewis

banais [banɪʃ] *nf* wedding reception; *gen* bainnse [bãĩʃə] *pl* bainnsean [bãĩʃən]

Banbh [banav] *pnf* Banff; *gen* Bhanbh [vanav]

banca [baŋgə] *nm* bank; *pl* ~n [baŋgən]

bann [bauN] *nm* band; *gen* ~a [baNə] *pl* ~an [baNən]

bàr [ba:r] *nm* bar; *gen* bàir [ba:rʲ] *pl* ~aichean [ba:rɪçən]

barail [baral] *nf* surmise; *gen* baralach [baraLəx] *pl* ~ean [baralən]

baraille [barɪLʲə] *nf* barrel; *pl* ~an [barɪLʲən]

bargan [baragan] *nm* bargain; *gen* & *pl* bargain [baragɛNʲ]

bàrd [ba:Rd] *nm* poet; *gen* & *pl* bàird [ba:Rdʲ] • bana-bhàrd [bana va:Rd] *nf* poetess; *gen* & *pl* bana-bhàird [bana va:Rdʲ]

bàrdachd [ba:Rdəxg] *nf* poetry

barr [baR] *nm* cream; *gen* ~a [baRə] *pl* ~an [baRən]

Barrach [baRəx] *nm* a person from Barra; *gen* & *pl* Barraich [baRɪç]

barrachd [baRəxg] *nf* more ("more-ness")

Barraigh [baRaj] *pnm* Barra; *gen* Bharraigh [vaRaj]

barrall [baRəL] *nf* shoelace; *gen* barraill [baRɪLʲ] *pl* ~an [baRəLən]

bas [bas] *nf* palm; *gen* boise [boʃə] *pl* basan [basən]

bàs [ba:s] *nm* death; *gen* bàis [ba:ʃ] *pl* ~an [ba:sən]

bàsaich [ba:sɪç] 1 *v* to die; 2 *vn* & *nm* bàsachadh [ba:səxəɣ] dying; *gen* bàsachaidh [ba:səxɪ]

basgaid [basgadʲ] *nf* basket; *gen* ~e [basgadʲə] *pl* ~ean [basgadʲən]

bata [bahdə] *nm* stick; *pl* ~ichean [bahdɪçən]

bàta [ba:hdə] *nm* & *nf* boat; *pl* ~ichean [ba:hdɪçən]

bàthadh [ba:həɣ] *vn* & *nm* drowning; *gen* bàthaidh [ba:hɪ] *pl* bàthaidhean [ba:hɪ.ən]

beachd [bɛxg] *nm* opinion; *pl* ~an [bɛxgən]

beag [beg] *adj* small; *pl* ~a [begə] 1ˢᵗ *comp* lugha [Luɣə] 2ⁿᵈ *comp* lughaide [Luɣɪdʲə]

beagan [began] *nm* a little ("littleness"); *gen* beagain [begɛNʲ]

bealach [bjaLəx] *nm* passage; *gen* bealaich [bjaLɪç] *pl* bealaichean [bjaLɪçən]

beairteach [bjaRʃdʲəx] *adj* rich; *comp* beairtiche [bjaRʃdʲɪçə]

bean [bɛn] *nf* wife; *gen* mnatha [mrã.ə] *dat* mnaoi [mrũj] *pl* mnathan [mrã.ən] *gen pl* bhan [van] • ~-stiùiridh [bɛnʲʃdʲu:rʲɪ] female director

beannachd [bjaNəxg] *nf* blessing; *pl* ~an [bjaNəxgən]

beàrn [bja:RN] *nf* gap; *gen* beàirn [bja:RNʲ] *pl* ~an [bja:RNən]

Beàrnaraigh [bja:RNəraj] *pnm* Berneray; *gen* Bheàrnaraigh [vja:RNəraj]

Beasag [besag] *pnf* Bessie; *gen* Bheasag [vesag] *voc* a Bheasag [ə vesag]

beatha [bɛhə] *nf* life

bèicear [bɛ:çgʲɛr] *nm* baker; *gen* bèiceir [bɛ:çgʲɛrʲ] *pl* ~an [bɛ:çgʲɛrən] • ~eachd [bɛ:çgʲɛrəxg] baking

being [beiŋʲgʲ] *nf* bench; *gen* ~e [beiŋʲgʲə] *pl* ~an [beiŋʲgʲən]

beinn [beiNʲ] *nf* mountain; *gen* ~e [beNʲə] *pl* beanntan
[bjauNdən] • A' Bheinn Mhór [ə veiNʲ vo:r] Benmore • A'
Bheinn Bhàn [ə veiNʲ va:n] Benvane • ~ a' Bhaoghla
[beNʲə vɣ:Lə] Benbecula • ~ na h-Iolaire
[beiNʲ nə hjuLɪrʲə] Benyellary • ~ Nibheis [be'Nʲivɪʃ] Ben
Nevis

beò [bjɔ:] *adj* alive; *pl* ~tha [bjɔ:.ə]

beul [biaL] *nm* mouth; *gen* & *pl* beòil [bjɔ:l] • ~-aithris [biaLərʲɪʃ]
folklore, oral tradition

Beurla [be:RLə] *nf* English (language); *gen* na ~ [nə be:RLə] • A'
Bheurla [ə ve:RLə] English

Bhatarsaigh [vahdəRsaj] *pnm* Vatarsay

Bhatarsach [vahdəRsəx] *nm* a person from Vatersay; *gen* & *pl*
Bhatarsaich [vahdəRsɪç]

Bheilg, a' ~ [ə velegʲ] *pnf* Belgium; *gen* na Beilge [nə belegʲə]

bho [vo] *prep* from; *def prep* bhon an [vonəNⁱ] *def prep pl*
bho na [vonə] *conjugated* bhuam [vuəm] bhuat [vuəhd]
bhuaidhe [vuəjə] bhuaipe [vuəhbə] bhuainn [vuəNʲ]
buaibh [vuəv] bhuapa [vuəhbə] • ~ chionn ghoirid
[vo çu:N ɣɣrʲɪdʲ] recently

Bhreatainn [ə vrʲɛhdɪNʲ veg] *pnf* Brittany; *gen* na Breatainne Bige
  Bheag, a' ~ [nə brʲɛhdɪNʲə bigʲə]

biadh [biəɣ] 1 *v* to feed 2 *vn* & *nm* ~adh [biəhəɣ] feeding 3 *nm*
food; *gen* bìdh [bi:]

bìd [bi:dʲ] 1 *v* to bite 2 *vn* & *nm* ~eadh [bi:dʲəɣ] biting

bile [bilə] *nf* lip; *pl* ~an [bilən]

bileag [bilag] *nf* leaflet; *gen* bileige [bilɛgʲə] *pl* ~an [bilagən]

bìoball [bi:bəL] *nm* bible; *gen* & *pl* bìobaill [bi:bɪLʲ]

bith [bih] *nf* existence; *pl* ~ean [bihən] • sam ~ [səm bih] at all

blais [bLaʃ] 1 *v* to taste 2 *vn* & *nm* blasad [bLasəd] tasting

blàr [bLa:r] *nm* battlefield; *gen* & *pl* blàir [bLa:rʲ]

blàth [bLa:] *adj* warm; *pl* ~a [bLa:.ə] *comp* blàithe [bLa:jə]

blàthach [bLa:həx] *nf* buttermilk; *gen* & *pl* blàthaich [bLa:hɪç]

bliadhna [bliəNə] *nf* year; *pl* ~ichean [bliəNɪçən] • A' Bhliadhna Ùr
[ə vliə Nu:r] New Year • ~ Mhath Ùr [bliəNə va u:r]
Happy New Year

bó [bo:] *nf* cow; *gen* & *pl* bà [ba:] *gen pl* bhó [vo:]

boc [bɔxg] *nm* buck; *gen* & *pl* buic [buçgʲ]

bòc	[bɔːxg] 1 *v* prance 2 *vn & nm* bòcadh [bɔːxgəɣ] *gen* bòcaidh [bɔːxgɪ]
bochd	[bɔxg] *adj* poor; *pl* ~a [bɔxgə]
bodach	[bɔdəx] *nm* old man; *gen & pl* bodaich [bɔdɪç] • ~-ròcais [bɔdəxˈRɔːxgɪʃ] scarecrow
Bòdach	[bɔːdəx] *nm* a person from Bute; *gen & pl* Bòdaich [bɔːdɪç]
bog	[bog] *adj* soft; *pl* ~a [bogə] *comp* buige [buigʲə]
bogaich	[bogɪç] 1 *v* to soak 2 *vn & nm* bogachadh [bogəxəɣ] soaking; *gen* bogachaidh [bogəxɪ]
bogha	[bo.ə] *nm* bow; *pl* ~nnan [bo.əNən] • ~-frois [bo.əˈfrɔʃ] rainbow
boglach	[bogLəx] *nf* quagmire; *gen* boglaiche [bogLɪçə] *pl* boglaichean [bogLɪçən]
bogsa	[bogsə] *nm* box; *pl* ~ichean [bogsɪçən] • ~-litreach [bogsəˈLʲihdrəx] letter-box
Bòid	[bɔːdʲ] *pn* Bute; *gen* Bhòid [vɔːdʲ]
bòidheach	[bɔːjəx] *adj* beautiful; *comp* bòidhche [bɔːçə]
boinne	[boNʲə] *nf* drop; *pl* ~an [boNʲən]
bonaid	[bonadʲ] *nf* bonnet; *gen* ~e [bonadʲə] *pl* ~ean [bonadʲən]
boireann	[borʲəN] *adj* female; *comp* boirinne [borʲɪNʲə]
boireannach	[borʲəNəx] *nm* woman; *gen & pl* boireannaich [borʲəNɪç]
bonn	[bouN] *nm* base; *gen & pl* buinn [buiNʲ]
borbair	[borɔbɛrʲ] *nm* barber; *pl* ~ean [borɔbɛrʲən]
bòrd	[bɔːRd] *nm* table; *gen & pl* bùird [buːRdʲ] • ~-sanais [bɔRdˈsanɪʃ] notice board
bòtann	[bɔːhdəN] *nm* wellington; *gen* bòtainn [bɔːhdɪNʲ] *pl* ~an [bɔːhdəNən]
botal	[bohdəL] *nm* bottle; *gen & pl* botail [bohdəl]
Both Càrna	[bohˈkaːRnə] *pnm* Muckairn; *gen* Bhoth Càrna [vohˈkaːRnə]
bracaist	[braxgɪʃdʲ] *nf* breakfast; *gen* ~e [braxgɪʃdʲə] *pl* ~an [braxgɪʃdʲən]
bradan	[bradan] *nm* salmon; *gen & pl* bradain [bradɛNʲ]
bràghad	[braː.əd] *nm* upper part; *gen* bràghaid [braː.ɪdʲ] *pl* ~an [braː.ədən] • ~ Albainn [braːdˈaLabɪNʲ] Breadalbane
bràigh	[braːj] *nm* brae; *gen* ~e [braːjə] *pl* ~achan [braːjəxən] • Am ~ Riabhach [əm braːj Rɪəvəx] Braeriach • ~ Mharr [brajˈvaːR] Braemar
brat	[brahd] *nm* mantle; *gen* brait [brahdʲ] *pl* ~an [brahdən]

brath	[brah] *nm* advantage; *gen* ~a [brahə]
bràth	[bra:] *nm* judgement; *gen* ~a [bra:.ə]
bràthair	[bra:hərʲ] *nm* brother; *gen* bràthar [bra:hər] *pl* bràithrean [bra:rʲən]
breabadair	[brʲɛbədɛrʲ] *nm* weaver; *pl* ~ean [brʲɛbədɛrʲən]
breac	[brʲɛxg] *nm* trout; *gen* & *pl* bric [brʲiçgʲ]
brèagha	[brʲia.ə] *adj* lovely
Breatann	[brʲɛhdəN] *pnf* Britain; *gen* Bhreatainn [vrʲɛhdɪNʲ]
breith	[brʲeh] see at end of wordlist
Brìde	[brʲi:dʲə] *pnf* Brigit; *voc* a Bhrìde [ə vrʲi:dʲə]
briogais	[brʲigɪʃ] *nf* trousers; *gen* ~e [brʲigɪʃə] *pl* ~ean [brʲigɪʃən]
briosgaid	[brʲisgɪdʲ] *nf* biscuit; *gen* ~e [brʲisgɪdʲə] *pl* ~ean [brʲisgɪdʲən]
bris	[brʲiʃ] 1 *v* to break 2 *vn* & *nm* ~eadh [brʲiʃəɣ] breaking; *gen* ~idh [brʲiʃɪ]
brisgean	[brʲiʃgʲan] *nm* gristle; *gen* & *pl* brisgein [brʲiʃgʲɛNʲ]
briste	[brʲiʃdʲə] *adj* broken
brochan	[brɔxan] *nm* porridge; *gen* & *pl* brochain [brɔxɛNʲ]
bròg	[brɔ:g] *nf* shoe; *gen* bròige [brɔ:gʲə] *pl* ~an [brɔ:gən] • ~-chuibhle [brɔg'xwilə] rollerskate
Bròlas	[brɔ:Ləs] *pnm* Brolass; *gen* Bhròlais [vrɔ:Lɪʃ]
brònach	[brɔ:nəx] *adj* sad; *comp* brònaiche [brɔ:nɪçə]
brot	[brɔhd] *nm* soup; *gen* ~a [brɔhdə] *pl* ~an [brɔhdən]
bruach	[bruəx] *nf* bank (of a river etc); *gen* bruaich [bruəç] *pl* bruaichean [bruəçən]
bruidhinn	[bri.ɪNʲ] 1 *v* to speak; *fut* bruidhnidh [bri:nɪ] *fut rel* bhruidhneas [vri:nəs] 2 *vn* & *nf* bruidhinn [bri.ɪNʲ]
bruis	[bruʃ] *nf* brush; *gen* ~e [bruʃə] *pl* ~eachan [bruʃəxən]
brùth	[bru:] 1 *v* to press 2 *vn* & *nm* ~adh [bru:.əɣ] pressing; *gen* ~aidh [bru:.ɪ]
buachaille	[buəxɪLʲə] *nm* cowherd; *pl* ~an [buəxɪLʲən]
buail	[buəl] 1 *v* to hit 2 *vn* & *nm* bualadh [buəLəɣ] hitting; *gen* bualaidh [buəLɪ] *pl* bualaidhean [buəLɪ.ən]
buaireadh	[buərʲəɣ] *nm* temptation; *gen* buairidh [buərʲɪ]
buannaich	[buəNɪç] 1 *v* to win 2 *vn* & *nm* buannachadh [buəNəxəɣ] winning; *gen* buannachaidh [buəNəxɪ]
bucaid	[buxgadʲ] *nf* bucket; *gen* ~e [buxgadʲə] *pl* ~eachan [buxgadʲən]
buidhe	[bujə] *adj* yellow

buidsear   [budʲʃɛr] *nm* butcher; *gen* buidseir [budʲʃɛrʲ] *pl* ~an
              [budʲʃɛrən]
buileach   [buləx] *adj* complete
buin   [buNʲ] 1 *v* to belong to 2 *vn* & *nm* ~eadh [buNʲəɣ]
              belonging to; *gen* ~idh [buNʲɪ]
buinig   [buNʲɪgʲ] 1 *v* to win 2 *vn* & *nm* ~eadh [buNʲɪgʲəɣ] winning
buntàta   [bənˈtahdə] *nm* potato
bus   [bəs] *nm* bus; *pl* ~aichean [bəsɪçən]
bùth   [bu:] *nf* shop; *gen* ~a [bu.ə] *pl* ~an [bu:.ən]

COLL [kɔuL]

cab   [kab] *nm* gab; *gen* & *pl* caib [kaib]
cabar   [kabər] *nm* pole; *gen* & *pl* cabair [kabɪrʲ] • ~ féidh
              [kabərˈfe:] antlers
cabhag   [kavag] *nf* hurry; *gen* cabhaige [kavɛgʲə]
cadal   [kadəL] *nm* sleep; *gen* cadail [kadəl]
cadha   [ka.a] *nm* ravine; *pl* ~ichean [ka.ɪçən]
caibideil   [kabɪdʲal] *nf* chapter; *gen* ~e [kabɪdʲalə] *pl* ~ean
              [kabɪdʲalən]
caidil   [kadʲɪl] 1 *v* to sleep 2 *vn* & *nm* cadal [kadəL] sleep,
              sleeping; *gen* cadail [kadəl]
càil   [ka:l] *nm* anything
caileag   [kalag] *nf* girl; *gen* caileige [kalɛgʲə] *pl* ~an [kalagən]
Cailean   [kalan] *pnm* Colin; *gen* Chailein [xalɛNʲ] *voc* a Chailein
              [ə xalɛNʲ]
caill   [kaiLʲ] 1 *v* to lose 2 *vn* & *nm* call [kauL] loosing, loss; *gen*
              ~ [kaiLʲ] • air chall [ɛrʲ xauL] lost
cailleach   [kaLʲəx] *nf* old woman; *gen* cailliche [kaLʲɪçə] *pl* ~an
              [kaLʲəxən]
cailleachail [kaLʲəxal] *adj* old womanish; *comp* ~e [kaLʲəxalə]
Caimbeul   [kaimbəL] *pnm* Campbell
A' Chaingis   [ə xɛŋʲgʲɪʃ] *nf* Pentecost; *gen* na Caingis [nə kɛŋʲgʲɪʃ]
cairt   [kaRʃdʲ] *nf* card; *gen* ~each [kaRʃdʲəx] *pl* ~ean [kaRʃdʲən] •
              ~-phuist [kaRʃdʲˈfuʃdʲ] postcard • ~-shiubhail
              [kaRʃdʲˈhju.əl] passport
cairteal   [kaRʃdʲal] 1 *nm* quarter 2 *v* to quarter 2 *vn* & *nm* ~adh
              [kaRʃdʲaləɣ] quartering
càise   [ka:ʃə] *nf* cheese; *pl* ~an [ka:ʃən]
caismeachd   [kaʃməxg] *nf* alarm; *pl* ~an [kaʃməxgən]

caisteal	[kaʃdʲaL] *nm* castle; *gen* caisteil [kaʃdʲɛl] *pl* ~an [kaʃdʲaLən] • ~-gainmhich [kaʃdʲaL'gɛnɛvɪç] sandcastle
càite	[ka:hdʲə] *interr* where? • ~ an…? [ka:hdʲ əN⁽ʲ⁾] where…?
caitligeach	[kahdligəx] *adj* catholic; *comp* caitligiche [kahdlɪgʲɪçə]
cala	[kaLə] *nm* harbour; *pl* calachan [kaLəxən]
Calanais	[kaLanɪʃ] *pn* Callanish; *gen* Chalanais [xaLanɪʃ]
calma	[kaLamə] *adj* brave
Calum	[kaLəm] *pnm* Calum; *gen* Chaluim [xaLəm] *voc* a Chaluim [ə xaLəm]
caman	[kaman] *nm* (shinty) stick; *gen* & *pl* camain [kamɛNʲ]
camara	[kamərə] *nm* camera; *pl* ~than [kamərə.ən]
camas	[kaməs] *nm* cove; *gen* camais [kamɪʃ] *pl* ~an [kaməsən]
campa	[kaumbə] *nm* camp; *pl* ~ichean [kaumbɪçən]
campaich	[kaumbɪç] 1 *v* to camp 2 *vn* & *nm* ~adh [kaumbəɣ] camping; *gen* ~idh [kaumbɪ]
Camshron	[kamarən] *pnm* Cameron
can	[kan] 1 *v* to say 2 *vn* & *nm* ~tainn [kandɪNʲ] saying
cana	[kanə] *nm* can; *pl* ~ichean [kanɪçən]
Canada	[kanadə] *pnf* Canada; *gen* Chanada [xanadə]
Canaigh	[kanaj] *pnm* Canna; *gen* Chanaigh [xanaj]
cànan	[ka:nan] *nm* language; *gen* & *pl* cànain [ka:nɛNʲ]
caogad	[kɯ:gəd] *num* fifty
caoin	[kɯ:Nʲ] 1 *v* to weep 2 *vn* & *nm* ~eadh [kɯ:Nʲəɣ] weeping; *gen* ~idh [kɯ:Nʲɪ]
caol	[kɯ:L] *adj* narrow; *pl* ~a [kɯ:Lə] *comp* caoile [kɯ:lə]
caolas	[kɯ:Ləs] *nm* strait; *gen* caolais [kɯ:Lɪʃ] *pl* ~an [kɯ:Ləsən]
caomh	[kɯ:v] *adj* gentle; *pl* ~a [kɯ:və] *comp* caoimhe [kɯjə]
caora	[kɯ:rə] *nf* sheep; *gen* ~ach [kɯ:rəx] *pl* ~ich [kɯ:rɪç]
capall	[kahbəL] *nm* small horse; *gen* & *pl* capaill [kahbɪLʲ] • ~coille [kahbəL'kɣLʲə] capercailie
car	[kar] *nm* turn; *gen* cuir [kurʲ] *pl* ~an [karən]
càr	[ka:r] *nm* car; *gen* càir [ka:rʲ] *pl* ~aichean [ka:rɪçən]
carabhan	[karavan] *nm* caravan; *gen* carabhain [karavɛNʲ] *pl* ~aichean [karavanɪçən]
càraich	[ka:rɪç] 1 *v* to fix 2 *vn* & *nm* ~adh [ka:rəɣ] fixing; *gen* ~idh [ka:rɪ]
càraid	[ka:radʲ] *nf* couple; *gen* ~e [ka:radʲə] *pl* ~ean [ka:radʲən]
caraid	[karɪdʲ] *nm* friend; *pl* càirdean [ka:Rdʲən]
carbad	[karabəd] *nm* vehicle; *gen* carbaid [karabɪdʲ] *pl* ~an [karabədən]

Carghas, an ~	[əŋ karaɣəs] *nm* Lent; *gen* a' Charghais [ə xaraɣɪʃ]
càrn	[ka:RN] *nm* heap; *gen* & *pl* cùirn [ku:RNʲ] • An ~ Gorm
	[əŋ ka:RN gɔrɔm] Cairngorm
cas	[kas] *nf* leg; *gen* coise [kɔʃə] *pl* ~an [kasən] • an cois
	[əŋ kɔʃ] accompanying
casadaich	[kasədɪç] *nf* coughing
cat	[kahd] *nm* cat; *gen* & *pl* cait [kɛhdʲ]
Cataibh	[kahdəv] *pnm* Sutherland; *gen* Chataibh [xahdəv]
cath	[kah] *nm* battle; *gen* ~a [kahə] *pl* ~an [kahən]
càth	[ka:] *nf* chaff; *gen* ~a [ka:.ə]
cathair	[kahɪrʲ] *nf* city; *gen* cathrach [karəx] *pl* cathraichean
	[karɪçən]
Catrìona	[kaˈtriənə] *pnf* Catherine; *voc* a Chatrìona [ə xaˈtriənə]
cead	[kʲed] *nm* permission; *pl* ~an [kʲedən]
ceangail	[kɛ̃.ə̃l] 1 *v* to tie 2 *vn* & *nm* ceangal [kɛ̃.ə̃L] tying; *gen* ~
	[kɛ̃.ə̃l]
ceann	[kʲauN] *nm* head; *gen* & *pl* cinn [kʲi:Nʲ] • ~-bhaile
	[kʲaNəvalə] capital • ~-cropaig [kʲaNˈkrɔhbɛgʲ] stuffed
	cod-head • ~ Locha [kʲaNˈLɔxə] Kinloch • ~ Loch Gilb
	[kʲaNLɔxˈgʲilib] Lochgilphead • ~-suidhe [kʲauNˈsujə]
	president • ~-uidhe [kʲaNˈujə] destination
ceannaich	[kʲaNɪç] 1 *v* to buy 2 *vn* & *nm* ceannach [kʲaNəx] buying;
	gen ~ [kʲaNɪç]
ceap	[kʲɛhb] *nm* cape; *gen* cip [kʲihb] *pl* ~an [kʲɛhbən] • ~
	Breatainn [kʲɛhˈbrʲɛhdɪNʲ] Cape Breton
ceapaire	[kʲɛhbɛrʲə] *nm* sandwich; *pl* ~an [kʲɛhbɛrʲən]
cearc	[kʲɛrg] *nf* chicken; *gen* circe [kʲirʲkʲə] *pl* ~an [kʲɛrgən]
ceàrdach	[kʲa:Rdəx] *nm* smithy; *gen* ceàrdaich [kʲa:Rdɪç] *pl* ~ean
	[kʲa:Rdɪçən]
ceàrnag	[kʲa:RNag] *nf* square; *gen* ceàrnaige [kʲa:RNɛgʲə] *pl* ~an
	[kʲa:RNagən]
cearr	[kʲa:R] *adj* wrong; *pl* & *comp* ~a [kʲaRə]
ceart	[kʲaRʃd] 1 *nm* right 2 *adj* correct; *pl* ~a [kʲaRʃdə]
ceathrad	[kʲɛrəd] *num* fourty
ceathramh	[kʲɛrəv] *num* fourth
ceathrar	[kʲɛrər] *nm* four (people)
céic	[kʲe:çgʲ] *nm* cake; *gen* ~e [kʲe:çgʲə] *pl* ~ean [kʲe:çgʲən]
céile	[kʲe:lə] *nm* partner, spouse; *pl* ~an [kʲe:lən] • ri chéile
	[rʲi çe:lə] together
céilidh	[kʲe:lɪ] *nf* visit, ceilidh; *gen* ~e [kʲe:lɪ.ə] *pl* ~ean [kʲe:lɪ.ən]

Ceilteach	[kʲeldʲəx] 1 *adj* Celtic 2 *nm* Celt; *gen* & *pl* Ceiltich [kʲeldʲɪç]
ceistear	[kʲeʃdʲɛr] *nm* questioner; *gen* ceisteir [kʲeʃdʲɛrʲ] *pl* ~an [kʲeʃdʲɛrən]
ceithir	[kʲɛhɪrʲ] *num* four; *counting form* a ~ [ə kʲɛhɪrʲ]
ceòl	[kʲɔːL] *nm* music; *gen* ciùil [kʲuːl] • ~-mór [kʲɔLˈmoːr] pibroch
ceòlmhor	[kʲɔːLvər] *adj* musical; *comp* ceòlmhoire [kʲɔːLvərʲə]
ceud	[kʲiəd] *num* hundred; *pl* ~an [kʲiədən]
ceudamh	[kʲiədəv] *num* hundredth
ceum	[kʲeːm] *nm* step, degree; *gen* ~a [kʲeːmə] *pl* ~annan [kʲeːməNən]
Chàisg, a' ~	[ə xaːʃgʲ] *nf* Easter; *gen* na Càisge [nə kaːʃgʲə]
Chomraich, a' ~	[ə xomərɪç] *pnf* Applecross; *gen* na Comraich [nə komərɪç]
Chòrn, a' ~	[ə xɔːRN] *pnf* Cornwall; *gen* na Còirne [nə kɔːRNʲə]
Chuimrigh, a' ~	[ə xɯmuɾʲɪ] *pnf* Wales; *gen* na Cuimrigh [nə kɯmuɾʲɪ]
Chuimris, a' ~	[ə xɯmuɾʲɪʃ] *pnf* Welsh (language); *gen* na Cuimrise [nə kɯmuɾʲɪʃə]
ciad	[kʲiəd] *num* first • a' chiad [ə çiəd] the first
ciall	[kʲiəL] *nf* sense; *gen* céille [kʲeːLʲə]
ciamar	[kʲimar] *interr* how? • ~ a...? [kʲimar ə] how...?
cidhe	[kʲi.ə] *nf* quay; *pl* ~an [kʲi.ən]
cidsin	[kʲidʲʃɪn] *nf* kitchen; *pl* ~ean [kʲidʲʃɪnən]
cill	[kʲiːLʲ] *nf* churchyard; *gen* ~e [kʲiːLʲə] *pl* ~tean [kʲiːLʲdʲən] • ~ Mhearnaig [kʲiːLʲˈvɛːRNɛgʲ] Kilmarnock • ~ MoChumaig [kʲiːLʲməˈxumɛgʲ] Kilmahumaig • ~ Rìmhinn [kʲiːLʲˈriːvɪNʲ] St Andrews
cileagram	[kʲiləgram] *nm* kilogram; *pl* ~an [kʲiləgramən]
Cinn Tìre	[kʲiNʲˈtʲiːrʲə] *pnm* Kintyre; *gen* Chinn Tìre [çiNʲˈtʲiːrʲə]
cinneadh	[kʲiNʲəɣ] *nm* race; *gen* cinnidh [kʲiNʲɪ] *pl* cinnidhean [kʲiNʲɪ.ən]
cìobair	[kʲiːbɛrʲ] *nm* shepherd; *pl* ~ean [kʲiːbɛrʲən]
ciontach	[kʲiNdəx] *adj* guilty; *comp* ciontaiche [kʲindɪçə] • neo-chiontach [NʲɔçəNdəx] innocent
cìr	[kʲiːrʲ] *nf* comb; *gen* cìre [kʲiːrʲə] *pl* ~ean [kʲiːrʲən]
ciste	[kʲiʃdʲə] *nf* kist; *pl* ~eachan [kʲiʃdʲəxən]
clach	[kLax] *nf* stone; *gen* cloiche [kLɔçə] *pl* ~an [kLaxən]
clachair	[kLaxɛrʲ] *nm* stonemason; *pl* ~ean [kLaxɛrʲən]
clachan	[kLaxan] *nm* hamlet; *gen* clachain [kLaxɛNʲ] *pl* ~an [kLaxanən]

cladach	[kLadəx] *nm* shore; *gen* cladaich [kLadɪç] *pl* cladaichean [kLadɪçən]
cladhaich	[kLɣ.ɪx] 1 *v* to dig 2 *vn* & *nm* cladhach [kLɣ.əx] digging; *gen* ~ [kLɣ.ɪç]
claidheamh	[kLajəv] *nm* sword; *gen* claidheimh [kLajəv] *pl* ~an [kLajəvən]
clann	[kLauN] *nf* children; *gen* cloinne [kLɣNʲə] • clàr-bìdh [kLarʹbiː] menu
clàr	[kLaːr] *nm* board; *gen* & *pl* clàir [kLaːrʲ]
clàrsach	[kLaːRsəx] *nm* harp; *gen* clàrsaich [kLaːRsɪç] *pl* clàrsaichean [kLaːRsɪçən]
cléireach	[kleːrʲəx] *nm* clerk; *gen* & *pl* cléirich [kleːrʲɪç]
clì	[kliː] *adj* left
clò	[kLɔː] *nm* cloth, tweed; *gen* ~tha [kLɔː.ə] *pl* ~than [kLɔː.ən] • ~-mór [kLɔʹmoːr] Harris Tweed
clobha	[kLo.ə] *nm* tong; *pl* -chan [kLo.əxən]
clò-bhuail	[kLɔʹvuəl] 1 *v* to print 2 *vn* & *nm* clò-bhualadh [kLɔʹvuəLəɣ] print, printing; *gen* clò-bhualaidh [kLɔʹvuəLɪ] *pl* clò-bhualaidhean [kLɔʹvuəLɪ.ən]
cluas	[kLuəs] *nf* ear; *gen* cluaise [kLuəʃə] *pl* ~an [kLuəsən]
cluich	[kLuç] 1 *nf* play; *gen* ~e [kLuçə] *pl* ~ean [kLuçən] 2 *v* to play 3 *vn* & *nf* ~e [kLuçə] playing
cnap	[krãhb] *nm* lump; *gen* cnaip [krɛ̃hb] *pl* cnapan [krãhbən]
Cnapadal	[krãhbədaL] *pnm* Knapdale; *gen* Chnapadail [xrãhbədal]
cnatan	[krãhdan] *nm* a cold; *gen* cnatain [krãhdɛNʲ]
cnoc	[krɔ̃xg] *nm* hill; *gen* & *pl* cnuic [krũ̃çgʲ] • An ~ Mór [ən krɔ̃xg moːr] Knockmore • ~ a' Chapaill [krɔ̃xg ə xahbɪLʲ] Cnoc a' Chapuill
cnocan	[krɔ̃xgan] *nm* little hill; *gen* & *pl* cnocain [krɔ̃xgɛNʲ] • An ~ Dubh [ən krɔ̃xgan du] Knockando
Cnòideart	[krɔ̃ːdʲəRʃd] *pnm* Knoydart; *gen* Chnòideirt [xrɔ̃ːdʲəRʃdʲ]
có	[koː] *interr* who? • ~ a...? [koː] who...? short co [kɔ] • co-dhiù [kɔʹjuː] anway • co mheud [kɔʹviad] how many?
còcaireachd	[kɔːxgɛrʲəxg] *nf* cooking
cofaidh	[kɔfɪ] *nm* coffee; *pl* ~ean [kɔfɪ.ən]
cóig	[koːgʲ] *num* five; counting form a cóig [ə koːgʲ]
Cóigeach	[koːgʲəx] *pnf* Coigach; *gen* Cóigich [koːgʲɪç]
cóigeamh	[koːgʲəv] *num* fifth
cóignear	[koːgʲər] *nm* five (people)
coileach	[kɣləx] *nm* cockerel; *gen* & *pl* coilich [kɣlɪç]

coille [kɤLʲə] *nf* forest; *pl* coilltean [kɤiLʲdʲən]

coimhead [kõjad] 1 *v* to look 2 *vn* & *nm* ~ [kõjad] looking; *gen* coimhid [kõjɪdʲ]

coimhearsnachd [kõjəRsnəxg] *nf* community; *pl* ~an [kõjəRsnəxgən]

coinean [kɔNʲan] *nm* rabbit; *gen* coinein [kɔNʲɛNʲ] *pl* ~an [kɔNʲanən]

Coinneach [kɤNʲəx] *pnm* Kenneth; *gen* Choinnich [xɤNʲɪç] *voc* a Choinnich [ə xɤNʲɪç]

còinneach [kɔːNʲəx] *nf* moss; *gen* còinnich [kɔːNʲɪç]

coinneal [kɤNʲəL] *nf* right; *gen* coinnle [kɤ̃ĩLʲə] *pl* coinnlean [kɤ̃ĩLʲən]

coinneamh [kɤNʲəv] *nf* meeting; *gen* coinneimh [kɤNʲəv] *pl* ~an [kɤNʲəvən] • mu choinneamh [məˈxɤNʲəv] opposite

coinnich [kɤNʲɪç] 1 *v* to meet 2 *vn* & *nm* coinneachadh [kɤNʲəxəɣ] meeting

còir [kɔːrʲ] *nf* right; *gen* còrach [kɔːrəx] *pl* còraichean [kɔːrɪçən]

coirce [kɔrʲçgʲə] *nm* oats

coire [kɔrʲə] *nm* kettle; *pl* ~achan [kɔrʲəxən]

coisich [kɔʃɪç] 1 *v* to walk 2 *vn* & *nf* coiseachd [kɔʃəxg] walking

Cola [kɔLə] *pn* Coll; *gen* Chola [xɔLə]

co-là [koˈLaː] *nm* anniversary; *pl* ~-làithean [koˈLaːjən]

cola-deug [kɔLaˈdʲiag] *nf* fortnight

colaiste [kɔLaʃdʲə] *nf* college; *pl* colaistean [kɔLaʃdʲən]

Colbhasa [kɔLɔ.əsə] *pnm* Colonsay; *gen* Cholbhasa [xɔLɔ.əsə]

coltach [kɔLdəx] *adj* similar; *comp* coltaiche [kɔLdɪçə]

coma [komə] *adj* indifferent

comain [komɛNʲ] *nf* obligation; *gen* ~e [komɛNʲə] *pl* ~ean [komɛNʲən] • 'nad chomain [nad xomɛNʲ] indebted to you

comann [koməN] *nm* association; *gen* & *pl* comainn [komɪNʲ]

comar [komər] *nm* confluence; *gen* comair [komɪrʲ] *pl* ~an [komərən] • ~ nan Allt [komər nə NauLd]

cofhurtail [kõ.əRʃdal] *adj* comfortable; *comp* ~e [kõ.əRʃdalə]

Còmhghall [kõːɣəL] *pnm* Cowal; *gen* Chòmhghaill [xõːɣɪLʲ]

comhairle [kõ.əRlə] *nf* advice, council; *pl* ~an [kõ.əRlən] • ~ nan Eilean Siar [kõ.əRlə nə Nʲelan ʃiər] Western Isles Council

comhairliche [kõ.əRlɪçə] *nm* councillor; *pl* ~an [kõ.əRlɪçən]

còmhla [kõːLə] 1 *nf* shutter; *pl* ~ichean [kõːLɪçən] 2 *adv* together

còmhradh [kõːraɣ] *nm* conversation; *gen* còmhraidh [kõːraj] *pl* còmhraidhean [kõːrajən]

companach	[kɔumbanəx] *nm* companion; *gen* & *pl* companaich [kɔumbanɪç]
connrag	[kɔuNrag] *nm* consonant; *gen* connraige [kɔuNrɛgʲə] *pl* ~an [kɔuNragən]
cor	[kɔr] *nm* circumstance; *gen* coir [kɔrʲ]
còrd	[kɔːRd] 1 *v* to enjoy, to agree 2 *vn* & *nm* ~adh [kɔːRdəɣ] enjoying, agreement; *gen* ~aidh [kɔːRdɪ] *pl* ~aidhean [kɔːRdɪ.ən]
corp	[kɔrb] *nm* body; *gen* & *pl* cuirp [kurʲb]
corr	[kɔːR] *nm* rest
cosgais	[kɔsgɪʃ] *nf* cost; *gen* ~e [kɔsgɪʃə] *pl* ~ean [kɔsgɪʃən]
còta	[kɔːhdə] *nm* coat; *pl* ~ichean [kɔːhdɪçən]
cothrom	[kɔrəm] *nm* chance; *gen* cothruim [kɔrəm] *pl* ~an [kɔrəmən]
crann	[krauN] *nm* plough, mast; *gen* & *pl* cruinn [kruiNʲ] • ~-ola [kraˈNɔLə] oilrig
crannchur	[kraNaxər] *nm* lottery; *gen* crannchuir [kraNaxərʲ]
craobh	[krɯːv] *nf* tree; *gen* craoibhe [krɯivə] *pl* ~an [krɯːvən]
crath	[krah] 1 *v* to shake 2 *vn* & *nm* ~adh [krahəɣ]; *gen* ~aidh [krahɪ]
creach	[krʲɛx] 1 *v* to plunder 2 *vn* & *nm* ~adh [krʲɛxəɣ] plundering; *gen* ~aidh [krʲɛxɪ]
creag	[krʲeg] *nf* cliff; *gen* creige [krʲegʲə] *pl* ~an [krʲegən] • ~ an Daraich [krʲegəNˈdarɪç] Craigendarroch • ~ Phàdraig [krʲegˈfaːdrɪgʲ] Craig Phadrig
creid	[krʲedʲ] 1 *v* to believe 2 *vn* & *nm* ~sinn [krʲedʲʃɪNʲ] believing
creutair	[krʲeːhdɪrʲ] *nm* creature; *pl* ~ean [kreːhdɪrʲən]
cridhe	[krʲi.ə] *nm* heart; *pl* ~achan [krʲi.əxən]
crìoch	[krʲiəx] *nf* border; *gen* crìche [krʲiːçə] *pl* ~an [krʲiəxən] • Na ~an [nə krʲiəxən] The Borders
crodh	[kro] *nm* cattle; *gen* cruidh [krɯj]
crogan	[krogan] *nm* jar; *gen* & *pl* crogain [krogɛNʲ]
croit	[krɔhdʲ] *nf* croft; *gen* ~e [krɔhdʲə] *pl* ~ean [krɔhdʲən]
croitear	[krɔhdʲɛr] *nm* crofter; *gen* croiteir [krɔhdʲɛrʲ] *pl* ~an [krɔhdʲɛrən]
croitearachd	[krɔhdʲɛrəxg] *nf* crofting
Cromba	[krɔumba] *pnm* Cromarty; *gen* Chrombaigh [xrɔumbaj]
crònan	[krɔːnan] *nm* croon; *gen* crònain [krɔːnɛNʲ]
cruaidh	[kruəj] *adj* hard; *pl* & *comp* ~e [kruəjə]

crùb   [kruːb] 1 *v* to crouch 2 *vn* & *nm* ~adh [kruːbəɣ] crouching;
              gen ~aidh [kruːbɪ]

cruinnich [krɯNʲɪç] 1 *v* to gather 2 *vn* & *nm* cruinneachadh
              [krɯNʲəxəɣ] gathering; *gen* cruinneachaidh [krɯNʲəxɪ] *pl*
              cruinneachaidhean [krɯNʲəxɪ.ən]

cruthaich [kruhɪç] 1 *v* to create 2 *vn* & *nm* cruthachadh [kruhəxəɣ]
              creating; *gen* cruthachaidh [kruhəxɪ]

cù   [kuː] *nm* dog; *gen* & *pl* coin [kɔNʲ] *gen pl* chon [xɔn]

cuach   [kuəx] *nf* bowl; *gen* cuaich [kuəç] *pl* ~an [kuəxən]

cuairt   [kuəRʃdʲ] *nf* circuit; *gen* ~e [kuəRʃdʲə] *pl* ~ean [kuəRʃdʲən]

cuan   [kuən] *nm* ocean; *gen* cuain [kuəNʲ] *pl* ~tan [kuəNdən]

cudrom   [kudrəm] *nm* weight; *gen* cudroim [kudrəm]

cudromach [kudrəməx] *adj* important; *comp* cudromaiche
              [kudrəmɪçə]

cuibhle   [kuilə] *nf* wheel; *pl* cuibhlichean [kuilɪçən]

cuideachd [kudʲəxg] 1 *nf* company; *pl* ~an [kudʲəxgən] 2 *adv* also

cuideam   [kudʲəm] *nm* weight; *gen* cuideim [kudʲəm]

cuidich   [kudʲɪç] 1 *v* to help 2 *vn* & *nm* cuideachadh [kudʲəxəɣ]
              helping; *gen* cuideachaidh [kudʲəxɪ]

cùil   [kuːl] *nf* corner; *gen* ~e [kuːlə] *pl* ~tean [kuːldʲən]

cuileag   [kulag] *nf* fly; *gen* cuileige [kulɛgʲə] *pl* ~an [kulagən]

cuilean   [kulan] *nm* puppy; *gen* cuilein [kulɛNʲ] *pl* ~an [kulanən]

Cuiltheann, an ~ [ən kuluhəN] *pnm* The Cuillins

cuimhne   [kũĩNʲə] *nf* memory

cuimhnich [kũĩNʲɪç] 1 *v* to remember 2 *vn* & *nm* cuimhneachadh
              [kũĩNʲəxəɣ]

cuine   [kuNʲə] *interr* when? • cuine a...? [kuNʲ ə] when...?

cuingichte [kũĩŋʲgʲɪçdʲə] *adj* restricted

cuir   [kurʲ] 1 *v* to put 2 *vn* & *nm* cur [kur] putting; *gen* ~ [kurʲ]

cùirt   [kuːRʃdʲ] *nf* court; *gen* ~e [kuːRʃdʲə] *pl* ~ean [kuːRʃdʲən]

cùirtear   [kuːRʃdʲɛr] *nm* curtain; *gen* cùirteir [kuːRʃdʲɛrʲ] *pl* ~an
              [kuːRʃdʲɛrən]

cùl   [kuːL] *nm* back; *gen* cùil [kuːl] *pl* cùiltean [kuːldʲən]

cultar   [kuLdər] *nm* culture; *gen* cultair [kuLdɪrʲ] *pl* ~an
              [kuLdərən]

cum   [kuːm] 1 *v* to keep 2 *vn* & *nf* ~ail [kumal] holding; *gen*
              ~alach [kumaLəx]

cumhang   [kũ.əŋg] *adj* narrow; *comp* cumhainge [kũ.əŋʲgʲə]

cunnart   [kuNaRʃd] *nm* danger; *gen* cunnairt [kuNaRʃdʲ] *pl* ~an
              [kuNaRʃdən]

cunnt	[kuːNd] 1 *v* to count 2 *nm & vn* ~adh [kuːNdəɣ]; *gen* ~aidh [kuːNdɪ]
cupa	[kuhbə] *nm* cup; *pl* ~nnan [kuhbəNən]
curran	[kuRan] *nm* carrot; *gen & pl* currain [kuRɛNʲ]
cùrsa	[kuːRsə] *nm* course; *pl* ~ichean [kuːRsɪçən] • ~-taice [kuRsəˈtaçɡʲə] support-course
cur-seachad	[kurˈʃaxəd] *nm* hobby; *pl* ~an [kurˈʃaxədən]
cus	[kus] *nm* too many, too much ("too muchness")
cuthag	[ku.ag] *nf* cuckoo; *gen* cuthaige [ku.ɛgʲə] *pl* ~an [ku.agən]

DAIR [darʲ]

dà	[daː] *num* two; *counting form* a dhà [ə ɣaː] • ~ dheug [daː ʝiag] 12 • ~ fhichead [daː içəd] 40
dà fhicheadamh	[daː içədəv] *num* fourtieth
dachaigh	[daxɪ] *nf* home; *gen* ~e [daxɪ.ə] *pl* ~ean [daxɪ.ən]
dad	[dad] *nm* anything
dail	[dal] *nf* dale; *gen* dalach [daLəx] *pl* dalaichean [daLɪçən]
dàil	[daːl] *nf* delay; *gen* dàlach [daːLəx] *pl* dàlaichean [daːLɪçən]
Danmhairg, an ~	[əN danavɪrʲgʲ] *pnf* Denmark; *gen* na Danmhairge [nə danavɪrʲgʲə]
damhan-allaidh	[davaˈnaLɪ] *nm* spider; *gen & pl* damhain-allaidh [davɛˈNʲaLɪ]
dannsa	[dãũNsə] *nm* dance; *pl* ~chan [dãũNsəxən]
daolag	[dɯːLag] *nf* beetle; *gen* daolaige [dɯːLɛgʲə] *pl* ~an [dɯːLagən]
daor	[dɯːr] *adj* expensive; *pl* ~a [dɯːrə] *comp* daoire [dɯːrʲə]
dara	[darə] see dàrna
dàrna	[daːrnə] *num* second
dath	[dah] *nm* colour; *gen* ~a [dahə] *pl* ~an [dahən]
de	[də] *prep* of (partitive); *short* a [ə] *def prep* dhen an [ʝɛnəNⁱ] *def prep pl* dhe na [ʝɛnə] conjugated dhìom [ʝiəm] dhìot [ʝiəhd] dheth [ʝɛh] dith [ʝih] dhinn [ʝiːNʲ] dhibh [ʝiv] diubh [ʝuː]
dé	[dʲeː] *interr* what? • ~ a...? [dʲeː] what...?
deagh	[dʲoː] *adj* good
dealanach	[dʲaLanəx] *nm* lightning; *gen & pl* dealanaich [dʲaLanɪç]
dealbh	[dʲɛLɛv] *nm* picture; *gen* deilbh [dʲelɪv] *pl* ~an [dʲɛLɛvən] • ~-chluich [dʲɛLɛvxLəç] play (act)

dealbhadair   [dʲɛLɛvədɛrʲ] *nm* designer; *pl* ~ean [dʲɛLɛvədɛrʲən]

dèanta   [dʲiandə] *adj* done

dearbh   [dʲɛrɛv] 1 *adj* same; *pl* ~a [dʲɛrɛvə] 2 *v* affirm; *vn* ~adh [dʲɛrɛvəɣ]

dearc   [dʲɛrg] *nf* berry; *pl* ~an [dʲɛrgən]

dearg   [dʲɛrɛg] *adj* red; *pl* ~a [dʲɛrɛgə] *comp* deirge [dʲerʲegʲə]

deas   [dʲes] 1 *nf* South • a ~ [ə dʲes] southerly 2 *adj* right; *pl* ~a [dʲesə] *comp* deise [dʲeʃə]

deich   [dʲeç] *num* ten; *counting form* a ~ [ə dʲeç] • ~ ar fhichead [dʲeç ər içəd] 30

deicheamh   [dʲeçəv] *num* tenth

deichnear   [dʲeçnər] *nm* ten (people)

déideadh   [dʲedʲəɣ] *nm* toothache; *gen* déididh [dʲedʲɪ] *pl* déididhean [dʲe:dʲɪ.ən]

deigh   [dʲej] *nf* ice; *gen* ~e [dʲejə]

déilig (ri)   [dʲe:lɪgʲ rʲɪ] 1 *v* to deal (with) 2 *vn* & *nm* déiligeadh [dʲe:lɪgʲəɣ] dealing; *gen* déiligidh [dʲe:lɪgʲɪ]

deireadh   [dʲerʲəɣ] *nm* end; *gen* deiridh [dʲerʲɪ] *pl* deiridhean [dʲerʲɪ.ən] • ~-seachdainn [dʲerʲəˈʃɛxgɪNʲ] weekend

deise   [dʲeʃə] *nf* suit; *pl* ~an [dʲeʃən] • ~-shnàmha [dʲeʃəˈnaːvə] swimsuit

deiseil   [dʲeʃal] *adj* ready; *comp* ~e [dʲeʃalə]

deoch   [dʲɔx] *nf* drink; *gen* dighe [dʲi.ə] *pl* ~an [dʲɔxən]

deuchainn   [dʲiaxɪNʲ] *nf* test; *gen* deuchainne [dʲiaxɪNʲə] *pl* ~ean [dʲiaxɪNʲən]

dhachaigh   [ɣaxɪ] *adv* homeward

dian   [dʲian] *adj* intense; *pl* ~a [dʲianə] *comp* déine [dʲe:nə] • ~-chùrsa [dʲianxursə] intensive course

DiarDaoin   [dʲəRˈduːNʲ] *nm* Thursday

di-beathte   [dʲɪˈbɛhdʲə] *adj* welcome

dìcheall   [dʲiːçəL] *nm* diligence; *gen* dìchill [dʲiːçɪLʲ]

DiCiadain   [dʲɪˈkʲiadɛNʲ] *nm* Wednesday

DiDómhnaich   [dʲɪˈdõːnɪç] *nm* Sunday

DihAoine   [dʲɪˈhuːNʲə] *nm* Friday

dìleas   [dʲiːləs] *adj* loyal; *comp* dìlse [dʲiːlʃə]

DiLuain   [dʲɪˈLuəNʲ] *nm* Monday

DiMàirt   [dʲɪˈmaːRʃdʲ] *nm* Tuesday

dìnnear   [dʲiːNʲər] *nf* dinner; *gen* ~ach [dʲiːNʲərəx] *pl* ~an [dʲiːNʲərən]

dìollaid   [dʲiəLɪdʲ] *nf* saddle; *gen* ~e [dʲiəLɪdʲə] *pl* ~ean [dʲiəLɪdʲən]

diombach   [dʲũːmbəx] *adj* annoyed; *comp* diombaiche [dʲũːmbɪçə]

dìreach [dʲiːrʲəx] *adj* just, direct; *comp* dìriche [dʲiːrʲɪçə]

DiSathairne [dʲɪˈsahəRNʲə] *nm* Saturday

dìsinn [dʲiːʃɪNʲ] *nf* die; *gen* dìsne [dʲiːʃnə] *pl* dìsnean [dʲiːʃnən] dice

dìthean [dʲihan] *nm* flower; *gen* dìthein [dʲiːhɛNʲ] *pl* ~an [dʲiːhanən]

dithis [dʲi.ɪʃ] *nf* two (people)

Diùra [dʲuːra] *pnm* Jura; *gen* Dhiùra [ʝuːra]

Diùrach [dʲuːrax] *nm* a person from Jura; *gen* & *pl* Diùraich [dʲuːrɪç]

dlùth [dLuː] *adj* close; *pl* ~a [dLuː.ə] *comp* dlùithe [dLuːjə]

do 1 [də] *prep* to; *short* a [ə] *def prep* dhan an [ɣanəNʲ⁽ⁱ⁾] *def prep pl* dha na [ɣanə] conjugated: dhomh [ɣõ] dhut [ɣuhd] dha [ɣaː] dhi [ʝiː] dhuinn [ɣɯiNʲ] dhuibh [ɣɯiv] dhaibh [ɣaiv] • a dh'ionnsaigh... [ə ʝuːNsɪ] against...

do 2 [də] *poss pron* your; before vowel d' [d]: do mhàthair [də vaːhərʲ] ⇨ d' athair [dahərʲ]

dòcha [dɔːxə] *adj* probable • 's ~ [sdɔːxə] probably

dòchas [dɔːxəs] *nm* hope; *gen* dòchais [dɔːxɪʃ] *pl* ~an [dɔːxəsən]

dòigh [dɔːj] *nf* method; *gen* ~e [dɔːjə] *pl* ~ean [dɔːjən]

dòigheil [dɔːjal] *adj* satisfactory; *comp* ~e [dɔːjalə]

doimhneachd [dõĩnəxg] *nf* depth

doirbh [dɤrʲəv] *adj* difficult; *pl* ~e [dɤrʲəvə] *comp* dorra [dɔRə]

dòirt [dɔːRʃdʲ] 1 *v* to pour 2 *vn* & *nm* dòrtadh [dɔːRʃdəɣ] pouring; *gen* dòrtaidh [dɔːRʃdɪ]

Doilidh [dɔlɪ] *pnf* Dolly; *gen* Dhoilidh [ɣɔlɪ] *voc* a Dhoilidh [ə ɣɔlɪ]

Dòmhnall [dõː.əL] *pnm* Donald; *gen* Dhòmhnaill [ɣõː.ɪLʲ] *voc* a Dhòmhnaill [ə ɣõː.ɪLʲ]

dona [dɔnə] *adj* bad; 1st *comp* miosa [misə] 2nd *comp* miste [miʃdʲə]

donn [douN] *adj* brown; *pl* ~a [dɔNə] *comp* duinne [dɯNʲə]

Donnchadh [doNoxəɣ] *pnm* Duncan; *gen* Dhonnchaidh [ɣoNoxɪ] *voc* a Dhonnchaidh [ə ɣoNoxɪ]

doras [dɔrəs] *nm* door; *gen* dorais [dɔrɪʃ] *pl* dorsan [dɔrsən]

dorcha [dɔrɔxə] *adj* dark; *comp* duirche [durʲɪçə]

dotair [dohdɛrʲ] *nm* doctor; *pl* ~ean [dohdɛrʲən]

dragh [drɤɣ] *nm* bother

draibh [draiv] 1 *v* to drive 2 *vn* & *nm* ~eadh [draivəɣ] driving

dràma [draːma] *nm* drama; *pl* ~nnan [draːmaNən]

drama [dramə] *nm* dram; *pl* ~nnan [draməNən]

draoidh [drɤj] *nm* druid; *pl* ~ean [drɤjən]

dreasa [dresə] *nf* dress; *pl* ~ichean [dresɪçən]

droch	[drɔx] *prefixed adj* bad
drochaid	[drɔxɪdʲ] *nf* bridge; *pl* ~ean [drɔxɪdʲən] • ~ an Aonachain [drɔxɪdʲ ə NɯːnəxɛNʲ] Spean Bridge
drùdhag	[druː.ag] *nf* drop; *gen* drùdhaige [druː.ɛgʲə] *pl* ~an [druː.agən]
druim	[drɯim] *nm* back; *gen* droma [dromə] *pl* dromannan [droməNən] • An ~ Buidhe [əN drɯim bujə] Drumbuie
duais	[duəʃ] *nf* prize; *gen* ~e [duəʃə] *pl* ~ean [duəʃən]
dual-chainnt	[duəL xãĩNʲdʲ] *nf* dialect; *gen* ~e [duəL xãĩNʲdʲə] *pl* ~ean [duəL xãĩNʲdʲən]
dualchas	[duəLxəs] *nm* heritage; *gen* dualchais [duəLxɪʃ]
dùbailte	[duːbaldʲə] *adj* double
dubh	[du] *adj* black; *pl* ~a [du.ə] *comp* duibhe [dɯjə]
dubhan	[du.an] *nm* hook; *gen* dubhain [du.ɛNʲ]
dùil	[duːl] *nf* hope; *gen* ~e [duːlə] *pl* ~tean [duːldʲən]
duilleag	[dɯLʲag] *nf* leaf, page; *gen* duilleige [dɯLʲɛgʲə] *pl* ~an [dɯLʲagən]
duileasg	[duləsg] *nm* dulse; *gen* duilisg [dulɪʃgʲ]
duilich	[dulɪç] *adj* sorry; *comp* duilghe [dɯlɯjə]
dùin	[duːNʲ] 1 *v* to close 2 *vn* & *nm* dùnadh [duːnəɣ] closing, closure; *gen* dùnaidh [duːnɪ] *pl* dùnaidhean [duːnɪ.ən]
dùinte	[duːNʲdʲə] *adj* closed
duine	[dɯNʲə] *nm* 1 person 2 husband; *pl* daoine [dɯːNʲə]
dùisg	[duːʃgʲ] 1 *v* to awake 2 *vn* & *nm* dùsgadh [duːsgəɣ] awakening; *gen* dùisgidh [duːsgɪ]
dùn	[duːn] *nm* fortress; *gen* & *pl* dùin [duːNʲ] • An ~ Beag [əN duːn beg] Dunbeg • An ~ Mór [əN duːn moːr] Dunmore • ~ Bheagan [dunˈvegan] *pnm* Dunvegan • ~ Déagh [dunˈdʲeː] *pnm* Dundee • ~ Éideann [dunˈeːdʲəN] *pnm* Edinburgh • ~ Dòmhnaill [dunˈdõː.ɪLʲ] Dundonald • ~ Tuilm [dunˈtɯlɯm] Duntulm
dùrachd	[duːrəxg] *nf* compliments; *pl* ~an [duːrəxgən]
Dùrar	[duːrər] *pnm* Duror; *gen* Dhùrair [ɣuːrɪrʲ]
dusan	[dusan] *nm* dozen; *gen* & *pl* dusain [dusɛNʲ]
dùthaich	[duː.ɪç] *nf* country; *gen* dùthcha [duːxə] *pl* dùthchannan [duːxəNən] • ~ MhicAoidh [duː.ɪç ĩçˈgɯj] North Sutherland

EADHA [ɛɣə]

e	[ɛ] *pron* he, it; *emph* esan [esən]
each	[ɛx] *nm* horse; *gen* & *pl* eich [eç]
Eachann	[ɛxəN] *pnm* Hector; *gen* & *voc* Eachainn [ɛxɪNʲ]
eachdraidh	[ɛxdrɪ] *nf* history; *gen* ~e [ɛxdrɪ.ə] *pl* ~ean [ɛxdrɪ.ən]
Eadailt, an ~	[ə Nʲedaldʲ] *pnf* Italy; *gen* na h-Eadailte [nə hedaldʲə]
eagal	[egəL] *nm* fear; *gen* eagail [egəl] • tha an t-~ orm [haNʲ tʲegəL ɔrɔm] I am afraid
eaglais	[egLɪʃ] *nf* church; *gen* ~e [egLɪʃə] *pl* ~ean [egLɪʃən]
ealain	[jaLɛNʲ] *nf* art; *gen* ~e [jaLɛNʲə]
Ealasaid	[jaLəsɛdʲ] *pnf* Elizabeth
earbsach	[ɛrɛbsəx] *adj* confident; *comp* earbsaiche [ɛrɛbsɪçə] • mì-~ [mĩ: ɛrɛbsəx] mistrustful
Eairdsidh	[ɛːRdʲʃɪ] *pnm* Archie
ear	[ɛr] *nf* east • an ~ [ə Nʲɛr] easterly
earball	[ɛrɛbəL] *nm* tail; *gen* & *pl* earbaill [ɛrɛbɪLʲ]
Earra Ghàidheal	[ɛRəˈɣɛː.əL] *pnm* Argyll
earrach	[jaRəx] *nm* Spring; *gen* earraich [jaRɪç] • as t-~ [əs tʲɛRəx] in Spring
éibhinn	[eːvɪNʲ] *adj* funny; *comp* éibhinne [eːvɪNʲʲ]
éideadh	[eːdʲəɣ] *nm* uniform; *gen* éididh [eːdʲɪ] *pl* éididhean [eːdʲɪ.ən]
Eige	[egʲə] *pn* Eigg
eigin	[egʲɪn] *adj* some • rud~ [Rudɪgʲɪn] something
éiginn	[eːgʲɪNʲ] *nf* distress; *gen* ~e [eːgʲɪNʲ]
Eilbheis, an ~	[ə Nʲelevɪʃ] *pnf* Switzerland; *gen* na h-Eilbheise [nə helevɪʃ]
eile	[elə] *adj* other
eilean	[elan] *nm* island; *gen* eilein [elɛNʲ] *pl* ~an [elanən] • an t-~ Dubh [əNʲ tʲelan du] the Black Isle • an t-~ Sgiathanach [əNʲ tʲelan sgʲiəhənəx] *gen* an Eilein Sgiathanaich [ə NʲelɛNʲ sgʲiəhənɪç] • na h-~an an Iar [nə helanən ə Nʲiər] The Western Isles; *gen* nan ~an an Iar [nə Nʲelanən ə Nʲiər]
eileanach	[elanəx] *nm* islander; *gen* & *pl* eileanaich [elanɪç]
Eilidh	[elɪ] *pnf* Helen
einnsean	[ẽĩNʲʃan] *nm* engine; *gen* einnsein [ẽĩNʲʃɛNʲ] *pl* ~an [ẽĩNʲʃanən]
Éiphit, an ~	[ə Nʲeːfɪdʲ] *pnf* Egypt; *gen* na h-Éiphite [na heːfɪdʲə]

éirich	[eːrʲɪç] 1 v to rise 2 vn & nf éirigh [eːrʲɪ] rising, rise
Éirinn	[eːrʲɪNʲ] pnf Ireland; gen Éireann [eːrʲəN]
Eirisgeigh	[erʲɪʃgaj] pnm Eriskay
éist	[eːʃdʲ] 1 v to listen 2 vn & nf ~eachd [eːʃdʲəxg] listening
Eóghann	[joːəN] pnm Ewen; gen & voc Eóghainn [joːˌɪNʲ]
eòlach	[joːLəx] adj acquainted; comp eòlaiche [joːLɪçə]
eòlaichea	[joːLɪçə] nm expert; pl eòlaichean [joːLɪçən]
eugh	[eːv] 1 v to shout 2 vn & nf ~achd [eːvəxg] shouting
eun	[ian] nm bird; gen & pl eòin [joːNʲ]

FEÀRN [fjaːRN]

fa	[fa] prep under (only as prefix) • ~ leth [fa leh] particular
facal	[faxgəL] nm word; gen facail [faxgɪl] pl faclan [faxgLən]
faclair	[faxgLɛrʲ] nm dictionary; pl ~ean [faxgLɛrʲən]
fad	[fad] nm length; gen faide [fadʲə] • fhad 's a... [ad sə] as long as...
fàd	[faːd] nm (piece of) peat; gen & pl fàid [faːdʲ]
fada	[fadə] adj long; comp nas fhaide [nə sadʲə]
fadachd	[fadəxg] nf longing
fadal	[fadəL] nm weariness; gen fadail [fadəl]
fadalach	[fadəLəx] adj late; comp fadalaiche [fadəLɪçə]
fàg	[faːg] 1 v to leave 2 vn & nf ~ail [faːgal] leaving
faiceallach	[façgʲəLəx] adj careful; comp faiceallaiche [façgʲəLɪçə]
faicheil	[façal] adj showy; comp faicheile [façalə]
faighnich	[fɤɪnɪç] 1 v to ask 2 vn & nf faighneachd [fɤɪnəxg] asking
fàilte	[faːldʲə] nf welcome
faire	[farʲə] nf vigil
fàire	[faːrʲə] nf horizon
fairich	[farʲɪç] 1 v to feel 2 vn & nf faireachdainn [farʲəxgɪNʲ] feeling; pl faireachdainnean [farʲəxgɪNʲən]
faisg	[faʃgʲ] adj near; pl & comp ~e [faʃgʲə]
fàisg	[faːʃgʲ] 1 v to squeeze 2 vn & nm fàsgadh [faːsgəɣ]; gen [faːsgɪ]
falamh	[faLəv] adj empty; comp falaimhe [faLɪvə]
falbh	[faLav] 1 v to leave 2 vn & nm ~ [faLav] leaving
falt	[faLd] nm hair; gen fuilt [fuldʲ]
fang	[faŋg] nm cattle pen; gen faing [faiɲgʲ] pl ~an [faŋgən]
faochag	[fɯːxag] nf whelk; gen faochaige [fɯːxɛgʲə] pl ~an [fɯːxagən]

faod [fɯːd] 1 *defective v* may; *fut* ~aidh [fɯːdɪ] *fut rel* dh'fhaodas [ɣɯːdəs]

faoileag [fɯːlag] *nf* seagull; *gen* faoileige [fɯːlɛgʲə] *pl* ~an [fɯːlagən]

far [far] *rel part* where • ~ an robh e [far ə Rɔ ɛ] where he was

farpais [farbɪʃ] *nf* competition; *gen* ~e [farbɪʃə] *pl* ~ean [farbɪʃən]

fàs [faːs] 1 *v* to grow 2 *vn & nm* ~ [faːs] growing; *gen* fàis [faːʃ]

fasgadh [fasgəɣ] *nm* shelter; *gen* fasgaidh [fasgɪ] *pl* fasgaidhean [fasgɪ.ən]

feadhainn [fjɤɣɪNʲ] *nf* some, the ones

feamainn [fɛmɪNʲ] *nf* seaweed; *gen* feamad [fɛməd]

feannag [fjaNag] *nf* crow; *gen* feannaig [fjaNɛgʲ] *pl* ~an [fjaNagən]

fear [fɛr] *nm* man; *gen & pl* fir [firʲ] *voc sing* fhir [irʲ] *voc pl* fheara [ɛrə] • na Fir Chlis [nə firʲ xliʃ] the Northern Lights • ~-lagha [fɛrˈLɤɣə] (male) lawyer • ~-teagaisg [fɛrˈtʲegɪʃgʲ] teacher

Fearchar [fɛrɛxər] *pnm* Farquhar; *gen & voc* Fhearchair [ɛrɛxɪrʲ]

Fearghas [fɛrɛɣəs] *pnm* Fergus; *gen & voc* Fhearghais [ɛrɛɣɪʃ]

feasgar [fesgər] *nm* afternoon; *gen* feasgair [fesgɪrʲ] *pl* ~an [fesgərən]

féileadh [feːləɣ] *nm* kilt; *gen* féilidh [feːlɪ] *pl* féilidhean [feːlɪ.ən]

féis [feːʃ] *nf* festival; *gen* ~e [feːʃə] *pl* ~ean [feːʃən]

feith [feh] 1 *v* to wait 2 *vn & nm* feitheamh [fehəv] waiting; *gen* feithimh [fehɪv]

feòil [fjɔːl] *nf* meat; *gen* feòla [fjɔːLə]

feuch [fiax] 1 *v* to attempt 2 *vn & nf* ~ainn [fiaxɪNʲ] attempt, trying; *pl* ~ainnean [fiaxɪNʲən]

feum [feːm] 1 *defective v* to have to; *fut* ~aidh [feːmɪ] *fut rel* dh'fheumas [ʝeːməs]

feur [fiar] *nm* grass; *gen & pl* feòir [fjɔːrʲ]

feusag [fiasag] *nf* beard; *gen* feusaig [fiasɛgʲ] *pl* ~an [fiasagən]

feusgan [fiasgan] *nm* mussel; *gen & pl* feusgain [fiasgɛNʲ]

fhathast [ha.əsd] *adv* yet

fhéin [heːn] *pron* self

fiach [fiax] *nm* due, rate; *gen* féich [feːç] *pl* ~an [fiaxən] • chan fhiach e [xa Nʲiax ɛ] it's not worth it • 's fhiach e [ʃiax ɛ] it's worth it

fiadh [fiaɣ] *nm* deer; *gen & pl* féidh [feːj]

fiadhaich	[fiə.ɪç] *adj* wild; *comp* ~e [fiə.ɪçə]
fichead	[fiçəd] *num* twenty
ficheadamh	[fiçədəv] *num* twentieth
fidheall	[fi:.əL] *nf* fiddle; *gen* fidhle [fi:lə] *pl* fidhlean [fi:lən]
fidhleir	[fi:lɛrʲ] *nm* fiddler; *pl* ~ean [fi:lɛrʲən]
fileanta	[filəNdə] *adj* fluent
film	[filim] *nm* film; *pl* ~ichean [filimɪçən]
fiodh	[fiɣ] *nm* wood; *gen* ~a [fiɣə]
fion	[fiən] *nm* wine; *gen* ~a [fiənə]
fionn	[fju:N] *adj* fair; *pl & comp* ~a [fiNə]
Fhionnlainn, an ~	[ə Nʲũ:NLɪNʲ] *pnf* Finland; *gen* na Fionnlainne [nə fju:NLɪNʲə]
Fhraing, an ~	[ə Nraiɲʲgʲ] *nf* France; *gen* na F" Fhrainge [nə fraiɲʲgʲə]
fios	[fis] *nm* knowledge; *pl* ~an [fisən] • gun fhiosta [gə nisdə] unbeknown
fiosrachadh	[fisrəxəɣ] *nm* information; *gen* fiosrachaidh [fisrəxɪ]
fireann	[firʲəN] *adj* male; *comp* fireannaiche [firʲəNɪçə]
firinn	[fi:rʲɪNʲ] *nf* truth
fiughar	[fju.ər] *nm* expectation; *gen* fiughair [fju.ɪrʲ]
flaitheas	[fLahəs] *nm* heaven; *gen* flaitheis [fLahɪʃ]
fliuch	[flux] *adj* wet; *pl* ~a [fluxə] *comp* fliche [fliçə]
flùr	[fLu:r] *nm* flower; *gen* flùir [fLu:rʲ] *pl* ~aichean [fLu:rɪçən]
fo	[fo] *prep* under; *def prep* fon an [fonəN⁽ʲ⁾] *def prep pl* fo na [fonə] conjugated fodham [fo.əm] fodhad [fo.əd] fodha [fo.ə] foidhpe [foihbə] fodhainn [fo.ɪNʲ] fodhaibh [fo.ɪv] fodhpa [fohbə]
foghainn	[fo.ɪNʲ] 1 *v* to suffice; *fut* foghnaidh [fo:nɪ] *fut rel* dh'fhoghnas [ɣo:nəs] 2 *vn & nm* foghnadh [fo:nəɣ] sufficing
foghar	[fɣvər] *nm* Autumn; *gen* foghair [fɣvɪrʲ] • as t-fhoghar [əs dɣvər] in Autumn
foghlam	[fo:Ləm] *nm* education; *gen* foghlaim [fo:Ləm]
foillsich	[fɣiLʲʃɪç] 1 *v* to publish 2 *vn & nm* foillseachadh [fɣiLʲʃəxəɣ] publishing, publication; *gen* foillseachaidh [fɣiLʲʃəxɪ] *pl* foillseachaidhean [fɣiLʲʃəxɪ.ən]
fois	[foʃ] *nf* leisure; *gen* ~e [foʃə]
follais	[foLɪʃ] *nf* publicness
fón	[fo:n] 1 *nm* phone; *pl* ~aichean [fo:nɪçən] 2 *v* to phone 3 *vn & nm* ~adh [fo:nəɣ] phoning
fonn	[fouN] *nm* tune; *gen & pl* fuinn [fuiNʲ]

forc [fɔrg] *nf* fork; *gen* fuirc [furʲgʲ] *pl* ~an [fɔrgən]

fortanach [fɔRʃdanəx] *adj* fortunate; *comp* fortanaiche [fɔRʃdanɪçə]

fosgail [fɔsgəl] 1 *v* to open; *fut* fosglaidh [fɔsgLɪ] *fut rel*
dh'fhosglas [ɣɔsgLəs] 2 *vn* & *nm* fosgladh [fɔsgLəɣ]
opening; *gen* fosglaidh [fɔsgLɪ] *pl* fosglaidhean
[fɔsgLɪ.ən]

fosgailte [fɔsgɪldʲə] *adj* open

Fraingis [franʲgʲɪʃ] *nf* French; *gen* ~e [franʲgʲɪʃə]

Frangach [frangəx] *adj* French; *comp* Frangaiche [frangɪçə]

fraoch [frɯːx] *nm* heather; *gen* fraoich [frɯːç]

fras [fras] *nf* shower; *gen* froise [frɔʃə] *pl* ~an [frasən]

freagair [frʲegɪrʲ] 1 *v* to answer 2 *vn* & *nf* ~t [frʲegəRʃdʲ] answering,
answer; *gen* ~e [frʲegəRʃdʲə] *pl* ~ean [frʲegəRʃdʲən]

freagarrach [frʲegəRəx] *adj* suitable; *comp* freagarraiche [frʲegəRɪçə]

Friseal [frʲiʃəL] *pnm* Fraser; *gen* Fhriseil [rʲiʃəl]

fuaim [fuəm] *nf* sound; *gen* fuaime [fuəimə] *pl* ~ean [fuəimən]

fuaimreag [fuəimrʲag] *nf* vowel; *gen* fuaimreig [fuəimrʲɛgʲ]; *pl* ~an
[fuəimrʲagən]

fuar [fuər] *adj* cold; *pl* ~a [fuərə] *comp* fhuaire [uərʲə]

fuasgail [fuəsgəl] 1 *v* release 2 *vn* & *nm* fuasgladh [fuəsgLəɣ]
releasing, solution; *gen* fuasglaidh [fuəsgLɪ]

fuasgailte [fuəsgɪldʲə] *adj* agile

fuil [ful] *nf* blood; *gen* fala [faLə]

fuineadair [fuNʲədɛrʲ] *nm* baker; *pl* ~ean [fuNʲədɛrʲən]

fuirich [furʲɪç] 1 *v* to live (in a place) 2 *vn* & *nm* fuireach [furʲəx]
living; *gen* fuirich [furʲɪç]

furasta [furəsdə] *adj* easy; *comp* nas fhasa [nə sasə]

GORT [gɔRʃd]

gabh [gav] 1 *v* to take 2 *vn* & *nf* ~ail [gahal] taking; *gen* ~alach
[gahaLəx] *pl* ~alaichean [gahaLɪçən] • ~ mo leisgeul
[gə mə leʃgʲəL] excuse me

gach [gax] *indef pron* every

Gàidheal [gɛː.əL] *nm* Gael; *gen* & *pl* Gàidheil [gɛː.əl]

Gàidhealach [gɛː.əLəx] *adj* Gaelic

Gàidhlig [gaːlɪgʲ] *pnf* & *adj* Gaelic

gainmheach [gãnãvəx] *nf* sand; *gen* gainmhich [gãnãvɪç]

gàire [gaːrʲə] 1 *nf* laughter

gàireachdainn [gaːrʲəxgɪNʲ] 1 *nf* laughter 2 *vn* laughing

gairm [gɤrʲɤm] 1 v to call 2 vn & nf call; gen ~e [gɤrʲɤmə] pl ~ean [gɤrʲɤmən]

gàirnealaireachd [ga:RNʲəLɛrʲəxg] nf gardening

Gall [gauL] nm Lowlander; gen & pl Goill [gɤiLʲ]

Gallaibh [gaLəv] pnm Caithness; gen Ghallaibh [ɣaLəv]

Galltachd [gauLdəxg] pnf Lowlands

gann [gauN] adj scarce; comp gainne [gaNʲə]

gaoth [gɯː] nf wind; gen gaoithe [gɯːhə] pl ~an [gɯːhən]

garaids [garɪdʲʃ] nf garage; pl ~ean [garɪdʲʃən]

gàrradh [ga:Rəɣ] nm garden, yard; gen gàrraidh [ga:Rɪ] pl gàrraidhean [ga:Rɪ.ən] • ~ iarainn [ga:Rəɣ iəRɪNʲ] shipyard

garbh [garav] adj rough; pl ~a [garavə] comp gairbhe [garʲavə]

gas [gas] 1 nm gas; pl ~an [gasən] 2 nf stalk; gen gaise [gaʃə] pl ~an [gasən]

gasta [gasdə] adj handsome

geal [gʲaL] adj white; pl ~a [gʲaLə] comp gile [gʲilə]

gealach [gʲaLəx] nf moon; gen gealaich [gʲaLɪç] pl gealaichean [gʲaLɪçən]

geall [gʲauL] 1 v to promise 2 vn & nm ~adh [gʲaLəɣ] promise, promising; gen geallaidh [gʲaLɪ] pl geallaidhean [gʲaLɪ.ən]

geama [gʲɛmə] nm game; pl ~nnan [gʲɛməNən]

geamair [gʲɛmɛrʲ] nm gamekeeper; pl ~ean [gʲɛmɛrʲən]

geamhradh [gʲãũrəɣ] nm Winter; gen geamhraidh [gʲãũrɪ] • anns a' gheamhradh [as ə jãũrəɣ] in Winter

geansaidh [gʲɛnsɪ] nm jersey; pl ~ean [gʲɛnsɪ.ən]

gearastan [gʲɛrasdan] nm garrison; gen gearastain [gʲɛrasdɛNʲ] pl ~an [gʲɛrasdanən] • An ~ [ən gʲɛrasdan] Fort William

Gearmailtis [gʲɛrɛmaldʲɪʃ] nf German (language); gen ~e [gʲɛrɛmaldʲɪʃə]

gearr [gʲa:R] 1 v to cut 2 vn & nm ~adh [gʲaRəɣ] cutting; gen ~aidh [gʲaRɪ] pl ~aidhean [gʲaRɪ.ən] 3 adj short; pl ~a [gʲaRə] 1st comp giorra [gʲiRə] 2nd comp giorraide [gʲiRɪdʲə] • ~a-mhuc [gʲaRə vuxg] guine pig

Gearrloch [gʲa:RLɔx] pnm Gairloch; gen Ghearrloch [ja:RLɔx]

geata [gʲɛhdə] nm gate; pl ~chan [gʲɛhdəxən]

ged [gad] conj although • ~ a... [gad ə] although...

ge-tà [gəˈta:] conj though

geur [gʲiar] adj sharp; pl ~a [gʲiarə] comp géire [gʲe:rʲə]

Ghàidhealtachd, a' ~ [ə ɣɛː.əLdəxg] *nf* The Highlands; *gen* na Gàidhealtachd [nə gɛː.əLdəxg]

Ghréig, a' ~ [ə ɣrʲeːgʲ] *pnf* Greece; *gen* na Gréige [nə grʲeːgʲə]

gille [gʲiLʲə] *nm* lad; *pl* ~an [gʲiLʲən]

GilleEasbaig [gʲiˈLʲesbɪgʲ] *pnm* Archibald; *gen* GhilleEasbaig [ʝiˈLʲesbɪgʲ] *voc* a GhilleEasbaig [ə ʝiˈLʲesbɪgʲ]

gin [gʲin] *nf* any, anyone

Giogha [gʲi.ə] *pnm* Gigha; *gen* Ghiogha [ʝi.ə]

glac [gLaxg] 1 *v* to grasp 2 *vn & nm* glacadh [gLaxgəɣ] grasping; *gen* glacaidh [gLaxgɪ]

glainne [gLaNʲə] *nf* glass; *pl* ~achan [gLaNʲəxən]

glais [gLaʃ] 1 *v* to lock 2 *vn & nm* glasadh [gLasəɣ] locking

glan [gLan] 1 *adj* clean; *pl* ~a [gLanə] *comp* glaine [gLaNʲə] 2 *v* to clean 3 *vn & nm* ~adh [gLanəɣ] cleaning; *gen* ~aidh [gLanɪ]

glaodh [gLɯː] 1 *v* to shout 2 *vn & nm* ~aich [gLɯː.ɪç] shouting

glas [gLas] *nf* lock; *gen* glaise [gLaʃə] *pl* ~an [gLasən]

Glaschu [gLasəxu] *pnf* Glasgow; *gen* Ghlaschu [ɣLasəxu]

glasraich [gLasrɪç] *nf* vegetables

glé [gleː] *adv* very

gleann [glauN] *nm* glen; *gen* glinne [gliNʲə] *pl* ~tan [glãũNdən] • An ~ Dubh [ən glɛuN du] Glendhu • ~a Comhan [glɛNəˈkõ.ən] Glencoe • ~ Eilg [glɛNʲelɪgʲ] Glenelg • ~ Sìdh [glɛNʲʃiː] Glenshee

gleoc [glɔxg] *nm* clock; *pl* ~an [glɔxgən]

glic [gliçgʲ] *adj* clever; *pl & comp* ~e [gliçgʲə]

gloine [gLʏNʲə] *nf* glass; *pl* ~achan [gLʏNʲəxən]

gnìomhachas [grʲĩə̃vəxəs] *nm* industry; *gen* gnìomhachais [grʲĩə̃vəxɪʃ] *pl* ~an [grʲĩə̃vəxəsən]

gnothach [grõ.əx] *nm* business; *gen* gnothaich [grõ.ɪç] *pl* gnothaichean [grõ.ɪçən]

gob [gob] *nm* beak; *gen* guib [gɯib] *pl* ~an [gobən]

gobha [go.ə] *nm* (black)smith; *gen* ~inn [go.ɪNʲ] *pl* goibhnean [gɣinən]

goid [gɣdʲ] 1 *v* to steal 2 *vn & nf* ~ [gɣdʲ] stealing; *gen* ~e [gɣdʲə]

goilf [gɔlf] *nm* golf

goireas [gɣrʲəs] *nm* facility; *gen* goireis [gɣrʲɪʃ] ~an [gɣrʲəsən]

goirt [gɔRʃdʲ] *adj* sore; *pl & comp* ~e [gɔRʃdʲə]

gòrach [gɔːrəx] *adj* silly (fem nouns only); *comp* gòraiche

[gɔ:rɪçə]

gorm [gɔrɔm] *adj* blue; *pl* ~a [gɔrɔmə] *comp* guirme [guɾʲumə]

gràmar [gra:mər] *nm* grammar; *gen* gràmair [gra:mɪrʲ]

grànda [grã:Ndə] *adj* ugly

Grannd [grãũNd] *pnm* Grant

greas [gres] 1 *v* to hurry 2 *vn* & *nm* ~adh [gresəɣ] hurrying

greim [grʲeim] *nm* bite; *gen* ~e [grʲemə] *pl* ~eannan [grʲeməNən]

grian [grʲian] *nf* sun; *gen* gréine [grʲe:nə] *pl* ~an [grʲianən]

Griomasaigh [grʲiməsaj] *pnm* Grimsay; *gen* Ghriomasaigh [ɣrʲiməsaj]

grod [grɔd] *adj* rotten; *pl* ~a [grɔdə] *comp* groide [grɔdʲə]

gruag [gruəg] *nf* hair; *gen* gruaige [gruəgʲə] *pl* ~an [gruəgən]

gruagaire [gruəgɛrʲə] *nm* hairdresser; *pl* ~an [gruəgɛrʲən]

grunn [gru:N] *nm* batch; *gen* ~a [gruNə] *pl* ~an [gruNən]

gruth [gruh] *nm* crowdie; *gen* gruith [grih]

gu [gə] *prep* to; *def prep* chun an [xunəN⁽ʲ⁾] *def prep pl* chun na [xunə] conjugated thugam [hugəm] thugad [hugəd] thuige [huɡʲə] thuice [huçɡʲə] thugainn [hugɪNʲ] thugaibh [hugɪv] thuca [huxgə] • ~ bràth [gə bra:x] forever • ~ do làimh chearr [gə də Laiv ça:R] to your left • ~ do làimh cheart [gə də Laiv çaRʃd] to your right • ~ do làimh chlì [gə də Laiv çli:] to your left • ~ do làimh dheis [gə də Laiv jeʃ] to your right • ~ léir [gə Lʲe:rʲ] totally • ~ sealladh sealbh ort! [gə ʃaLəɣ ʃaLav ɔRʃd] Goodness!

guga [gugə] *nm* young gannet; *pl* ~chan [gugəxən]

gun [gəN⁽ʲ⁾] *conj* that • ~ ith thu [gə Nʲiç u] that you will eat • ~ òl thu [gə Nɔ:L u] that you will drink

gùn [gu:n] *nm* gown; *gen* gùin [gu:Nʲ] *pl* gùintean [gu:Nʲdʲən]

gunna [guNə] *nm* gun; *pl* ~chan [guNəxən]

guth [guh] *nm* voice; *gen* gutha [guhə] *pl* guthan [guhən]

h-UATH [huə]

hama [hamə] *nf* ham; *pl* ~ichean [hamɪçən]

Hearach [hɛrəx] *nm* a person from Harris; *gen* & *pl* Hearaich [hɛrɪç]

IODH [jɣɣ]

i [i] *pron* she, her; *emph* ise [iʃə]

iad [iəd] *pron* they, them; *emph* iadsan [iədsən]

Iain [i.aNʲ] *pnm* Ian

iar [iər] *nf* west • an ~ [ə Nʲiər] westerly

iarnaig [iəRNɪgʲəɣ] 1 *v* to iron 2 *vn* & *nf* ~eadh [iəRNɪgʲəɣ] ironing

iarr [iəR] 1 *v* to want 2 *vn* & *nm* ~aidh [iəRɪ] wanting, request; *pl* ~aidhean [iəRɪ.ən]

iarrtas [iəRdəs] *nm* demand; *gen* iarrtais [iəRdɪʃ] *pl* ~an [iəRdəsən]

iasg [iasg] *nm* fish; *gen* & *pl* éisg [e:ʃgʲ]

iasgach [iasgəx] *nm* fishing; *gen* iasgaich [iasgɪç]

I Chaluim Chille [ixaLəm'çiLʲə] *pnf* Iona

idir [idʲɪrʲ] *adv* at all

ifrinn [ifrʲɪNʲ] *nf* hell; *pl* ~ean [ifrʲɪNʲən]

Ìle [i:lə] *pnf* Islay

im [i:m] *nm* butter; *gen* ime [imə]

inbhir [iNʲɪrʲ] *nm* estuary; *pl* ~ean [iNʲɪrʲən] • An t-~ Beag [əNʲ tʲiNʲɪrʲ beg] Inverbeg • ~ Àir [iNʲɪrʲ'a:rʲ] Air • ~ Aora [iNʲɪrʲ'ɯ:rə] Inverary • ~ Nàrann [iNʲɪrʲ'na:rəN] Nairn • ~ Nis [iNʲɪrʲ'niʃ] Inverness

ìne [i:Nʲə] *nf* fingernail; *pl* ~an [i:Nʲən]

inneal [iNʲaL] *nm* instrument; *gen* inneil [iNʲɛl] *pl* ~an [iNʲaLən]

innis [ĩ:ʃ] 1 *v* to tell 2 *vn* & *nf* innse [ĩ:ʃə] telling

innis [inɪʃ] *nf* isle; *gen* innse [ĩ:ʃə] *pl* innseachan [ĩ:ʃəxən] • ~ Choluim [inɪʃ'xɔLəm] Inchcolm

Innseanach [ĩ:ʃanəx] 1 *nm* Indian; *gen* & *pl* innseanaich [ĩ:ʃanɪç] 2 *adj* indian; *comp* innseanaiche [ĩ:ʃanɪçə]

inntinneach [ĩ:NʲdʲɪNʲəx] *adj* interesting; *comp* inntinniche [ĩ:NʲdʲɪNʲɪçə]

iomadh [iməɣ] *nm* many; *gen* iomaidh [imɪ] • 's iomadh [ʃiməɣ] many a…

iomain [imɛNʲ] *nf* shinty; *gen* iomaine [imɛNʲə]

iomair [imɪrʲ] 1 *v* to row 2 *vn* & *nm* iomradh [imirəɣ] rowing; *gen* iomraidh [imirɪ]

Iomhar [ĩəvər] *pnm* Ivor; *gen* & *voc* Iomhair [ĩəvɪrʲ]

iomradh [imirəɣ] *nm* report; *gen* iomraidh [imiraj] *pl* iomraidhean [imirajən]

ionad [inəd] *nm* place; *gen* ionaid [inɪdʲ] *pl* ~an [inədən] • ~-slàinte [inəd'sLa:Nʲdʲə] health centre • ~-spòrs [inəd'sbɔ:rs] sports centre

ionga see ìne

iongnadh [ĩəNəɣ] *nm* amazement; *gen* iongnaidh [ĩəNɪ]

ionnsaich	[jũːNsɪç] 1 *v* to attack, to learn 2 *vn* & *nm* ionnsachadh [jũːNsəxəɣ] learning, attacking
Ìosa	[iəsə] *pnm* Jesus
is	[ɪs] *v* to be (with noun/pronoun predicate)
ist	[iʃdʲ] *excl* shush! *pl* ~ibh [iʃdʲɪv]
Iseabail	[iʃəbal] *pnf* Ishbel, Isobel
ìseal	[iːʃəL] *adj* low; *comp* ìsle [iːʃlə]
itealag	[içdʲaLag] *nf* kite; *gen* itealaig [içdʲaLɛgʲ] *pl* ~an [içdʲaLagən]
ith	[iç] 1 *v* to eat 2 *vn* & *nf* ~e [içə] eating
iuchair	[juxɪrʲ] *nf* key; *gen* iuchrach [juxrəx] *pl* iuchraichean [juxrɪçən]

LUIS [Luʃ]

là	[Laː] *nm* day (used in certain compounds) • ~ Bealltainn [Laː bjauLdɪNʲ] May Day • Là na Sàbaid [Laː nə saːbɪdʲ] Sunday
labhair	[Lavɪrʲ] 1 *v* to utter 2 *vn* & *nf* ~t [LavɪRʃdʲ] uttering
lachdann	[LaxgəN] *adj* tawny; *comp* lachdainne [LaxgɪNʲə]
Lachlann	[LaxLəN] *pnm* Lachlan; *gen* Lachlainn [LaxLɪNʲ] *voc* a Lachlainn [ə LaxLɪNʲ]
lag	[Lag] *adj* weak; *pl* ~a [Lagə] *comp* laige [Lagʲə]
lagaich	[Lagɪç] 1 *v* to weaken 2 *vn* & *nm* lagachadh [Lagəxəɣ] weakening; *gen* lagachaidh [Lagəxɪ]
laghach	[Lɤ.əx] *adj* decent; *comp* laghaiche [Lɤ.ɪçə]
làidir	[Laːdʲɪrʲ] *adj* strong; *comp* ~e [Laːdʲɪrʲə]
laigh	[Laj] 1 *v* to lie 2 *vn* & *nf* ~e [Lajə] lying
làir	[Laːrʲ] *nf* mare; *gen* làrach [Laːrəx] *pl* làraichean [Laːrɪçən] • ~-mhaide [Larʲʲvadʲə] seesaw
làitheil	[Laːjal] *adj* daily
làmh	[Laːv] *nf* hand; *gen* làimhe [Laivə] *pl* ~an [Laːvən]
làn	[Laːn] *adj* full; *pl* ~a [Laːnə] *comp* làine [LaːNʲə] • ~ dì do bheatha [Laːn dʲi: də vɛhə] you're very welcome
lanntair	[LãũNdɛrʲ] *nm* lantern; *pl* ~ean [LãũNdɛrʲən]
laochan	[Luːxan] *nm* good lad; *gen* & *pl* laochain [LuːxɛNʲ]
làr	[Laːr] *nm* floor; *gen* & *pl* làir [Laːrʲ]
làrna-mhàireach	[LaːRNə vaːrʲəx] *adv* following morning
las	[Las] 1 *v* to ignite 2 *vn* & *nm* ~adh [Lasəɣ] igniting; *gen* ~aidh [Lasɪ]

latha	[La.ə] *nm* day; *pl* làithean [La:jən]
Latharna	[LahəRNə] *pnm* Lorne
le	[le] *prep* with; *def prep* leis an [leʃəNⁱ⁾] *def prep pl* leis na [leʃnə] conjugated leam [loum] leat [lɛhd] leis [leʃ] leatha [lɛ.ə] leinn [leiNʲ] leibh [leiv] leotha [lɔ.ə]
leabaidh	[Lʲebɪ] *nf* bed; *gen* leapa [Lʲɛhbə] *pl* leapannan [LʲɛhbəNən]
leabhar	[Lʲɔ.ər] *nm* book; *gen* leabhair [Lʲɔ.ɪrʲ] *pl* leabhraichean [Lʲɔ:rɪçən] • ~-lann [Lʲɔ.əRLəN] library • ~-sgoile [Lʲɔ.ər'sgolə] school book
leac	[Lʲɛxg] *nf* slab; *gen* lice [Lʲiçgʲə] *pl* ~an [Lʲɛxgən] • An ~ [ə Lʲɛxg] The Lecht
leag	[Lʲeg] 1 *v* to fell 2 *vn & nm* ~adh [Lʲegəɣ] felling; *gen* ~aidh [Lʲegɪ]
Leamhnachd	[Lʲãũnəxg] *pnf* Lennox; *gen* ~ [lãũnəxg]
lean	[Lʲɛn] 1 *v* to follow 2 *vn & nm* ~tainn [LʲɛndɪNʲ] following
leann	[LʲauN] *nm* ale; *gen* ~a [LʲaNə] *pl* ~tan [LʲauNdən]
leatas	[Lʲɛhdəs] *nm* lettuce; *gen* leatais [Lʲɛhdɪʃ] *pl* ~an [Lʲɛhdəsən]
leathann	[LʲɛhəN] *adj* broad; *comp* leathainne [LʲɛhɪNʲə]
leig	[Lʲegʲ] 1 *v* to let 2 *vn & nf* ~eil [Lʲegʲal] letting; *gen* ~ealach [LʲegʲəLəx]
léine	[Lʲe:nə] *nf* shirt; *pl* léintean [Lʲe:ndʲən]
leithid	[Lʲehɪdʲ] *nf* equivalant; *gen* ~e [Lʲehɪdʲə] *pl* ~ean [Lʲehɪdʲən]
leitir	[Lʲehdʲɪrʲ] *nf* hillslope; *gen* leitreach [Lʲehdrəx] *pl* leitrichean [Lʲehdrɪçən] • ~ Fhionnlaigh [Lʲehdʲɪrʲʲjũ:NLaj] Letterfinlay
Leòdhas	[Lʲɔ:.əs] *pnm* Lewis; *gen* Leòdhais [Lʲɔ:.ɪʃ]
Leòdhasach	[Lʲɔ:.əsəx] *nm* a person from Lewis; *gen & pl* Leòdhasaich [Lʲɔ:.əsɪç]
leòr	[Lʲɔ:r] *nf* sufficiency; *gen* leòir [Lʲɔ:rʲ] • gu leòr [gə Lʲɔ:r] enough
leth	[Lʲeh] *nm* half • ~ dusan [Lʲeh dusan] half a dozen • ~ fhacal [Lʲe haxgəL] clue • ~ phinnt [Lʲeh fĩ:Nʲdʲ] half a pint • ~ uair [Lʲe huərʲ] half an hour
leud	[Lʲiad] *nm* width; *pl* ~an [Lʲiadən]
leudaich	[Lʲiadɪç] 1 *v* to extend 2 *vn & nm* leudachadh [Lʲiadəxəɣ] extending; *gen* leudachaidh [Lʲiadəxɪ]

leugh	[Lʲeːv] 1 *v* to read 2 *vn* & *nm* ~adh [Lʲeːvəɣ] reading; *gen* ~aidh [Lʲeːvɪ] *pl* ~aidhean [Lʲeːvɪ.ən]
leum	[Lʲeːm] 1 *v* to jump 2 *vn* & *nm* jumping, jump; *gen* ~a [Lʲeːmə] *pl* ~an [Lʲeːmən]
liath	[Lʲiə] *adj* grey (hair or fur); *pl* ~a [Lʲiə.ə] *comp* léithe [Lʲeː.ə]
linne	[LʲiNʲə] *nf* firth; *pl* ~achan [LʲiNʲəxən] • ~ Chluaidh [LʲiNʲə'xLuəj] Firth of Clyde
lìon	[Lʲiən] 1 *v* to fill 2 *vn* & *nm* ~adh [Lʲiənəɣ] filling 3 *nm* net; *gen* lìn [Lʲiːn] *pl* ~tan [LʲiəNdən]
Lìonacleit	[Lʲiənəklehdʲ] *pnf* Liniclete; *gen* ~ [lʲiənəklehdʲ]
lios	[Lʲis] *nm* garden; *gen* ~a [Lʲisə] *pl* ~an [Lʲisən] • ~ Mór [Lʲis'moːr] Lismore
Liosach	[Lʲisəx] *nm* a person from Lismore; *gen* & *pl* Liosaich [Lʲisɪç]
lite	[Lʲihdʲə] *nf* porrige
Lìte	[Lʲiːhdʲə] *pnf* Leith; *gen* ~ [liːhdʲə]
litir	[Lʲihdʲɪrʲ] *nf* letter; *gen* litreach [Lʲihdrəx] *pl* litrichean [Lʲihdrɪçən]
litrich	[Lʲihdrɪç] 1 *v* to spell 2 *vn* & *nm* litreachadh [Lʲihdrəxəɣ] spelling
loch	[Lɔx] *nm* loch; *gen* ~a [Lɔxə] *pl* ~an [Lɔxən] • An ~ Dubh [ə Lɔx du] Lochdhu • ~ Abar [Lɔx'abər] Lochaber • ~ Aillse [Lɔx'aiLʲʃə] Lochalsh • ~ Laomainn [Lɔx'LuːmɪNʲ] Loch Lomond • ~ na Creige [Lɔx nə krʲegʲə] Loch na Creige • ~ nam Madadh [Lɔx nə madəɣ] Lochmaddy • ~ Nis [Lɔx'nʲiʃ] Loch Ness • ~ Mhùrlaig [Lɔx'vuːRLɛgʲ] Loch Morlich • ~ Raonasa [Lɔx'ruːnəsə] Lochranza
lochan	[Lɔxan] *nm* little loch; *gen* & *pl* lochain [LɔxɛNʲ]
Lochlann	[LɔxLəN] *pnf* Scandinavia; *gen* Lochlainn [LɔxLɪNʲ]
loidhne	[Lɤinə] *nf* line; *pl* ~achan [Lɤinəxən]
loisg	[Lɔʃgʲ] 1 *v* to burn 2 *vn* & *nm* losgadh [Lɔsgəɣ] burning; *gen* losgaidh [Lɔsgɪ]
lòn	[Lɔːn] *nm* marshy meadow; *gen* lòin [LɔːNʲ] *pl* lòintean [LɔːNʲdʲən]
long	[Lɔuŋg] *nf* ship; *gen* luinge [Luiŋʲgʲə] *pl* ~an [Lɔuŋgən]
lorg	[Lɔrɔg] 1 *v* to find 2 *vn* & *nm* ~ [Lɔrɔg] finding; *gen* luirg [Lurʲɪgʲ]
luach	[Luəx] *nm* value
luath	[Luə] *adj* quick; *pl* ~a [Luə.ə] *comp* luaithe [Luəjə]

lùbach	[Lu:bəx] *adj* winding; *comp* lùbaiche [Lu:bɪçə]
luch	[Lux] *nf* mouse; *gen* ~a [Luxə] *pl* ~an [Luxən]
lùchairt	[Lu:xɪRʃdʲ] *nf* palace; *gen* ~e [Lu:xɪRʃdʲə] *pl* ~ean [Lu:xɪRʃdʲən]
luchd	[Luxg] see neach
Lunnainn	[LuNɪNʲ] *pnf* London
lus	[Lus] *nm* plant; *gen* luis [Luʃ] *pl* ~an [Lusən] • ~ a' chrom-chinn [Lus ə xrɔumçɪNʲ] daffodil • ~-gréine [Lus'grʲe:nə] sunflower

MUIN [muNʲ]

ma	[ma] *conj* if; with copula mas [mas] & [maʃ] • mas e [ma ʃɛ:] if it is
mac	[maxg] *nm* son; *gen* & *pl* mic [miçgʲ] • ~ a' Phearsain [maxgə'fɛrsɛNʲ] MacPherson • MacAmhlaigh [max'gãũLɪ] MacAulay • MacArtair [max'gaRʃdɪrʲ] MacArthur • MacAsgaill [max'gasgɪLʲ] MacAskill • ~ a' Ghobhainn [maxg ə ɣo.ɪNʲ] Smith • ~ an t-Saoir [maxg ən tuː:rʲ] Macintyre • MacAonghais [max'gũnũɪʃ] MacInnes • MacDhòmhnaill [maxg'ɣɔ̃:.ɪLʲ] MacDonald • MacDhùghaill [maxg'ɣu:.ɪLʲ] MacDougall • MacFhionghain [max'gʲiniɣɛNʲ] MacKinnon • MacGilleEathain [maxgʲɪ'Lʲɛ.ɛNʲ] MacLean • MacGillelosa [maxgʲɪ'Lʲiəsə] Gillies • MacGilleMhoire [maxgʲiLʲə'vorʲə] Gilmore • MacGumaraid [max'gumərɪdʲ] Montgomery • MacIomhair [max'gʲiəvɪrʲ] MacIver • MacMhathain [maxg'vahɛNʲ] MacMahon • MacNeacail [max'grɛ̃xgal] Nicholson • MacNèill [max'grɛ̃:Lʲ] MacNeill • MacPhàrlain [maxg'fa:RLɛNʲ] MacFarlane • MacRath [max'grah] MacRae • MacThòmais [max'kɔ:mɪʃ] Thomson
machair	[maxɛrʲ] *nf* machair; *gen* machrach [maxrəx] *pl* machraichean [maxrɪçən]
madainn	[madɪNʲ] *nf* morning; *gen* maidne [maNʲə] *pl* ~ean [madɪNʲən]
maighdeann	[mɤidʲəN] *nf* maid, virgin; *gen* maighdinn [mɤidʲɪNʲ] *pl* maighdinnean [mɤidʲɪNʲən]
Maighread	[majrʲəd] *pnf* Margaret; *gen* Maighreid [majrʲɪdʲ] *voc* a Mhaighread [ə vajrʲəd]

maighstir	[maiʃdʲɪrʲ] *nm* master; *pl* ~ean [maiʃdʲɪrʲən]
màileid	[ma:lɪdʲ] *nf* suitcase; *gen* ~e [ma:lɪdʲə] *pl* ~ean [ma:lɪdʲən]
maille	[maLʲə] *nf* delay
mair	[marʲ] 1 *v* to last 2 *vn* & *nm* ~eann [marʲəN] lasting
Mairead	see **Maighread**
Màiri	[ma:rʲɪ] *pnf* Mary; *voc* a Mhàiri [ə va:rʲɪ]
maistir	[maʃdʲɪrʲ] *nm* stale urine
mala	[maLə] *nf* eyebrow; *pl* ~ichean [maLɪçən]
màla	[ma:Lə] *nf* bag; *pl* ~n [ma:Lən]
Manainn	[manɪNʲ] *pnf* (Isle of) Man; *gen* Mhanainn [vanɪNʲ]
manaidsear	[manɪdʲʃɛr] *nm* manager; *gen* manaidseir [manɪdʲʃɛrʲ] *pl* ~an [manɪdʲʃɛrʲən]
mansa	[mansə] *nm* manse; *pl* ~ichean [mansɪçən]
mapa	[mahbə] *nm* map; *pl* ~ichean [mahbɪçən]
mar	[mar] *prep* as • ~ sin [maRʲʃin] like that
marag	[marag] *nf* pudding; *gen* maraig [marɛgʲ] *pl* ~an [maragən]
marbh	[marav] *adj* dead; *pl* ~a [maravə], *comp* mairbhe [mɛrʲɛvə]
marcaich	[margɪç] 1 *v* to ride 2 *vn* & *nm* marcachd [margəxg] riding
margadh	[maragəɣ] *nm* market; *gen* margaidh [maragɪ] *pl* margaidhean [maragɪ.ən]
Marsaili	[maRsalɪ] *pnf* Marjory; *gen* Marsaili [maRsalɪ] *voc* a Mharsaili [ə vaRsalɪ]
Màrtainn	[ma:RʃdɪNʲ] *pnm* Martin; *gen* Mhàrtainn [va:RʃdɪNʲ] *voc* a Mhàrtainn [ə va:RʃdɪNʲ]
mar-tha	[marˈha:] same as **mu thràth** (qv)
Mata	[mahdə] *pnm* Matthew; *gen* Mhata [vahdə] *voc* a Mhata [ə vahdə]
ma-tà	[maˈta:] *conj* in that case
math	[ma] *adj* good; *pl* ~a [ma.ə] 1st *comp* nas fhearr [nə ʃa:R] 2nd *comp* as fheairrde [ə ʃa:Rdʲə] • is fhearr leam [ə ʃa:R ləm] I prefer • ~ fhéin! [ma he:n] great!
ma-thà	[maˈha:] *conj* in that case
màthair	[ma:hərʲ] *nf* mother; *gen* màthar [ma:hər] *pl* màthraichean [ma:rɪçən]
meadhan	[mi.an] *nm* middle; *gen* meadhain [mi.ɛNʲ] *pl* ~an [mi.anən] • ~-latha [mianˈLa.ə] midday
meadhanach	[mi.anəx] *adj* medium; *comp* meadhanaiche [mi.anɪçə]
meall	[mjauL] *nm* lump, round hill; *gen* & *pl* mill [mi:Lʲ] • Am ~ Mór [ə mjauL mo:r] Meallmore
mear	[mɛr] *adj* merry; *pl* ~a [mɛrə] *comp* meire [merʲə]

meas	[mes] *nm* 1 esteem 2 fruit
measg	[mesg] *n* midst • am measg [ə'mesg] in the midst
measgaich	[mesgɪç] 1 *v* to mix 2 *vn* & *nm* measgachadh [mesgəxəɣ] mixing
meirleach	[mɛ:Rləx] *nm* thief; *gen* & *pl* meirlich [mɛ:Rlɪç]
Meudarloch	[miadəRLɔx] *pnm* Benderloch; *gen* Mheudarloch [viadəRLɔx]
meur	[miar] *nm* finger; *gen* & *pl* meòir [mjɔ:rʲ]
Mhorbhairne, a' ~	[ə vɔrɔ.əRNʲə] *pnf* Morvern; *gen* na Morbhairne [nə mɔrɔ.əRNʲə]
mi	[mi] *pron* I, me; *emph* mise [miʃə]
Mìcheal	[mi:çəL] *pnm* Michael; *gen* Mhìcheil [vi:çɪl] *voc* a Mhìcheil [ə vi:çɪl]
mì-fhortanach	[mi: ɔRʃdanəx] *adj* unfortunately; *comp* mì-fhortanaiche [mi: ɔRʃdanɪçə]
mìlsean	[mi:lʃan] *nm* sweet, desert; *gen* mìlsein [mi:lʃɛNʲ] *pl* ~an [mi:lʃanən]
mì-mhodh	[mi:voɣ] *nm* impertinence; *gen* ~a [mi:voɣə] *pl* ~an [mi:voɣən]
mìle	[mi:lə] *num* thousand; *pl* mìltean [mi:ldʲən]
mìleamh	[mi:ləv] *num* thousandth
milis	[milɪʃ] *adj* sweet; *comp* mìlse [mi:lʃə]
millean	[miLʲan] *nm* million; *pl* ~an [miLʲanən]
milleanamh	[miLʲənəv] *num* millionth
min	[min] *nf* flour; *gen* ~e [minə]
mìn	[mi:n] *adj* soft; *pl* & *comp* ~e [mi:nə]
mìnich	[mi:nɪç] 1 *v* to explain 2 *vn* & *nm* mìneachadh [mi:nəxəɣ] explaining
ministear	[minɪʃdʲɛr] *nm* minister; *gen* ministeir [minɪʃdʲɛrʲ] *pl* ~an [minɪʃdʲɛrən]
mionach	[minəx] *nm* entrails; *gen* mionaich [minɪç]
mionaid	[minadʲ] *nf* minute; *gen* ~e [minadʲə] *pl* ~ean [minadʲən]
mìos	[miəs] *nm* month; *pl* ~an [miəsən]
miotag	[mihdag] *nf* glove; *gen* miotaige [mihdɛgʲə] *pl* ~an [mihdagən]
Miughalaigh	[mju.əLaj] *pnm* Mingulay; *gen* Mhiughalaigh [vju.əLaj]
mo	[mə] *poss pron* my; before vowel m' [m]: m' athair [mahərʲ] • ~ chreach! [mə xrʲɛx] oh dear!
moch	[mɔx] *adj* early; *pl* ~a [mɔxə] *comp* moiche [mɔçə]
mòd	[mɔ:d] *nm* mod; *gen* mòid [mɔ:dʲ] *pl* mòdan [mɔ:dən]

modh   [moɣ] *nm* manner; *gen* ~a [moɣə] *pl* ~an [moɣən] •
              ~ cainnte [moɣ kaiNʲdʲə] manner of speaking

modhail   [moɣal] *adj* polite; *comp* ~e [moɣalə] • mì-mhodhail
              [mĩː voɣal] impolite

Moireabh [morʲəv] *pnm* Moray; *gen* Mhoireibh [vorʲəv]

Moireach [morʲəx] *pnm* Murray; *gen* Mhoirich [vorʲɪç]

Moireastan [morʲəsdan] *pnm* Morrison; *gen* Mhoireastain [vorʲəsdɛNʲ]

mol   [moL] 1 *v* to praise 2 *vn* & *nm* ~adh [moLəɣ] praise,
              praising; *gen* ~aidh [moLɪ] *pl* ~aidhean [moLɪ.ən]

monadh   [monəɣ] *nm* mountain moor; *gen* monaidh [monɪ] *pl*
              monaidhean [monɪ.ən] • Am ~ Ruadh [ə monəɣ Ruəɣ]
              the Cairngorms

mór   [moːr] *adj* big; *pl* ~a [moːrə] 1st *comp* motha [mo.ə] 2nd
              comp móid [moːdʲ]

mór-chuid [moːrxədʲ] *nf* majority; *pl* ~-chodaichean [moːrxədɪçən]

Mórag   [moːrag] *pnf* Morag; *gen* Móraig [moːrɛgʲ] *voc* a Mhórag
              [ə voːrag]

móran   [moːran] *nm* much, a lot of; *gen* mórain [moːrɛNʲ]

Mòrar   [moːrər] *pnm* Morar; *gen* Mhòrair [võːrərʲ]

mormhair [morovarʲ] *nm* lord mayor; *pl* ~an [morovarʲən]

mothaich [mo.ɪç] 1 *v* to notice 2 *vn* & *nm* mothachadh [mo.əxəɣ]
              noticing; *gen* mothachaidh [mo.əxɪ]

mu   [ma] *prep* about; *def prep* mun an [manəNⁱ⁽ʲ⁾] *def prep pl*
              mu na [manə] conjugated umam [uməm] umad [uməd]
              uime [uɯmə] uimpe [uɯimbə] umainn [umɪNʲ] umaibh
              [umɪv] umpa [ũːmbə] • ~ dhèidhinn [mə je.ɪNʲ] about

muasgan-caol [muəsganˈkɯːL] *nm* prawn; *gen* muasgain-chaoil
              [muəsgɛNʲˈxɯːl] *pl* muasgain-chaola [muəsgɛNʲˈxɯːLə]

muc   [muxg] *nf* pig; *gen* muice [muçgʲə] *pl* ~an [muxgən]

muga   [mugə] *nm* mug; *pl* ~ichean [mugɪçən]

Mùideart [muːdʲəRʃd] *pnm* Moidart; *gen* Mhùideirt [vuːdʲəRʃdⁱ]

Muile   [mulə] *pnm* Mull; *gen* Mhuile [vulə]

Muileach [muləx] *nm* a person from Mull; *gen* & *pl* Muilich [mulɪç]

muileann [muləN] *nm* mill; *gen* muilinn [mulɪNʲ] *pl* muillean
              [muiLʲən]

muillear [muiLʲɛr] *nm* miller; *gen* muilleir [muiLʲɛrʲ] *pl* ~an
              [muiLʲɛrən]

muin   [muNʲ] *nf* back part • air ~ [ɛrʲ muNʲ] mounted on

mùin   [muːNʲ] *v* & *vn* to urinate, urinating

muinntir [mũĩNʲdʲɪrʲ] *nf* folk; *gen* ~e [mũĩNʲdʲɪrʲə] *pl* ~ean

[mũĩN^jd^jɪr^jən]

muir   [mur^j] *nm* sea; *gen (nf)* mara [marə] *pl (nf)* marannan
              [marəNən]

mullach   [muLəx] *nm* roof; *gen & pl* mullaich [muLɪç]

mur   [mar] *conj* if not

murt   [muRʃd] *nm* murder; *gen & pl* muirt [muRʃd^j]

Murchadh   [muruxəɣ] *pnm* Murdo; *gen* Mhurchaidh [vuruxɪ] *voc* a
              Mhurchaidh [ə vuruxɪ]

mus   [mas] *conj* before

NUIN [NuN^j]

Na Hearadh   [nə hɛrəɣ] *pn* Harris
na ¹   [na] *adv* (do) not
na ²   [na] relative particle that, that which
nach   [nax] 1 neg *interr* (is) not?, (are) not?, (was) not? etc 2
                  neg conj that (is) not, that (was) not etc

na h-Innseachan   [nə hĩːʃəxən] *pnf pl* India
naidheachd   [Nɛ.əxg] *nf* news; *pl* ~an [Nɛ.əxgən]
nàiseanta   [NaːʃəNdə] *adj* national
nan   [naN^(j)] *part* if
naochad   [Nɯːxəd] *num* ninety
naoidh   [Nɯj] *num* nine; *counting form* a ~ [ə Nɯj]
naoidheamh   [Nɯjəv] *num* ninth
naomhaich   [Nɯːvɪç] 1 *v* to hallow 2 *vn & nm* naomhachadh
                  [Nɯːvəxəɣ] hallowing; *gen* naomhachaidh [Nɯːvəxɪ]
naonar   [Nɯːnər] *nm* nine (people)
Narann   [NarəN] *pn* Nairn; *gen* ~ [narəN]
nas   [nas] *comp* more
neach   [N^jɛx] *nm* person; *pl nm* luchd [Luxg] • luchd-
                  ionnsachaidh [Lux'g^juːNsəxɪ] learners • [Lux'gobrəx]
                  staff • ~-treòrachaidh [N^jɛx'trɔːrəxɪ] guide • luchd-turais
                  [Lux'turɪʃ] tourists
nèamh   [N^jɛːv] *nm* heaven; *gen* nèimh [N^jɛːv] *pl* ~an [N^jɛːvən]
neoini   [N^jɔnɪ] *nm* zero; *counting form* a ~ [ə N^jɔnɪ]
neònach   [N^jɔːnəx] *adj* weird; *comp* neònaiche [N^jɔːnɪçə]
neapaigear   [N^jɛhbɪg^jɛr] *nm* handkerchief; *gen* neapaigeir [N^jɛhbɪg^jɛr^j]
                  pl ~an [N^jɛhbɪg^jɛrən]
nì   [N^jiː] *nm* thing; *pl* nithean [N^jihən]
Niall   [N^jiaL] *pnm* Neil; *gen* Nèill [nɛːL^j] *voc* a Nèill [ə nɛːL^j]

Nic	[Nʲiçgʲ] *nf* daughter of (in surnames) • ~ a' Phearsain [Nʲiçgʲə'fɛrsɪNʲ] MacPherson • NicAmhlaigh [Nʲiç'gãūLɪ] MacAulay • NicArtair [Nʲiç'gaRʃdɪrʲ] MacArthur • NicAsgaill [Nʲiç'gasgɪLʲ] MacAskill • ~ a' Ghobhainn [Nʲiçgʲ ə ɣo.ɪNʲ] Smith • ~ an t-Saoir [Nʲiçgʲ ən tuːrʲ] Macintyre • NicAonghais [Nʲiç'gũnũɪʃ] MacInnes • NicDhòmhnaill [Nʲiçgʲ'ɣõ:.ɪLʲ] MacDonald • NicDhùghaill [Nʲiçgʲ'ɣu:.ɪLʲ] MacDougall • NicFhionghain [Nʲiç'gʲiniɣɪNʲ] MacKinnon • NicGilleEathain [Nʲiçgʲɪ'Lʲɛ.ɛNʲ] MacLean • NicGillelosa [Nʲiçgʲɪ'Lʲiəsə] Gillies • NicGilleMhoire [NʲiçgʲiLʲə'vorʲə] Gilmore • NicGumaraid [Nʲiç'gumərɪdʲ] Montgomery • Niclomhair [Nʲiç'gʲiəvɪrʲ] MacIver • NicMhathain [NʲiçgʲivahɛNʲ] MacMahon • NicNeacail [Nʲiç'grɛ̃xgal] Nicholson • NicNèill [Nʲiç'grʲɛ̃:Lʲ] MacNeill • NicPhàrlain [Nʲiçgʲ'fa:RLɪNʲ] MacFarlane • NicRath [Nʲiç'grah] MacRae • NicThòmais [Nʲiç'kɔ:mɪʃ] Thomson
nigh	[Nʲi] 1 *v* to wash 2 *vn* & *nm* ~e [Nʲi.ə] washing • ~eadaireachd [Nʲi.ədɛrʲəxg] washing
nighean	[Nʲi.an] *nf* daughter; *gen* nighinn [Nʲi.ɪNʲ] *pl* ~an [Nʲi.anən]
Nirribhidh	[NʲiRɪvɪ] *pnf* Norway; *gen* ~e [niRɪvɪ.ə]
no	[nɔ] *conj* or
nochd	[Nɔxg] 1 *v* to appear 2 *vn* & *nm* ~adh [Nɔxgəɣ] appearing
Nollaig, an ~	[ə NɔLɛgʲ] *nf* Christmas; *gen* na Nollaig [nə NɔLɛgʲ]
not	[Nɔhd] *nm* pound (currency); *pl* ~aichean [Nɔhdɪçən]
nuair	[Nuərʲ] *conj* when • ~ a... [Nuərʲ ə] when...

ONN [ɔuN]

o	[o] & [ɔ] *prep* see bho
obair	[obɪrʲ] 1 *v* to work 2 *nf* work; *gen* obrach [obrəx] *pl* obraichean [obrɪçən] • ~-fhighe [obɪrʲi.ə] knotwork
òban	[ɔ:ban] *nm* a little bay; *gen* & *pl* òbain [ɔ:bɛNʲ] • An t-~ [əN tɔ:ban] Oban *gen* an Òbain [ə Nɔ:bɛNʲ]
obh obh!	[o vov] *excl* oh dear!
obraich	[obrɪç] 1 *v* to work 2 *vn* & *nm* obrachadh [obrəxəɣ] working; *gen* obrachaidh [obrəxɪ]
ochd	[ɔxg] *num* eight; *counting form* a h-~ [ə hɔxg]
ochdad	[ɔxgəd] *num* eighty
ochdamh	[ɔxgəv] *num* eighth
ochdnar	[ɔxgnər] *nm* eight (people)

òg [ɔːg] *adj* young; *pl* ~a [ɔːgə] *comp* òige [ɔːgʲə]

oidhche [ɣ̃jçə] *nf* night; *pl* ~annan [ɣ̃jçəNən] • ~ Challainn [ɣ̃jçəˈxaLɪNʲ] Hogmanay • ~ na Bliadhna Ùire [ɣ̃jçə nə bləˈNuːrʲə] New Year's Eve • ~ Shamhna [ɣ̃jçəˈhãūnə] Halloween • ~ Luain [ɣ̃jçəˈLuəNʲ] Monday night • ~ Mhàirt [ɣ̃jçəˈvaːRʃdʲ] Tuesday night • ~ Chiadain [ɣ̃jçəˈçiədɛNʲ] Wednesday night • ~ ArdAoin [ɣ̃jçəRˈduːNʲ] Thursday night • ~ hAoine [ɣ̃jçəˈhuːNʲə] Friday night • ~ Shathairne [ɣ̃jçəˈhahəRNʲə] Saturday night • ~ Dhòmhnaich [ɣ̃jçəˈɣõːnɪç] Sunday night

oifigeach [ɔfɪgʲəx] *adj* official; *comp* oifigich [ɔfɪgʲɪç]

oifis [ɔfɪʃ] *nf* office; *gen* ~e [ɔfɪʃə] *pl* ~ean [ɔfɪʃən] • ~ a' phuist [ɔfɪʃ ə fuʃdʲ] post office

Oighrig [ɣirʲɪgʲ] *pnf* Effie

òigridh [ɔːgʲrʲɪ] *nf* youth

oileanach [ɣlanəx] *nm* student; *gen* & *pl* [ɣlanɪç] • ban-~ [ban ɣlanəx] *nf* female student; *gen* ban-oileanaich [ban ɣlanɪç] *pl* mnathan-~ [mrã.ən ɣlanəx]

oilthigh [ɔlhəj] *nm* university; *pl* ~ean [ɔlhəjən]

oir [ɔrʲ] *conj* because

òir [ɔːrʲ] *adj* golden

òirleach [ɔːRləx] *nf* inch; *gen* & *pl* òirlich [ɔːRlɪç]

oisean [ɔʃan] *nm* corner, nook; *gen* oisein [ɔʃɛNʲ] *pl* ~an [ɔʃanən]

òl [ɔːL] 1 *v* to eat 2 *vn* & *nm* ~ [ɔːL] drinking

ola [ɔLə] *nf* oil; *pl* ~ichean [ɔLɪçən]

Òlaind, an ~ [ə NɔːLandʲ] *pnf* Holland; *gen* na h-Òlainde [nə hɔːLandʲə]

olc [ɔLg] *adj* evil; *pl* ~a [ɔLgə] *comp* uilc [ɯlgʲ]

onair [ɔnarʲ] *nf* honour

òr [ɔːr] *nm* gold; *gen* òir [ɔːrʲ]

orains [ɔrənʃ] *adj* orange; *comp* ~e [ɔrənʃə]

orainsear [ɔranʃɛr] *nm* orange; *gen* orainseir [ɔranʃɛrʲ] *pl* ~an [ɔranʃɛrən]

òran [ɔːran] *nm* song; *gen* & *pl* òrain [ɔːrɛNʲ]

Orasa [ɔrəsə] *pnm* Oronsay

òrd [ɔːRd] *nm* hammer; *gen* & *pl* ùird [uːRdʲ]

òrdag [ɔːRdag] *nf* thumb; *gen* òrdaige [ɔːRdɛgʲə] *pl* ~an [ɔːRdagən]

òrdugh [ɔːRdu] *nm* order; *gen* òrduigh [ɔːRdɪ] *pl* òrduighean [ɔːRdɪ.ən]

os cionn [ɔs kʲuːN] *prep* above

ostail	[ɔsdal] *nf* hostel; *gen* ~e [ɔsdalə] *pl* ~ean [ɔsdalən] • ~-òigridh [ɔsdaˈlɔːgʲrʲɪ] youth hostel
ospadal	[ɔsbədəL] *nm* hospital; *gen* ospadail [ɔsbədəl] *pl* ~an [ɔsbədəLən]

PEITH [peh]

Pabaigh	[pabaj] *pnm* Pabay; *gen* Phabaigh [fabaj]
paca	[paxgə] *nm* pack; *pl* ~nnan [paxgəNən]
pacaid	[paxgɪdʲ] *nf* packet; *pl* ~ean [paxgɪdʲən]
Pàdraig	[paːdrɪgʲ] *pnm* Patrick; *gen* Phàdraig [faːdrɪgʲ] *voc* a Phàdraig [ə faːdrɪgʲ]
paidhir	[pa.ɪrʲ] *nf* pair; *gen* paidhreach [pairʲəx] *pl* paidhrichean [pairʲɪçən]
pàigh	[paːj] 1 *v* to pay 2 *vn* & *nm* ~eadh [paːjəɣ] paying
pailteas	[paldʲəs] *nm* plenty (of); *gen* pailteis [paldʲɪʃ]
pàipear	[pɛːhbɛr] *nm* paper; *gen* pàipeir [pɛːhbɛrʲ] *pl* ~an [pɛːhbɛrʲən] • ~-naidheachd [pɛhbɛrˈnɛ.əxg] newspaper
Pàislig	[paːʃlɪgʲ] *pnf* Paisley; *gen* Phàislig [faːʃlɪgʲ]
pàiste	[paːʃdʲə] *nf* child; *pl* ~ean [paːʃdʲən]
Paras	[parəs] *pnm* Paris; *gen* Pharas [farəs]
pàrant	[paːrəNd] *nm* parent; *gen* pàraint [paːrɪNʲdʲ] *pl* ~an [paːrəndən]
pàrlamaid	[paːRLəmɪdʲ] *nf* parliament; *gen* ~e [paːRLəmɪdʲə] *pl* ~ean [paːRLəmɪdʲən]
pasaidear	[pasɪdʲɛr] *nm* passenger; *gen* pasaideir [pasɪdʲɛrʲ] *pl* ~an [pasɪdʲɛrən]
pathadh	[pa.əɣ] *nm* thirst; *gen* pathaidh [pa.ɪ] • tha am ~ orm [ham pa.əɣ ɔrɔm] I am thirsty
Peairt	[pɛRʃdʲ] Perth; *gen* Pheairt [fɛRʃdʲ]
peanasaich	[pɛnəsɪç] 1 *v* to punish 2 *vn* & *nm* peanasachadh [pɛnəsəxəɣ] punishing; *gen* peanasachaidh [pɛnəsəxɪ]
peann	[pjauN] *nm* pen; *gen* & *pl* pinn [piːNʲ]
peant	[pɛnd] *nm* paint; *gen* ~a [pɛndə] *pl* ~aichean [pɛndɪçən]
peasair	[pesɪrʲ] *nf* pea; *gen* peasrach [pesrəx] *pl* ~ean [pesɪrʲən]
peasan	[pesan] *nm* brat; *gen* & *pl* peasain [pesɛNʲ]
peata	[pɛhdə] *nm* pet; *pl* ~ichean [pɛhdɪçən]
Peigi	[pegʲɪ] *pnf* Peggy; *voc* a Pheigi [ə fegʲɪ]
peitean	[pehdʲan] *nm* jumper; *gen* peitein [pehdʲɛNʲ] *pl* ~an [pehdʲanən]

Peutan	[pe:hdan] *pnm* Beaton; *gen* Pheutain [fe:hdɛNʲ]
Phòlainn, a' ~	[ə fɔ:LɪNʲ] *pnf* Poland; *gen* na Pòlainne [nə pɔ:LɪNʲə]
Phortagail, a' ~	[ə fɔRʃdəgal] *pnf* Portugal; *gen* na Portagaile [na pɔRʃdəgələ]
pinc	[piŋʲkʲ] *adj* pink; *pl* & *comp* ~e [piŋʲkʲə]
pinnt	[pĩ:Nʲdʲ] *nm* pint; *pl* ~ean [pĩ:Nʲdʲən]
pìob	[pi:b] *nf* pipe; *gen* ~a [pi:bə] *pl* ~an [pi:bən] • a' phìob-mhòr [ə fibˈvo:r] bagpipes
piobar	[pibɛr] *nm* pepper; *gen* piobair [pibɛrʲ] *pl* ~an [pibɛrʲən]
pìobaire	[pi:bɛrʲə] *nm* piper; *pl* ~ean [pi:bɛrʲən]
pìobaireachd	[pi:bɛrʲəxg] *nf* piping
pìos	[pi:s] *nm* piece; *gen* ~a [pi:sə] *pl* ~an [pi:sən]
piseag	[piʃag] *nf* kitten; *gen* piseige [piʃɛgʲə] *pl* ~an [piʃagən]
piuthar	[pju.ər] *nf* sister; *gen* peathar [pɛhər] *pl* peathraichean [pɛrɪçən]
plana	[pLanə] *nm* plan; *pl* ~ichean [pLanɪçən]
plèan	[plɛ:n] *nm* airplane; *pl* ~aichean [plɛ:nɪçən]
poblachd	[pobLəxg] *nf* republic; *pl* ~an [pobLəxgən]
poca	[pɔxgə] *nm* bag; *pl* ~nnan [pɔxgəNən] • ~-cadail [pɔxgəˈkadal] sleeping bag
pòcaid	[pɔ:xgɪdʲ] *nf* pocket; *gen* ~e [pɔ:xgɪdʲə] *pl* ~ean [pɔ:xgɪdʲən]
pòg	[pɔ:g] 1 *nf* kiss; *gen* pòige [pɔ:gʲə] *pl* ~an [pɔ:gən] 2 *v* to kiss 2 *vn* & *nm* ~adh [pɔ:gəɣ]
poileas	[pɔləs] *nm* police; *gen* poilis [pɔlɪʃ]
poit	[pɔhdʲ] *nf* pot; *gen* ~e [pɔhdʲə] *pl* ~ean [pɔhdʲən]
pònair	[pɔ:nɪrʲ] *nf* bean; *gen* pònarach [pɔ:nərəx] *pl* ~ean [pɔ:nɪrʲən]
port	[pɔRʃd] *nm* 1 harbour 2 tune; *gen* & *pl* puirt [puRʃdʲ] • ~-a-beul [pɔRʃd a bial] mouth music • ~-adhair [pɔRʃdˈa.ɪrʲ] airport • ~ Rìgh [pɔRʃdˈri:] Portree
pòs	[pɔ:s] 1 *v* to marry 2 *vn* & *nm* ~adh [pɔ:səɣ] marrying, wedding; *gen* ~aidh [pɔ:sɪ] *pl* ~aidhean [pɔ:sɪ.ən]
pòsta	[pɔ:sdə] *adj* married
post	[pɔsd] *nm* post; *gen* puist [puʃdʲ]
prais	[praʃ] *nf* pot; *gen* ~e [praʃə] *pl* ~ean [praʃən]
prìosanach	[prʲi:sanəx] *nm* prisoner; *gen* & *pl* prìosanaich [prʲi:sanɪç]
prìs	[prʲi:ʃ] *nf* price; *gen* ~e [prʲi:ʃə] *pl* ~ean [prʲi:ʃən]
punnd	[pũ:Nd] *nm* pound; *gen* & *pl* puinnd [pũ:Nʲdʲ]

put	[puhd] 1 *v* to push 2 *vn & nm* ~adh [puhdəɣ] pushing; *gen* ~aidh [puhdɪ]
putan	[puhdan] *nm* button; *gen* putain [puhdɛNʲ] *pl* ~an [puhdanən]

RUIS [Ruʃ]

Raghnaid	[Rɤːnɪdʲ] *pnf* Rachel; *voc* a Raghnaid [ə rɤːnɪdʲ]
Raghnall	[Rɤ̃ː.əL] *pnm* Ronald; *gen* Raghnaill [rɤ̃ː.ɪLʲ] *voc* a Raghnaill [ə rɤ̃ː.ɪLʲ]
raineach	[RaNʲəx] *nf* fern; *gen* rainich [RaNʲɪç] • ~ [RaNʲəx] Rannoch
ràithe	[Raːjə] *nf* season; *pl* ~an [Raːjən]
rannsaich	[RãũNsɪç] 1 *v* to research 2 *vn & nm* rannsachadh [RãũNsəxəɣ] researching; *gen* rannsachaidh [RãũNsəxɪ]
rath	[Rah] *nm* luck; *gen* ~a [Rahə]
ràth	[Raː] *nm* raft; *gen* ~a [Raː.ə] *pl* ~an [Raː.ən]
rathad	[Ra.əd] *nm* road; *gen* rathaid [Ra.ɪdʲ] *pl* rathaidean [Ra.ɪdʲən]
Ratharsair	[Ra.əRsɛrʲ] *pnm* Raasay; *gen* ~ [ra.əRsɛrʲ]
ré	[reː] *prep* during
reamhar	[Rãũ.ər] *adj* fat; *comp* reamhra [Rãũrə]
reic	[Reçgʲ] 1 *v* to sell 2 *vn & nm* ~ [Reçgʲ] selling • ~eadair [Reçgʲədɛrʲ] salesperson
rèidio	[Rɛːdʲɔ] *nm* radio; *pl* ~than [Rɛːdʲɔ.ən]
reòiteag	[Rɔːhdʲag] *nf* ice cream; *gen* reòiteig [Rɔːhdʲɛgʲ] *pl* ~an [Rɔːhdʲagən]
reul	[ReːL] *nf* star; *gen* réile [Reːlə] *pl* ~tan [ReːLdən]
ri	[rʲi] *prep* to; *def prep* ris an [rʲiʃəN⁽ʲ⁾] *def prep pl* ris na [rʲiʃnə] • rium [rʲium] riut [rʲuhd] ris [rʲiʃ] rithe [rʲi.ə] rinn [rʲiːNʲ] ribh [rʲiːv] riutha [rʲu.ə]
riabhach	[Riəvəx] *adj* brindled; *comp* riabhaiche [Riəvɪçə]
riaghailt	[Riə.əldʲ] *nf* rule; *pl* ~ean [Riə.əldʲən]
rìoghachd	[Riə.əxg] *nf* kingdom; *pl* ~an [Riə.əxgən] • An ~ Aonaichte [ə Riə.əxg ɯːnɪçdʲə] the United Kingdom
rionnag	[RuNag] *nf* star; *gen* rionnaige [RuNɛgʲə] *pl* ~an [RuNagən]

ro	[rɔ] *prep* before; *def prep* ron an [rɔnəN⁽ʲ⁾] *def prep pl* ~ na [rɔnə] • romham [rõ.əm] romhad [rõ.əd] roimhe [rõjə] roimhpe [rõihbə] romhainn [rõ.ɪNʲ] romhaibh [rõ.ɪv] romhpa [rõhbə]
roinn	[RʏiNʲ] *nf* department; *gen* ~e [RʏNʲə] *pl* ~ean [RʏNʲən]
Roinn Eòrpa, an ~	[ə Rʏi Nʲɔːrbə] *pnf* Europe; *gen* na Roinn Eòrpa [nə Rʏi Nʲɔːrbə]
rola	[RɔLə] *nm* roll; *pl* ~n [RɔLən]
ròpa	[Rɔːhbə] *nm* rope; *pl* ~ichean [Rɔːhbɪçən]
ruadh	[Ruəɣ] *adj* red (hair or fur); *pl* ~a [Ruəɣə] *comp* ruaidhe [Ruəjə]
Ruaraidh	[Ruərɪ] *pnm* Rory; *gen* ~ [ruərɪ] *voc* a ~ [ə ruərɪ]
rubha	[Ru.ə] *nm* headland; *pl* ~nnan [Ru.əNən] • An ~ [ə Ru.ə] Point/Rhu(e)
rud	[Rud] *nm* thing; *pl* ~an [Rudən]
rùda	[Ruːdə] *nm* ram (animal); *pl* ~chan [Ruːdəxən]
ruige	[Rɯgʲə] *prep* until; gu ~ [gə Rɯgʲə] until
Ruis, an ~	[ə Ruʃ] *pnf* Russia; *gen* na Ruise [nə Ruʃə]
Ruiseanach	[Ruʃənəx] *nm* Russian; *gen* & *pl* Ruiseanaich [Ruʃənɪç]
Ruisis	[Ruʃɪʃ] *pnf* Russian (language); *gen* ~e [Ruʃɪʃə]
ruith	[Rɯj] 1 *v* to run 2 *vn* & *nf* ~ [Rɯj] running; *gen* ~e [Rɯjə]
rum	[Ruːm] 1 *nm* room; *gen* ruim [Rɯim] *pl* ~annan [RuməNən] 2 *pn* Rum; *gen* Ruma [Rumə] • ~-cadail [Rumˈkadəl] bedroom • ~-ionnlaid [RumˈjũːNLɪdʲ] bathroom
rùn	[Ruːn] *nm* secret; *gen* rùin [RuːNʲ] *pl* rùintean [RuːNʲdʲən]

SAIL [sal]

sabaid	[sabɪdʲ] *nf* fight; *gen* ~e [sabɪdʲə] *pl* ~ean [sabɪdʲən]
sàbaid	[saːbɪdʲ] *nf* sabbath; *gen* ~e [saːbɪdʲə] *pl* ~ean [saːbɪdʲən] • Là na Sàbaid [Laː nə saːbɪdʲ] Sunday
sabhal	[so.əL] *nm* barn; *gen* sabhail [so.ɪl] *pl* ~an [so.əLən]
sagart	[sagəRʃd] *nm* priest; *gen* sagairt [sagəRʃdʲ] *pl* ~an [sagəRʃdən]
saighdear	[sʏidʲɛr] *nm* soldier; *gen* saighdeir [sʏidʲɛrʲ] *pl* ~an [sʏidʲɛrən]
saill	[saiLʲ] *nf* grease; *gen* ~e [saLʲə]
salach	[saLəx] *adj* dirty; *comp* salaiche [saLɪçə]
salann	[saLəN] *nm* salt; *gen* & *pl* salainn [saLɪNʲ]

salm	[saLam] *nm* psalm; *gen* & *pl* sailm [salam]
sàmhach	[sa:vəx] *adj* quiet; *comp* sàmhaiche [sa:vɪçə]
samhradh	[sãũrəɣ] *nm* Summer; *gen* samhraidh [sãũrɪ] • as t-~ [əs dãũrəɣ] in Summer
sanas	[sanəs] *nm* sign; *gen* sanais [sanɪʃ] *pl* ~an [sanəsən] • ~-reic [sanəs'Reçg] advertisement
saoghal	[sɯ:.əL] *nm* world; *gen* saoghail [sɯ:.əl] *pl* ~an [sɯ:.əLən]
saoil	[sɯ:l] 1 *v* to think 2 *vn* & *nf* ~sinn [sɯ:lʃɪN] thinking
saor	[sɯ:r] 1 *nm* joiner; *gen* & *pl* saoir [sɯ:r] 2 *adj* free; *pl* ~a [sɯ:rə] *comp* saoire [sɯ:rə] • ~-làithean [sɯ:RLajən] holidays
sàraich	[sa:rɪç] 1 *v* to bother 2 *vn* & *nm* sàrachadh [sa:rəxəɣ] bothering; *gen* sàrachaidh [sa:rəxɪ]
Sasainn	[sasɪN] *pnf* England; *gen* Shasainn [hasɪN]
Sasannach	[sasəNəx] *nm* a person from England; *gen* & *pl* Sasannaich [sasəNɪç]
sàsar	[sa:sər] *nm* saucer; *gen* sàsair [sa:sɪr] *pl* ~an [sa:sərən]
seacaid	[ʃɛxgɪd] *nf* jacket; *gen* ~e [ʃɛxgɪdə] *pl* ~ean [ʃɛxgɪdən]
seachad	[ʃɛxəd] *adv* past
seachd	[ʃɛxg] *num* seven; *counting form* a ~ [ə ʃɛxg]
seachdad	[ʃɛxgəd] *num* seventy
seachdain	[ʃɛxgɪN] *nf* week; *gen* ~e [ʃɛxgɪNə] *pl* ~ean [ʃɛxgɪNən]
seachdamh	[ʃɛxgəv] *num* seventh
seachdnar	[ʃɛxgnər] *nm* seven (people)
seal	[ʃɛL] *nm* while; *gen* ~a [ʃɛLə] *pl* ~an [ʃɛLən]
seall	[ʃauL] 1 *v* to show 2 *vn* & *nm* ~adh [ʃaLəɣ] showing, view; *gen* ~aidh [ʃaLɪ]
Sealtainn	[ʃaLdɪN] *pnf* Shetland; *gen* Shealtainn [hjaLdɪN]
seamrag	[ʃɛmɛrag] *nf* clover; *gen* seamraige [ʃɛmɛrɛgə] *pl* ~an [ʃɛmɛragən]
sean	[ʃɛn] *adj* old; *pl* ~a [ʃɛnə] *comp* sine [ʃinə]
seanair	[ʃɛnar] *nm* grandfather; *pl* ~ean [ʃɛnarən]
seanmhair	[ʃɛnavər] *nf* grandmother; *pl* ~ean [ʃɛnavərən]
seann	[ʃauN] *adj (prefixed)* old
Seapan, an t-~	[əN tʲɛhbən] *pnf* Japan; *gen* na Seapaine [nə ʃɛhbɪNə]
searbh	[ʃɛrɛv] *adj* sour; *pl* ~a [ʃɛrɛvə] *comp* seirbhe [ʃɛrʲevə]
searbhadair	[ʃɛrɛvədɛr] *nm* towel; *pl* ~ean [ʃɛrɛvədɛrən]
searrag	[ʃɛRag] *nf* flask; *gen* searraige [ʃɛRɛgə] *pl* ~an [ʃɛRagən]
seas	[ʃes] 1 *v* to stand 2 *vn* & *nm* ~amh [ʃesəv] standing; *gen*

~aimh [ʃesəv]

seasgad [ʃesgəd] *num* sixty

sèimh [ʃɛ:v] *adj* calm; *pl* & *comp* sèimhe [ʃɛ:və]

seinn [ʃeiNʲ] 1 *v* to sing 2 *vn* & *nf* ~ [ʃeiNʲ] singing;
gen ~e [ʃeNʲə]

seinneadair [ʃeNʲədɛrʲ] *nm* singer; *pl* ~ean [ʃeNʲədɛrʲən]

seirbheis [ʃerʲevɪʃ] *nf* service; *gen* ~e [ʃerʲevɪʃə] *pl* ~ean [ʃerʲevɪʃən]

séithear [ʃe:.ər] *nf* chair; *gen* sèitheir [ʃe:.ɪrʲ] *pl* sèithrichean
[ʃe:rʲɪçən]

seo [ʃɔ] *dem pron* this

seòbhrach [ʃɔ:rəx] *nf* primrose; *gen* seòbhraich [ʃɔ:rɪç] *pl*
seòbhraichean [ʃɔ:rɪçən]

seòl [ʃɔ:L] 1 *v* to sail 2 *vn* & *nf* ~adh [ʃɔ:Ləɣ] sailing, address;
gen ~aidh [ʃɔ:Lɪ] 3 *nm* sail; *gen* & *pl* siùil [ʃu:l]

seòlta [ʃɔ:Ldə] *adj* cunning

seòmar [ʃɔ:mər] *nm* room; *gen* seòmair [ʃɔ:mɪrʲ] *pl* seòmraichean
[ʃɔ:mɪçən] • ~-cadail [ʃɔmər'kadəl] bedroom • ~-ionnlaid
[ʃɔmər'jũ:NLɪdʲ] bathroom • ~-leughaidh [ʃɔmər'Lʲe:vɪ]
reading-room • ~-suidhe [ʃɔmər'sujə] living room

Seonag [ʃɔnag] *pnf* Joan; *gen* Seonaig [ʃɔnɛgʲ] *voc* a Sheonag
[ə hjɔnag]

Seònaid [ʃɔ:nɪdʲ] *pnf* Janet; *voc* a Sheònaid [ə hjɔ:nɪdʲ]

Seonaidh [ʃɔnɪ] *pnm* Johnny; *gen* Sheonaidh [hjɔnɪ] *voc* a
Sheonaidh [ə hjɔnɪ]

Seòras [ʃɔ:rəs] *pnm* George; *gen* Sheòrais [hjɔ:rɪʃ] *voc* a
Sheòrais [ə hjɔ:rɪʃ]

seòrsa [ʃɔ:Rsə] *nm* sort; *pl* ~ichean [ʃɔ:Rsɪçən]

Seumas [ʃe:məs] *pnm* James; *gen* Sheumais [he:mɪʃ] *voc* a
Sheumais [ə he:mɪʃ]

sgadan [sgadan] *nm* herring; *gen* & *pl* sgadain [sgadɛNʲ]

sgàilean [sga:lan] *nm* umbrella; *gen* sgàilein [sga:lɛNʲ] *pl* ~an
[sga:lanən]

Sgalpaigh [sgaLbaj] *pnm* Scalpay

sgarbh [sgarav] *nm* cormorant; *gen* & *pl* sgairbh [sgɛrʲɛv]

Sgarp, an ~ [ə sgarb] *pn* Scarp

sgeilp [sgʲelb] *nf* shelf; *gen* ~e [sgʲelbə] *pl* ~ean [sgʲelbən]

sgeul [sgʲiaL] *nm* tale; *gen* sgeòil [sgʲɔ:l] *pl* ~an [sgʲiaLən]

sgian [sgʲian] *nf* knife; *gen* sgéine [sgʲe:nə] *pl* sgeanan [sgʲɛnən]
• ~-arain [sgʲə'narɛNʲ] bread-knife • ~-dubh [sgʲən'du]
skean dhu

sgillinn [sgⁱiLʲɪNʲ] *nf* penny; *pl* ~ean [sgⁱiLʲɪNʲən]

sgioba [sgⁱibə] *nm* team; *pl* ~n [sgⁱibən]

sgioblaich [sgⁱibLɪç] 1 *v* to tidy (up) 2 *vn* & *nm* sgioblachadh [sgⁱibLəxəɣ] tidying (up); *gen* sgioblachaidh [sgⁱibLəxɪ]

sgiort [sgⁱɤRd] *nm* skirt; *gen* ~a [sgⁱɤRdə] *pl* ~aichean [sgⁱɤRdɪçən]

sgìos [sgⁱiːs] *nf* fatigue

sgìth [sgⁱiː] *adj* tired; *pl* & *comp* ~e [sgⁱiː.ə]

Sgitheanach [sgⁱi.ənəx] *nm* a person from Skye; *gen* & *pl* Sgiathanaich [sgⁱi.ənɪç]

sgoil [sgɔlʲ] *nf* school; *gen* ~e [sgɔlə] *pl* ~tean [sgɔldʲən] • ~-àraich [sgɔlˈaːrɪç] nursery

sgoinneil [sgɤNʲal] *adj* terrific; *comp* ~e [sgɤNʲalə]

sgoth [sgɔh] *nf* skiff; *gen* ~a [sgɔhə] *pl* ~an [sgɔhən]

sgòth [sgɔː] *nf* cloud; *pl* ~an [sgɔː.ən]

sgrìob [sgrⁱiːb] *nf* excursion; *gen* ~a [sgrⁱiːbə] *pl* ~an [sgrⁱiːbən]

sgrìobh [sgrⁱiːv] 1 *v* to write 2 *vn* & *nm* ~adh [sgrⁱiːvəɣ] writing; *gen* ~aidh [sgrⁱiːvɪ] *pl* ~aidhean [sgrⁱiːvɪ.ən]

sgrìobhaiche [sgrⁱiːvɪçə] *nm* writer; *pl* ~an [sgrⁱiːvɪçən]

sguab [sguəb] 1 *v* to sweep 2 *vn* & *nm* ~adh [sguəbəɣ] sweeping; *gen* ~aidh [sguəbɪ]

sguir [sgurⁱ] 1 *v* to stop 2 *vn* & *nm* sgur [sgur] stopping

sgurr [sguːR] *nm* sharp steep hill; *gen* ~a [sguRə] *pl* ~an [sguRən] • Sgurr Alastair [sguˈRaLəsdɪrⁱ] Sgùrr Alasdair

shuas [huəs] *adv* up (location)

sia [ʃia] *num* six; *counting form* a ~ [ə ʃia]

sian [ʃian] *nf* stormy weather; *gen* sìne [ʃiːnə] *pl* ~tan [ʃiandən]

sianar [ʃianər] *nm* six (people)

siathamh [ʃia.əv] *num* sixth

sibh [ʃiv] *pron* you (plural); *emph* sibhse [ʃiːvʃə]

sìde [ʃiːdʲə] *nf* weather

sil [ʃil] 1 *v* to drip 2 *vn* & *nm* sileadh [ʃiləɣ]; *gen* silidh [ʃilɪ]

sin [ʃin] *dem prom* that

sìn [ʃiːn] 1 *v* to stretch 2 *vn* & *nm* ~eadh [ʃiːnəɣ] stretching

Sìn, an t-~ [əNʲ tʲiːn] *pnf* China; *gen* na Sìne [nə ʃiːnə]

Sìne [ʃiːnə] *pnf* Jane; *voc* a Shìne [ə hiːnə]

sinn [ʃiNʲ] *pron* we, us; *emph* sinne [ʃiNʲə]

sìon [ʃiən] *nm* anything

sionnach [ʃuNəx] *nm* fox; *gen* & *pl* sionnaich [ʃuNɪç]

sìorraidh [ʃiəRɪ] *adj* eternal

sìos	[ʃiəs] *adv* down (motion away from speaker)
sìthean	[ʃi.an] *nm* fairy mound; *gen* sìthein [ʃi.ɛNʲ] *pl* ~an [ʃi.anən]
siùcar	[ʃuːxgər] *nm* sugar; *gen* siùcair [ʃuːxgɪrʲ] *pl* siùcairean [ʃuːxgɪrʲən]
siubhail	[ʃu.al] 1 *v* to travel 2 *vn & nm* siubhal [ʃu.əL] travelling *gen* ~ [ʃu.al]
siud	[ʃid] *dem pron* that (yon)
siuga	[ʃugə] *nf* jug; *pl* ~ichean [ʃugɪçən]
slabhraidh	[sLauɪ] *nf* chain; *pl* ~ean [sLauɪ.ən]
slàinte	[sLaːNʲdʲə] *nf* health
slaodach	[sLɯːdəx] *adj* slow; *comp* slaodaiche [sLɯːdɪçə]
slat	[sLahd] *nf* yard (measure); *gen* slaite [sLahdʲə] *pl* ~an [sLahdən] • ~-iasgaich [sLahdˈiəsgɪç] fishing rod
slige	[ʃligʲə] *nf* shell; *pl* ~an [ʃligʲən]
sloinneadh	[sLɤNʲəɣ] *nm* surname; *gen* sloinnidh [sLɤNʲɪ] *pl* sloinnidhean [sLɤNʲɪ.ən]
sluagh	[sLuəɣ] *nm* crowd; *gen* sluaigh [sLuəj] *pl* slòigh [sLɔːj] *gen pl* slògh [sLɔːɣ] • ~-ghairm [sLuəɣ ɤrʲɯm] slogan
sluig	[sLɯgʲ] 1 *v* to swallow 2 *vn & nm* slugadh [sLugəɣ] *gen* slugaidh [sLugɪ]
smaoinich	[smɯːNʲɪç] 1 *v* to think 2 *vn & nm* smaoineachadh [smɯːNʲəxəɣ] thinking; *gen* smaoineachaidh [smɯːNʲəxɪ]
sméid	[smeːdʲ] 1 *v* to wave 2 *vn & nm* sméideadh [smeːdʲəɣ] waving; *gen* sméididh [smeːdʲɪ]
smid	[smidʲ] *nf* syllable; *gen* ~e [smidʲə] *pl* ~ean [smidʲən]
smoc	[smɔxg] 1 *v* to smoke 2 *vn & nm* ~adh [smɔxgəɣ]
snàmh	[sNaːv] 1 *v* to swim 2 *vn & nm* ~ [sNaːv] swimming; *gen* ~a [sNaːvə]
snàth	[sNaː] *nm* wool yarn; *gen* ~a [sNaː.ə] *pl* snàithean [sNaːjən]
sneachd	[ʃNʲɛxg] *nm* snow; *gen* ~a [ʃNʲɛxgə]
snèap	[ʃNʲɛːhb] *nf* turnip; *gen* snèipe [ʃNʲɛːhbə] *pl* ~an [ʃNʲɛːhbən]
snog	[sNog] *adj* nice; *pl* ~a [sNogə] *comp* snoige [sNɤgʲə]
Sòthaigh	[sɔː.aj] *pnm* Soay; *gen* Shòthaigh [hɔː.aj]
soilleir	[sɤLʲɪrʲ] *adj* bright; *comp* ~e [sɤLʲɪrʲə]
soitheach	[sɤ.əx] 1 *nf* vessel 2 *nm* dish; *gen* soithich [sɤ.ɪç] *pl* soithichean [sɤ.ɪçən]

solas [sɔLəs] *nm* light; *gen* solais [sɔLɪʃ] *pl* ~an [sɔLəsən] • ~- sràide [sɔLə'sdra:dʲə] street light

sòlas [sɔːLəs] *nm* consolation; *gen* sòlais [sɔːLɪʃ]

sònraichte [sɔːnrɪçdʲə] *adj* special

spàin [sbaːNʲ] *nf* spoon; *gen* ~e [sbaːNʲə] *pl* ~ean [sbaːNʲən]

Spàinn, an ~ [ə sbaːNʲ] *pnf* Spain; *gen* na Spàinne [nə sbaːNʲə]

Spàinnis [sbaːNʲɪʃ] *pnf* Spanish (language); *gen* ~e [sbaːNʲɪʃə]

spidean [sbidʲan] *nm* pinnacle; *gen* & *pl* spidein [sbidʲɛNʲ]

sporan [sbɔran] *nm* sporran, purse; *gen* & *pl* sporain [sbɔrɛNʲ]

spòrs [sbɔːRs] *nf* sport; *gen* ~a [spɔːRsə] *pl* ~achan [sbɔːRsəxən]

spreadh [sbrʲɛ] 1 *v* to explode 2 *vn* & *nm* ~adh [sbrʲɛ.əɣ]

sràid [sdra:dʲ] *nf* street; *pl* ~ean [sdra:dʲən]

stampa [sdãũmbə] *nf* stamp; *pl* ~ichean [sdãũmbɪçən]

srath [sdrah] *nm* wide valley; *gen* ~a [sdrahə] *pl* ~an [sdrahən] • An ~ Mór [ə sdrah moːr] Strathmore • ~ Chluaidh [sdra'xLuəj] Strathclyde • ~ Spé [sdra'sbeː] Strathspey

sreang [sdrɛŋg] *nf* string; *gen* sreinge [sdreŋʲgʲə] *pl* ~an [sdrɛŋgən]

sreothartaich [sdrɔhəRʃdɪç] *nf* sneezing; *gen* ~e [sdrɔhəRʃdɪçə]

sreap [sdrɛhb] 1 *v* to climb 2 *vn* & *nm* ~adh [sdrɛhbəɣ] climbing; *gen* ~aidh [sdrɛhbɪ]

sròn [sdrɔːn] *nf* nose; *gen* sròine [sdrɔːNʲə] *pl* sròintean [sdrɔːNʲdʲən] • An t-Sròn Reamhar [əN trɔːn rãũ.ər] Straenrar

Sruighlea [sdruila] *pnm* Stirling; *gen* Shruighlea [ruila]

sruth [sdruh] *nm* stream; *gen* ~a [sdruhə] *pl* ~an [sdruhən]

stàball [sdaːbəL] *nm* stable; *gen* & *pl* stàbaill [sdaːbɪLʲ]

stad [sdad] 1 *v* to cease 2 *vn* & *nm* ~ [sdad] ceasing; *gen* staid [sdadʲ]

staighre [sdɤirʲə] *nf* stair; *gen* ~ach [sdɤirʲəx] *pl* staighrichean [sdɤirʲɪçən]

stàilinn [sdaːlɪNʲ] *nf* steel

stais [sdaʃ] *nf* moustache; *gen* staise [sdaʃə] *pl* staisean [sdaʃən]

stàit [sdaːhdʲ] *nf* state; *gen* stàite [sdaːhdʲə] *pl* stàitean [sdaːhdʲən] • Na Stàitean Aonaichte [nə sdaːhdʲən ɯːnɪçdʲə] The United States

stéisean [sdeːʃən] *nm* station; *gen* stéisein [sdeːʃɛNʲ] *pl* ~an [sdeːʃənən]

Steòrnabhagh	[ʃdʲɔːRNəvaɣ] *pnm* Stornoway; *gen* Steòrnabhaigh [ʃdʲɔːRNəvaj]
stiall	[ʃdʲiaL] 1 *v* to scourge 2 *vn* & *nm* stialladh [ʃdʲiaLəɣ] scourging
stiùirich	[ʃdʲuːrʲɪç] 1 *v* to direct 2 *vn* & *nm* stiùireadh [ʃdʲuːrʲəɣ] directing, instruction; *gen* stiùiridh [ʃdʲuːrʲɪ] *pl* stiùiridhean [ʃdʲuːrʲɪ.ən]
stòbha	[sdɔːvə] *nf* stove; *pl* ~chan [sdɔːvəxən]
stocainn	[sdɔxgɪNʲ] *nf* sock; *pl* ~ean [sdɔxgɪNʲən]
stoirm	[sdɤrʲɤm] *nf* storm; *gen* ~e [sdɤrʲɤmə] *pl* ~ean [sdɤrʲɤmən]
stòr	[sdɔːr] *nm* store; *gen* & *pl* stòir [sdɔːrʲ]
Suain, an t-~	[əN tuəNʲ] *pnf* Sweden; *gen* na Suaine [nə suəNʲə]
stuama	[sduəmə] *adj* sober • neo-~ [Nʲɔ'sduəmə] not sober
stùc	[sduːxg] *nf* (mountain) horn; *gen* stùic [sduːçgʲ] *pl* ~an [sduːxgən] • ~ a' Ghobhainn [sduxgə'ɣo.ɪNʲ] Stuckagowan
streap	see sreap
Suaineart	[suəNʲəRd] *pnm* Sunart; *gen* Shuaineirt [huəNʲəRdʲ]
suas	[suəs] *adv* upwards (motion away from speaker)
suidh	[sɯj] *v* to sit; *vn* & *nf* ~e [sɯjə]
suidheachan	[sɯjəxan] *nm* seat; *gen* & *pl* suidheachain [sɯjəxɛNʲ]
suidhich	[sɯjɪç] 1 *v* to situate 2 *vn* & *nm* suidheachadh [sɯjəxəɣ] situating; *gen* suidheachaidh [sɯjəxɪ]
sùil	[suːl] *nf* eye; *gen* sùla [suːLə] *pl* ~ean [suːlən]

TEINE [tʲenə]

tachair	[taxɪrʲ] 1 *v* to happen; *fut* tachraidh [taxrɪ] *fut re/* thachras [haxrəs] 2 *vn* & *nf* tachairt [taxɪRʃdʲ] happening
tadhail	[tɤ.əl] 1 *v* to frequent 2 *vn* & *nm* tadhal [tɤ.əL] frequenting
tagh	[tɤɣ] 1 *v* to choose 2 *vn* & *nm* ~adh [tɤ.əɣ] choosing; *gen* ~aidh [tɤ.ɪ] • ~adh pàrlamaid [tɤ.əɣ paːRləmɪdʲ] parliamentary election
taghta	[tɤːɣdə] *adj* excellent
taic	[taçgʲ] *nf* support; *gen* ~e [taçgʲə]
taiceil	[taçgʲal] *adj* supportive; *comp* ~e [taçgʲalə]

taigh	[tɤj] *nm* house; *gen* ~e [tɛhə] *pl* ~ean [tɛhən] • ~ an Uillt [təˈNɯiLʲdʲ] Taynuilt • ~-beag [təˈbeg] toilet • ~-bìdh [təˈbiː] restaurant • ~ na Bruaich [tɤj nə bruəç] Tighnabruaich • ~-cluich [təˈkLuç] theatre • ~-dhealbh [təˈjɛLɛv] cinema • ~-òsta [təˈjɔːsdə] hotel • ~-seinnse [təˈʃeiNʲʃə] pub • ~-staile [təˈsdalə] distillery • ~-tasgaidh [təˈtasgɪ] museum
tairg	[tɛrʲɛgʲ] 1 *v* to offer 2 *vn & nf* ~sinn [tɛrʲɛgʲʃɪNʲ] offering
tàirneanach	[taːRNʲanəx] *nm* thunder; *gen* tàirneanaich [taːRNʲanɪç]
taisbean	[taʃbən] 1 *v* to present 2 *vn & nm* ~adh [taʃbənəɤ] presenting, exhibition; *gen* ~aidh [taʃbənɪ] *pl* ~aidhean [taʃbənɪ.ən]
talamh	[taLəv] *nm* land; *gen nf* talmhainn [taLəvɪNʲ] *pl* ~an [taLəvən]
tana	[tanə] *adj* thin; *comp* taine [tanə]
taobh	[tɯːv] *nf* side; *gen* taoibhe [tɯivə] *pl* ~an [tɯːvən]
tapadh	[tahbəɤ] *nm* cleverness; *gen* tapaidh [tahbɪ] • ~ leat [tahbə lɛhd] thank you
Tarasaigh	[tarəsaj] *pnm* Taransay; *gen* Tharasaigh [harasaj]
tarraing	[taRɪŋʲgʲ] 1 *v* to pull; *fut* tàirnidh [taːrNʲɪ] *fut rel* thàirneas [haːrNʲəs] 2 *vn & nf* tarraing [taRɪŋʲgʲ]; *gen* tàirne [taːrNʲə] *pl* tàirnean [taːrNʲən]
tarsainn	[taRsɪNʲ] *adv* across
té	[tʲeː] *nf* (female) one • ~ eile [tʲelə] the other (female one)
teagaisg	[tʲegɪʃgʲ] 1 *v* to teach 2 *vn & nm* teagasg [tʲegəsg] teaching; *gen* ~ [tʲegɪʃgʲ]
teagamh	[tʲegəv] *nm* doubt; *gen* teagaimh [tʲegəv] *pl* ~an [tʲegəvən]
teaghlach	[tʲɤːLəx] *nm* family; *gen* teaghlaich [tʲɤːLɪç] *pl* teaghlaichean [tʲɤːLɪçən]
teanga	[tʲɛŋgə] *nf* tongue; *pl* ~nnan [tʲɛŋgəNən]
teann	[tʲauN] *adj* tight; *pl* ~a [tʲaNə] *comp* teinne [tʲeNʲə]
Teàrlach	[tʲaːRLəx] *pnm* Charles; *gen* Theàrlaich [hjaːRLɪç] *voc* a Theàrlaich [ə hjaːRLɪç]
teich	[tʲeç] 1 *v* to escape 2 *vn & nm* ~eadh [tʲeçəɤ] escaping; *gen* ~idh [tʲeçɪ]
teine	[tʲenə] *nf* fire; *pl* teintean [tʲeNʲdʲən]
teth	[tʲeh] *adj* hot; *pl* teatha [tʲe.ə] *comp* teotha [tʲɔ.ə]
thall	[hauL] *adv* over there (location distant from speaker)

thar	[har] *prep* across; *def prep* thar an [har əN⁽ʲ⁾] *def prep pl* thar na [har nə] conjugated tharam [harəm] tharad [harəd] thairis [harʲɪʃ] thairte [haRʃdʲə] tharainn [harɪNʲ] tharaibh [harɪv] tharta [haRʃdə]
theirig	[herʲɪgʲ] *v imp def* go!
thu	[u] *pron* you; *emph* thusa [usə] *unlenited* tu [du] *unlenited emph* tusa [dusə]
thugainn	[hugɪNʲ] *v imp def* come! *pl* thugnaibh [hugnɪv]
tighearna	[tʲi.əRNə] *nm* lord; *pl* ~an [tʲi.əRNən]
tilg	[tʲilig] 1 *v* to throw 2 *vn & nm* ~eadh [tʲiligʲəɣ]
till	[tʲi:Lʲ] 1 *v* to return 2 *vn & nm* ~eadh [tʲiLʲəɣ] return; *gen* ~idh [tʲiLʲɪ]
tim	[tʲi:m] *nf* time; *gen* time [tʲimə] *pl* ~eannan [tʲiməNən]
timcheall	[tʲimiçəL] *adv* around
tinn	[tʲi:Nʲ] *adj* ill; *pl & comp* ~e [tʲiNʲə]
tiodhlac	[tʲiəLəg] *nm* present; tiodhlaic [tʲiəLɪgʲ] *pl* ~an [tʲiəLəgən]
tiodhlacadh	[tʲiəLəgəɣ] *nm* burial, funeral; *gen* tiodhlacaidh [tʲiəLəgɪ] *pl* tiodhlacaidhean [tʲiəLəgɪ.ən]
tiodhlaic	[tʲiəLɪgʲ] 1 *v* to bury 2 *vn & nm* ~eadh [tʲiəLɪçgʲəɣ]
tiormaich	[tʲirimɪç] 1 *v* to dry (up) 2 *vn & nm* tiormachadh [tʲiriməxəɣ] drying (up); *gen* tiormachaidh [tʲiriməxɪ]
tìr	[tʲi:rʲ] *nf* country; *gen* ~e [tʲi:rʲə] *pl* ~ean [tʲi:rʲən] • na ~ean Ìsle [nə tʲi:rʲən i:ʃlə] the Netherlands
Tiridhe	[tʲirʲɪ.ɪ] *pnf* Tiree; *gen* Thiridhe [hirʲɪ.ɪ]
Tirisdeach	[tʲirʲɪʃdʲəx] *nm* a person from Tiree; *gen & pl* Tirisdich [tʲirʲɪʃdʲɪç]
tiugh	[tʲu] *adj* thick; *pl* ~a [tʲu.ə] *comp* tighe [tʲi.ə]
tlachd	[tLaxg] *nf* pleasure
tlachdmhor	[tLaxgvər] *adj* pleasant; *comp* tlachdmhoire [tLaxgvərʲə]
tobar	[tobər] *nf* well; *gen* tobrach [tobrəx] *pl* tobraichean [tobrɪçən]
todhar	[to.ər] *nm* manure; *gen* todhair [to.ɪrʲ]
tog	[tog] 1 *v* to lift 2 *vn & nf* ~ail [togal] lifting, building; *gen* ~alach [togaLəx] *pl* ~alaichean [togaLɪçən]
togair	[togɪrʲ] 1 *v* to be inclined 2 *vn & nm* togradh [togrəɣ] inclination; *gen* tograidh [togrɪ] *pl* tograidhean [togrɪ.ən] • na thogras tu [nə hogrəs du] whatever you want
toigh	[tʏj] *adj* agreeable • is ~ leam [sdʏ ləm] I like • an ~ leam? [əN tʏ ləm] do I like? • 's toigh! [sdʏl] I do
toil	[tol] *nf* desire; *gen* toile [tolə]

toilichte	[tɔlɪçdʲə] *adj* happy
toiseach	[tɔʃəx] *nm* beginning; *gen* & *pl* toisich [tɔʃɪç]
tòisich	[tɔːʃɪç] 1 *v* to begin 2 *vn* & *nm* tòiseachadh [tɔːʃəxəɣ] beginning; *gen* tòiseachaidh [tɔːʃəxɪ]
toradh	[tɔrəɣ] *nm* result; *gen* toraidh [tɔrɪ] *pl* toraidhean [tɔrɪ.ən] • a thoradh [ə hɔrəɣ] because
Tormod	[tɔrɔməd] *pnm* Norman; *gen* Thormoid [hɔrɔmɪdʲ] *voc* a Thormoid [ə hɔrɔmɪdʲ]
torr	[tɔːR] *nm* heap, imposing hill, a lot (of); *gen* ~a [tɔRə] *pl* ~an [tɔRən] • An ~ Gorm [əN tɔːR gɔrɔm] Torgorm
tràigh	[traːj] *nf* beach; *gen* tràghad [traː.əd] *pl* ~ean [traːjən]
trang	[traŋg] *adj* busy; *pl* ~a [traŋgə] *comp* trainge [traŋʲgʲə]
trannsa	[trãũNsə] *nf* corridor; *pl* ~chan [trãũNsəxən]
tràth	[traː] 1 *nm* tense; *gen* tràith [traːj] *pl* ~an [traː.ən] 2 *adj* early; *pl* ~a [traː.ə] *comp* tràithe [traːjə]
trèan	[trɛːn] *nf* train; *pl* ~aichean [trɛːnɪçən]
treas	[tres] *num* third
treòraich	[trɔːrɪç] 1 *v* to guide 2 *vn* & *nm* treòrachadh [trɔːrəxəɣ] guiding, guidance; *gen* treòrachaidh [trɔːrəxɪ] *pl* treòrachaidhean [trɔːrəxɪ.ən]
trì	[triː] *num* three; *counting form* a ~ [ə triː]
tric	[triçgʲ] *adj* often; *pl* & *comp* ~e [triçgʲə]
trithead	[tri.əd] *num* thirty
tritheamh	[tri.əv] see treas
triubhas	[tru.əs] *nm* trews; *gen* triubhais [tru.ɪʃ] *pl* ~an [tru.əsən]
triùir	[truːrʲ] *nf* three (people)
tro	[trɔ] *prep* through; *def prep* tron an [trɔnəN(j)] *def prep pl* tro na [trɔnə] conjugated tromham [trõ.əm] tromhad [trõ.əd] troimhe [trõjə] troimhpe [trõjhbə] tromhainn [trõ.ɪNʲ] tromhaibh [trõ.ɪv] tromhpa [trõhbə]
trobhad	[tro.əd] *v def* come! *pl* ~aibh [tro.ədɪv]
troigh	[trɤj] *nf* foot (measure); *gen* ~e [trɤjə] *pl* ~ean [trɤjən]
trom	[trɔum] *adj* heavy; *pl* ~a [trɔmə] *comp* truime [trʉmə]
truagh	[truəɣ] *adj* sad; *pl* ~a [truəɣə] *comp* truaighe [truəjə]
truinnsear	[trũĩNʲʃɛr] *nm* plate; *gen* truinnseir [trũĩNʲʃɛrʲ] *pl* ~an [trũĩNʲʃɛrən]
tuath	[tuə] *nf* north • a ~ [ə tuə] northerly
tuathanach	[tuəhanəx] *nm* farmer; *gen* & *pl* tuathanaich [tuəhanɪç]
tuathanas	[tuəhanəs] *nm* farm; *gen* tuathanais [tuəhanɪʃ] *pl* ~an [tuəhanəsən] • ~-éisg [tuəhanəs'eːʃgʲ] fish-farm

tubaiste	[tubaʃdʲə] *nf* accident; *pl* ~an [tubaʃdʲən]
tubhailt	[tu.aldʲ] *nf* towel; *gen* tubhailte [tu.aldʲə] *pl* tubhailtean [tu.aldʲən]
tuig	[tɯgʲ] 1 *v* to understand 2 *vn* & *nf* tuigsinn [tɯgʲʃɪNʲ] understanding; *gen* tuigsinne [tɯgʲʃɪNʲə]
tuilleadh	[tɯLʲəɣ] *nm* extra
tuit	[tuhdʲ] 1 *v* to fall 2 *vn* & *nm* tuiteam [tuhdʲəm] falling, fall; *gen* tuiteim [tuhdʲəm] *pl* tuiteaman [tuhdʲəmən]
tulach	[tuLəx] *nm* small green hill; *gen* tulaich [tuLɪç] *pl* tulaichean [tuLɪçən] • Tulach Eòghain [tuLəxˈjɔ:.ɛNʲ] Tullichewen
tunnag	[tuNag] *nf* duck; *gen* tunnaige [tuNɛgʲə] *pl* ~an [tuNagən]
tur	[tur] *adj* absolute
tùr	[tu:r] *nm* tower; *gen* & *pl* tùir [tu:rʲ]
turas	[turəs] *nm* journey; *gen* turais [turɪʃ] *pl* tursan [tursən]
turasachd	[turəsəxg] *nf* tourism
turasaiche	[turəsɪçə] *nm* traveller; *pl* ~an [turəsɪçən]

UILEANN [uləN]

uabhas	[uəvəs] *nm* horror; *gen* uabhais [uəvɪʃ]
uabhasach	[uəvəsəx] *adj* terrible; *comp* uabhasaiche [uəvəsɪçə]
uachdar	[uəxgər] *nm* surface; *gen* uachdair [uəxgɪrʲ] *pl* ~an [uəxgərən]
uaine	[uəNʲə] *adj* green
uair	[uərʲ] *nf* hour; *gen* uarach [uərəx] *pl* ~ean [uərʲən] • ~eannan [uərʲəNən] sometimes • an uairsin [əˈNuəRʃɪn] then
uaireadair	[uərʲədɛrʲ] *nm* watch; *pl* ~ean [uərʲədɛrʲən]
uamh	[ũəv] *nf* cave; *gen* ~a [ũəvə] *pl* ~an [ũəvən]
uasal	[uəsəL] *adj* noble; *comp* uaisle [uəʃlə]
ubhal	[u.əL] *nm* apple; *gen* ubhail [u.al] *pl* ùbhlan [u:Lən]
ugh	[u] *nf* egg; *gen* uighe [ɯjə] *pl* uighean [ɯjən]
ùghdar	[u:dər] *nm* author; *gen* ùghdair [u:dɪrʲ] *pl* ~an [u:dərən]
Uibhist	[ɯi.ɪʃdʲ] *pnf* Uist; *pl* na h-~ean [nə hɯi.ɪʃdʲən] • ~ a Deas [ɯi.ɪʃdʲ ə dʲes] South Uist • ~ a Tuath [ɯi.ɪʃdʲ ə tuə] North Uist
Uibhisteach	[ɯi.ɪʃdʲəx] *nm* a person from Uist; *gen* & *pl* Uibhistich [ɯi.ɪʃdʲɪç]
uile	[ulə] *adj* all • a h-~ [ə xulə] every

Uilinis   [ulɪnɪʃ] *pn* Ullinish
Uilleam   [uᴸiam] *pnm* William; *gen* & *voc* Uilleim [uᴸiam]
ùine   [uːNiə] *nf* time; *pl* ~achan [uːNiəxən]
uinneag   [uᴺiag] *nf* window; *gen* uinneige [uᴺiɛgiə] *pl* ~an
                   [uᴺiagən]
uisge   [uʃgiə] *nm* water; *pl* ~achan [uʃgiəxən] • ~-beatha
                   [uʃgiə'bɛhə] • ~ Spé [uʃgiə'sbeː] River Spey • ~ Tatha
                   [uʃgiə'taː.ə] River Tay
Ùistean   [uːʃdian] *pnm* Hugh; *gen* & *voc* Ùistein [uːʃdiɛNi]
Ulabul   [uᴸəbəᴸ] *pn* Ullapool; *gen* Ulabuil [uᴸəbəl]
Ulbha   [uᴸuvə] *pnm* Ulva
ullaich   [uᴸɪç] 1 *v* to prepare 2 *vn* & *nm* ullachadh [uᴸəxəɣ]
                   preparing, preparation; *gen* ullachaidh [uᴸəxɪ] *pl*
                   ullachaidhean [uᴸəxɪ.ən]
Ùna   [uːnə] *pnf* Una
ùr   [uːr] *adj* new; *pl* ~a [uːrə] *comp* ùire [uːriə]
ur   [ər] *poss pron* see ur n-
ur n-   [ər] *poss pron* your; ur n-athair [ər nahəri]; n- is lost
                   before any consonant: ur taigh [ər tɤj] your house
ùrnaigh   [uːRNɪ] *nf* prayer; *gen* ~e [uːRNɪ.ə] *pl* ~ean [uːRNɪ.ən]
urrainn   [uRɪNi] *nf* ability; *short* urra [uRə] • 's ~ dhomh...
                   [suRɪNi ɣõ] I can... • an urra dhut... [ə NuRə ɣuhd] can
                   you...?

The Irregular Verbs

Rather than put these in the wordlist, I've listed them separately because it will be easier for you to find what you're looking for. Remember, this is about pronunciation so I'm only giving you the basic meaning of the root for the most part. You will learn what form means what as you progress with your Gaelic.

I have also not listed the passive/impersonal forms because once you have mastered the forms listed here, the pronunciation of all remaining forms is easy to figure out.

Where a form is in grey, it means that form is not normally used but substituted with a regular verb (given in italics).

ABAIR 'say'

Fut	their [herʲ]	a' their [ə herʲ]	abair [abɪrʲ]
	canaidh [kanɪ]	*a chanas* [ə xanəs]	*can* [kan]
Pres	ag ràdh [ə graː]		
Past	thuirt [huRʃdʲ]		duirt [duRʃdʲ]
	thubhairt [hu.əRʃdʲ]		dubhairt [du.əRʃdʲ]

Imp	abram	abair	abradh	abramaid	abraibh
	[abrəm]	[abɪrʲ]	[abrəɣ]	[abrəmɪdʲ]	[abrɪv]

Cond	theirinn	theireadh	theireamaid
	[herʲɪNʲ]	[herʲəɣ]	[herʲəmɪdʲ]
	abrainn	abradh	abramaid
	[abrɪNʲ]	[abrəɣ]	[abrəmɪdʲ]
	c(h)anainn	*c(h)anadh*	*c(h)anamaid*
	[kanɪNʲ]	[kanəɣ]	[kanəmɪdʲ]

BEIR 'bear'

Fut	beiridh [berʲɪ]	a bheireas [ə verʲəs]	beir [berʲ]
Pres	a' breith [ə brʲeh]		
Past	rug [rug]		do rug [də rug]

Imp	beiream	beir	beireadh	beireamaid	beiribh
	[berʲəm]	[berʲ]	[berʲəɣ]	[berʲəmɪdʲ]	[berʲɪv]

Cond	bheirinn	bheireadh	bheireamaid
	[verʲɪNʲ]	[verʲəɣ]	[verʲəmɪdʲ]
	beirinn	beireadh	beireamaid
	[berʲɪNʲ]	[berʲəɣ]	[berʲəmɪdʲ]

BI 'be' (1)

Fut	bidh [bi]	a bhios [ə viəs]	bi [bi]
	bithidh [bi.ɪ]	a bhitheas [ə vi.əs]	
Pres	tha [ha]	bheil [vel]	eil [el]
Past	bha [va]		robh [Rɔ]

Imp	bitheam	bi	bitheadh	bitheamaid	bithibh
	[bi.əm]	[bi]	[bi.əɣ]	[bi.əmɪdʲ]	[bi.ɪv]

Cond	bhithinn	bhitheadh	bhitheamaid
	[vi.ɪNʲ]	[vi.əɣ]	[vi.əmɪdʲ]
	bithinn	bitheadh	bitheamaid
	[bi.ɪNʲ]	[bi.əɣ]	[bi.əmɪdʲ]
		bhiodh	bhiomaid
		[vjɤɣ]	[viəmɪdʲ]
		biodh	biomaid
		[bjɤɣ]	[biəmɪdʲ]

CLUINN 'hear'

Fut	cluinnidh [kLɯNʲɪ] a chluinneas [ə xLɯNʲəs] cluinn [kLɯiNʲ]
Pres	a' cluinntinn [ə kLɯiNʲdʲɪNʲ]
Past	chuala [xuəLə] cuala [kuəLə]

Imp	cluinneam [kLɯiNʲəm]	cluinn [kLɯiNʲ]	cluinneadh [kLɯNʲəɣ]	cluinneamaid [kLɯNʲəmɪd]	cluinnibh [kLɯNʲɪv]

Cond	chluinninn [xLɯNʲiNʲ]	chluinneadh [xLɯNʲəɣ]	chluinneamaid [xLɯNʲəmɪdʲ]
	cluinninn [kLɯNʲiNʲ]	cluinneadh [kLɯNʲəɣ]	cluinneamaid [kLɯNʲəmɪdʲ]

DÈAN 'do'

Fut	nì [niː] a nì [ə niː] dèan [dʲian]
Pres	a' dèanamh [dʲianəv]
Past	rinn [rɣiNʲ] do rinn [də rɣiNʲ]

Imp	dèanam [dʲianəm]	dèan [dʲian]	dèanadh [dʲianəɣ]	dèanamaid [dʲianəmɪdʲ]	dèanaibh [dʲianɪv]

Cond	dhèanainn [jianɪNʲ]	dhèanadh [jianəɣ]	dhèanamaid [jianəmɪdʲ]
	dèanainn [dʲianɪNʲ]	dèanadh [dʲianəɣ]	dèanamaid [dʲianəmɪdʲ]

FAIC 'see'

Fut	chì [çiː]	a chì [ə çiː]	faic [fɛçgʲ]
Pres	a' faicinn [ə fɛçgʲɪNʲ]		
Past	chunnaic [xuNɪgʲ]		faca [faxgə]

Imp	faiceam	faic	faiceadh	faiceamaid	faicibh
	[fɛçgʲəm]	[fɛçgʲ]	[fɛçgʲəɣ]	[fɛçgʲəmɪdʲ]	[fɛçgʲɪv]

Cond	chithinn	chitheadh	chitheamaid
	[çi.ɪNʲ]	[çi.əɣ]	[çi.əmɪdʲ]
	faicinn	faiceadh	faiceamaid
	[fɛçgʲɪNʲ]	[fɛçgʲəɣ]	[fɛçgʲəmɪdʲ]

FAIGH 'get'

Fut	gheibh [ʝev]	a gheibh [ə ʝev]	faigh [faj]
Pres	a' faighinn [ə fajɪNʲ]		
Past	fhuair [huərʲ]		d' fhuair [duərʲ]

Imp	faigheam	faigh	faigheadh	faigheamaid	faighibh
	[fajəm]	[faj]	[fajəɣ]	[fajəmɪdʲ]	[fajɪv]

Cond	gheibhinn	gheibheadh	gheibheamaid
	[ʝevɪNʲ]	[ʝevəɣ]	[ʝevəmɪdʲ]
	faighinn	faigheadh	faigheamaid
	[fajɪNʲ]	[fajəɣ]	[fajəmɪdʲ]

IS 'be' (2)

Pres	is [ɪs] 's e [ʃɛ]	as [əs]	-
Past	bu [bə] b' e [bɛ]	a bu [ə bə] a b' [ə b]	bu [bə] b' [b]

Cond	bu [bə] b' e [bɛ]

RACH 'go'

Fut	théid [he:dʲ]	a théid [ə he:dʲ]	déid [dʲe:dʲ]
Pres	a' dol [ə dɔL]		
Past	chaidh [xaj]		deach [dʲɛx]

Imp	racham [Raxəm] theirigeam [herʲɪgʲəm] na deirigeam [na dʲerʲɪgʲəm]	rach [Rax] theirig [herʲɪgʲ] na deirig [na dʲerʲɪgʲ]	rachadh [Raxəɣ] theirigeadh [herʲɪgʲəɣ] na deirigeadh [na dʲerʲɪgʲəɣ]	rachamaid [Raxəmɪdʲ] theirigeamaid [herʲɪgʲəmɪdʲ] na deirigeamaid [na dʲerʲɪgʲəmɪdʲ]	rachaibh [Raxɪv] theirigibh [herʲɪgʲɪv] na deirigibh [na dʲerʲɪgʲɪv]

Cond	rachainn [raxɪNʲ] rachainn [RaxɪNʲ]	rachadh [raxəɣ] rachadh [Raxəɣ]	rachamaid [raxəmɪdʲ] rachamaid [Raxəmɪdʲ]

RUIG 'arrive'

Fut	ruigidh [Rɯgʲɪ]	a ruigeas [ə rɯgʲəs]	ruig [Rɯgʲ]
Pres	a' ruigsinn [ə RɯgʲʃɪNʲ]		
Past	ràinig [raːnɪgʲ]		do ràinig [də raːnɪgʲ]

Imp	ruigeam	ruig	ruigeadh	ruigeamaid	ruigibh
	[Rɯgʲəm]	[Rɯgʲ]	[Rɯgʲəɣ]	[Rɯgʲəmɪdʲ]	[Rɯgʲɪv]

Cond	ruiginn	ruigeadh	ruigeamaid
	[rɯgʲɪNʲ]	[rɯgəɣ]	[rɯgʲəmɪdʲ]
	ruiginn	ruigeadh	ruigeamaid
	[RɯgʲɪNʲ]	[Rɯgəɣ]	[Rɯgʲəmɪdʲ]

THIG 'come'

Fut	thig [higʲ]	a thig [ə higʲ]	dig [dʲigʲ]
Pres	a' tighinn [ə tʲi.ɪNʲ]		
Past	thàinig [haːnɪgʲ]		dàinig [daːnɪgʲ]

Imp	thigeam	thig	thigeadh	thigeamaid	thigibh
	[higʲəm]	[higʲ]	[higʲəɣ]	[higʲəmɪdʲ]	[higɪv]
	na digeam	na dig	na digeadh	na digeamaid	na digibh
	[na dʲigʲəm]	[na dʲigʲ]	[na dʲigʲəɣ]	[na dʲigʲəmɪdʲ]	[na dʲigʲɪv]

Cond	thiginn	thigeadh	thigeamaid
	[higʲɪNʲ]	[higʲəɣ]	[higʲəmɪdʲ]
	diginn	digeadh	digeamaid
	[dʲigʲɪNʲ]	[dʲigʲəɣ]	[dʲigʲəmɪdʲ]

THOIR 'give'

Fut	bheir [verʲ]		a bheir [ə verʲ]	doir [dɔrʲ]
Pres	a' toirt [ə tɔRʃdʲ] a' tabhairt [ə tɔ.əRʃdʲ]			
Past	thug [hug]			dug [dug]

Imp	thoiream [horʲəm] na doiream [na dorʲəm]	thoir [horʲ] doir [dɔrʲ]	thoireadh [horʲəɣ] doireadh [dɔrʲəɣ]	thoireamaid [horʲəmɪdʲ] doireamaid [dɔrʲəmɪdʲ]	thoiribh [horʲɪv] doiribh [dɔrʲɪv]

Cond	thoirinn [horʲɪNʲ] doirinn [dɔrʲɪNʲ] thugainn [hugɪNʲ] dugainn [dugɪNʲ]	thoireadh [horʲəɣ] doireadh [dɔrʲəɣ] thugadh [hugəɣ] dugadh [dugəɣ]	thoireamaid [horʲəmɪdʲ] doireamaid [dɔrʲəmɪdʲ] thugamaid [hugəmɪdʲ] dugamaid [dugəmɪdʲ]

II.   Appendix II - Conversion charts

There aren't many 'mainstream' Gaelic publications which give a guide to pronunciation throughout. Even fewer use a reliable system of indicating pronunciation and most use an ad-hoc system based loosely on English syllables. This is generally dubbed 'adopted pronunciation'. These systems, which incidentally don't even agree with each other, are about as reliable as reducing the instructions to use '275gr butter, 125gr sugar, 125gr finely ground hazelnuts and 350gr plain flour[83]' to 'mix some butter, sugar, nuts and flour'… Which one would you rather follow for your Christmas baking?

Given that you have invested all this time and effort into learning the sounds of Gaelic and a reliable way of putting them into writing you might find the conversion charts below useful. It relates the other systems to the symbols used in this book.

I have only selected those which are in common use these days[84] and which are also reliable. Most others just don't work. Be particularly wary of the 'pronunciation guides' in MacLennan's and MacAlpine's dictionaries (see bibliography)! And of course any of those books using English syllables to give "pronunciation".

---

[83] This, incidentally, is my grandma's famous recipe for Vanilla Kipferl. Melt the butter, mix all ingredients well and form a thick sausage. Wrap in clingfilm and put in the fridge overnight. Cut off slices and form small crescent (no bigger than a AA battery) with your hands and place on a greased tray. Bake for about 15-20 minutes at 100°C until firm-ish but don't let them get brown. Take out of the oven and immediately roll in a mixture of icing sugar (100gr) and vanilla sugar (40gr). Like Gaelic pronunciation they're a bit tricky to get right but when you do, they're stunning!

[84] As of early 2011

Black, R. *Cothrom Ionnsachaidh,* University of Edinburgh

Cothrom Ionnsachaidh has been around for a while, its first edition came
out in 1984 and it has been republished several times since. The author
uses standard IPA with a few modifications so I'm only giving you the
symbols which are different

RB	ə	ə:	ʎ	ʎ:	əi	əi	b, p	bʲ	mʲ
	ɤ	ɤː	ɯ	ɯː	ɤi	ɯi	b	bj	mj
RB	ŋ, ŋk	ŋʲ, ŋʲkʲ	r	rʲ	fʲ	vʲ	ç	ɹ	-
	ng	nʲgʲ	r	rʲ	fj	vj	hj	R	.

The two confusing things about this transcription variant are that:

- at the beginning of a word [b], [d] and [g] are written as [b], [d] and [g]
  but elsewhere in a word as [p], [t] and [k].

- [ə] is used for "our" [ɤ] in stressed syllables but [ə] in unstressed
  syllables.

He also uses an extra **r** symbol, the [ɹ] (same as in Standard English
rock [ɹɔk] for the Gaelic [R] that occurs before **l** and **d**, for example *bòrd*
[boːɹd].

Up until lesson 5 all new vocabulary (and some more) is transcribed into
IPA. From then on it occurs less frequently but makes appearances at
strategic intervals. On the whole, the pronunciation guide is reliable and
useful.

Buchanan, D. *Gaelic-English, English-Gaelic Dictionary,* Geddes &
Grosset

The merits of the dictionary aside, it does have a reliable pronunciation
guide. It's a system which has a 1 to 1 correspondence to the IPA. The
reasons it's not straightforward IPA is that the publisher felt some
symbols looked too alien. Here's a list of the symbols which are different:

BD	ī	ē	ɛ̄	ā	ɔ̄	ō	o̱	ō̱	ū	u̱	ū̱	o̱i
	iː	eː	ɛː	aː	ɔː	oː	ɤ	ɤː	uː	ɯ	ɯː	ɤi

BD	u̱i	py	by	t'	d'	k'	g'	my	ng	ng'	N'	L'
	ɯi	pj	bj	tʲ	dʲ	kʲ	gʲ	mj	ŋg	ŋʲgʲ	Nʲ	Lʲ

BD	r'	fy	vy	š	ch	ch'	gh	gh'	hy
	rʲ	fj	vj	ʃ	x	ç	ɣ	ʝ	hj

Other notes: it doesn't use ['] to indicate a stressed syllable but instead
puts the stressed syllable in bold letters if necessary. Mostly safe to use.

Dieckhoff, H. *A Pronouncing Dictionary of Scottish Gaelic,* Gairm 1932 (reprint 1992)

This dictionary has both advantages and disadvantages. As a dictionary, it is neither very big nor does it give much in the way of explanations or examples and the pronunciations given were obtained from speakers of Glen Garry Gaelic (Glen Garry in Knoydart, not Glen Garry in Aberdeenshire). Its good points are a fairly reliable pronunciation guide and – something which no other dictionary has so far attempted – the pronunciation of genitive and plural forms is given for many headwords.

DH	i	i:	*i*	é	é:	è	è:	ə	ò, o	ò:	ó	ó:
	(ü)	(ü:)				(æ)	(æ:)	(ɐ)				
DH	i	i:	ɪ	e	e:	ɛ	ɛ:	ə	ɔ	ɔ:	o	o:

DH	ö	ö:	y	y:	i:a	i:ə	u:a	öi	ui:	èu	ou:	éi
DH	ɤ	ɤ:	ɯ	ɯ:	ia	iə	ue	ɤi	ɯi	au	ɔu	ei

DH	p	*b*	b	tc	*d'j*	*k'j*	*g'j*	m	ng	ng	N'	n, n'
									ngg	ngg'*j*		
DH	pj	b	bj	tˡ	dʲ	kʲ	gʲ	mj	ŋg	ŋ'gʲ	Nʲ	n

DH	L'	l, l'	r'	f	v	v	S	K	*c*	G	*j*
					(w)	*(w)*					
DH	Lʲ	l	rʲ	fj	v	vj	ʃ	x	ç	ɣ	i̠

His description has some additional symbols such as ɐ, æ and ü ([ɨ] in IPA). For our purposes they are considered identical to the sounds next to which they are given, for example [ɐ] is treated as [ə]. He uses italics because in certain loanwords he uses the non-italic letters to indicate English sounds, for example Gaelic *beag* [*bég*] vs English *beg* [bɛg]. Nasal vowels are indicated with an asterisk: **ia*** for [ĩã]

Bearing in mind the somewhat dialectal nature of this dictionary's sources, on the whole it is a fairly helpful dictionary when it comes to pronunciation once you get your head around the slightly odd symbols he uses. Safe to use once you get used to it.

Klevenhaus, M. *Lehrbuch der schottish-gälischen Sprache,* Buske 2008

This new textbook for German learners of Gaelic has a fairly extensive chapter on pronunciation. The pronunciation guide uses exactly the same symbols as Blas na Gàidhlig uses, so it's safe to use.

Ó Maolalaigh, R. *Scottish Gaelic in Three Months,* Hugo 1997 & *Scottish Gaelic in Twelve Weeks,* Birlinn 2008

This book (both the original edition and the more recent one) is one of the rare exceptions which not only gives you very good overview of how Gaelic works but also uses a very reliable pronunciation guide. With a few minor exceptions where alternate symbols are used, the author uses unabridged IPA symbols for maximum accuracy. Again, I've only given you the symbols which are different:

ÓM	i	d̪	ŋ	ŋʲ	n̪	ɲ	ɫ	ʎ	ꞧ	ɾ	ɾʲ	-
	ɪ	d	ng	ŋʲgʲ	N	Nʲ	L	Lʲ	R	r	rʲ	.

Nasal vowels are marked in the standard IPA way, for example [ã], if necessary. There are no overlaps or inconsistencies so it's safe and reliable to use and the only thing one could possible bemoan is the fact that not all vocabulary is given in IPA.

III.   Appendix III - Key to the exercises

Key to Exercise 40

Vowel Set 01

	[e]	[eː]	[ɛ]	[ɛː]
01		beːm		
02			bɛn	
03	leʃ			
04				pɛː
05			gʲɛr	
06				gɛː
07		leːm		
08	kʲed			
09			ʃɛL	
10	̺jeh			

Vowel Set 02

	[o]	[oː]	[ɔ]	[ɔː]
01			mɔhdʲ	
02		boː		
03				krɔː
04				sglɔː
05		moːr		
06	gob			
07			kɔl	
08				tɔːR
09			bɔʃ	
10	bog			

Vowel Set 03

	[a]	[aː]	[ɛ]	[ɛː]
01			gʲɛn	
02				pɛː
03	ar			
04		dʲaːR		
05	kal			
06			fɛr	
07				mɛː
08		maːs		
09	taxg			
10			drɛx	

Vowel Set 04

	[i]	[iː]	[ə]	[e]
01			ər	
02		biː		
03	ʃi			
04				leʃ
05	kʲi			
06			əN	
07				mes
08		brʲiː		
09	miçgʲ			
10			nə	

Vowel Set 05

	[ɯ]	[ɯː]	[u]	[uː]
01			kus	
02				ʃuːl
03			stuxg	
04		mɯːL		
05				Ruː
06	ɯʃ			
07			hug	
08		brɯːn		
09	kɯNʲ			
10				kluː

Key to Exercise 41

	labial	dental	alveolar	palatal	velar	nasal
si<u>p</u>	☑					
<u>f</u>lit	☑					
<u>t</u>ime			☑			
<u>c</u>reel					☑	
<u>y</u>oung				☑		
ee<u>l</u>			☑			
<u>g</u>one					☑	
<u>d</u>ish			☑			
bon<u>n</u>y			☑			☑
bo<u>th</u>er		☑				
<u>b</u>airn	☑					
<u>r</u>ain			☑			
sti<u>ck</u>					☑	
wi<u>d</u>th		☑				
mer<u>r</u>y			☑			
ba<u>g</u>					☑	
<u>th</u>is		☑				
<u>m</u>ush	☑					☑
bu<u>ng</u>					☑	☑
<u>g</u>ob					☑	
<u>w</u>eek	☑					
<u>k</u>irk					☑	
<u>h</u>ive	☑					
lo<u>ch</u>					☑	
cousi<u>n</u>			☑			☑

Key to Exercise 86

01. mə xas ⇒ [k]	11. mə nɯːv ⇒ [N] or [Nʲ]
02. mə hɤj ⇒ [s] or [t]	12. mə fɔːxgɪdʲ ⇒ [p]
03. mə lebɪ ⇒ [Lʲ]	13. mə hɔLəs ⇒ [s] or [t]
04. mə voː ⇒ [b] or [m]	14. mə hjuːxgər ⇒ [ʃ] or [tʲ]
05. mə çauN ⇒ [kʲ]	15. mə jɔːrʲ ⇒ [dʲ] or [gʲ]
06. muːdər ⇒ [f] or [uː]	16. mə ɤob ⇒ [d] or [g]
07. mə ɤah ⇒ [d] or [g]	17. mə fjuər ⇒ [pj]
08. mə raːv ⇒ [R]	18. mə jensɪ ⇒ [dʲ] or [gʲ]
09. mə varag ⇒ [b] or [m]	19. mə ned ⇒ [N] or [Nʲ]
10. mə hjɔːL ⇒ [ʃ] or [tʲ]	20. meːdal ⇒ [f] or [eː]

Key to Exercise 87

	Lenited ⇒ Past	Unlenited ⇒ Order
01	xurʲ miʃə (I put)	
02		mɔL miʃə (praise ME!)
03		gɤl miʃə (boil ME!)
04	faʃgʲ miʃə (I folded)	
05	hɯgʲ miʃə (I understood)	
06		Riərɪç miʃə (satisfy ME!)
07		kurʲ miʃə (put ME!)
08	ɣɤinɪç miʃə (I asked)	
09	ɣɤl miʃə (I boiled)	
10	vɔL miʃə (I praised)	
11		fɤinɪç miʃə (ask ME!)
12	riərɪç miʃə (I satisfied)	
13		Nʲi miʃə (wash ME!)
14	ni miʃə (I washed)	
15	ɣuːNʲ miʃə (I closed)	
16		tɯgʲ miʃə (understand ME!)
17		duːNʲ miʃə (close ME!)
18		paʃgʲ miʃə (fold ME!)

Key to Exercise 88

01 Seo mo chiad bhriogais fhada.

02 Thuit torr fhir bheaga gheala an-sin.

03 An do bhris e tro dhoras mór leis a' gheimhleag mhór ghobhlach?

04 Chuir mi d' fhìdheall shnog air ghleus dhut.

05 A Thormoid bhig bhìodaich, tha e ro dhaor!

06 Sin a' bhó bheag dhonn as fhaisge ort.

07 'S beag orm do dhroch chainnt shalach shàrachail

08 Tha mo chéile airson sgoil mhór Ghàidhlig a thogail.

09 Chan fhaigh sinn deagh leabaidh bhog ron ath mhìos.

10 'S e gnìomh a dhearbhas mar a chanas a sheanair.

11 Cha mhi a chluinneas tu air a' bheinn mhór chas ghlas ud.

12 Sin a' cheist ghòrach as fhaide a thog e 'nam chlas a-riamh.

Key to Exercise 89

01 mo cheann	10 a' chiad chas	19 mo thòn
02 dà chas	11 bu mhór	20 cha do thog
03 gun dealbh	12 bhon bhó	21 cha tog
04 aon taigh	13 cha dùin	22 aon nead
05 leis an luchag	14 bu toil	23 bu diùid
06 bhon dùn	15 gun chliù	24 mo leabaidh [Lʲ] ⇒ [l]
07 sa chàr	16 cha mhol	25 seann duine
08 aon mhàs	17 a' chiad duilleag	26 dath an fhir
09 seann dùthaich	18 dath an taighe	27 cha ghearr

Key to Exercise 90

02 Cha do bhìd na coin thana dhonna ud mo chat.

03 Bha móran dhaoine sa bhaile bheag sàmhach ud.

04 Ciamar a l'eughas mi sin gun solas 'nam sheòmar beag?

05 Cha phòs a' bhean bheag ghrinn sin do sheann bhràthair.

06 A Mhàiri bheag, tha thu 'gam shìor shàrachadh le do bheachdan.

07 An do thuit am prìomh mhinistear air a' bhrat sleamhnach seo?

08 Tha a dheagh chaman ris an doras trom ghorm.

09 Chan fhaca mi briseadh an dorais thruim ghuirm.

10 Cha tusa am fear a tha glé glé thoilichte leis a' chat mhór dubh.

11 Cha mhise an té a tha toilichte leis an droch cho-dhùnadh seo.

12 Bh²uail dà pheilear tron bhalla tiugh bhuidhe fo mo phiuthar.

[1] Lenited from [Lʲ] to [l] but not visible in the orthography.

[2] Lenited by the past tense particle *do* which is dropped at the beginning of phrase.

Key to Exercise 91

eala	dhìth	earrach	iuchair
dhìol	dhìom	dh'fhios	cidhe
guidhe	dh'Inbhir Nis	ghin	dh'ith
iùil	eòrna	ghearr	ghiomach
dhiùlt	ghéill	Eòlaigearraidh	ghiùlain

Key to Exercise 93

01	kLauN	kLɯNʲə	12	ma:L	ma:l
02	baLax	baLɪç	13	puhdan	puhdɛNʲ
03	marag	marɛgʲ	14	kur	kurʲ
04	bɔxg	bɯçgʲ	15	mɔnəɣ	mɔnɪ
05	frɯ:x	frɯ:ç	16	kas	kaʃə
06	aran	arɛNʲ	17	ɛRəN	ɛRɪNʲ
07	slahd	slɛhdʲə	18	brɔ:g	brɔ:gʲə
08	kʲɔ:L[1]	kʲu:l	19	bauL	bɯiLʲ
09	ba:ɣ[2]	ba:j	20	karax	karɪç
10	kʲauN	kʲi:Nʲ	21	ahər	ahərʲ
11	mo:r	mo:rʲ	22	fad	fadʲ

[1] The result of [L] palatalising in 8, 12 and 19 is not the same. The clue here is in the normal spelling system where [L] spelled with a double ll palatalised to [Lʲ] whereas the [L] written with a single l palatalises to [l]. In this case, 8 *ceòl* [kʲɔ:L] ⇒ *ciùil* [kʲu:l] and 12 *màl* [ma:L] ⇒ *màil* [ma:l] but 19 *ball* [bauL] ⇒ *buill* [bɯiLʲ].

[2] After a back vowel, [ɣ] normally turns into [j] when it is palatalised. Note that the [əɣ] ending changes to [j] when palatalised.

Key to Exercise 94

ha ku: səN xaːr	tha cù san chàr
ha NʲaNag ʃɔ moːr	tha an fheannag seo mór
ha ku: səN tɤj	tha cù san taigh
ha ku: egʲ ə Nʲɛr	tha cù aig an fhear
ha ku: ɛrʲ ə Nʲiar	tha cù air an fheur
ha xalag ʃɔ moːr	tha a' chaileag seo mór
ha vɛn ʃɔ moːr	tha a' bhean seo mór
ha ku: egʲ ə Nad	tha cù aig an ad
ha ku: ɛrʲ ə Nʲelan	tha cù air an eilean
har nahərʲ əʲʃɔ	tha ur n-athair an-seo
ha ku: egʲ ə NɯNʲag	tha cù aig an uinneag
ha Nʲiːdʲag ʃɔ moːr	tha an fhìdeag seo mór
ha Nʲɔːrag ʃɔ moːr	tha an fheòrag seo mór
har naran mah	tha ar n-aran math
ha elan sə Nʲɛr	tha eilean san ear

Key to Exercise 95

01. leʃ ə Nad	leis an fhad / ad
02. dʲɔx nə Nɤjən	deoch nan naoidhean / aoighean
03. sə Nʲɛr	san fhear / ear
04. ȷe NuəLəx	dhen nuallach / uallach
05. gu Narʲɪç u	gun nàirich / àirich thu
06. ɛrʲ ə NaLd	air an fhalt / alt
07. rʲiʃ ə Nʲɛx	ris an neach / each
08. ɔ Naː	on fhàth / àth
09. trɔ NʲɛRʃd	tron fheart / neart
10. sə Nʲesan	san fheasan / easan / neasan

Key to Exercise 96

01. tha i san ìochdar	16. tha m' uchd / muc ann
02. dath an aoil	17. tha cù air an fhearann / earann mhór
03. tha bainne san ùth	18. seo d' obair
04. tha d' fhiach mór	19. 's i m' eudail
05. tha fear san fhear/ear	20. tha thu air an eilean
06. tha falt air Niall	21. thig e san luchar
07. cuir uisge air an fhùdar / ùghdar	22. tha i gun éis / fhéis
08. seo dath / d' ath	23. tha clach air an athair / nathair
09. leis an neart / fheart seo	24. bhon oide
10. éist ris an arm / fharam	25. tha gath san fheòil
11. fhuair mi m' àrach	26. thoir seo dhan each / dha neach
12. is dona an uaill	27. tha bó air an fheur / iar
13. gabh d' anail	28. tha an ad aig an fhéill
14. tha seo gun éifeachd	29. tha d' ad / dad an-seo
15. air an anart	30. leis an adhbhar / fhaobhar seo

Key to Exercise 97

01.	I came forward	cautiously	and giving ear	as I came	heard someone	rattling with dishes	and a little dry eager cough	that came in fits	but there was	no sound of speech	and not a dog barked.
02.	The door	as well as I could see it	in the dim light	was a great piece of wood	all studded with nails	and I lifted my hand	with a faint heart	under my jacket	and knocked once.
03.	Then I stood	and waited.
04.	The house	had fallen	into a dead silence	a whole minute passed away	and nothing stirred	but the bats overhead.
05.	I knocked again	and hearkened again.
06.	By this time	my ears	had grown so accustomed	to the quiet	that I could hear	the ticking of the clock	inside	as it slowly counted out	the seconds	but whoever was	in that house	kept deadly still	and must have held	his breath.
07.	I was	in two minds	whether to run away	but anger	got the upper hand	and I began instead	to rain kicks and buffets	on the door	and to shout out aloud	for Mr Balfour.
08.	I was	in full career	when I heard	the cough	right overhead	and jumping back	and looking up	beheld a man's head	in a tall nightcap	and the bell mouth of a blunderbuss	at one of the first-storey windows.

Key to Exercise 100

Listen to the recording and underline the syllable or word which bears the stress.

01.	a-mhàin	[əvaːNʲ]	02.	dùinte	[duːndʲə]
03.	bruidhinn	[briɪNʲ]	04.	dìomhair	[dʲiəvɪrʲ]
05.	amannan	[aməNən]	06.	eagalach	[egəLəx]
07.	casan	[kasən]	08.	móran	[moːran]
09.	MacAoidh	[maxgɯj]	10.	a-steach	[əʃdʲɛx]
11.	taighean	[tajən]	12.	Dùn Barra	[dunbaRə]
13.	ciallachadh	[kʲiaLəxəɣ]	14.	cabadaich	[kabədɪç]
15.	an-diugh	[əndʲu]	16.	mearachd	[mɛrəxg]
17.	balaich	[baLɪç]	18.	caistealan	[kaʃdʲəLən]
19.	athraichean	[arɪçən]	20.	lus	[Lus]

Key to Exercise 101

01.	DihAoine	dʲɪˈhɯːNʲə	02.	taigh-òsta	təˈjɔːsdə
03.	leabhraichean	Lʲɔːɾɪçən	04.	cunbhalach	kunuvəLəx
05.	NicGilleRuaidh	NiçgʲiLʲəˈruəj	06.	agamsa	agəmsə
07.	atharraich	ahəRɪç	08.	a-null	əˈNuːL
09.	an-uiridh	əˈNurʲɪ	10.	dèanamh	dʲiənəv
11.	Dùn Bheagan	dunˈvegan	12.	caileagan	kalagən
13.	craobhan	krɯːvən	14.	Inbhir Theòrsa	ɪNʲɪrʲˈhjɔːRsə
15.	beanntan	bjauNdən	16.	a-nuas	əˈNuəs
17.	margaideachd	maragɪdʲəxg	18.	tìr-mór	tʲirʲˈmoːr
19.	buntàta	bənˈtaːdə	20.	freagarrach	frʲegəRəx

Key to Exercise 102

One stress	Two stresses
a redshank	a red shank
freeclimbing	free climbing
livestock	live stock
a redneck	a red neck
a stonefish	a stone fish
a stagparty	a stag party
a blackhead	a black head
a blackbird	a black bird
a running joke	a running joke
the goldenrod	the golden rod
a green finch	a greenfinch

Key to Exercise 103

	'normal' word, stress on first syllable	hyphen, stress on the 'important' word	capital letters, stress on the 'important' word	exception
01. cuimhneachadh	☑			
02. an-diugh		☑		
03. MacGumaraid			☑	
04. buntàta				☑
05. DiSathairne			☑	
06. taigh-dhealbh		☑		
07. a-null		☑		
08. Dùn Dèagh			☑	
09. grad-shealladh		☑		
10. a-réir		☑		
11. DiCiadaoin			☑	
12. NicGilleMhìcheil			☑	
13. clàraichte	☑			
14. an-uiridh		☑		
15. drannd-eun		☑		
16. puinnseanachadh	☑			
17. NicAoidh			☑	
18. cnoc-faire		☑		
19. ban-tighearna				☑
20. Inbhir Nis			☑	

Key to Exercise 104

	1st vowel	2nd vowel	3rd vowel	4th vowel
01. còisirean	stressed	unstressed	unstressed	
02. amannan	stressed	unstressed	unstressed	
03. an-diugh	unstressed	stressed		
04. ball-coise	unstressed	stressed		
05. càraichean	stressed	unstressed	unstressed	
06. cuideachadh	stressed	unstressed	unstressed	
07. MacDhòmhnaill	unstressed	stressed	unstressed	
08. fuaradairean	stressed	unstressed	unstressed	unstressed
09. inntinniche	stressed	unstressed	unstressed	unstressed
10. mac Dhòmhaill	stressed	stressed	unstressed	
11. deasachaidhean	stressed	unstressed	unstressed	unstressed
12. DiarDaoin	unstressed	stressed		
13. oillteachadh	stressed	unstressed	unstressed	
14. caolachadh	stressed	unstressed	unstressed	
15. cothroman	stressed	unstressed	unstressed	

03: hyphen ⇒ stress not on the expected syllable; 04 hyphen ⇒ stress not on the expected syllable; 07: one word, two capital letters ⇒ stress not on the expected syllable; 10: two words, only one capital letter ⇒ stress on the expected syllable; 12: one word, two capital letters ⇒ stress not on the expected syllable; 15: two words, two capital letters ⇒ stress not on the expected syllable.

Key to Exercise 105

01. bothan		ɔ	
02. cìsean	ə		
03. pàganaich	aː		
04. maoineachadh			ɯː
05. aran			a
06. adhbrannan			ɤː
07. toileachadh	ə		
08. taigh-tasgaidh			ɪ
09. muinntireas		ɯi	
10. muladach			ə
11. sgrìobhadair	iː		
12. freagarrachadh	ɛ		
13. clachan		a	
14. buannachadh			uə
15. ime		i	

Key to Exercise 106

01 taigh-dhealbh	02 mór-thìr	03 glaine-fìona
04 taigh-dubh	05 brat-ùrlair	06 dealbh-chluich
07 sgian-arain	08 meanbh-chuileag	09 àrd-sgoil
10 uisge-beatha	11 taigh-mór	12 cas-bheart
13 mór-chùiseach	14 sgoil-àraich	15 taigh-tasgaidh
16 bun-sgoil	17 coileach-dubh	18 slat-iasgaich

03: a wine-glass ⟺ a glass of wine; 04 a blackhouse ⟺ a black house; 07 a breadknife ⟺ a knife made of bread; 11 a mansion ⟺ a big house; 17 a blackcock ⟺ a black cockerel.

Key to Exercise 107

01. dùnadh	du:nəɣ	02. aran	aran
03. urras	uRəs	04. togail	togal
05. cothrom	kɔRəm	06. sitig	ʃihdʲɪgʲ
07. móran	mo:ran	08. caileag	kalag
09. cailleach	kaLʲəx	10. toman	toman
11. leabhar	Lʲɔ.ər	12. Donnchadh	doNoxəɣ
13. cupa	kuhbə	14. craobhan	krɯ:vən
15. balaich	baLɪç	16. beagan	began
17. càise	ka:ʃə	18. dìochuimhnich	dʲiəxənɪç
19. boireann	borʲəN	20. boireannach	borʲəNəx
21. corra	kɔRə	22. tunnag	tuNag
23. sgoile	sgɔlə	24. sgoiltean	sgoldʲən
25. sgileil	sgʲilal	26. ceannard	kʲauNəRd
27. dèanamh	dʲianəv	28. éiridh	e:rʲɪ
29. aiseag	aʃəg	30. litir	Lʲihdʲɪrʲ
31. bochdainn	boxgɪNʲ	32. beinne	beNʲə
33. peantadh	pɛndəɣ	34. càirdeil	ka:Rdʲal
35. ceartas	kʲaRʃdəs	36. dhùineas	ɣu:nəs
37. cinnteach	kʲi:Nʲdʲəx	38. dùinidh	du:Nʲɪ
39. rachainn	raxɪNʲ	40. bhathar	vahər

Key to Exercise 109

01	Tha e athair ás an Òban agus tha iad a' dol ann a-nochd.
02	Bha uinneagan na h-eaglaise àrd briste on oidhche ud.
03	Cha bhi e toilichte idir is tu a' bualadh a-òrdag cho cruaidh.
04	Is urrainn dhut maille a chur air le bith a' cur seo an-sin.
05	Leum e a-mach air an uinneag agus chan fhaca e an cù.
06	Thàinig i an-seo an-diugh is chan fhalbh i gu DiSathairne.
07	Thig an-seo is chì thu a' bhó as motha a chunnaic thu a-riamh!
08	A Ailig, am faca e an trod a bha eatarra an-seo dà bhliadhna air ais?
09	Bu àbhaist dhomh a dhol ann ach sguir mi dheth dà latha air ais.
10	Dé an dath a tha air na cait bheaga a fhuair thu an-raoir?

Key to Exercise 111

		Fionnlagh Fada		
òrdag	colgag	[fjũ:NLəɣ fadə]	mac an aba	lùdag bheag
[ɔ:Rdag]	[kɔLɔgag]	Màiri Fhada	[maxg ə Nabə]	[Lu:dag veg]
		[maːrʲɪ adə]		
	balbhag	an gunna fada	mac an t-sradaich	lùdag bheag an airgid
	[baLavag]	[əŋ guNə fadə]	[maxg əN tradɪç]	[Lu:dag veg ə
			nic an t-sradaich	Nɛrʲɛgʲɪdʲ]
			[Nʲiçgʲ əN tradɪç]	
	tolgag	ceanna-fead		coiteag
	[tɔLɔgag]	[kʲaNəˈfed]		[kɣihdʲag]
	sgealbag	gille fada		plaosgag
	[sgʲaLabag]	[gʲiLʲə fadə]		[pLɯ:sgag]

Key to Exercise 112

gog gog gag gàg	gòrag gòrag	fearaman faraman
[gog gog gag gaːg]	[goːrag goːrag]	[fɛrəman farəman]
cnàg cnàg	chu sil ì chu sil ò	mó mó
[krãːg krãːg]	[xuʃɪlˈi: xuʃɪlˈɔː]	[mõː mõː]
af af	hi homh homh	meig meig
[af af]	[hĩ hõ hõ]	[megʲ megʲ]
mè mè	ràc ràc	fais
[mɛ̃ mɛ̃]	[Raːxg Raːxg]	[faʃː]
miamh miamh	guileag guileag	mhàg mhàg
[mjãũ mjãũ]	[gulag gulag]	[vãːg vãːg]
gog a ghuidhe ghaoidhe	gug gùg	u i o homh
[gog ə ɣujə ɣɯjə]	[gug guːg]	[uiɔ hõ]
dùrd dùrd	siu-chù siu-chù	gnost gnost
[duːRd duːRd]	[ʃuˈxu: ʃuˈxu:]	[grõsd grõsd]

Key to Exercise 115

	Phrase	
01.	va muː əˈʃɪn	bha am bùth an-sin
02.	rˠiNʲ i ŋʲgʲeːm	rinn i an ceum/geum
03.	ha Nʲes əˈʃin	tha an deas/eas/neas/teas an-sin
04.	ʃɔ m hɔuL	seo am poll
05.	ʃɔ N hɔuL	seo an toll
06.	va maxg agəd mah	bha am bac/mac/paca agad math
07.	ʃin ə ŋruh	sin an cruth/gruth
08.	stɔ ləm dah nə mjauN	's toil leam dath nam beann/beann/peann
09.	mə Nʲesəx ʃɔ	mun deasach/teasach
10.	ʃɔ ŋʲgʲed agəm	seo an cead/gead agam
11.	xuNə ʃiNʲ ə NuəLəx	chunnaic sinn an nuallach/t-uallach
12.	ha m bian dɔnə	tha am bian/pian dona
13.	xa tˠ ləm ə ŋauL ʃɔ	cha toil leam an gall/call seo
14.	ʃin ə Nʲeːd	sin an deud/teud/t-eud
15.	xuəLə mi mə Nʲɛxgɛrʲəxg	chuala mi mun deachdaireachd/teachdaireachd

Key to Exercise 116

01. seachdain	02. fàilidhean	03. tànaiste	04. deifrich
05. cilltean	06. banais	07. isean	08. fighe
09. faoin	10. giobach	11. rùisgte	12. tèarainn
13. cìsean	14. eilean	15. geòidh	16. daoine
17. leabaidh	18. mìneachadh	19. eile	20. cnuic
21. Éireannach	22. leòman	23. leisgeadair	24. ròlaisteach
25. sònraichte	26. teagaisg	27. ùineachan	28. ciste
29. cruithneach	30. falmhaich	31. geamannan	32. aiseag
33. bochdainn	34. làthaireachd	35. caileige	36. urram
37. nighean	38. bràigh	39. ainmich	40. feòragan

In addition to the underlined slender consonants, this key also shows the entire slender groups highlighted in grey.

01. seachdain	02. fàilidhean	03. tànaiste	04. deifrich
05. cilltean	06. banais	07. isean	08. fighe
09. faoin	10. giobach	11. rùisgte	12. tèarainn
13. cìsean	14. eilean	15. geòidh	16. daoine
17. leabaidh	18. mìneachadh	19. eile	20. cnuic
21. Éireannach	22. leòman	23. leisgeadair	24. ròlaisteach
25. sònraichte	26. teagaisg	27. ùineachan	28. ciste
29. cruithneach	30. falmhaich	31. geamannan	32. aiseag
33. bochdainn	34. làthaireachd	35. caileige	36. urram
37. nighean	38. bràigh	39. ainmich	40. feòragan

Key to Exercise 117

ceann [kʲauN]	fead [fed]	cama [kamə]
‣ beann [bjauN]	‣ cead [kʲed]	‣ ama [amə]
‣ seann [ʃauN]	‣ nead [Nʲed]	‣ hama [hamə]
‣ deann [dʲauN] ...	‣ cnead [krʲēd]	‣ drama [dramə]
BUT	BUT	BUT
‣ fireann [firʲəN]	‣ airgead [ɛrʲɛgʲəd]	‣ stuama [sduəmə]
‣ boireann [borʲəN] ...	‣ uiread [urʲəd]	‣ tuama [tuəmə]
caorach [kɯːrəx]	beinn [beiNʲ]	feum [feːm]
‣ maorach [mɯːrəx]	‣ seinn [ʃeiNʲ]	‣ ceum [kʲeːm]
‣ daorach [dɯːrəx]	‣ leinn [leiNʲ]	‣ leum [Lʲeːm]
‣ Paorach [pɯːrəx]	‣ teinn [tʲeiNʲ]	‣ teum [tʲeːm]
	NOT	NOT
	‣ mèinn [mɛːNʲ]	‣ luath-cheum [Luəçem]
	‣ Scoitbheinn [sgɔhdʲveNʲ]	‣ Cuingleum [kũĩləm]
gaol [gɯːL]	ciùil [kʲuːl]	mac [maxg]
‣ craol [krɯːL]	‣ siùil [ʃuːl]	‣ sac [saxg]
‣ caol [kɯːL]	‣ shiùil [hjuːl]	‣ bac [baxg]
‣ aol [ɯːL]	‣ iùil [juːl]	‣ srac [sdraxg]
		NOT
		‣ currac [kuRəg]
		‣ tìodhlac [tʲiəLəg]
tinn [tʲiːNʲ]	achadh [axəɣ]	each [ɛx]
‣ binn [biːNʲ]	‣ aideachadh [adʲəxəɣ]	‣ speach [sbɛx]
‣ cinn [kʲiːNʲ]	‣ atharrachadh [ahəRəxəɣ]	‣ creach [krʲɛx]
‣ dinn [dʲiːNʲ]	‣ ciallachadh [kʲiəLəxəɣ]	‣ deach [dʲɛx]
BUT	BUT	NOT
‣ éiginn [eːgʲɪNʲ]	‣ adhbrann [ɤːbrəN]	‣ bileach [biləx]
‣ broinn [brɤiNʲ]	‣ seadh [ʃɤɣ]	‣ imeach [iməx]
fileanta [filəNdə]	cluinn [kLɯiNʲ]	sgeul [sgʲiaL]
‣ bitheanta [bihəNdə]	‣ tuinn [tɯiNʲ]	‣ beul [biaL]
‣ puinnseanta [pũĩNʲʃəNdə]	‣ fuinn [fɯiNʲ]	‣ reul [RiaL]
‣ coileanta [kɔləNdə]	‣ cruinn [krɯiNʲ]	‣ neul [NʲiaL]
NOT		NOT
‣ beantainn [bɛndɪNʲ]		‣ Caimbeul [kaimbəL]
‣ leantail [Lʲɛndal]		‣ leisgeul [LʲeʃgʲəL]

Key to Exercise 118

Long Vowel/Diphthong	Short Vowel
[kauL] [kauLdɪNʲ] [kauLdəx] • call calltainn calltach	[kaLə] • calla
[bauN] [bauNdə] • bann bannta	[baNə] • banna
[Lɔum] [Lɔumnəxg] • lom lomnochd	[Lomə] [Lomɐy] • loma lomadh
[glauN] [glauNdən] [glauNdɪv] [glauNdal] • gleann gleanntan gleanntaibh gleanntail	[glaNə] [glaNan] [glaNəx] • gleanna gleannan gleannach
[kaiLʲdʲə] [kaiLʲ] [kaiLʲdʲəx] • caillte caill caillteach	[xaLʲɐy] • chailleadh
[sgɣiNʲ] • sgoinn	[sgɣNʲal] [sgɣNʲə] • sgoinneil sgoinne
[ku:m] [kū:mdʲə] • cum cumte	[kumal] [kumɐy] [kumadal] • cumail cumadh cumadail
[i:m] • im	[imə] [iməx] • ime imeach
[kū:Ndəy] [kū:Ndəs] • cunntadh cunntas	
[pɔuLdəx] [pɔuL] • polltach poll	[pɔLan] [pɔLag] [pɔLəx] • pollan pollag pollach
[gauL] [gauLdəxg] [gauLdə] • gall galltachd gallta	[gaLə] • galla
[tʲi:Nʲ] • tinn	[tʲiNʲəs] [tʲiNʲəd] • tinneas tinnead
[kʲiNʲ] [kʲī:Nʲdʲə] [kʲī:NʲdʲɪNʲ] • cinn cinnte cinntinn	[kʲiNʲɐy] [kʲiNʲəs] • cinneadh cinneas
[bja:R] [bja:Rdə] [bja:Rdəx] • bearr bearrta bearrtach	[bjaRɐy] [bjaRədərʲ] • bearradh bearradair
[dʲa:Rs] [dʲa:Rsəy] [dʲa:Rsəx] • dearrs dearrsadh dearrsach	
[aum] • am	[amə] [aməNən] • ama amannan
[kLūiNʲdʲɪNʲ] [kLɯiNʲ] [kLūiNʲdʲər] • cluinntinn cluinn cluinntear	[xLɯNʲɐy] [xLɯNʲɪNʲ] • chluinneadh chluinninn
[Lū:N] • lunn	[LuNəx] [LuNə] • lunnach lunna
[fjū:N] [fjū:NLəx] • fionn fionnlach	[fjuNər] [fjuNɐy] • fionnar fionnadh
[fɣiLʲ] • foill	[fɣLʲə] [fɣLʲər] • foille foillear
[tʲi:Lʲ] [tʲi:LʲdʲɪNʲ] • till tilltinn	[tʲiLʲɐy] [hiLʲɪNʲ] • tilleadh thillinn
[gʲauL] [gʲauLdɪNʲ] [jauL] [gʲauLdə] [gʲauLdənəs] • geall gealltainn gheall geallta gealltanas	[gʲaLɐy] • gealladh
[kāīNʲdʲ] [kāīNʲdʲə] [kāīNʲdʲən] [kāīNʲdʲəxg] • cainnt cainnte cainntean cainnteachd	

[sba:R] [sba:Rdə] • sparr sparrta	[sbaRəɣ] [sbaRan] • sparradh sparran
[greim] • greim	[grʲeməɣ] [grʲemɪç] [grʲemɪrʲ] • greimeadh greimich greimir
[ʃeiNʲ] [heiNʲ] • seinn sheinn	[ʃeNʲə] [ʃeNʲədɛrʲ] • seinne seinneadair
[tɔ:R] • torr	[tɔRəɣ] [tɔRan] [tɔRanəx] • torradh torran torranach
[prõũNdəx] [prɔuN] [prõũNdal] • pronntach pronn pronntail	[prɔNəɣ] [prɔNədərʲ] [prɔNəs] • pronnadh pronnadair pronnas

Key to Exercise 119

		All Front	All Back	Front ⇒ Back	Back ⇒ Front
01.	ku:L		☑		
02.	ʃɛ:	☑			
03.	mil	☑			
04.	ʃia			☑	
05.	guh		☑		
06.	RɤiNʲ				☑
07.	ʃi:	☑			
08.	aum		☑		
09.	Lɔh		☑		
10.	kʲed	☑			

Exercise 120

01 beanntan	[bjauNdən]	11 beagan	[began]
02 fear	[fɛr]	12 bioran	[biran]
03 fiù	[fju:]	13 thig	[higʲ]
04 bealach	[bjaLəx]	14 meall	[mjauL]
05 mearachd	[mɛrəxg]	15 fiadh	[fiaɣ]
06 mèinn	[mɛ:Nʲ]	16 bìd	[bi:dʲ]
07 a shiùcar	[ə hju:xgər]	17 feòrag	[fjɔ:rag]
08 mo bheò	[mə vjɔ:]	18 Miughalaigh	[mju.əLaj]
09 beantainn	[bɛndɪNʲ]	19 glé theann	[gle: hjauN]
10 feasgar	[fesgər]	20 peacadh	[pɛxgəɣ]

Exercise 121

01 teine	[tʲenə]	11 gloine	[gLɤNʲə]
02 gin	[gʲin]	12 raineach	[RaNʲəx]
03 coin	[kɔNʲ]	13 mìnich	[miːnɪç]
04 céin	[kʲeːn]	14 cainb	[kɛnɛb]
05 cuin	[kuNʲ]	15 mòine	[mɔːNʲə]
06 càineadh	[kaːNʲəɣ]	16 a bhuineas	[ə vuNʲəs]
07 DihAoine	[dʲɪˈhɯːNʲə]	17 duine	[dɯNʲə]
08 ainm	[ɛnɛm]	18 ciùineas	[kʲuːNʲəs]
09 fhéin	[heːn]	19 inis	[inɪʃ]
10 tuineach	[tɯNʲəx]	20 caoineadh	[kɯːNʲəɣ]

Exercise 122

	Ending marking an agent	Cannot be split
01 fuineadair	*fuin* 'bake' and **-eadair**	
02 seanmhair		☑
03 abair		☑
04 boghadair	*bogha* 'bow' and **-adair**	
05 crùnair	*crùn* 'crown' and **-air**	
06 acair		☑
07 fuaradair	*fuar* 'cold' and **-adair**	
08 reiceadair	*reic* 'sell' and **-eadair**	
09 onair		☑
10 socair		☑
11 stiùireadair	*stiùir* 'rudder' and **-eadair**	
12 dìobair		☑
13 mair		☑
14 nigheadair	*nigh* 'wash' and **-eadair**	
15 frasair	*fras* 'shower' and **-air**	

Appendix IV - The Guide to Reading Gaelic   479

IV.   Appendix IV - The Guide to Reading Gaelic

I guess technically this is more of a chapter than an appendix but it's easier to find for reference right at the end of the book so here is it.

As I've explained, in many ways the Gaelic writing system is pure genius. As a result, one can actually provide a step-by-step guide to pronouncing Gaelic. So in this section I will take you through the rules one by one and explain to you how they work.

> Remember this book uses a more traditional spelling
>
> as it is the only system that reliably indicates
>
> pronunciation from a learner's point of view.

Because of the regularity of the writing system, you should be able to determine the correct pronunciation of a word by looking at its written form in the vast majority of cases. The rest are mostly exceptions, the most important of which we looked at in 5.6.16.

To begin with you need to understand the following things:

- The difference between broad and slender (see 5.2). In the Guide a capital C stands for ANY broad consonant and V for ANY broad vowel. C' stands for ANY slender consonant and V' for any slender vowel. Examples:

  - o **nnC** refers to a **nn** which is followed by any broad consonant, for example *beanntan, ionnraic, Fionnlagh*...

  - o **VthV** refers to a **th** which is surrounded by broad vowels, for example *athair, mothaich, mathanas*...

  - o **g'** refers to any slender **g**, for example: *geal, giomach, bige*...

- An asterisk * means that the letter represents a lenited sound in the spoken language which is not shown in the written language (see 4.5). Examples:

  o *n means an n that has been lenited, for example *mo neart, do nàbaidh*...

  o *r means an r that has been lenited, for example *mo Ruaraidh, mo ràmh*...

- The use of the hyphen -. A hyphen is used to indicate the presence of any letter or combination of letters. So it can stand for a single consonant or vowel or several consonants or vowels. It simply indicates that 'something **has** to be here'. Examples:

  o c- means a broad c (no apostrophe) which has to be followed by something, for example *càr, casan, cù*...

  o -iu- means an iu which has to be preceded by something and followed by something, for example *an-diugh, siubhal, fliuch*...

- The use of brackets ( ). Brackets are used to indicate that a letter or letters might be there, but don't have to be. For example (i) means that an i might be there but doesn't have to be, (-) means that something might be there but doesn't have to be. Examples:

  o ua(i) means an ua which may or may not be followed by an i, for example: *uan, uaine, gruamach*...

  o (-)eu means an eu which may or may not be preceded by any letter, for example: *ceum, eudail, seud*...

- Remember stress usually falls on the first syllable of a word (the 'first part'). Therefore all other syllables are generally unstressed (see also 4.12.1).

- If two or more rules apply, the more specific one applies. This shouldn't be a problem as the Guide gives you the specific rules first and then the general ones. For example, in the word *bog*, there are two rules which could apply: (-)o + g(-) or (-)o + C ELSEWHERE. But because the more specific rule is listed first (the one which deals with **o** before **g**, **b** or **m**) you're going to find the correct, more specific rule first - as long as you start at the top and don't jump rules.

- Where there is more than one vowel in sequence, the whole sequence is treated as a unit. Examples:

    o in *cuimhne* the vowel groups are **ui** and **e**

    o in *gaoithe* the vowel groups are **aoi** and **e**

    o in *iobairt* the vowel groups are **io** and **ai**

    o Something similar applies to consonants. All lenited consonants (**bh**, **ch**, **dh**, **fh**, **gh**, **mh**, **ph**, **sh**, **th**), double **ll**, **nn** and **rr** and **ng** are treated as one unit. There are certain other consonant combinations which get 'special treatment' but because of how they are listed in the Guide, you can't miss them anyway.

This actually looks more complicated than it is. You'll begin to get a feel for how to read these rules quite quickly when we look at them one by one.

Now, whenever you are trying to figure out an unfamliar word, there are two crucial questions you have to ask yourself straight away. So to begin with, I'd ask you to photocopy the next page before you go on. Alternatively retype them on your computer and print them out. If you don't, it will take you a lot longer to find the right sound and you will make a lot more mistakes.

CONSONANTS

When you're looking at a consonant,

you <u>must</u> ask yourself

IS IT BROAD OR SLENDER?

If it's broad,

expect a plain consonant (d, t, s, L, N, r, ɣ…)

If it's slender,

expect a palatal consonant (dʲ, tʲ, ʃ, Lʲ, Nʲ, rʲ, ʝ…)

VOWELS

When you're looking at a vowel,

you <u>must</u> ask yourself

IS IT STRESSED OR UNSTRESSED?

If it's stressed,

expect an 'interesting' vowel (i, ɛ, ei, au, aː, eː…)

If it's unstressed,

expect a 'boring' vowel (ə, ɪ)

Here's an example of how this works step by step using a nice and simple word like **doras** to begin with.

- As the first letter in **doras** is **d** ask yourself the Crucial Question about consonants and then go to the d section.

- The first four entries deal with **dh** so you can ignore them. The next option on offer is **(-)d(-)**. This translates as 'something may be there, followed by a broad **d** and something may come after'. In **doras** we have nothing in front of the **d** but something following so this is our first sound: [**d**].

- The next letter is **o** so ask yourself the Crucial Question and then go to the **o** section. The first three entries concern **ò** or **ó** so we can ignore them because there is no accent marker anywhere in **doras**. The next set deals with **oi**, which we can ignore too as we're just looking for an **o**. The next entries look at **o** but in all cases this **o** has to be followed by certain letters: **llV(-)**, **nnV(-)** etc. There is no specific match for our **o** until we get to **O15** which says **(-)o(-) + C ELSEWHERE**. This translates as 'something may be there followed by **o** followed by a broad consonant'. This is exactly what we have in **doras** so our **o** is pronounced [ɔ].

- Next letter is **r**. Crucial Question, broad or slender? Since it is next to **o** and **a**, we know it's a broad **r**. Looking under the **r** section we find that the first entry looks at a lenited ***r** at the start of a word so we ignore that. The next entry also looks at initial **r-** so we ignore that and also the next entries for double **-rr(-)** and for **-rt(-)** and **-rd(-)**. The last entry is **-r(-)**. This reads: has to be something in front of a single broad r, possibly something after it. Which is what we have in **doras** so our **r** is: [r]

- Next is the **a**. The answer to the Crucial Question is 'Unstressed' because this **a** is not in the first part of the word so it must be unstressed. There is only one entry for **a UNSTRESSED** at the end of the a section: [ə].

- Last we need an **s**. Since it is next to a, we know it's a broad **s**. There's only one entry that fits: **(-)s(-)**. This means it's a broad **s** which 'may have something in front and may have something behind it'. In the case of **doras**, we have something in front and nothing behind so we're ok.

This means our word **doras** is pronounced [dɔrəs].

Now this was admittedly slow going. But you will find that as you do this more often, you will remember the most common rules very quickly and speed up considerably once you've internalised the patterns. And remember the hints in the section on using rhymes (see 5.5), which will also help you figure out correct pronunciation much more quickly.

A

A01	(-)à(i)(-)		[aː]

When **à** or **ài**, which may be preceded and/or followed by other letters occur, you get long [aː]. There are a small number of exceptions (like *Gàidheal* and *pàipear*). Note that some dialects have a tendency to turn many **ài** combinations into [ɛː].

Examples:

àrach	[aːrəx]	àite	[aːdʲə]
làr	[Laːr]	càite	[kaːhdʲə]
bà	[baː]	a-mhàin	[əˈvaːNʲ]

STRESSED

A02	(-)aoi + b(-), bh(-), dh(-), m(-), mh(-), gh(-), dh(-)		[ɣ]

When you get **aoi** in a stressed syllable, possibly after some letters, you most commonly get the [ɣ] sound if they are followed by one of the above labials or **gh/dh**.

Examples:

craoibhe	[krɣjə]	aoigh	[ɣj]
daoimean	[dɣiman]	naoidhean	[Nɣjan]
faoighe	[fɣjə]	claoidh	[kLɣj]

STRESSED

A03	(-)ao(i)-		[ɯː]

When the previous rule doesn't apply, **ao** and **aoi** at the beginning or in the middle of a word are both pronounced [ɯː].

Examples:

aosta	[ɯːsdə]	aois	[ɯːʃ]
gaol	[gɯːL]	taois	[tɯːʃ]
faodaidh	[fɯːdɪ]	maoil	[mɯːl]

STRESSED

A04   (-)ai +   ll, nn, m   [ai]

          llC(-), nnC(-), mC(-)   [ai]

This rule deals with **ai** (optionally with letters in front of it) which is
followed either by:

- **ll**, **nn** or **m** without anything following them, that is, at the end of
  a word
- **ll**, **nn** or **m** which are immediately followed by a consonant and
  optionally more letters

In all cases the pronunciation will be [ai].

Examples:

aill	[aiLʲ]	aillse	[aiLʲʃə]
caill	[kaiLʲ]	aimbeart	[ãĩmbəRʃd]
crainn	[kraiNʲ]	bainnse	[bãĩNʲʃə]

STRESSED

A05   (-)a +   ll, nn, m   [au]

          llC(-), nnC(-), mC(-)   [au]

This rule deals with **au** (optionally with letters in front of it) which is
followed either by:

- **ll**, **nn** or **m** without anything following them, that is, at the end of
  a word
- **ll**, **nn** or **m** which are immediately followed by a consonant and
  optionally more letters

In all cases the pronunciation will be [au].

Examples:

call	[kauL]	calltainn	[kauLdɪNʲ]
ann	[auN]	annta	[ãũNdə]
cam	[kaum]	campa	[kãũmbə]

STRESSED

A06   (-)a(i) +   rd(-), rl(-), rn(-), rr, rrC(-)   VAR: à   [aː]

You get long [aː] if **a** or **ai** are followed by

- double **rr** at the end of a word
- double **rr** which is immediately followed by a consonant and possibly more letters
- **rd**, **rl** or **rn** which may be then followed by any other letters

The vowels affected by these consonants are sometimes written as **à** but this isn't necessary as it's totally predictable when the **a** will be long. Not using the grave also avoids the problem of having to remove the grave when vowels are added to a word, for example *barr* [baːR] & *barra* [baRə] vs *bàrr* [baːR] and *barra* [baRə].

STRESSED

Examples:

à barr	[baːR]	àrd	[aːRd]
à sparr	[sbaːR]	càrn	[kaːRN]
à Farr	[faːR]	àirde	[aːRdʲə]

A07   (-)ai + [h] [x] [ç]   [ɛ]

When the **ai** group, possibly with letters in front of it, is followed by one of the guttural fricatives [h] [x] or [ç], you usually get [ɛ].

STRESSED

Examples:

faicinn	[fɛçgʲɪNʲ]	craiceann	[krɛçgʲəN]
cait	[kɛhdʲ]	slait	[sLɛhdʲ]
aice	[ɛçgʲə]	caitheamh	[kɛhəv]

A08 (-)ai + ghC(-)   [ɣ]

When **ai**, either preceded by other letters or not, is followed by **gh** and another consonant immediately after, the pronunciation will be [ɣ]. Other letters may follow but won't affect the pronunciation of the **ai**. This rules operates in conjunction with rule G09.

Examples:

saighdear	[sɣidʲɛr]	maighdeann	[mɣidʲəN]
saighde	[sɣidʲə]	maighdeag	[mɣidʲag]
slaightear	[sLɣidʲɛr]	faighnich	[fɣinɪç]

STRESSED

A09 (-)a + dhC(-), ghC(-)   [ɣː]

When *a,* either preceded by other letters or not, is followed by **gh** or **dh** and another consonant immediately after, the pronunciation will be [ɣː]. Other letters may follow but won't affect the pronunciation of the **a**.

Examples:

adhbrann	[ɣːbrəN]	laghdaich	[Lɣːdɪç]
adhbhar	[ɣːver]	adhlac	[ɣːLag]
Fadhlainn	[fɣːLɪNʲ]	adhradh	[ɣːrəɣ]

STRESSED

A10 (-)a + dh(V-), gh(V-)   [ɣ]

In a stressed syllable, when a (possibly with letters in front of it) is followed by **dh** or **gh** at the end or alternatively by a vowel and possibly more letters, then you get a short [ɣ].

Examples:

laghach	[Lɣ.əx]	adha	[ɣ.ə]
aghaidh	[ɣ.ɪ]	adharc	[ɣ.ərg]
taghadh	[tɣ.əɣ]	radharc	[Rɣ.ərg]

STRESSED

A

A11	(-)ai +	lb(-), lbh(-), lch(-), lg(-), lgh(-), lm(-), lmh(-)	[ε-ε]
		nb(-), nbh(-), nch(-), ngh(-), nm(-), nmh(-)	[ε-ε]
		rb(-), rbh(-), rch(-), rg(-), rgh(-), rm(-), rmh(-)	[ε-ε]
		ml(-), mr(-), ms(-), mch(-)	[ε-ε]

When the **ai** group, possibly with letters in front of it, is involved in a helping vowel appearing, this is most commonly [ε-ε]. Other letters may follow.
Note that although [ε-ε] is the most common denominator, **ai** in this environment is far from uniform, the most common alternative being [ε-a].

STRESSED

Examples:

airgead	[ɛrʲɛgʲəd]	tairbh	[tɛrʲɛv]
ainm	[ɛnɛm]	cainb	[kɛnɛb]
aimsir	[ɛmɛʃɪrʲ]	gairbhe	[gɛrʲɛvə]

A12	(-)a +	lb(-), lbh(-), lch(-), lg(-), lgh(-), lm(-), lmh(-)	[a-a]
		nb(-), nbh(-), nch(-), ngh(-), nm(-), nmh(-)	[a-a]
		rb(-), rbh(-), rch(-), rg(-), rgh(-), rm(-), rmh(-)	[a-a]
		ml(-), mr(-), ms(-), mch(-)	[a-a]

When **a**, possibly with letters in front of it, is involved in a helping vowel appearing, you get [a-a]. Other letters may follow.

STRESSED

Examples:

Alba	[aLabə]	margadh	[maragəɣ]
Banbh	[banav]	garbh	[garav]
arm	[aram]	amlach	[amaLəx]

A13   (-)a(i)(-) ELSEWHERE   [a]

This rule means that if an **a** or **ai**, either at the start of a word or following letters and optionally with letters following, does not fit any of the other rules above, it will most commonly be pronounced [a] in a stressed syllable.

STRESSED

Examples:

acras	[axgrəs]	aiseag	[aʃəg]
aran	[aran]	aifreann	[afrʲəN]
athair	[ahərʲ]	caileag	[kalag]

A14   -ail(-)   [al]

This ending in an unstressed syllable will usually have clear [a]. Other letters may follow.

UNSTRESSED

Examples:

togail	[togal]	fearail	[fɛral]
anail	[anal]	laghaileachd	[Lɤɣaləxg]
caochail	[kɯːxal]	mórail	[moːral]

A15   -ag(-), -an(-)   [a]

These two endings in an unstressed syllable will have clear [a]. Remember that in the case of **-an** that only applies when it's not a plural ending (see 4.12.5)! Other letters may follow.

UNSTRESSED

Examples:

beagan	[began]	putag	[puhdag]
balachan	[baLəxan]	corrag	[kɔRag]
curran	[kuRan]	marag	[marag]

A16	-aig(-)		[εgʲ]
	-ain(-)		[εNʲ]

When - in an unstressed syllable - the endings **-ag** and **-an** are slenderised for whatever reason, you get [ε]. Other letters may follow the **-aig** and **-ain**.

Examples:

beagain	[begεNʲ]	putaige	[puhdεgʲə]
balachain	[baLəxεNʲ]	corraige	[kɔRεgʲə]
currain	[kuRεNʲ]	maraige	[marεgʲə]

(margin: UNSTRESSED)

A17	-aigh(-)		[aj]

In an unstressed syllable **-aigh** will be [aj], both when it is at the end of a word or when more letters follow. This ending is most common in surnames and place names.

Examples:

Barraigh	[baRaj]	Pabaigh	[pabaj]
Stròmaigh	[sdrɔːmaj]	MacAmhlaigh	[maxˈgãũLaj]
Rònaigh	[Rɔːnaj]	ìomhaigh	[iəvaj]

(margin: UNSTRESSED)

A18	-aich(-)		[ɪ]
	-aidh		[ɪ]

The **-ai-** in the above endings in an unstressed syllable will be [ɪ]. If other letters follow the **-aidh** then you get [ɪj].

Examples:

glasaidh	[gLasɪ]	cungaidhean	[kuŋgɪjən]
aghaidh	[ɣ.ɪ]	leasaichidh	[Lʲesɪçɪ]
margaidhean	[maragɪjən]	abaich	[abɪç]

(margin: UNSTRESSED)

A19   -ai(-) + PALATAL ([dʲ] [gʲ] [Lʲ] [Nʲ] [rʲ] [ʃ])   [ɪ]

In an unstressed syllable **ai**, which may or may not be followed by other letters, will be [ɪ] if followed by a phonetically palatal sound.

Examples:

balaich	[baLɪç]	Pàdraig	[paːdrɪgʲ]
caraid	[karɪdʲ]	abair	[abɪrʲ]
acainn	[axgɪNʲ]	a Raghnaill!	[ə rɤː.ɪLʲ]

UNSTRESSED

A20   -a(i)(-) ELSEWHERE   [ə]

In an unstressed syllable **a**, which may or may not be followed by other letters, will be [ə] when none of the previous rules apply.

Examples:

balach	[baLəx]	cùraim	[kuːrəm]
lomarra	[LoməRə]	altraim	[aLdrəm]
balla	[baLə]	foghlaim	[fɤːLəm]

UNSTRESSED

B01 (-)V̀bhC(-)   [ ]

When you have a vowel that is marked long followed by a broad **bh** which itself is followed immediately by another consonant, the **bh** is silent. Other letters may come in front of the long vowel and follow the consonant but have no effect.

This spelling rule is handled a bit messily by some so you may want to check a dictionary. For example, the word for 'swallow' can be found as *gobhlan* and *gòbhlan* (both [gɔ:Lan]). If you find any cases of a spelling with the grave, then assume it should be present in all cases.

Examples:

dùbhlan	[du:Lan]	cùbhraidh	[ku:rɪ]
siùbhlach	[ʃu:Ləx]	dòbhran	[dɔ:ran]
ùbhlan	[u:Lən]	seòbhrag	[ʃɔ:rag]

B R O A D

B02 (-)VV / V: + bhV(-)   [v]

This slightly complicated looking rule looks worse than it is. It means that when you get a **bh** following a diphthong or a long vowel and get another vowel after it, the **bh** will usually still be pronounced [v].

This only happens after 'natural' diphthongs and long vowels, as in where the spelling tells you directly that it's a diphthong or long vowel. The kind of diphthong you get in rule B01 doesn't count here.

Examples:

uabhasach	[uəvəsəx]	craobhan	[krɯ:vən]
treubhan	[tre:vən]	faobhar	[fɯ:vər]
buabhall	[buəvəL]	àbhaist	[a:vɪʃdʲ]

B R O A D

B03	-bhC(-)		[u]

If rule B01 does not apply and you have a broad **bh** immediately followed by another consonant, with letters in front and possibly after, then the **bh** will turn into an [u] vowel.

Examples:

cabhsair	[kausɪrʲ]	slabhraidh	[sLaurɪ]
sabhs	[saus]	bobhla	[bɔuLə]
labhrach	[Laurəx]	abhlann	[auLəN]

B R O A D

B04	(-)VbhV(-)		[.]

This rule affects **bh** that is caught between two vowels, possibly with other sounds coming before and after. Such a **bh** will usually result in hiatus (4.3). There are quite a few exceptions to this rule as it can also still be [v] and on occasion [u].

Examples:

abhainn	[a.ɪNʲ]	rubha	[Ru.ə]
ubhal	[u.əL]	diabhal	[dʲiə.əL]
gobhar	[go.ər]	cobhair	[ko.ɪrʲ]

B R O A D

B05	(-)bh(-) ELSEWHERE		[v]

This means that in all those cases where none of the previous rules about **bh** have applied, you can assume that it's going to be [v], both at the start and at end of words.

Examples:

bhàsaich	[va:sɪç]	craobh	[krɯ:v]
bhuail	[vuəl]	taobh	[tɯ:v]
bhagair	[vagɪrʲ]	falbh	[faLav]

B R O A D

B06   (-)b(-)   [b]

This rule deals with the remaining cases of broad **b**. It means that you can expect a broad **b** to be [b] both at the start, in the middle and at the end of words.

Examples:

baga	[bagə]	cabar	[kabər]
balla	[baLə]	gob	[gob]
aba	[abə]	òb	[ɔːb]

BROAD

B07   (-) + u(:) ɯ(:) o(:) ɤ(:) ɔ(:) a(:) uə + bh'   [iv]

When a slender **bh** is preceded by a back vowel or back diphthong and the **bh** is at the end of the word then you get [iv]. Other letters may come in front.

Examples:

dhaibh	[ɣaiv]	luibh	[lɯiv]
dhuibh	[ɣɯiv]	draibh	[draiv]
bhuaibh	[vuəiv]	saoibh	[sɤiv]

SLENDER

B08   (-)Vbh'C(-)   [i]

When a slender **bh** is between a vowel and a consonant, it is usually [i].

Examples:

cuibhreann	[kuirʲəN]	aoibhneas	[ɤiNʲəs]
duibhre	[dɯirʲə]	coibhneil	[kɤiNʲal]
aibhne	[aiNʲə]	cuibhle	[kɯilə]

SLENDER

B09   (-)Vbh'V(-)   [j]

SLENDER

When a slender **bh** is between vowels, normally the outcome is a [j]. Common exceptions are the name *Daibhidh* [daivɪ], recent loanwords like *cleabhar* [klɛvər] and *draibhear* [draivɛr] and high register words like *sléibhe* [ʃLʲeːvə].

Examples:

sùibheag	[suːjag]	duibhe	[dɯjə]
luibhean	[Lɯjən]	cuibheas	[kujəs]
MaRuibhe	[maˈrujə]	luibheach	[Lɯjəx]

B10   u(ː) ɯ(ː) o(ː) ɤ(ː) ɔ(ː) a(ː) au + bh'   [iv]

SLENDER

A slender **bh** after a back vowel at the end of the word is normally [iv] in a stressed syllable.

Examples:

dhaibh	[ɣaiv]	saoibh	[sɤiv]
luibh	[Lɯiv]	ruibh	[rɯiv]
draibh	[draiv]	craoibh	[krɤiv]

B11   bh' + u(ː) ɯ(ː) o(ː) ɤ(ː) ɔ(ː) a(ː) au (-)   [vj]

SLENDER

When you get slender **bh** at the start of a word and it is followed by a back vowel (long, short or diphthong) you get a [vj].

Examples:

bheòthaich	[vjɔː.ɪç]	fo bheanntan	[fɔ vjauNdən]
bhiodh	[vjɤɣ]	dà bhiùg	[daː vjuːg]
Bheàrnaraigh	[vjaːRNəraj]	bhearr	[vjaːR]

B12	bhl'		[vl]
	bhr'		[vrʲ]

When a slender **bh** is followed by an **l** or **r**, then the broad/slender rule does not apply to the bh and it will always be [v].

Examples:

bhleoghann	[vlɔ.əN]	glé bhrèagha	[gle: vrʲia.ə]
bhleadraig	[vledrɪgʲ]	glé bhreò	[gle: vrʲɔ:]
bhliadhna	[vliəNə]	dà bhriathar	[da: vrʲiəhər]

S L E N D E R

B13	(-)bh'(-) ELSEWHERE		[v]

This means that in all those cases where none of the previous rules about **bh** apply, you can assume that it's going to be [v].

Examples:

bhìd	[vi:dʲ]	uairibh	[uərʲɪv]
bhithinn	[vi.ɪNʲ]	cùlaibh	[ku:Lɪv]
a bhean	[ə vɛn]	Gallaibh	[gaLɪv]

SLENDER

B14	b' + u(:) ɯ(:) o(:) ɣ(:) ɔ(:) a(:) au (-)		[bj]

When you get slender **b** at the start of a word and it is followed by any type of back vowel you get a [bj].

Examples:

beòthaich	[bjɔ:.ɪç]	beanntan	[bjãũNdən]
biodh	[bjɣɣ]	bearr	[bja:R]
Beàrnaraigh	[bja:RNəraj]	biùg	[bju:g]

SLENDER

B15   (-) + uː ɯː oː ɤː ɔː aː uə + b'(-)   [ib]

When a slender **b** is preceded by a long back vowel or back diphthong then you get [ib]. Other letters may come in front and/or behind the whole group.

Examples:

sglàib	[sgLaːib]	lùib	[Luːib]
slàibeach	[sLaːibəx]	lùibeach	[Luːibəx]
sguaib	[sguəib]	ròibean	[Rɔːiban]

B16   bl'   [bl]
b r'   [brʲ]

When a slender **b** is followed by an **l** or **r**, then the broad/slender rule does not apply to the **b** and it will always be [b].

Examples:

bleoghann	[blɔ.əN]	brèagha	[brʲia.ə]
bleadraig	[bledrɪgʲ]	breò	[brʲɔː]
bliadhna	[bliəNə]	briathar	[brʲiəhər]

B17   (-)b'(-) ELSEWHERE   [b]

This deals with all remaining cases of slender **b** not covered by the other rules. It means that when you get slender **b** at the beginning, in the middle or at the end of a word in any other environment, it's simply going to be [b].

Examples:

beaga	[begə]	rib	[Rib]
bile	[bilə]	biadh	[biəɣ]
ribe	[Ribə]	beinn	[beiNʲ]

C01 cn-   [kr~]

When you have a **c** at the start of a word followed by an **n** (and then more letters), the **n** will change to an [r] in pronunciation and the next vowel will be nasal. The nasality here is important to maintain the distinction with words that start with **cr**, for example *cràbhach* [kra:vəx] 'devout' and *cnàmhach* [krã:vəx] 'bony'.

Examples:

cnag	[krãg]	cnò	[krɔ̃:]
cnàmh	[krã:v]	cnuimh	[krũiv]
cnoc	[krɔ̃xg]	cnuaic	[krũə̃çgʲ]

B R O A D

C02 (-)Vc(-)   [xg]

This rule tells you that when you get a broad **c** after a vowel in the middle or at the end of a word, you will get a pre-aspirated group: [xg]. This only applies in stressed syllables.

Examples:

aca	[axgə]	muclach	[muxgLəx]
diùc	[dʲu:xg]	glac	[gLaxg]
faca	[faxgə]	mac	[maxg]

B R O A D

C03 (-)Vc(-)   [g]

In an unstressed syllable, if you have a **c** after a vowel you do not get pre-aspiration. Cases of this are rare.

Examples:

adhlac	[ɤ:Ləg]	tìodhlac	[tʲiəLəg]

B R O A D

C04   -chd(-)   [xg]

When you get **-chd** either in the middle or at the end of a word, it will be [xg]. So in spite of the spelling, pairs like *sloc* and *slochd* are pronounced exactly the same.

Examples:

achd	[axg]	a-nochd	[əˈNɔxg]
uchd	[uxg]	achdan	[axgən]
beachd	[bɛxg]	cleachdadh	[klɛxgəɣ]

BROAD

C05   chn-   [xr̃]

This rule is very similar to C01. When you have a **ch** at the start of a word followed by an **n** (and then more letters), the **n** will change to a [r] in pronunciation and the next vowel will be nasal. The nasality here can be used to maintain the distinction with words that start with **chr**, for example *chràbhach* [xra:vəx] 'devout' and *chnàmhach* [krã:vəx] 'bony'.

Examples:

dà chnag	[da: xrãg]	dà chnò	[da: xrɔ̃:]
dà chnàmh	[da: xrã:v]	dà chnuimh	[da: xrũiv]
dà chnoc	[da: xrɔ̃xg]	dà chnuaic	[da: xrũ̃ə̃çgʲ]

BROAD

C06   (-)ch(-) ELSEWHERE   [x]

This rule tells you that when all previous rules about broad **ch** do not apply, the pronunciation will be [x] at the beginning, in the middle and at the end of words.

Examples:

chaidh	[xaj]	cochall	[kɔxəL]
chosg	[xɔsg]	ach	[ax]
machair	[maxɪrʲ]	loch	[Lɔx]

BROAD

C07   -Cc(-)   [g]

When broad **c** is preceded by another consonant and other letters, possibly followed by more letters, the **c** will weaken to a [g]. Many speakers have an extra [x] sound in **lc** and **rc** groups, for example: *olc* [ɔLxg].

Examples:

olc	[ɔLg]	banca	[baŋgə]
adharc	[ɣ.ərg]	ascaoin	[asgɪNʲ]
àrc	[aːrg]	falcag	[faLgag]

(side margin: BROAD)

C08   c- ELSEWHERE   [k]

If broad **c** is at the beginning of words elsewhere, it will simply be [k].

Examples:

cas	[kas]	corr	[kɔːR]
caran	[karan]	crag	[krag]
còir	[kɔːrʲ]	clann	[kLauN]

(side margin: BROAD)

C09   cn'-   [krʲ~]

This rule is very similar to C01. When you have a slender **c** at the start of a word followed by an **n** (and then more letters), the **n** will change to a [rʲ] in pronunciation and the next vowel will be nasal. As in C01 and C05, the nasality is important here. Note that the [k] is just a broad [k], the broad/slender difference doesn't apply here.

Examples:

cneasta	[krʲẽsdə]	cneas	[krʲẽs]
cnead	[krʲẽd]	Cnìp	[krʲĩ:hb]
cneutag	[krʲĩãhdag]	cniadaich	[krʲĩədɪç]

(side margin: SLENDER)

C10 cl'-   [kl]

cr'-   [krʲ]

When you get a slender **cl** or **cr** group at the beginning of a word, the broad/slender rules don't apply to the **c** and it will always be broad [k].

Examples:

cleas	[kles]	cridhe	[krʲi.ə]
clisg	[kliʃgʲ]	crios	[krʲis]
clì	[kli:]	creag	[krʲeg]

SLENDER

C11 (-)Vc'(-)   [çgʲ]

This rule is very similar to C02. This rule tells you that when you get a slender **c** after a vowel, either at the start, in the middle or at the end of a word, you will get a pre-aspirated group: [çgʲ]. This also only applies in stressed syllables.

Examples:

ic	[içgʲ]	reic	[Reçgʲ]
mic	[miçgʲ]	faicinn	[fɛçgʲɪNʲ]
lic	[Lʲiçgʲ]	craiceann	[krɛçgʲəN]

SLENDER

C12 (-)Vc'(-)   [gʲ]

In an unstressed syllable, if you have a slender **c** after a vowel you do not get pre-aspiration. Case of this are rare also.

Examples:

| adhlaic | [ɣ:Lɪgʲ] | tìodhlaic | [tʲiəLɪgʲ] |
| ionnraic | [jũNərɪgʲ] | ceimic | [kʲemɪgʲ] |

SLENDER

C13 -chd'(-)   [çgʲ]

When you get slender **-chd** either in the middle or at the end of a word, it will be [çgʲ]. This is rather rare and most frequently appears as a spelling variant where **-ic** and **-ichd** are confused because the pre-aspiration in **-ic** makes it sounds exactly like **-ichd**.

Examples:

clìchd (clìc)	[kliːçgʲ]	gloichd (gloic)	[gLɔçgʲ]
araichd	[arɪçgʲ]	imrichd	[imirʲɪçgʲ]
buaichd (buaic)	[buəçgʲ]	sginichd	[sgʲinɪçgʲ]

C14 chn'-   [xrʲ˜]

This rule is very similar to C09. When you have a slender **ch** at the start of a word followed by an **n** (and then more letters), the **n** will change to an [rʲ] in pronunciation and the next vowel will be nasal. Note that the **ch** is just a broad [x], the broad/slender difference doesn't apply here.

Examples:

glé chneasta	[gleː xrʲẽsdə]	dà chneas	[da: xrʲẽs]
dà chnead	[da: xrʲẽd]	Chnìp	[xrʲĩːhb]
dà chneutag	[da: xrʲĩãhdag]	chniadaich	[xrʲĩədɪç]

C15 chl'-   [xl]

     chr'-   [xrʲ]

When you get a slender **chl** or **chr** group, the broad/slender rules don't apply to the **ch** and it will always be broad [x].

Examples:

dà chleas	[da: xles]	dà chridhe	[da: xrʲi.ə]
glé chlisg	[gleː xliʃgʲ]	dà chrios	[da: xrʲis]
bhon a' chlì	[vɔnə xliː]	dà chreag	[da: xrʲeg]

C16 (-)ch'(-) ELSEWHERE   [ç]

This means that when no other specific rules exist for slender **ch**, it will be [ç] anywhere else.

Examples:

chì	[çiː]	faiche	[façə]
cheumnaich	[çeːmnɪç]	aidich	[adʲɪç]
abaichead	[abɪçəd]	fairich	[farʲɪç]

S L E N D E R

C17 -Cc'(-)   [gʲ]

When a slender **c** is preceded by another consonant, then it will weaken to [gʲ]. Many speakers have an extra [ç] sound in **lc** and **rc** groups, for example: *circe* [kʲirʲçgʲə].

Examples:

cailc	[kalgʲ]	circe	[kʲirʲgʲə]
pàirc	[paːrʲgʲ]	failcean	[falgʲan]
uircean	[urʲgʲan]	coirce	[kɔrʲgʲə]

S L E N D E R

C18 c'V(-)   [kʲ]

When slender **c** appears at the start of a word and is followed by a vowel, it will be pronounced [kʲ].

Examples:

ceòl	[kʲɔːL]	ciùin	[kʲuːNʲ]
ceum	[kʲeːm]	cìs	[kʲiːʃ]
cearr	[kʲaːR]	cill	[kʲiːLʲ]

SLENDER

D

D01 (-)VdhV(-)   [.]

This complicated looking rule just means that when you get a broad **dh** between vowels, then it is most likely going to be pronounced as hiatus. Note the common exception *modhail* [mɔɣal].

Examples:

adha	[ɣ.ə]	odhar	[o.ər]
cladhadh	[kLɣ.əɣ]	crudha	[kru.ə]
bodhar	[bo.ər]	rudhadh	[Ru.əɣ]

BROAD

D02 (-)VdhC(-)   [ ]

After a short vowel (never a diphthong) when you get a broad **dh** which is immediately followed by a consonant, then the **dh** itself will be silent. Check the individual vowels for the effect this has on the vowel.

Examples:

adhbrann	[ɣːbraN]	bliadhna	[bliəNə]
adhbhar	[ɣːver]	adhlac	[ɣːLəg]
laghdaich	[Lɣːdɪç]	adhradh	[ɣːrəɣ]

BROAD

D03 (-)V̄dh   [ ]

When **dh** follows a long vowel and the **dh** is at the end of the word, it will be silent.

Examples:

glaodh	[gLɯː]	sùdh	[suː]
gràdh	[graː]	sròdh	[sdrɔː]
ràdh	[Raː]	cràdh	[kraː]

BROAD

D04   -dh-   [ɣ]

B R O A D

When none of the previous rules about broad **dh** apply, it will be [ɣ].

Examples:

dha	[ɣa]	dhut	[ɣuhd]
dh'fhàs	[ɣaːs]	ruadh	[Ruəɣ]
dà dhùn	[daː ɣuːn]	moladh	[mɔLəɣ]

D05   (-)d(-)   [d]

BROAD

Broad **d** just on its own in all other cases will be [d].

Examples:

dà	[daː]	ad	[ad]
donn	[dɔuN]	badan	[badan]
dùn	[duːn]	aonad	[ɯːnəd]

D06   (-) u(ː) ɯ(ː) o(ː) ɤ(ː) ɔ(ː) a(ː) uə + dh'(V)   [j]

SLENDER

This rule is closely linked with D07. When slender **dh** follows a back vowel and is either at the end of a word or followed by a vowel, then you usually get a [j].

Examples:

buidhe	[bujə]	ùidh	[uːj]
buidheann	[bujəN]	aoidh	[ɤj]
draoidheachd	[drɤjəxg]	àigh	[aːj]

D

D07	(-) i(:) e(:) ɛ(:) + dh'V(-)		[.]
	dh'		[ ]

When you get slender **dh** after a front vowel and it is followed by a vowel, then you usually get hiatus. If it's at the end of the word, there is no sound.

Examples:

cidhe	[kʲi.ə]	déidh	[dʲeː]
cridhe	[krʲi.ə]	bìdh	[biː]
gléidheadh	[gleː.əɣ]	réidh	[Reː]

SLENDER

D08	dhr'-	[ɣr]
	dhl'-	[ɣl]

This is another instance where the broad/slender distinction has been broken. When a slender **dh** at the start of a word is followed by an **r** or **l**, it is pronounced [ɣ], as if it was broad. In case of a **dhr**, the **r** will also be broad. Other letters always follow but have no effect on the pronunciation.

Examples:

dà dhreuchd	[da: ɣriaxg]	dà dhreach	[da: ɣrɛx]
glé dhriùchdach	[gle: ɣru:xgəx]	dà dhlighe	[da: ɣli.ə]
do dhréin	[də ɣre:n]	dà dhleastanas	[da: ɣlesdənəs]

SLENDER

D09	dh'- ELSEWHERE	[ʝ]

In all cases where D08 doesn't apply, initial slender **dh** will be [ʝ] irrespective of what comes after it.

Examples:

a dhìth	[ə ʝi:]	dheth	[ʝeh]
dà dhinnear	[da: ʝi:Nʲər]	glé dhearg	[gle: ʝɛrɛg]
glé dhìleas	[gle: ʝi:ləs]	dhealaich	[ʝaLɪç]

SLENDER

D

D10	dr'-	[dr]
	dl'-	[dl]

Similar to D08 when a slender **d** at the beginning of a word is followed by an **r** or **l**, it will be pronounced like a broad [d]. In case of a **dr**, the **r** will also be broad.

Examples:

dreuchd	[driaxg]	dreach	[drɛx]
driùchdach	[dru:xgəx]	dlighe	[dli.ə]
dréin	[dre:n]	dleastanas	[dlesdənəs]

SLENDER

D11	(-)d'(-)	[dʲ]

Where the previous rules for slender **d** do not apply, it will be [dʲ] at the beginning, in the middle and at the end of a word.

Examples:

dearg	[dʲɛrɛg]	aidich	[adʲɪç]
deud	[dʲe:d]	oide	[ɤdʲə]
dìnnear	[dʲi:Nʲər]	abaid	[abɪdʲ]

SLENDER

E

E01 (-)èa + m, mh, p   [ɛː]

Either at the beginning or in the middle of a word in a stressed syllable **èa** is usually pronounced [ɛː].

STRESSED

Examples:

nèamh	[Nʲɛ̃ːv]	frèam	[frʲɛːm]
nèapaigear	[Nʲɛːhbɪgʲɛr]	sèamh	[ʃɛ̃ːv]
trèamhla	[trɛ̃ːvLa]	sèam	[ʃɛ̃ːm]

E02 (-)èa- ELSEWHERE   [ia]

Either at the beginning or in the middle of a word in a stressed syllable **èa** is going to be pronounced [ia].

STRESSED

Examples:

dèan	[dʲian]	tèarainte	[tʲiarɪNʲdʲə]
brèagha	[brʲia.ə]	èasgaidh	[iasgɪ]
crèadh	[krʲiaɣ]	fèath	[fia]

E03 (-)é(i)(-)   VAR: è(i)   [eː]

This rule states that when you get **é** or **éi** either at the beginning, in the middle or at the end of a word it will be pronounced [eː]. Note that there are variant spellings (especially GOC) where **é(i)** is spelled **è(i)** so it may be advisable to check in an older dictionary when you come across words with **è(i)**.

STRESSED

Examples:

éis	[eːʃ]	glé	[gleː]
éibhinn	[eːvɪɲ]	léir	[Lʲeːrʲ]
dé	[dʲeː]	séideadh	[ʃeːdʲəɣ]

E04	(-)ei- + rd(-), rl(-), rn(-), rr		VAR: è(i) [ɛː]

This rule tells you that when you get **ei** in a stressed syllable, possibly with letters in front of it, immediately followed by **rd**, **rl** or **rn** (possibly with letters after) or **rr** (at the end of the word), then you get a long [ɛː]. Note that there are variant spellings where **ei** is spelled **èi**. Since this is totally predictable, the accent here isn't necessary as you can see in many older publications which leave it out.

Examples:

mèirleach	[mɛːRləx]	gèirnean	[gʲɛːRNan]
spèirlig	[sbɛːRlɪgʲ]	smèirne	[smɛːRNə]
mèirdreach	[mɛːRdrəx]	mèirneal	[mɛːRnəL]

STRESSED

E05	(-)è(i)-	[ɛː]

This rule is in contrast with E03 but the principle is the same. When you get **è** or **èi** either at the beginning, in the middle or at the end of a word it will be pronounced [ɛː]. Note that in some modern spellings this spelling overlaps with **é(i)** so you may have to check with an older dictionary to be sure.

Examples:

gnè	[grʲɛ̃ː]	mèinn	[mɛːNʲ]
sèimh	[ʃɛ̃ːv]	snèip	[ʃNʲɛːhb]
bèicear	[bɛːçgʲɛr]	stèisean	[sdɛːʃan]

STRESSED

E06	eò(i)-	[jɔː]

When you have **eò** or **eòi** at the beginning of a word, then usually there will be a [j] sound in front of the [ɔː].

Examples:

eòlach	[jɔːLəx]	Eòghann	[jɔː.əN]
eòlas	[jɔːLəs]	eòin	[jɔːNʲ]
eòrna	[jɔːRnə]	eòrlain	[jɔːRlɛNʲ]

STRESSED

E

E07 -eò(i)-   [ɔː]

When you have **-eò** or **-eòi** after one or more consonants, it will simply be long [ɔː].

STRESSED

Examples:

ceò	[kʲɔː]	beò	[bjɔː]
seòl	[ʃɔːL]	feòir	[fjɔːrʲ]
breò	[brʲɔː]	meòir	[mjɔːrʲ]

E08 -eo(-)   [ɔ]

When you have **eo** in the stressed syllable of a word it will be pronounced as a short [ɔ].

In a few Gaelic words you get an **eo** in the unstressed syllable of a word as a result of a word with long **eò** having joined with another word or prefix. The result often is also a short [ɔ].

(UN)STRESSED

Examples:

seo	[ʃɔ]	sgleog	[sglɔg]
deoch	[dʲɔx]	aineol	[aNʲɔL]
cleoc	[klɔxg]	aindeoin	[aNʲɔn]

E09 (-)eu + m(-)   [eː]

This rule and the next deal with the issue of how to unscramble the different pronunciations of **eu**. When the **eu**, at the beginning or in the middle of a stressed syllable is followed by an **m** then it is most likely going to be [eː]. It will also be [eː] if the word is 'fancy'.

STRESSED

Examples:

beum	[beːm]	feum	[feːm]
ceum	[kʲeːm]	leum	[Lʲeːm]
Seumas	[ʃeːməs]	treun	[treːn]

E

E10 (-)eu- ELSEWHERE   [ia]

When E09 does not apply, the **eu** is most likely going to be pronounced as an [ia] diphthong.

Examples:

ceud	[kʲiad]	deuchainn	[dʲiaxɪNʲ]
meud	[miad]	deug	[dʲiag]
reubadh	[Riabəɣ]	eun	[ian]

STRESSED

E11 (-)ei + lb(-), lbh(-), lch(-), lg(-), lgh(-), lm(-), lmh(-)   [e-e]
nb(-), nbh(-), nch(-), ngh(-), nm(-), nmh(-)   [e-e]
rb(-), rbh(-), rch(-), rg(-), rgh(-), rm(-), rmh(-)   [e-e]
ml(-), mr(-), ms(-), mch(-)   [e-e]

When **ei**, possibly with letters in front of it, is involved in a helping vowel appearing, you get [e-e]. Other letters may follow.

Examples:

seilbh	[ʃelev]	eirbhir	[erʲevɪrʲ]
seilcheag	[ʃeleçag]	seirbheis	[ʃerʲevɪʃ]
eilgheadh	[elejəɣ]	meirg	[merʲegʲ]

STRESSED

E12	(-)ei + ll, nn, m		[ei]
	llC(-), nnC(-), mC(-)		[ei]

This rule deals with **ei** (possibly with letters in front of it) which is followed either by:

- **ll**, **nn** or **m** without anything following them, that is, at the end of a word
- **ll**, **nn** or **m** which are immediately followed by a consonant and optionally more letters

In all cases the pronuciation will be [ei].

Examples:

beinn	[beiNʲ]	greim	[grʲeim]
seinn	[ʃeiNʲ]	teinntean	[tʲeiNʲdʲan]
spreill	[sbrʲeiLʲ]	einnsean	[eiNʲʃan]

E13	(-)e(i)(-) ELSEWHERE		[e]

When you get

- **e** at the end of a one-syllable word
- **ei** either at the beginning of a word or following some letters, immediately followed by another slender consonant

it will be pronounced [e]. Other letters may follow but don't have to.

Examples:

le	[le]	greimeag	[grʲemag]
eile	[elə]	seillean	[ʃeLʲan]
ceist	[kʲeʃdʲ]	seinneadair	[ʃeNʲədɛrʲ]

E14 ea + [L], [R]   [j]

At the beginning of a word if **ea** is followed by a dark [L] or [R] then the word will start with a [j] glide. The vowel itself varies and is covered in rules E15, E17, E18 and E19.

STRESSED

Examples:

eala	[jaLə]	earrach	[jaRəx]
ealain	[jaLɛNʲ]	earr	[ja:R]
ealbh	[jɛLɛv]	earlas	[ja:RLəs]

E15 (-)ea + lb(-), lbh(-), lch(-), lg(-), lgh(-), lm(-), lmh(-)   [ɛ-ɛ]

nb(-), nbh(-), nch(-), ngh(-), nm(-), nmh(-)   [ɛ-ɛ]

rb(-), rbh(-), rch(-), rg(-), rgh(-), rm(-), rmh(-)   [ɛ-ɛ]

ml(-), mr(-), ms(-), mch(-)   [ɛ-ɛ]

When **ea**, possibly with letters in front of it, is involved in a helping vowel appearing, you get [ɛ-ɛ]. Other letters may follow. You will also hear [ɛ-a] instead of [ɛ-ɛ] quite a lot. Just be consistent about which one you choose yourself.

STRESSED

Examples:

dealbh	[dʲɛLɛv]	Fearghas	[fɛrɛɣəs]
seanchaidh	[ʃɛnɛxɪ]	seanmhair	[ʃɛnɛvərʲ]
dearg	[dʲɛrɛg]	seamrag	[ʃɛmɛrag]

| E16 | (-)ea + | bh | [ɔ] |
| | | bhV(-) | [ɔ.] |

After an **eabh** group at the end of a word, the **ea** will be [ɔ], if another vowel follows (and maybe more letters) then you get hiatus as well.

STRESSED

Examples:

treabh	[trɔ]	feabhas	[fjɔ.əs]
treabhadh	[trɔ.əɣ]	seabhag	[ʃɔ.ag]
leabhar	[Lʲɔ.ər]	steabhag	[ʃdʲɔ.ag]

E17	(-)ea +	ll, nn	[au]
		llC(-), nnC(-)	[au]
		bhC(-), dhC(-), mhC(-)	[au]

When **ea** in a stressed syllable (possibly with letters in front of it) is followed either by:

- **ll** or **nn** without anything following them, that is, at the end of a word
- **ll** or **nn** which are immediately followed by a consonant and optionally more letters
- **bh**, **dh** or **mh** which are immediately followed by a consonant and optionally more letters

the pronunciation in all cases will be [au]. Note that in cases of **mhC** nasalisation usually also appears.

STRESSED

Examples:

seall	[ʃauL]	gleanntan	[glauNdən]
sealltainn	[ʃauLdɪNʲ]	leamhrag	[Lʲãũrag]
gleann	[glauN]	geamhradh	[gʲãũrəɣ]

E18   (-)ea(i) + rd(-), rl(-), rn(-), rr, rrC(-)   VAR: eà   [aː]

This rule tells you that when, possibly after some letter, you get **ea** in a stressed syllable immediately followed by

- **rd**, **rl** or **rn** (possibly with letters after)
- **rr** at the end of the word
- **rr** followed by a consonant (possibly with more letters after)

then you get a long [aː].

Note that there are variant spellings (especially GOC) where **ea** is spelled **eà**, even before **rr**. Since this is totally predictable, the accent here isn't really necessary as you can see in many older publications which don't use it. Because it is so well-established, I have stuck to using **à** before **rl**, **rd** and **rn**. However, as it's misleading before **rr**, I have stuck to the traditional convention of not writing it.

STRESSED

Examples:

ceàrnag	[kʲaːRnag]	geàrrte	[gʲaːRdʲə]
ceàrr	[kʲaːR]	deàrrsadh	[dʲaːRsəɣ]
Teàrlach	[tʲaːRLəx]	's fheàirrde	[ʃaːRdʲə]

E19   (-)ea + [L]V(-), [N]V(-), [R]-   NOT before helping   [a]
      vowel

When the previous rules about **ea** do not apply and (possibly after some initial letters)

- you get dark [L] or [N] followed by a vowel and possibly some more letters
- [R] which is followed by some letters

then you get short [a]. This does **NOT** apply in rules involving the helping vowel (such as E15).

STRESSED

Examples:

bealach	[bjaLəx]	ceannach	[kʲaNəx]
sealladh	[ʃaLəɣ]	ceart	[kʲaRʃd]
gealladh	[gʲaLəɣ]	gearradh	[gʲaRəɣ]

E20 (-)ea + dh(V-), gh(V-)   [ɣ]

When an **ea** (potentially with letters in front of it) is in a stressed syllable that is followed by a **dh** or **gh** either at the end of the word or followed by a vowel and possibly other letters, you usually get an [ɣ] vowel. There are quite a few exceptions, most notably the word *meadhan* [mi.an].

Examples:

seadh	[ʃɣɣ]	an eadh?	[ə Nʲɣɣ]
feadh	[fjɣɣ]	feadhainn	[fjɣɣɪNʲ]
leagh	[Lʲɣɣ]	leaghadh	[Lʲɣ.əɣ]

STRESSED

E21 (-)ea + dhC(-), ghC(-)   [ɣ:]

When an **ea** (potentially with letters in front of it) is in a stressed syllable that is followed by a **dh** or **gh** followed by a consonant (and possibly other letters), you get a long [ɣ:] vowel.

Examples:

teaghlach	[tʲɣ:Ləx]	greadhnachas	[grʲɣ:nəxəs]
Cille Mheadhrain	[kʲiLʲəˈvjɣ:rɛNʲ]	gleadhraich	[glɣ:rɪç]
teadhraichean	[tʲɣ:rɪçən]	meadhrach	[mjɣ:rəx]

STRESSED

E22 (-)ea + s(-), d(-), g(-)   [e]

When **ea** (potentially with letters in front of it) in a stressed syllable is followed by a **s**, **d** or **g** either at the end of the word or followed by other letters, it will be pronounced [e].

Examples:

eas	[es]	ceadaich	[kʲedɪç]
measail	[mesal]	beag	[beg]
eadar	[edər]	leag	[Lʲeg]

STRESSED

E

E23 (-)ea(i)- ELSEWHERE   [ε]

In all those cases where the previous rules about *ea* in a stressed syllable do not apply **ea** will be pronounced [ε] at the beginning of a word or following other letter or letters and always followed by more letters. Note this rule most frequently contrasts with E22.

Examples:

eabar	[ɛbər]	geama	[gʲɛmə]
each	[ɛx]	fear	[fɛr]
creach	[krʲɛx]	Peairt	[pɛRʃdʲ]

STRESSED

E24 -eil(-)   [al]

This ending in an unstressed syllable will have clear [a]. Other letters may follow.

Examples:

ainmeil	[ɛnɛmal]	cridheil	[krʲi.al]
caisteil	[kaʃdʲal]	fritheil	[frʲihal]
cianail	[kʲianal]	sgoinneil	[sgɣNʲal]

UNSTRESSED

E25 -eid(-)   [adʲ]

This ending in an unstressed syllable will have clear [a]. Other letters may follow.

Examples:

aiseid	[aʃadʲ]	réisimeid	[Reːʃɪmadʲ]
ròsaid	[Rɔːsadʲ]	ribheid	[Rivadʲ]
boineid	[bɔnadʲ]	aimhreid	[ãĩrʲadʲ]

UNSTRESSED

E

E26	-eag(-)		[ag]
	-ean(-)		[an]

These two endings in an unstressed syllable will almost always have clear [a]. Remember that in the case of **-ean** that only applies when it's not a plural ending (see 4.12.5)! Other letters may follow. The main exception for **-eag** is *aiseag* [aʃəg].

UNSTRESSED

Examples:

Ailean	[alan]	caileag	[kalag]
Cailean	[kalan]	boiseag	[bɔʃag]
binnean	[biNʲan]	binneag	[biNʲag]

E27	-ea-	[ə]

When you get **ea** in an unstressed syllable (which means it is always preceded by other letters) and always followed by another letter or letters, then it will most frequently be pronounced as a weak [ə]. The only common exceptions to this are some of the special endings discussed in chapter 4.12.5 such as the diminutives **-eag** and **-ean**.

UNSTRESSED

Examples:

cuireadh	[kurʲəɣ]	àbhaisteach	[aːvɪʃdʲəx]
bitheanta	[bihəNdə]	inneal	[iNʲəL]
tuilleadh	[tuLʲəɣ]	fidheall	[fiː.əL]

E28	-eig(-)		[εgʲ]
	-ein(-)		[εNʲ]

When in an unstressed syllable the endings **-eag** and **-ean** are slenderised for whatever reason, you get [ε]. Other letters may follow.

UNSTRESSED

Examples:

Ailein!	[alεNʲ]	caileige	[kalεgʲə]
A Chailein!	[ə xalεNʲ]	boiseige	[bɔʃεgʲə]
binnein	[biNʲεNʲ]	binneige	[biNʲεgʲə]

E29	-e(i)(-)		[ə]

When you get **e(i)** in an unstressed syllable at the end of a word then it will be pronounced as a weak [ə]. Note that this [ə] is always in danger of disappearing (see 4.13).

UNSTRESSED

Examples:

càise	[ka:ʃə]	àite	[a:hdʲə]
eaglaise	[egLɪʃə]	céile	[kʲe:lə]
cidhe	[kʲi.ə]	buille	[buLʲə]

F

F01	fhl-		[L]
	fhr-		[r]

Broad fh at the beginning of a word in these groups will be silent. Even though **l** and **r** are therefore the first sounds of such words, they will behave as if they were in the middle of a word so you get [L] (there's only one broad l, remember?) and weak [r].

BROAD

Examples:

dà fhlasg	[da: Lasg]	dà fhras	[da: ras]
dà fhlath	[da: Lah]	dà fh ròg	[da: rɔːg]
glé fhlagach	[gle: Lagəx]	dà fhraoch	[da: rɯːx]

F02	(-)fh-	[ ]

Broad **fh** either at the beginning of a word or in the middle is going to be totally silent in almost all cases. Fully dropping a sound feels weird to many people but it's no weirder than dropping the **k** in knife. The only exceptions are *fhuair* [huərʲ] (and other forms of the verb which begin with *fhua-*), *fhathast* [ha.əsd] and *fhalla* [haLə].

BROAD

Examples:

(a) fhalt	[aLd]	d' fhàileadh	[da:ləɣ]
(a) fhuil	[ul]	co-fharpais	[kɔ'arbɪʃ]
(a) fhear	[ɛr]	dh'fhalbh	[ɣaLav]

F03	(-)f(-)	[f]

Broad **f** either at the beginning of a word, in the middle or at the end is going to be simply [f] in all cases.

BROAD

Examples:

falt	[faLd]	diofar	[dʲifər]
fuil	[ful]	riof	[Rif]
gafann	[gafəN]	graf	[graf]

F

F04	fhl'-		[l]
	fhr'-		[r]

When you have a slender **fhl** or **fhr** group, the broad/slender rules don't apply to the **fh** and it will always behave like a broad **fh**. In a lenited **fhr** group the **r** behaves rather oddly and is usually a weak but non-palatal [r].

SLENDER

Examples:

fhreagair	[reɡɪrʲ]	dà fhleasgach	[da: lesɡəx]
dà fhreiceadan	[da: reçɡʲədan]	dà fhleadh	[da: lɤɣ]
dà fhrìth	[da: ri:]	glé fhliuch	[gle: lux]

F05	fh' + u(:) ɯ(:) o(:) ɤ(:) ɔ(:) a(:) au	[j]

When broad **fh** is lenited (see F01 and F02) it completely disappears. But the two different kinds of slender **f** behave differently depending on what comes after. As a slender **f** followed by a back vowel results in [fj] (see F08), when you lenited the **f** away you're left with a [j] at the start of the word. That's what this rule tells you.

SLENDER

Examples:

m' fheòil	[mjɔ:l]	glé fhiùghantach	[gle: ju:.əNdəx]
dà fheòrag	[da: jo:rag]	m' fheadhainn	[mjɤɣɪNʲ]
dà fheàrna	[da: ja:Rnə]	glé fhealltach	[gle: jauLdəx]

F06	fh' ELSEWHERE	[ ]

In those cases where F05 doesn't apply, slender lenited **fh** is going to be totally silent. That is, in front of front vowels such as [i] [i:] [e] [e:] [ɛ] [ɛ:] etc. The only exception is *fhéin* [he:n].

SLENDER

Examples:

glé fhiosrach	[gle: isrəx]	m' fheum	[me:m]
glé fhìrinneach	[gle: i:rʲɪNʲəx]	fheara!	[ɛrə]
dà fheadag	[da: edag]	dà fheusag	[da: iasag]

F07 | fl'- | [fl]
---

fr'- [frʲ]

When you have a slender **fl** or **fr** group, the broad/slender rules don't apply to the **f** and it will always behave like a broad **f**.

Examples:

freagair	[frʲegɪrʲ]	fleasgach	[flesgəx]
freiceadan	[frʲeçgʲədan]	fleadh	[flɤɣ]
frìth	[frʲiː]	fliuch	[flux]

SLENDER

F08 f ' + u(ː) ɯ(ː) o(ː) ɤ(ː) ɔ(ː) a(ː) au   [fj]

A slender **f** at the start of a word is followed by a back vowel, the resulting pronunciation is [fj].

Examples:

feòil	[fjɔːl]	fiùghantach	[fjuː.əNdəx]
feàrna	[fja:Rnə]	feadhainn	[fjɤɣɪNʲ]
feòrag	[fjɔːrag]	fealltach	[fjauLdəx]

SLENDER

F09 (-)f '(-) ELSEWHERE   [f]

In all cases where none of the other rules about slender **f** apply, it will simply be [f] both at the beginning of a word, in the middle or at the end.

Examples:

fiosrach	[fisrəx]	éifeachd	[eːfəxg]
feadag	[fedag]	taifeid	[tafɪdʲ]
feusag	[fiasag]	An Rif	[ə Rif]

SLENDER

F

G

G01 (-)VghV(-)   [.]

This means that when you get broad **gh** in between vowels, optionally with more letters in front and behind, the result is going to be hiatus in most cases. Some of the exceptions you're likely to encounter soon are *laghail* [Lɤɣal], *leughadh* [Lʲe:vaɣ] and *eughachd* [e:vəxg].

Examples:

bogha	[bo.ə]	sùghadh	[su:.əɣ]
aghaidh	[ɤ.ɪ]	leaghadh	[Lʲɤ.əɣ]
taghadh	[tɤ.əɣ]	deoghail	[dʲo.al]

G02 (-)VghC(-)   VAR: V̀   [ ]

After a short vowel (never a diphthong) when you get a **gh** which is immediately followed by a consonant, then then **gh** itself will be silent. Check the individual vowels for the effect this has on the vowel. Note that some people choose to write this combination with a grave over the vowel.

Examples:

ò roghnaich	[Ro:nɪç]	ò foghlam	[fo:Ləm]
ò foghnadh	[fo:nəɣ]	ù Dughlas	[du:Ləs]
ù lughdaich	[Lu:dɪç]	ù ughdar	[u:dər]

G03 (-)ugh
(-)ùgh

At the end of a word when you get **u** or **ù** before the broad **gh**, the **gh** is going to be silent.

Examples:

ugh	[u]	an-diugh	[əNʲ'dʲu]
sùgh	[su:]	òrdugh	[ɔ:Rdu]
brùgh	[bru:]	tiugh	[tʲu]

G

G04	ghn-		[ɣr̃]

This rule is similar to the rule about **chn-**. When you get broad **ghn-** at the beginning of a word, the **n** will become [r] and the next vowel will be nasal.

Examples:

dà ghnùis	[da: ɣrũːʃ]	dà ghnàths	[da: ɣrãːs]
dà ghnog	[da: ɣrõg]	dà ghnag	[da: ɣrãg]
dà ghnùst	[da: ɣrũːsd]	dà ghnàmhan	[da: ɣrãːvan]

BROAD

G05	(-)gh(-) ELSEWHERE		[ɣ]

In all other cases where G01-04 don't apply, **gh** is going to be [ɣ] both at the start and at the end of words.

Examples:

ghlan	[ɣLan]	àgh	[aːɣ]
ghoid	[ɣɤdʲ]	dragh	[drɤɣ]
truagh	[truəɣ]	laogh	[Lɯːɣ]

BROAD

G06	gn-		[gr̃]

This rule is similar to the rule about **cn-**. When you get broad **gn** at the beginning of a word, the **n** will become [r] and the next vowel will be nasal.

Examples:

gnùis	[grũːʃ]	gnàths	[grãːs]
gnog	[grõg]	gnag	[grãg]
gnùst	[grũːsd]	gnàmhan	[grãːvan]

BROAD

G

G07 (-)g(-)   [g]

In all other cases broad **g** at the beginning, in the middle and at the end of words will simply be [g].

Examples:

glas	[gLas]	magadh	[magəɣ]
gorm	[gɔrɔm]	bog	[bog]
baga	[bagə]	marag	[marag]

G08 i(:) e(:) ɛ(:) +   gh'V(-)   [.]
                gh'   [ ]

When a slender **gh** follows a front vowel and is then itself followed by another vowel (and potentially more letters), the **gh** is going to show up as hiatus. At the end of a word, slender **gh** will be silent following those vowels.

Examples:

tighinn	[tⁱi.ɪNʲ]	lighiche	[Lʲi.ɪçə]
leighis	[Lʲe.ɪʃ]	rìgh	[Ri:]
greigheach	[grʲe.əx]	léigh	[Lʲe:]

G09 -gh'C(-)   [i]

If you have a slender **gh** before a consonant, the **gh** will turn into ('vocalise') to [i].

Examples:

saighdear	[sɤidʲɛr]	maighdeann	[mɤidʲəN]
maighdeag	[mɤidʲag]	faighnich	[fɤinɪç]
slaightear	[sLɤidʲɛr]	oighre	[ɤirʲə]

G

G10 -gh'(V-)   [j]

If you have a slender **gh**
- between vowels
- or at the end of a word

then it will usually be [j]. If it is in an unstressed syllable, then it is a special ending and is silent, for example: *dachaigh* [daxɪ].

Examples:

laighe	[Lajə]	dòigh	[dɔːj]
aoigheachd	[ɤjəxg]	faigh	[faj]
bràigh	[braːj]	bloigheag	[bLɔjag]

SLENDER

G11 ghl'-   [ɣl]

ghr'-   [ɣrʲ]

When you get slender **ghl-** or **ghr-** at the beginning of a word, the broad/slender rules do not apply to the **gh** and it will always be a broad [ɣ].

Examples:

glé ghlic	[gle: ɣliçgʲ]	dà ghrian	[da: ɣrʲian]
ghleac	[ɣlɛxg]	dà ghreis	[da: ɣrʲeʃ]
dà ghleann	[da: ɣlauN]	glé ghreannach	[gle: ɣrʲɛNəx]

SLENDER

G12 ghn'-   [ɣrʲ˜]

This rule is similar to the rule about slender **chn-**. When you get slender **ghn-** at the beginning of a word, the broad/slender rules do not apply to the **gh** and it will always be a broad [ɣ]. The **n** will become [r] and the next vowel will be nasal.

Examples:

dà ghnìomh	[da: ɣrʲĩə̃v]	dà ghnè	[da: ɣrʲɛ̃:]
dà ghnìomhar	[da: ɣrʲĩə̃vər]	glé ghnèitheil	[gle: ɣrʲɛ̃.al]
glé ghnìomhach	[gle: ɣrʲĩə̃vəx]	dà ghnìobann	[da: ɣrʲĩə̃bən]

SLENDER

G

G13 gh'-   [ʝ]

Slender **gh-** at the beginning of a word is going to be [ʝ].

Examples:

mo ghiomach	[mə ʝiməx]	glé gheur	[gle: ʝiar]
dà gheas	[da: ʝes]	ghiùlain	[ʝu:LɛNʲ]
ghéill	[ʝe:Lʲ]	dà gheamhradh	[da: ʝãũrəɣ]

SLENDER

G14 gl'-   [gl]

gr'-   [grʲ]

When you get slender **gl-** or **gr-** at the beginning of a word, the broad/slender rules do not apply to the **g** and it will always be a broad [g].

Examples:

glic	[gliçgʲ]	grian	[grʲian]
gleac	[glɛxg]	greis	[grʲeʃ]
gleann	[glauN]	greannach	[grʲɛNəx]

SLENDER

G15 gn'-   [grʲ~]

This rule is similar to the rule about slender **cn-**. When you get slender **gn-** at the beginning of a word, the broad/slender rules do not apply to the *g* and it will be a broad [g], the **n** will become [r] and the next vowel will be nasal.

Examples:

gnìomh	[grʲĩ̃əv]	gnè	[grʲɛ̃:]
gnìomhar	[grʲĩ̃əvər]	gnèitheil	[grʲɛ̃:.al]
gnìomhach	[grʲĩ̃əvəx]	gnìobann	[grʲĩ̃əbən]

SLENDER

G16	(-)g'(-) ELSEWHERE		[gʲ]

In all those cases where the previous rules about slender **g** do not apply, at the beginning, in the middle and at the end of words it will be [gʲ].

Examples:

gille	[gʲiLʲə]	eige	[egʲə]
geama	[gʲɛmə]	leig	[Lʲegʲ]
sligeach	[ʃLʲigʲəx]	aisig	[aʃɪgʲ]

SLENDER

G

❋ ❋ ❋ ❋ ❋ ❋ ❋ ❋

H01	h-		[h]

The letter **h** rarely appears in the basic form of words in Gaelic, with the exception of place-names borrowed from Norse perhaps, and most commonly shows up after certain forms of the article, possessives and other particles.   Either way, there is no broad/slender difference with h at the beginning of a word.

Examples:

hama	[hamə]	Hiort	[hiRʃd]
na h-adan	[nə hadən]	na h-eaglaisean	[nə hegLɪʃən]
a h-aran	[ə haran]	a h-each	[ə hɛx]

I

I01	(-)io +	lb(-), lbh(-), lch(-), lg(-), lgh(-), lm(-), lmh(-)	[i-i]
		nb(-), nbh(-), nch(-), ngh(-), nm(-), nmh(-)	[i-i]
		rb(-), rbh(-), rch(-), rg(-), rgh(-), rm(-), rmh(-)	[i-i]
		ml(-), mr(-), ms(-), mch(-)	[i-i]

When io, possibly with letters in front of it, is involved in a helping vowel appearing, this is usually [i-i]. Other letters may follow.

The exact vowel combination can vary quite a bit from area to area and depending on what comes next, the most common alternatives being something like [i-ɪ] or [i-ə]. Remember the most important thing is to <u>have</u> an extra vowel!

STRESSED

Examples:

iomradh	[imirəɣ]	tiormaich	[tʲirimɪç]
ionmhas	[inivəs]	MacFhionghain	[max'gʲiniɣɛNʲ]
iomlan	[imiLan]	iomchaidh	[imixɪ]

I02	io + dhl(-), l(-), ll(-)	[ju]

When an **io** at the beginning of a word is followed by a **dhl**, **l** or **ll**, you usually pronounce this as [ju]. Other letters may follow.

STRESSED

Examples:

iodhlann	[juLəN]	iollagach	[juLagəx]
iolaire	[juLɪrʲə]	iolra	[juLrə]
iolach	[juLəx]	iola	[juLə]

| I03 | io + | nn- | | [ju] |
| | | nnC(-) | | [ju:] |

When an **io** at the beginning of a word is followed by **nn** you get a [ju] sound (other letters may follow the **io**). If the **nn** is followed by a consonant, the **io** will have a long [ju:] sound.

Examples:

ionnas	[juNəs]	ionnsramaid	[jũːNsdrəmɪdʲ]
ionnairidh	[juNɪrʲɪ]	ionnsaigh	[jũːNsɪ]
ionnsaich	[jũːNsɪç]	ionndrainn	[jũːNdrɪNʲ]

STRESSED

| I04 | -io + | llV(-), nnV(-) | VAR: iu | [u] |

This rule deals with non-initial **io** followed by **ll** or **nn** which are immediately followed by a vowel and optionally more letters
In all cases the pronunciation will be short [u]. Note that in some cases the spelling has started to catch up with the pronunciation, using **iu** instead of **io**.

Examples:

giollachd ^{iu}	[gʲuLəxg]	mionnaich	[mjuNɪç]
sgiollag	[sgʲuLag]	sionnach	[ʃuNəx]
fionnar	[fjuNər]	rionnag	[RuNag]

STRESSED

I05	(-)io +	ll, nn, rr	[u:]
		llC(-), nnC(-), rrC(-)	[u:]
		rd(-), rl(-), rn(-)	[u:]

This rule deals with **io** (possibly with letters in front of it) which is followed either by:

- **ll, nn** or **rr** at the end of the word
- **ll, nn** or **rr** which are immediately followed by a consonant and optionally more letters
- **rd, rl** or **rn**, optionally followed by other letters

This is usually very nasal if the **nn** is followed by a consonant.

Examples:

fionn	[fju:N]	tionndadh	[tʲũ:Ndəɣ]
os cionn	[ɔs kʲu:N]	sgiorrtachd	[sgʲu:Rdəxg]
lionn	[Lʲu:N]	giornalair	[gʲu:Rnəlɛrʲ]

STRESSED

I06	(-)ìo + b(-), bh(-)	[i:]

When you have **ìo** (possibly after other letters) followed by a **b** or *bh* and possibly more letters after, you get long [i:].

Examples:

sgrìob	[sgrʲi:b]	sgrìobh	[sgrʲi:v]
bìoball	[bi:bəL]	sìobhalta	[ʃi:vəLdə]
pìob	[pi:b]	prìobhaideach	[prʲi:vɪdʲəx]

STRESSED

I07	(-)ìo- ELSEWHERE	[iə]

If I06 does not apply, **ìo** is going to be pronounced [iə] in a stressed syllable, either at the beginning of a word or following some initial letters.

Examples:

ìoghnadh	[iənəɣ]	lìon	[Lʲiən]
ìoc	[iəxg]	cìoch	[kʲiəx]
ìosal	[iəsəL]	spìon	[sbiən]

STRESSED

I08   (-)ì(-) ELSEWHERE   [i:]

When none of the other rules about **ì** apply, then it will be simply
long [i:] in a stressed syllable at the beginning of a word or following
some initial letters.

STRESSED

Examples:

ìseal	[i:ʃəL]	cìr	[kʲi:rʲ]
ìne	[i:nə]	Sìne	[ʃi:nə]
ìre	[i:rʲə]	clì	[kli:]

I09   iù(i)(-)   [ju:]

This rule deals with **iù** and **iùi** at the beginning of a word. Both
combinations may be followed by other letters. There will usually be
a glide in pronunciation before the **iù(i)** so you get [ju:].

STRESSED

Examples:

iùil	[ju:l]	iùlag	[ju:Lag]
iùdhach	[ju:.əx]	iùl	[ju:L]
Poll Iù	[poL'ju:]	iùras	[ju:rəs]

I10   -iù(i)(-)   [u:]

When **iù** and **iùi** are preceded by other letters in a stressed syllable,
they will both just be [u:] in pronunciation.

STRESSED

Examples:

ciùineas	[kʲu:Nʲəs]	cliù	[klu:]
siùil	[ʃu:l]	fiù	[fju:]
stiùirich	[ʃdʲu:rʲɪç]	diù	[dʲu:]

I11	(-)iu(i) + ll, nn, m, rr	VAR: iù	[u:]
	llC(-), nnC(-), mC(-), rrC(-)		[u:]
	rd(-), rl(-), rn(-)		[u:]
	bhC(-), mhC(-)		[u:]

This rule deals with **iu** (possibly with letters in front of it) which is followed either by:

- **ll, nn, m** or **rr** at the end of a word
- **ll, nn, m** or **rr** followed immediately by another consonant and then optionally more letters
- **rd, rl** or **rn** which can be followed by more letters
- **bh** or **mh** immediately followed by a consonant and then optionally by more letters

In all cases the pronunciation will be long [u:]. As with A06 and E18, I'm sticking to the traditional spelling of not using the grave on **iù** before **rr** as it would lead to misleading spellings.

Examples:

ciurr (ciùrr)	[kʲu:R]	siùrdan	[ʃu:Rdan]
rium	[rʲu:m]	iùbhrach	[ju:rəx]
iunntachd	[jũ:Ndəxg]	piùrna	[pju:RNə]

STRESSED

I12	iu-	[ju]

When you get **iu** at the beginning of a word, it will be pronounced [ju]. This is not a very common initial combination.

Examples:

iutharn	[juhəRn]	iurpais	[jurbɪʃ]
iuchair	[juxɪrʲ]	iubhar	[ju.ər]
iullagach	[juLagəx]	iulla	[juLə]

STRESSED

I13	-iu-		[u]

An **iu** in a stressed syllable, with letters before it and after it, is just going to be a short [u] in pronunciation.

Examples:

fliuch	[flux]	tiugh	[tʲu]
siubhal	[ʃu.al]	piuthar	[pju.ər]
an-diugh	[əNʲˈdʲu]	triubhas	[tru.əs]

I14	(-)ia(i)(-) ELSEWHERE		[iə]

When you have **ia** or **iai** in a stressed syllable, either at the beginning or following some letters and optionally with more letters following, then it is most likely going to be [iə]. It can sometimes be [ia] but it's not possible to predict exactly.

Examples:

iarraidh	[iəRɪ]	miann	[miəN]
iar	[iər]	biadh	[biəɣ]
iarann	[iəRəN]	grian	[grʲiən]

I15	(-)i +	Ib(-), Ibh(-), Ich(-), Ig(-), Igh(-), Im(-), Imh(-)	[i-i]
		nb(-), nbh(-), nch(-), ngh(-), nm(-), nmh(-)	[i-i]
		rb(-), rbh(-), rch(-), rg(-), rgh(-), rm(-), rmh(-)	[i-i]
		ml(-), mr(-), ms(-), mch(-)	[i-i]

When **i**, possibly with letters in front of it, is involved in a helping vowel appearing, this is most commonly [i-i]. Other letters may follow.

Examples:

gilb	[gʲilib]	inbhe	[inivə]
imleag	[imilag]	tilg	[tʲiligʲ]
timcheall	[tʲimiçəL]	inghear	[inijər]

I

I16	(-)i +	ll, nn, m	VAR: ì	[iː]
		llC(-), nnC(-), mC(-)		[iː]
		(-)bhC(-)		[iː]

An **i** (possibly with letters in front of it) which is followed either by:

- **ll**, **nn** or **m** at the end of the word
- **ll**, **nn** or **m** which are immediately followed by a consonant and optionally more letters
- **bh** which is immediately followed by a consonant and optionally more letters

In all cases the pronuciation will be long [iː]. As explained in A06, E18 and I11, I'm avoiding the bad modern habit of using a grave over the **ì** as the length is totally predictable. If you do use the grave in such cases, you must remember not to write it when there is a vowel following as this will render the **i** short (see 5.6.2).

Examples:

ˈtill	[tʲiːLʲ]	ˈim	[iːm]
ˈfillte	[fiːLʲdʲə]	ˈimpidh	[iːmbɪ]
ˈbinn	[biːNʲ]	ˈsibhse	[ʃiːvʃə]

STRESSED

I17	(-)i(o)(-) ELSEWHERE	[i]

When none of the previous rules about combinations with **i** apply, both **i** and **io** in a stressed syllable are going to be [i]

Examples:

ciste	[kʲiʃdʲə]	lios	[Lʲis]
thig	[higʲ]	cille	[kʲiLʲə]
dlighe	[dli.ə]	ime	[imə]

STRESSED

I18 -i- UNSTRESSED			[ɪ]
A simple rule for **i** for a change. If you have **i** in an unstressed syllable, preceded and optionally followed by other letters, the pronunciation will be [ɪ].			
Examples:			
litir	[Lʲihdʲɪrʲ]	aisig	[aʃɪgʲ]
fuirich	[furʲɪç]	Màiri	[maːrʲɪ]
airidh	[arʲɪ]	neoini	[Nʲɔnɪ]

UNSTRESSED

I

L01	(-)l(-)		[L]
	-ll(-)		[L]

Broad l, irrespective of how many there are and in what place in the word it is will always be [L]. This includes positions where you might expect lenition.

Examples:

lag	[Lag]	balla	[baLə]
dà luchag	[da: Luxag]	call	[kauL]
mala	[maLə]	càl	[ka:L]

BROAD

L02	* l'-		[l]

A slender l at the beginning of a word which has been lenited (meaning if it comes after a word that causes lenition or is in a spot where words are normally lenited such as past tense verbs) will be pronounced as a weak [l].

Examples:

mo leabaidh	[mə lebɪ]	dà leac	[da: lɛxg]
do léine	[də le:nə]	leum e	[le:m ɛ]
dà lighiche	[da: li.ɪçə]	lìon e	[liən ɛ]

SLENDER

L03	l'-		[Lʲ]

A slender l at the beginning of a word which hasn't been lenited will be pronounced [Lʲ]. The only exception to this are the forms of le 'with' which have weak [l].

Examples:

leabaidh	[Lʲebɪ]	leac	[Lʲɛxg]
léine	[Lʲe:nə]	leum!	[Lʲe:m]
lighiche	[Lʲi.ɪçə]	lìon!	[Lʲiən]

SLENDER

L04	-ll'(-)		[Lʲ]	

A double slender **ll** which is in the middle or at the end of a word will always be pronounced as a palatal [Lʲ].

Examples:

gille	[gʲiLʲə]	cill	[kʲiːLʲ]
tilleadh	[tʲiLʲəɣ]	till	[tʲiːLʲ]
tuilleadh	[tɯLʲəɣ]	foill	[fɣiLʲ]

SLENDER

L05	-l'(-)		[l]	

A single slender **l** in the middle or at the end of a word will always be pronounced as a weak [l].

Examples:

gile	[gʲilə]	càil	[kaːl]
uile	[ulə]	anail	[anal]
baile	[balə]	toil	[tɔl]

SLENDER

L

M

M01 (-)mhC(-)   [˜]

A broad **mh** before a consonant will result in nasalisation on the preceding vowel. The **mh** itself is not pronounced anymore. The nasality as always can spread to other vowels too but that isn't obligatory.

Examples:

comhla	[kõ:Lə]	cùmhnant	[kũ:nənd]
comhradh	[kõ:rəɣ]	ùmhlachd	[ũ:Ləxg]
samhradh	[sãũrəɣ]	comhdach	[kõ:dəx]

BROAD

M02 (-) + u(:) o(:) ɔ(:) + mhV(-)   [˜.]

When you have **mh** in between vowels, it turns into hiatus if the vowel in front of the **mh** is one of those back vowels in the list above. Other letters may be in front and behind and the vowels near the **mh** usually have become nasal.

Examples:

cumhang	[kũ.əŋg]	comhairle	[kõ.əRLʲə]
cumhachd	[kũ.əxg]	dùmhail	[dũ:.al]
romham	[rõ.əm]	Còmhall	[kõ:.əL]

BROAD

M03 (-)mh(-) ELSEWHERE   [v]

Elsewhere (when M01 and M02 don't apply) broad **mh** is going to be [v]. It is often accompanied by nasalisation but not always.

Examples:

mhol	[voL]	nèamhaich	[Nʲɛ̃:vɪç]
glé mhór	[gle: vo:r]	làmh	[La:v]
amhach	[avəx]	àireamh	[a:rʲəv]

BROAD

M

M04 (-)m(-)   [m]

BROAD

A broad **m**, no matter where in a word it appears, will always be [m].

Examples:

mol	[mɔL]	seòmar	[ʃoːmər]
mór	[moːr]	lom	[Lɔum]
amar	[amər]	balgam	[baLagəm]

M05 mh' + u(:) ɯ(:) o(:) ɣ(:) ɔ(:) a(:) au (-)   [vj]

SLENDER

At the beginning of a word, slender **mh** will be pronounced [vj] if it is followed by a back vowel.

Examples:

mheall	[vjauL]	mo mhiùg	[mə vjuːg]
dà mheòir	[da: vjɔːrʲ]	dà mheann	[da: vjauN]
mheòraich	[vjɔːrɪç]	dà mheamhran	[da: vjãũran]

M06   mh' + ELSEWHERE   [v]

SLENDER

When M05 doesn't apply, initial slender **mh** will just be [v]

Examples:

mhill	[viːLʲ]	mhèilich	[vɛːlɪç]
mhìnich	[viːnɪç]	mheasgaich	[vesgɪç]
mheal	[vɛL]	mheuraich	[viarɪç]

M07   (-) i(:) e(:) ɛ(:) + mh'(-)   [v]

SLENDER

When you have a slender **mh** after a front vowel the **mh** will be [v]. Other letters may follow or precede the whole group.

Examples:

sèimh	[ʃɛːv]	gainmheach	[gɛnɛvəx]
sèimhich	[ʃɛːvɪç]	nimh	[Nʲĩv]
Cill Rìmhinn	[kʲiLʲ'riːvɪNʲ]	nimheil	[Nʲĩval]

M

M08 (-)mh'C'(-)   [˜ĩ]

Before another consonant (and possibly more letters), slender **mh**
will be pronounced [ĩ] with nearby nasality.

Examples:

gaimhleag	[gãĩlag]	làimhsich	[Lã:jʃɪç]
cuimhne	[kũĩNʲə]	nàimhdean	[Nã:ĩdʲən]
doimhne	[dy̆ĩnə]	aimhreit	[ãĩrʲadʲ]

SLENDER

M09 (-)mh'(-) ELSEWHERE   [˜j]

Elsewhere (between vowels or at the end of a word), slender **mh** will
usually be pronounced [j] with nearby nasality.

Examples:

coimhead	[kõjad]	coimheach	[kõjəx]
roimhe	[rõjə]	clòimh	[kLɔ̃:j]
troimhe	[trõjə]	uaimh	[ũə̃j]

SLENDER

M10 m' + u(:) ɯ(:) o(:) ɤ(:) ɔ(:) a(:) au (-)   [mj]

At the beginning of a word, slender **m** will be pronounced [mj] if it is
followed by a back vowel.

Examples:

meall	[mjauL]	miùg	[mju:g]
meòir	[mjɔ:rʲ]	meann	[mjauN]
meòraich	[mjɔ:rɪç]	meamhran	[mjã̃ũran]

SLENDER

M11 (-) u(:) ɯ(:) o(:) ɤ(:) ɔ(:) a(:) uə + m'(-)   [im]

When you have a slender **m** after a back vowel (and possible more letters) then you get an extra vowel before the m: [im].

Examples:

muime	[muimə]	daoimean	[dɤiman]
caime	[kaimə]	luime	[lɯimə]
maoim	[mɤim]	fuaim	[fuəim]

SLENDER

M12 (-)m'(-) ELSEWHERE   [m]

When none of the other rules about slender **m** at the beginning, in the middle or at the end of a word apply, then it will simply be [m].

Examples:

mìnich	[miːnɪç]	caismeachd	[kaʃməxg]
measgaich	[mesgɪç]	im	[iːm]
ime	[imə]	ainm	[ɛnɛm]

SLENDER

N

N01	* n-		[n]

A broad **n** at the beginning of a word which has been lenited (meaning if it comes after a word that causes lenition or is in a spot where words are normally lenited such as past tense verbs) will be pronounced as a weak [n].

Examples:

mo nàbaidh	[mə naːbɪ]	dà not	[daː nɔhd]
mo nàire	[mə naːrʲə]	glé nuadh	[gleː nuəɣ]
do nòs	[də nɔːs]	do nuallan	[də nuəLan]

BROAD

N02	n-		[N]

Broad **n** at the beginning of a word is, barring a few exceptions (see 5.6.16), always going to be strong [N].

Examples:

nàbaidh	[Naːbɪ]	not	[Nɔhd]
nàire	[Naːrʲə]	nuadh	[Nuəɣ]
nòs	[Nɔːs]	nuallan	[NuəLan]

BROAD

N03	-nn(-)		[N]

When you have a double **nn** in the middle or at the end of a word it will always be a strong [N]. Before a consonant this often is nasalised away in spoken Gaelic (for example *cunntas* [kũːdəs] instead of [kũːNdəs] but that's not something you have to do to have a good accent.

Examples:

gunna	[guNə]	fann	[fauN]
cunntas	[kũːNdəs]	srann	[sdrauN]
annasach	[aNəsəx]	comann	[koməN]

BROAD

N04 -ng(-)   [ŋg]

A broad **ng** in the middle or at the end of a word is usually going to be pronounced [ŋg]. In a few cases the **ng** has been nasalised away (see 5.6.16).

Examples:

long	[Lɔuŋg]	cumhang	[kũ.əŋg]
rung	[Ruŋg]	eang	[ɛŋg]
teanga	[tʲɛŋgə]	Frangach	[fraŋgəx]

BROAD

N05 -nt(-)   [Nd]

A single broad **n** followed by a **t** in the middle or at the end of a word will strengthen to [Nd].

Examples:

cantainn	[kaNdɪNʲ]	bitheantas	[bihəNdəs]
fantainn	[faNdɪNʲ]	fileanta	[filəNdə]
cumanta	[kuməNdə]	coileanta	[kɔləNdə]

BROAD

N06 -n(-)   [n]

A single broad **n** in the middle or at the end of a word is going to be weak [n]. The main exception to this are all forms of the definite article **an** or words which contain the definite article **an** (see 4.9).

Examples:

cana	[kanə]	can	[kan]
dùnadh	[du:nəɣ]	dùn	[du:n]
sona	[sɔnə]	son	[sɔn]

BROAD

N

N07 * n'-   [n]

A slender **n** at the beginning of a word which has been lenited
(meaning if it comes after a word that causes lenition or is in a spot
where words are normally lenited such as past tense verbs) will be
pronounced as a weak [n].

Examples:

mo nead	[mə ned]	dà neul	[da: niaL]
dà neasgaid	[da: nesgɪdʲ]	mo nighean	[mə ni.an]
do nèamh	[də nɛ̃:v]	dà nì	[da: ni:]

SLENDER

N08 n'-   [Nʲ]

A slender **n** at the beginning of a word which hasn't been lenited will
be pronounced [Nʲ]. There are a few exceptions (see page 368) but
not many.

Examples:

nead	[Nʲed]	neul	[NʲiaL]
neasgaid	[Nʲesgɪdʲ]	nighean	[Nʲi.an]
nèamh	[Nʲɛ̃:v]	nì	[Nʲi:]

SLENDER

N09 -nn'(-)   [Nʲ]

A slender **nn** in the middle or at the end of a word will be palatal [Nʲ].
The main exceptions are the forms of *innis* [ī:ʃ].

Examples:

cinneadh	[kʲiNʲəɣ]	beinn	[beiNʲ]
bainne	[baNʲə]	cinn	[kʲi:Nʲ]
beinne	[beNʲə]	tighinn	[tʲi.ɪNʲ]

SLENDER

N

N10 -ng'(-)   [ŋʲgʲ]

A slender **ng** will usually be pronounced as a palatal [ŋʲgʲ]. There are some cases where slender **ng** has nasalised away in the middle of a word, for example in *aingeal* [ãjəL].

Examples:

cuing	[kwiŋʲgʲ]	luinge	[lwiŋʲgʲə]
farsaing	[faRsɪŋʲgʲ]	Cingidh	[kʲiŋʲgʲɪ]
tarraing	[taRɪŋʲgʲ]	aingidh	[aiŋʲgʲɪ]

SLENDER

N11 (-) u(ː) ɯ(ː) o(ː) ɣ(ː) ɔ(ː) a(ː) ia uə + n'(-)   [Nʲ]

When a single slender **n** (including a group that has **n** in it) follows a back vowel, you get a palatal [Nʲ].

Examples:

càineadh	[kaːNʲəɣ]	coin	[kɔNʲ]
ùine	[uːNʲə]	uaine	[uəNʲə]
faoin	[fɯːNʲ]	cùirn	[kuːRNʲ]

SLENDER

N12 -n'(-)   [n]

When none of the other rules about single slender **n** in the middle or at the end of a word apply, then you just get weak [n]. Remember that some speakers have extended rule N11 to the long front vowels [iː] [eː] and [ɛː].

Examples:

léine	[Lʲeːnə]	sin	[ʃin]
gréine	[grʲeːnə]	fhéin	[heːn]
Sìne	[ʃiːnə]	lìn	[Lʲiːn]

SLENDER

O

O01   (-)ó(i)(-)   VAR: ò   [oː]

This rule deals with **ó** and **ói**, optionally with letters both in front and after. In all cases, this will be round [oː]. Note that in some modern spellings the **ó** has been replaced with **ò** throughout so you may want to check the spelling in an older dictionary.

Examples:

bó	[boː]	leóbag	[Lʲoːbag]
cóig	[koːgʲ]	mór	[moːr]
có	[koː]	ó	[oː]

STRESSED

O02   (-)o + rd(-), rl(-), rn(-), rr   VAR: ò   [ɔː]

When you get the letter **o**, possibly after some initial letters, in a stressed syllable and immediately followed by an **rd**, **rl** or **rn** (which may or may not be followed by other letters) or a double **rr** at the end of a word then you get a long [ɔː]. Note that some people put a grave over the vowel to show the length but since the length can be fully predicted from the consonants nearby, that's not really necessary.

Examples:

ò corr	[kɔːR]	dòrnan	[dɔːRNan]
ò torr	[tɔːR]	òrd	[ɔːRd]
dòrn	[dɔːRN]	dòrlach	[dɔːRLəx]

STRESSED

O03   (-)ò(i)(-)   [ɔː]

When you have **ò** or **òi**, optionally with letters both in front and after, it will be pronounced [ɔː]. Note that in some modern spellings O01 and O03 have been merged and are now ambiguous.

Examples:

òg	[ɔːg]	pòg	[pɔːg]
òran	[ɔːran]	beò	[bjɔː]
còisir	[kɔːʃɪrʲ]	ceò	[kʲɔː]

STRESSED

O04	(-)oi + llV(-), nnV(-)			[ɣ]

In a stressed syllable, possibly following some other initial letters, oi before **ll** and **nn** will be [ɣ] if there is a vowel immediately after. Other letters may follow.

Examples:

cloinne	[kLɣNʲə]	coille	[kɣLʲə]
coinnich	[kɣNʲɪç]	soilleir	[sɣLʲɪrʲ]
sgoinneil	[sgɣNʲal]	broilleach	[brɣLʲəx]

O05	(-)oi +	ll, nn, m	[ɣi]
		llC(-), nnC(-), mC(-)	[ɣi]
		bhC(-), dhC(-), ghC(-), mhC(-)	[ɣi]

This rule deals with **oi** (optionally with letters in front of it) which is followed either by:

- **ll**, **nn** or **m** without anything following them, that is, at the end of a word
- **ll**, **nn** or **m** which are immediately followed by a consonant and optionally more letters
- **bh**, **dh**, **gh** and **mh** which are immediately followed by a consonant and optionally more letters

In all cases the pronunciation will be [ɣi].

Examples:

roinn	[RɣiNʲ]	toinnte	[tɣiNʲdʲə]
foill	[fɣiLʲ]	doimhneachd	[dɣĩnəxg]
oillt	[ɣiLʲdʲ]	oighreachd	[ɣirʲəxg]

O

STRESSED

STRESSED

O

O06 (-)oi + mhV(-)   [õ]

When an **oi**, possibly after some letters, in a stressed syllable is followed by **mh** and then by a vowel and possibly some more letters, you get a nasal [õ].

Examples:

coimheach	[kõjəx]	coimhearsnach	[kõjəRsnəx]
roimhe	[rõjə]	troimhe	[trõjə]
coimhead	[kõjad]	croimheal	[krõjəL]

STRESSED

O07 (-)oi + bh(-), d(-), dh(-), gh(-)   [ɣ]
HIATUS   [ɣ]

This rule is as messy as it looks. The problem is that **oi**, which used to be [ɔ] across the board has been gradually developing into [ɣ] in Gaelic. However, the process is far from tidy, uniform or complete, especially with **oi** before **r** and **l**. So the above rule is broadly right but not universal. It's not a bad mistake to get this one wrong. Rule O04 is reliable by the way.

Examples:

goid	[gɣdʲ]	oighre	[ɣjrʲə]
oide	[ɣdʲə]	oidheam	[ɣjəm]
oidhche	[ɣ̆jçə]	soitheach	[sɣ.əx]

STRESSED

O

O08	(-)oi +	lb(-), lbh(-), lch(-), lg(-), lgh(-), lm(-), lmh(-)	[ɣ-ɣ]
		nb(-), nbh(-), nch(-), ngh(-), nm(-), nmh(-)	[ɣ-ɣ]
		rb(-), rbh(-), rch(-), rg(-), rgh(-), rm(-), rmh(-)	[ɣ-ɣ]
		ml(-), mr(-), ms(-), mch(-)	[ɣ-ɣ]

STRESSED

When rule O07 applies to the **oi** group and **oi** is [ɣ], then, if a helping vowel appears, this will give you [ɣ-ɣ]. Other letters may be in front of the whole group and/or follow.

Examples:

doirbh	[dɣrʲɣv]	Foirbeis	[fɣrʲɣbɪʃ]
doilgheas	[dɣlɣjəs]	soirbheas	[sɣrʲɣvəs]
coirb	[kɣrʲɣb]	stoirm	[sdɣrʲɣm]

O09	(-)oi +	c(-), ch(-), n(-), ng(-), p(-), rr(-), s(-), t(-)	[ɔ]
		ELSEWHERE	[ɔ]

STRESSED

In those cases when none of the previous rules about **oi** apply, it will usually have the default pronunciation of the letter **o** in Gaelic which is [ɔ]. Please read the note in O07 about the messy state of affairs between [ɣ] and [ɔ].

The first line of the rule is fairly consistent, so in those specific environments you very rarely get [ɣ] and can be confident it's [ɔ]. Anywhere else, you're best off consulting the Wordlist or checking with a native speaker. The word *coire* exemplifies this problem: it occurs both as [kɣrʲə] 'fault' and [kɔrʲə] 'kettle'.

Examples:

fois	[fɔʃ]	oirre	[ɔRə]
croin	[krɔNʲ]	coire	[kɔrʲə]
poit	[pɔhdʲ]	sgoil	[sgɔl]

O

O10	(-)o + ll, nn, m	[ɔu]
	llC(-), nnC(-), mC(-)	[ɔu]

This rule deals with **o** (optionally with letters in front of it) which is followed either by:

- **ll, nn** or **m** without anything following them, that is, at the end of a word
- **ll, nn** or **m** which are immediately followed by a consonant and optionally more letters

In all cases the pronunciation will be [ɔu].

Examples:

toll	[tɔuL]	tolltach	[tɔuLdəx]
conn	[kɔuN]	connlach	[kɔuNLəx]
lom	[Lɔum]	lomte	[Lɔumdʲə]

STRESSED

O11	(-)o + dhC(-), ghC(-)	VAR: ó & ò	[o:]

If, in a stressed syllable, **o** is followed by a **dh** or **gh** and then immediately another consonant, you get a long [o:]. Other letters may be in front of the **o** and at the end of the word.

Examples:

fóghnaidh	[fo:nɪ]	bóghlanach	[bo:Lənəx]
róghnaich	[Ro:nɪç]	deoghladair	[dʲo:Lədɛrʲ]
fóghlam	[fo:Ləm]	Cill Òdhrain	[kʲiLʲʼo:rɛNʲ]

STRESSED

O12	(-)o + HIATUS		[o]

When an **o**, possible after other letters, is followed by hiatus (meaning that there is a **bh**, **dh**, **gh**, **fh**, **mh** or **th** that is not pronounced anymore) then you usually get a round [o] instead of the open [ɔ].

Examples:

bogha	[bo.ə]	comharradh	[kõ.əRəɣ]
ogha	[o.ə]	foghain	[fo.ɪNʲ]
todhar	[to.ər]	gnothach	[grõ.əx]

STRESSED

O13	(-)o + g(-), b(-) mV(-)		[o]

When **o** (not **oi**) comes before **g** or **b** (followed by more letters) or **m** followed by a vowel, then you usually get a round [o].

Examples:

bog	[bog]	tog	[tog]
gob	[gob]	tobar	[tobər]
coma	[komə]	loma	[Lomə]

STRESSED

O14	(-)o +	lb(-), lbh(-), lch(-), lg(-), lgh(-), lm(-), lmh(-)	[ɔ-ɔ]
		nb(-), nbh(-), nch(-), ngh(-), nm(-), nmh(-)	[ɔ-ɔ]
		rb(-), rbh(-), rch(-), rg(-), rgh(-), rm(-), rmh(-)	[ɔ-ɔ]
		ml(-), mr(-), ms(-), mch(-)	[ɔ-ɔ]

When you have an **o** in an environment where a helping vowel appears, this will give you [ɔ-ɔ]. Other letters may be in front of the whole group and/or follow.

Examples:

borb	[bɔrɔb]	colchag	[kɔLɔxag]
dorcha	[dɔrɔxə]	dorgh	[dɔrɔɣ]
mormhair	[mɔrɔvɪrʲ]	gorm	[gɔrɔm]

STRESSED

O15 (-)o(-) ELSEWHERE [ɔ]

In all cases when none of the previous rules about **o** anywhere in the stressed syllable of a word apply, it will simply be [ɔ].

Examples:

sona	[sɔnə]	fo	[fɔ]
bothan	[bɔhan]	bodach	[bɔdəx]
donna	[dɔNə]	corrach	[kɔRəx]

STRESSED

O16 -o(-) [ə]

The letter **o** in an unstressed position does not occur very often and if it does, it normally obeys the rules that say that unstressed vowels are boring, so you get [ə]. The main exceptions to this rule are place names which end in **-bol** [bɔL] and **-phort** [fɔRʃd] and recent loanwords like *seileafon* [ʃeləfɔn].

Examples:

cothrom	[kɔrəm]	eaconomaidh	[ɛˈkɔnəmɪ]
cudromach	[kudrəməx]	lùthmhor	[Lu:vər]
aotrom	[ɯ:drəm]	almon	[aLamən]

UNSTRESSED

P01 (-)ph(-)   [f]

A broad **ph** anywhere in a word is going to be [f]. It's most commonly found at the beginning of a word as a result of leniting **p** but can occur elsewhere too.

Examples:

phòs	[fɔ:s]	phaisg	[faʃgʲ]
phàigh	[fa:j]	Euphort	[iafɔRʃd]
phut	[fuhd]	Sìophort	[ʃiəfɔRʃd]

BROAD

P02 (-)Vp(-)   [hb]

A broad **p** which comes after a vowel, possibly with other letters before and/or after will undergo pre-aspiration and come out as [hb].

Examples:

apa	[ahbə]	ùpraid	[u:hbrɪdʲ]
cupa	[kuhbə]	pàpa	[pa:hbə]
mapa	[mahbə]	ceap	[kʲɛhb]

BROAD

P03 -Cp(-)   [b]

When a broad **p**, following some other letters, comes directly after another consonant it will weaken to a [b]. Other letters may follow.

Examples:

sporan	[sbɔran]	cuspair	[kusbɪrʲ]
spadadh	[sbadəɣ]	Scarp	[sgarb]
campa	[kaumbə]	teampall	[tʲaumbəL]

BROAD

P

P04 p-   [p]

At the beginning of a word broad **p** will be pronounced [p].

Examples:

pòs	[pɔːs]	paisg	[paʃgʲ]
pàigh	[paːj]	partan	[paRʃdan]
put	[puhd]	Pabaigh	[pabaj]

BROAD

P05 phlʲ-   [fl]

phrʲ-   [frʲ]

The **ph** in a **phl** or **phr** group will always be just [f].

Examples:

dà phreas	[daː frʲes]	dà phriobaid	[daː frʲibɪdʲ]
dà phreachan	[daː frʲɛxan]	dà phrionnsa	[daː frʲũːNsə]
phriob	[frʲib]	do phrionnsabal	[də frʲũːNsəbəL]

SLENDER

P06 phʲ + u(ː) ɯ(ː) o(ː) ɣ(ː) ɔ(ː) a(ː) au (-)   [fj]

A lenited slender **ph** at the beginning of a word will be pronounced
[fj] if there is a back vowel coming after it.

Examples:

mo phiuthar	[mə fju.ər]	glé pheallagach	[gleː fjaLagəx]
dà phiòrna	[daː fjuːRnə]	phiòrr	[fjuːR]
glé phiullagach	[gleː fjuLagəx]	dà phiàno	[daː fjaːnɔ]

SLENDER

P07 (-)phʲ(-) ELSEWHERE   [f]

Elsewhere slender **ph** will be pronounced [f].

Examples:

glé phianail	[gleː fianal]	dà pheur	[daː fiar]
phill	[fiːLʲ]	pheanasaich	[fɛnəsɪç]
dà phiseag	[daː fiʃag]	An Éiphit	[ə Nʲeːfɪdʲ]

SLENDER

P08 plⁱ-   [pl]

pr'-   [prʲ]

The **p** in a **pl** or **pr** group will always be just [p].

Examples:

preas	[prʲes]	priobaid	[prʲibɪdʲ]
preachan	[prʲɛxan]	prionnsa	[prʲũ:Nsə]
priob	[prʲib]	prionnsabal	[prʲũ:NsəbəL]

SLENDER

P09 pⁱ + u(:) ɯ(:) o(:) ɤ(:) ɔ(:) a(:) au (-)   [pj]

A slender **p** at the beginning of a word will be pronounced [pj] if there is a back vowel coming after it.

Examples:

piuthar	[pju.ər]	peallagach	[pjaLagəx]
piòrna	[pju:Rnə]	piorr	[pju:R]
piullagach	[pjuLagəx]	peann	[pjauN]

SLENDER

P10 (-)Vpⁱ(-)   [hb]

A slender **p** which comes after a vowel, possibly with other letters before and/or after will undergo pre-aspiration and come out as [hb].

Examples:

cipean	[kʲihban]	drip	[drihb]
cuip	[kuihb]	Duipinn	[duihbɪNʲ]
suaip	[suəihb]	pàipear	[pɛ:hbɛr]

SLENDER

P

P (left margin tab)

P11 -Cp'(-)   [b]

When a slender **p**, following some other letters, comes directly after another consonant it will weaken to a [b]. Other letters may follow.

Examples:

oidhirp	[ɣ.ɪrb]	ceilp	[kʲelb]
cuirp	[kurʲb]	MacAilpein	[maxˈgalbɛNʲ]
scairp	[sgarʲb]	impis	[ĩːmbɪʃ]

SLENDER

P12 p' ELSEWHERE   [p]

Where none of the other rules about slender **p** apply, it will simply be [p].

Examples:

pianail	[pianal]	peur	[piar]
pill	[piːLʲ]	peanasaich	[pɛnəsɪç]
piseag	[piʃag]	peilear	[pelər]

SLENDER

R

R01 * r-   [r]

A broad **r** at the beginning of a word which has been lenited
(meaning if it comes after a word that causes lenition or is in a spot
where words are normally lenited such as past tense verbs) will be
pronounced as a weak [r].

Examples:

rannsaich	[rauNsıç]	ruaig	[ruəgʲ]
ràinig	[ra:nɪgʲ]	dà rùd	[da: ru:d]
dà ròn	[da: rɔ:n]	dà ròs	[da: rɔ:s]

B R O A D

R02 r-   [R]

When rule R01 does not apply, broad **r** at the beginning of a word is
going to be a strong [R]. The only exceptions to this rule are the
words listed on page 368.

Examples:

rannsaich!	[RauNsıç]	ruaig!	[Ruəgʲ]
ruigidh	[Rɯgʲɪ]	rùd	[Ru:d]
ròn	[Rɔ:n]	ròs	[Rɔ:s]

BROAD

R03 -rr(-)   [R]

Double broad **r** in the middle or at the end of a word will be
pronounced as strong [R].

Examples:

curran	[kuRan]	ciùrr	[kʲu:R]
Barraigh	[baRaj]	bàrr	[ba:R]
torrach	[tɔRəx]	tòrr	[tɔ:R]

BROAD

R

R04 -rt(-)   [Rʃd]

A single broad **r** in the middle or at the end of a word followed immediately by a **t** will be pronounced as [Rʃd]. Other letters may follow.

Examples:

furtach	[fuRʃdəx]	ceart	[kʲaRʃd]
dòrtadh	[dɔ:Rʃdəɣ]	neart	[NʲaRʃd]
cuartaich	[kuəRʃdɪç]	murt	[muRʃd]

BROAD

R05 -r + d(-), n(-), l(-), s(-)   [R]

When **r** comes before another dental (**d**, **n**, **l** and **s**) it will strengthen to [R]. The combination **rt** is covered in rule R04.

Examples:

àrd	[a:Rd]	càrn	[ka:RN]
bàrd	[ba:Rd]	cùrsa	[ku:Rsə]
bùrn	[bu:RN]	dòrlach	[dɔ:RLəx]

BROAD

R06 -r(-) ELSEWHERE   [r]

Single broad **r** in the middle or at the end of a word will be pronounced [r] in all places when the previous rules about broad **r** do not apply.

Examples:

aran	[aran]	cur	[kur]
cùramach	[ku:rəməx]	mar	[mar]
òran	[ɔ:ran]	cor	[kɔr]

BROAD

R

R07	* rʲ		[r]

As there is no difference between initial broad and slender **r**, they both behave the same so a slender **r** at the beginning of a word which has been lenited (meaning if it comes after a word that causes lenition or is in a spot where words are normally lenited such as past tense verbs) will be pronounced as a weak [r].

Examples:

dà rionnag	[da: ruNag]	rianaich	[rianɪç]
reic	[reçgʲ]	do rìgh	[dɔ ri:]
dà réis	[da: re:ʃ]	reòth	[rɔ:]

SLENDER

R08	rʲ-		[R]

As there is no difference between initial broad and slender **r**, they both behave the same so when rule R07 does not apply, slender **r** at the beginning of a word is going to be a strong [R]. The only exceptions to this rule are the words listed on page 368.

Examples:

rionnag	[RuNag]	rianaich!	[Rianɪç]
reic!	[Reçgʲ]	rìgh	[Ri:]
réis	[Re:ʃ]	reòth!	[Rɔ:]

SLENDER

R09	-rtʲ(-)		[Rʃdʲ]

A single slender **r** in the middle or at the end, followed immediately by a **t** will be pronounced as [Rʃdʲ]. Other letters may follow.

Examples:

cairteal	[kaRʃdʲal]	abairt	[abəRʃdʲ]
cuairtear	[kuəRʃdʲər]	cairt	[kaRʃdʲ]
pàirteach	[pa:Rʃdʲəx]	freagairt	[frʲegɪRʃdʲ]

SLENDER

R

R10 (-) u(:) ɯ(:) o(:) ɤ(:) ɔ(:) a(:) +   rn'(-)   [RNʲ]

When there is a back vowel before a slender **rn** group, the **r** will be a strong [R] and the n will also be strong [Nʲ].

Examples:

SLENDER

cùirn	[ku:RNʲ]	bùirn	[bu:RNʲ]
Gòirneag	[gɔ:RNʲag]	àirneis	[a:RNʲɪʃ]
A' Mhaoirne	[ə vɯ:RNʲə]	bàirneach	[ba:RNʲəx]

R11 -rʲ + d(-), n(-), l(-), s(-)   [R]

Slender **r** before another dental (**d, n, l** and **s**) will strengthen to [R].

Examples:

SLENDER

bàird	[ba:Rdʲ]	cùirn	[ku:RNʲ]
àird	[a:Rdʲ]	tùirse	[tu:Rʃə]
àirne	[a:RNʲə]	comhairle	[kõ.əRlə]

R12 -rʲ(-) ELSEWHERE   [rʲ]

Elsewhere single slender **r** will be pronounced [rʲ].

Examples:

SLENDER

gàire	[ga:rʲə]	cìr	[kʲi:rʲ]
coire	[kɔrʲə]	cuir	[kurʲ]
bùireadh	[bu:rʲəɣ]	abair	[abɪrʲ]

S01	shl-	[L]
	shr-	[r]

Lenited **sl** and **sr** will simply be [L] and [r]. Some speakers have more complicated things going on here but that isn't required across all dialects so you can do without it as a learner without sounding odd. Check section 5.6.4 about the **sr/str** spelling issue.

BROAD

Examples:

mo shròn	[mə rɔːn]	do shlàinte	[dɔ LaːNʲdʲə]
dà shrath	[daː rah]	dà shloc	[daː Lɔxg]
shraon	[rɯːn]	dà shlat	[daː Lahd]

S02	shn-	[n]

If you get broad lenited **shn** at the beginning of a word, all you get is a weak [n]. Some speakers have more complicated things going on here but that's not necessary for a good accent for a learner.

BROAD

Examples:

shnàmh	[naːv]	do shnaoisean	[dɔ nɯːʃan]
glé shnog	[gle: nog]	glé shnotach	[gle: nɔhdəx]
dà shnagan	[daː nagan]	do shnuadh	[dɔ nuəɣ]

S03	s(t)r-	[sdr]

A broad **st** or **str** at the start of a word will always be [sdr]. Check section 5.6.6 about the **sr/str** spelling issue.

BROAD

Examples:

sròn	[sdrɔːn]	stràc	[sdraːxg]
srath	[sdrah]	strap	[sdrahb]
sruth	[sdruh]	strìopach	[sdriːhbəx]

S04 sn- [sN]

If you get broad **sn** at the beginning of a word, the **n** will be strong.

Examples:

snàmh	[sNaːv]	snaoisean	[sNɯːʃan]
snog	[sNog]	snotadh	[sNɔhdəɣ]
snagan	[sNagan]	snuadh	[sNuəɣ]

BROAD

S05 sh- [h]

When none of the previous rules about lenited **sh** at the beginning of a word apply, it will simply be pronounced [h].

Examples:

ro shalach	[rɔ haLəx]	glé shona	[gleː hɔnə]
shàsaich	[haːsɪç]	mo shùilean	[mə huːlən]
ro shoilleir	[rɔ hɣLʲɪrʲ]	dà shaoghal	[daː hɯː.əL]

BROAD

S06 (-)st(-) VAR: sd [sd]

Broad **st** at the beginning, in the middle or at the end of a word is pronounced [sd]. The variant **sd** spelling is pronounced exactly the same.

Examples:

staran	[sdaran]	astar	[asdər]
stàth	[sdaː]	posta	[pɔsdə]
stuth	[sduh]	liosta	[Lʲisdə]

BROAD

S07 (-)s(-) ELSEWHERE   [s]

Broad **s** in all other positions (at the beginning, in the middle and at the end of words) is pronounced [s].

Examples:

sàr	[saːr]	fosgailte	[fɔsgəldʲə]
sùil	[suːl]	cus	[kus]
casan	[kasən]	fallas	[faʟəs]

BROAD

S08 shr'-   [r]

Lenited slender **shr** will simply be [r]. Some speakers have more complicated things going on here but that's not necessary for a good accent for a learner. Check section 5.6.6 about the **sr/str** spelling issue.

Examples:

dà shrian	[daː rian]	dà shreath	[daː rɛh]
shreap	[rɛhb]	glé shreamach	[gleː rɛməx]
do shreothart	[dɔ rɔhəRʃd]	glé shrianach	[gleː rianəx]

SLENDER

S09 shl'-   [l]

When you have a lenited slender **sl** group at the start of a word, all that is left is weak [l].

Examples:

shlìob	[liːb]	glé shleamhainn	[gleː lɛ̃vɪNʲ]
dà shlighe	[daː li.ə]	dà shleagh	[daː lɤɣ]
mo shliochd	[mə liəxg]	mo shléibhtean	[mə leːvdʲən]

SLENDER

S

S10 shn'-   [n]

When you have a lenited slender **sn** group at the start of a word, all that is left is weak [n].

Examples:

shnìomh	[niəv]	dà shnèap	[da: nɛ:hb]
shnigh	[ni]	mo shneachda	[mə nɛxgə]
glé shnigheach	[gle: ni.əx]	dà shneag	[da: neg]

SLENDER

S11 sh' + u(:) ɯ(:) o(:) ɤ(:) ɔ(:) a(:) au   [hj]

A lenited slender **sh** which is followed by a back vowel will have a glide, so you get [hj].

Examples:

dà shiùcar	[da: hju:xgər]	dà sheòmar	[da: hjo:mər]
sheòl	[hjɔ:L]	mo sheann aois	[mə hjauN ɯ:ʃ]
bho Sheoc	[vɔ hjɔxg]	dà sheagh	[da: hjɤɣ]

SLENDER

S12 sh'- ELSEWHERE   [h]

If none of the previous rules about lenited slender **sh** apply, then you get [h].

Examples:

mo shìol	[mə hiəL]	glé shean	[gle: hɛn]
shìn	[hi:n]	mo sheud	[mə he:d]
dà shiorram	[da: hiRəm]	glé shearbh	[gle: hɛrɛv]

SLENDER

S

S13 s(t)r'-   [sdr]

Because the broad/slender difference does not apply here, a slender **st** or **str** at the start of a word will also be [sdr]. Check page 358 about the **sr/str** spelling issue.

Examples:

srian	[sdrian]	strìochd	[sdriəxg]
sreap	[sdrɛhb]	strì	[sdri:]
sreothart	[sdrɔhəRʃd]	streup	[sdriahb]

SLENDER

S14 sp' +   u(:) ɯ(:) o(:) ɤ(:) ɔ(:) a(:) au (-)   [sbj]

sm' +   u(:) ɯ(:) o(:) ɤ(:) ɔ(:) a(:) au (-)   [smj]

In a slender **sm** or **sp** group at the beginning of a word the **s** will be broad [s]. The **m** and **p** will be [bj] and [mj] if they are followed by a back vowel.

Examples:

smeòrach	[smjɔ:rəx]	spiuthar	[sbjuhər]
smiùr	[smju:r]	spionnadh	[sbjuNəɤ]
smeòirn	[smjɔ:RNʲ]	speàrl	[sbja:RL]

SLENDER

S15 sg'-   [sgʲ]

In a slender **sg** group at the beginning of a word the **s** will be broad [s] and only the **g** will be palatal [gʲ].

Examples:

sgian	[sgʲian]	sgeir	[sgʲerʲ]
sgìth	[sgʲi:]	sgeadaich	[sgʲedɪç]
sgeulachd	[sgʲiaLəxg]	sgioba	[sgʲibə]

SLENDER

S

S16 sl'-   [ʃLʲ]

When you have a slender **sl** group at the start of a word, both letters will behave as if they were at the start of the word, so you get strong [Lʲ]. In some areas the **s** is broad but that's not necessary for a good accent for a learner.

SLENDER

Examples:

slìob	[ʃLʲiːb]	sleamhainn	[ʃLʲɛ̃vɪNʲ]
slighe	[ʃLʲi.ə]	sleagh	[ʃLʲɤɣ]
sliochd	[ʃLʲiəxg]	sléibhtean	[ʃLʲeːvdʲən]

S17 sn'-   [ʃNʲ]

When you have a slender **sn** group at the start of a word, both letters will behave as if they were at the start of the word, so you get strong [Nʲ]. In some areas the **s** is broad but that's not necessary for a good accent for a learner.

SLENDER

Examples:

snìomh	[ʃNʲiəv]	snèap	[ʃNʲɛːhb]
snigh	[ʃNʲi]	sneachda	[ʃNʲɛxgə]
snigheach	[ʃNʲi.əx]	sneag	[ʃNʲeg]

S18 (-)s'(-) ELSEWHERE   [ʃ]

When none of the other rules about slender **s** apply, then it will be pronounced [ʃ] at the beginning, in the middle and at the end of a word.

SLENDER

Examples:

seachdain	[ʃɛxgɛNʲ]	maise	[maʃə]
siùil	[ʃuːl]	ceist	[kʲeʃdʲ]
ciste	[kʲiʃdʲə]	cìs	[kʲiːʃ]

T01	t-sl-	[tL]
	t-sr-	[tr]
	t-sn-	[tr˜]

The definite article **an t-** causes lenition. In spite of the spelling, this also applies to **sl**, **sn** and **sr** groups. In the case of **t-sl** and **t-sr** this simply lenites away the **s**, resulting in [tL] and [tr] (as if they were written **t-shl** or **t-shr**). In the case of **t-sn**, leniting the **s** away results in **t + n**, which in Gaelic results in [tr˜].

BROAD

Examples:

air an t-slat	[ɛrʲ əN tLahd]	san t-sròn	[səN trɔːn]
san t-sloc	[səN tLɔxg]	air an t-snaois	[ɛrʲ əN trũːʃ]
air an t-sràid	[ɛrʲ əN traːdʲ]	air an t-snathainn	[ɛrʲ əN trãhɪNʲ]

| T02 | tn- | [tr˜] |

this is similar to groups like **cn** so at the beginning of a word the **n** will turn into [r] with nasalisation on nearby vowels. Words with **tn-** are very rare in Gaelic, except in the an **t-sn-** combination.

BROAD

Examples:

tnùth	[trũː]	tnachair	[trãxɪrʲ]
thnùthail	[trũː.al]	tnùthmhor	[trũːvər]
tnùthaire	[trũː.ɛrʲə]	tnùthach	[trũː.əx]

| T03 | (-)thC(-) | |

A broad **th** anywhere that is immediately followed by another consonant is silent. Some speakers do more complicated things to **thC-** at the start of a word but that doesn't happen everywhere so you don't have to worry about doing it yourself.

BROAD

Examples:

do thlachd	[dɔ Laxg]	dùthchasach	[duːxəsəx]
màthraichean	[maːrɪçən]	sruthlach	[sdruLəx]
cothrom	[kɔrəm]	lùths	[Luːs]

T

| T04 | V̄th + V- | [.] |
| | | [ ] |

A broad **th** results in hiatus if the first vowel is long (it does not apply to diphthongs) if there is another vowel coming after. At the end, it is silent.

Examples:

bùtha	[bu:.ə]	gaothach	[gɯ:.əx]
làthair	[La:.ɪrʲ]	gaoth	[gɯ:]
blàthaich	[bLa:.ɪç]	bùth	[bu:]

BROAD

| T05 | (-)th(-) ELSEWHERE | [h] |

When none of the previous rules about broad **th** apply, then is is usually [h]. If it occurs between vowels it can also sometimes be hiatus but since it's hard to predict, I'd advise you to check with a native speaker, the wordlist or a dictionary.

Examples:

thàinig	[ha:nɪgʲ]	cruth	[kruh]
athair	[ahərʲ]	tuath	[tuəh]
sgiathan	[sgʲiəhən]	latha	[La.ə]

BROAD

| T06 | (-)Vt(-) | [hd] |

A broad **t** which comes after a vowel, possibly with other letters before and/or after will undergo pre-aspiration and come out as [hd].

Examples:

put	[puhd]	bòtainn	[bɔ:hdɪNʲ]
cat	[kahd]	atach	[ahdəx]
cutadh	[kuhdəɣ]	còta	[kɔ:hdə]

BROAD

T07 -Ct(-)   [d]

When a broad **t** in the middle or at the end of a word is immediately
preceded by another consonant, you get a [d].

Examples:

allt	[auLd]	calltainn	[kauLdɪNʲ]
cunnt	[kũːNd]	gealltanas	[gʲauLdənəs]
sagart	[sagəRʃd]	taghta	[tɤɣdə]

BROAD

T08 t-   [t]

When none of the previous rules apply, a broad **t** at the start of a
word will be pronounced [t].

Examples:

taigh	[tɤj]	tòn	[tɔːn]
tarraing	[taRɪŋʲgʲ]	turas	[turəs]
tog	[tog]	tùr	[tuːr]

BROAD

T09 t-sl-   [tl]

t-sr-   [tr]

t-sn-   [tr̃]

The definite article an **t-** has leniting force. In spite of the spelling,
this also applies to **sl**, **sn** and **sr** groups. In the case of **t-sl** and **t-sr**
this simply lenites away the **s**, resulting in [tl] and [tr] (as if they were
written **t-shl** or **t-shr**). In the case of **t-sn**, leniting the **s** away results
in **t + n**, which in Gaelic results in [tr̃].

Examples:

air an t-sliabh	[ɛrʲ əN tliav]	air an t-sreath	[ɛrʲ əN trɛh]
air an t-sleagh	[ɛrʲ əN tlɤɣ]	air an t-sneachda	[ɛrʲ əN trɛ̃xgə]
air an t-srian	[ɛrʲ əN trian]	air an t-snighe	[ɛrʲ əN trĩ.ə]

SLENDER

T

T10 thl'-   [l]

thr'-   [r]

A lenited slender **thl** and **thr** group will result in weak [l] and [r]. Some speakers do more complicated things here but that doesn't happen everywhere so you don't have to worry about doing it yourself.

Examples:

do thligheachd	[dɔ li.əxg]	bho thrì	[vɔ riː]
do thliochdan	[dɔ lixgan]	dà threòir	[daː rɔːrʲ]
dà threabhaiche	[daː rɔ.ɪçə]	dà threud	[daː reːd]

SLENDER

T11 th' + u(ː) ɯ(ː) o(ː) ɤ(ː) ɔ(ː) aː au -   [hj]

At the beginning of a word a slender **th** will be pronounced [hj] if one of the above back vowels is immediately following. Other letters will follow.

Examples:

glé theòma	[gleː hjɔːmə]	thearn	[hjaːRn]
'ga theòdhadh	[gə hjɔː.əɣ]	dà thiurr	[daː hjuːR]
A Thearlaich!	[ə hjaːRLɪç]	glé theann	[gleː hjauN]

SLENDER

T12 -th'C(-)   [ ]

A slender **th** in the middle or at the end of a word that is immediately followed by another consonant is silent.

Examples:

creithleag	[krʲelag]	cruithneachd	[krɯN'əxg]
àithne	[aːNʲə]	aithreachas	[arʲəxəs]
breithneachadh	[brʲenəxəɣ]	lùiths	[Luːʃ]

SLENDER

T13 (-) iː eː ɛː + th'   [ ]

At the end of a word after the above long front vowels, slender **th** will be silent.

Examples:

dìth	[dʲiː]	léith	[Lʲeː]
sgìth	[sgʲiː]	sgéith	[sgʲeː]
sìth	[ʃiː]	fèith	[fɛː]

SLENDER

T14 (-) u(ː) ɯ(ː) o(ː) ɤ(ː) ɔ(ː) aː uə + th'V-   [j]

Between two vowels slender **th**, possibly followed by more letters, frequently turns into a [j] glide if the first vowel is one of the above back vowels.

Examples:

làithean	[Laːjən]	gaoithe	[gɤje]
luaithe	[Luəjə]	dlùitheachd	[dLuːjəxg]
ràithe	[Raːjə]	saoitheil	[sɤjal]

SLENDER

T15 (-)th'(-) ELSEWHERE   [h]

When none of the previous rules apply, slender **th** is usually [h]. If it occurs between vowels it can also sometimes be hiatus but since that is hard to predict, I'd advise you to check with a native speaker, the wordlist or a dictionary.

Examples:

thig	[higʲ]	frithealadh	[frʲihəLəɤ]
theasaich	[hesɪç]	bitheanta	[bihəNdə]
glé thiamhaidh	[gleː hĩə̃vɪ]	dithis	[dʲi.ɪʃ]

SLENDER

T16 tl'- [tl]

tr'- [tr]

Slender **tl** and **tr** will result in [tl] and [tr] because the broad/slender difference doesn't apply in these groups.

Examples:

tligheachd	[tli.əxg]	trì	[tri:]
tliochdan	[tlixgan]	treòir	[trɔ:rʲ]
treabhaiche	[trɔ.ɪçə]	treud	[tre:d]

SLENDER

T17 -Ct'(-) [dʲ]

When you have a consonant immediately before a slender **t** then you get [dʲ]. There will always be letters in front and possibly some after.

Examples:

leòinteach	[Lʲɔ:Nʲdʲəx]	slàinte	[sLa:Nʲdʲə]
mòinteach	[mɔ:Nʲdʲəx]	susbaint	[susbɪNʲdʲ]
Asainte	[asɪNʲdʲə]	smuaint	[smuəNʲdʲ]

SLENDER

T18 (-)Vt'(-) [hdʲ]

When you have a vowel directly in front of a slender **t** then you get pre-aspiration. Other letters may be in front and after the group.

Examples:

oiteag	[ɔhdʲag]	poit	[pɔhdʲ]
aiteamh	[ahdʲəv]	moiteil	[mɔhdʲal]
croit	[krɔhdʲ]	tuiteam	[tuhdʲəm]

SLENDER

T19	t'-		[tʲ]

Slender **t** at the beginning of a word will result in palatal [tʲ]. Note that in some spelling systems some of the irregular verb spellings are an exception to this rule (see 5.6.15).

SLENDER

Examples:

teas	[tʲes]	tearn	[tʲaːRn]
teagamh	[tʲegəv]	teòma	[tʲɔːmə]
tiamhaidh	[tʲĩə̃vɪ]	tiurr	[tʲuːR]

T

U01 (-)ua(i)(-)   [uə]

In a stressed syllable, possibly following some other initial letters, **ua** and **uai** will be pronounced [uə]. Other letters may follow.

Examples:

bhuam	[vuəm]	uaine	[uəNʲə]
cuan	[kuən]	bruaich	[bruəç]
gluasad	[gLuəsəd]	buail	[buəl]

STRESSED

U02 (-)u(i) + rd(-), rl(-), rn(-), rrC(-), rr   [u:]

When **u** or **ui** is followed by an **rd**, **rl**, **rn** and **rr** plus a consonant anywhere or by **rr** at the end of a word then you get a long [u:]. Once again, I'm following the traditional convention of not writing the grave before **rr** as it leads to misleading spellings (cf A06, E18, I11).

Examples:

bùrn	[bu:Rn]	bùird	[bu:Rdʲ]
cùrlach	[ku:RLəx]	ùird	[u:Rdʲ]
sgurr	[sgu:R]	tùirling	[tu:Rlɪŋʲg ʲ]

STRESSED

U03 (-)ù(i)(-)   [u:]

In a stressed syllable, possibly following some other initial letters, **ù** and **ùi** will be pronounced [u:]. Other letters may follow.

Examples:

dùn	[du:n]	dùin	[du:Nʲ]
glùn	[gLu:n]	cùil	[ku:l]
cùlaibh	[ku:Ləv]	sùilean	[su:lən]

STRESSED

U04	(-)u +	lb(-), lbh(-), lch(-), lg(-), lgh(-), lm(-), lmh(-)	[u-u]
		nb(-), nbh(-), nch(-), ngh(-), nm(-), nmh(-)	[u-u]
		rb(-), rbh(-), rch(-), rg(-), rgh(-), rm(-), rmh(-)	[u-u]
		ml(-), mr(-), ms(-), mch(-)	[u-u]

When you have an **u** in an environment where a helping vowel appears, this will give you [u-u]. Other letters may be in front of the whole group and/or follow.

Examples:

ulbhag	[uLuvag]	lurgann	[LurugəN]
cunbhalach	[kunuvəLəx]	furm	[furum]
urchair	[uruxɪrʲ]	mulghart	[muLuɣəRʃd]

U05	(-)u + llV(-), nnV(-), rrV(-), mV(-)	[u]

In a stressed syllable, possibly following some other initial letters, u before **ll**, **nn** and **m** will be [u] if there is a vowel immediately after. Other letters may follow.

Examples:

ullamh	[uLəv]	grunnach	[gruNəx]
mullach	[muLəx]	cumail	[kumal]
gunna	[guNə]	cumanta	[kuməNdə]

U

U06	(-)u +	ll, nn, m	[uː]
		llC(-), nnC(-), mC(-)	[uː]

This rule deals with **u** (optionally with letters in front of it) which is followed either by:

- **ll**, **nn** or **m** without anything following them, that is, at the end of a word
- **ll**, **nn** or **m** which are immediately followed by a consonant and optionally more letters

In all cases the pronunciation will be [uː]. Once again, since this lengthening is fully predictable, I'm not using the grave on these in line with the traditional system (cf A06, E17, I11, U02).

Examples:

a-null	[əˈNũːL]	sunnt	[sũːNd]
grunn	[grũːN]	cum	[kũːm]
cunnt	[kũːNd]	diumbach	[dʲũːmbəx]

STRESSED

U07	(-)u + dhC(-), ghC(-)	[uː]

In a stressed syllable, initially and following other initial letters you get a long [uː] if there is a **dh** or **gh** coming after which itself is immediately followed by another consonant. Other letters may follow but have no further effect.

Examples:

lughdaich	[Luːdɪç]	rudhraich	[Ruːrɪç]
Dughlas	[duːLəs]	Lughdan	[Luːdan]
ughdar	[uːdər]	Fughlaigh	[fuːLaj]

STRESSED

U08	(-)ui + llV(-), nnV(-), mV(-)		[ɯ]

In a stressed syllable, possibly following some other initial letters, **ui** before **ll**, **nn** and **m** will be [ɯ] if there is a vowel immediately after. Other letters may follow. Note that there is a certain amount of variation in the way native speakers deal with this group. Some have retained the older [u] pronunciation, so [u] is acceptable in many places too.

Examples:

tuilleadh	[tɯLʲəɣ]	cuinneag	[kɯNʲag]
duilleag	[dɯLʲag]	luime	[Lɯimə]
cluinneadh	[kLɯNʲəɣ]	muime	[mɯimə]

U09	(-)ui + ll, nn, m		[ɯi]
	llC(-), nnC(-), mC(-)		[ɯi]

This rule deals with **ui** (optionally with letters in front of it) which is followed either by:

- **ll**, **nn** or **m** without anything following them, that is, at the end of a word
- **ll**, **nn** or **m** which are immediately followed by a consonant and optionally more letters

In all cases the pronunciation will be [ɯi].

Examples:

tuill	[tɯiLʲ]	cluinntinn	[kLɯ̃ĩNʲdʲɪNʲ]
uillt	[ɯiLʲdʲ]	suim	[sɯim]
cluinn	[kLɯ̃ĩNʲ]	Luimneach	[Lɯimnəx]

U10	ui-		[ɯ]
	d, n, t, l, s + ui-		[ɯ]

This rule and the next deal with what is perhaps the messiest aspect of the Gaelic spelling system. The previous rules are reliable but U10 and U11 are only broadly indicative. Different speakers and dialects differ considerably from each other. So in the remaining cases of **ui** you will more often than not get [ɯ] if:

- the **ui** is at the beginning of a word
- if it follows a dental (**d, n, t, l** and **s**)

Examples:

uiseag	[ɯʃag]	duine	[dɯNʲə]
uisge	[ɯʃgʲə]	duilleag	[dɯLʲag]
tuiseal	[tɯʃəL]	suipear	[sɯihbər]

STRESSED

U11	-ui- l		[u]
	-ui- ELSEWHERE		[u]

Please also read the note under U10 about the problems with the remaining cases of **ui**. In the middle of a word, it will usually be [u] before a single l and more often than not in all other cases.

Examples:

buileach	[buləx]	buidhe	[bujə]
cuilean	[kulan]	bruis	[bruʃ]
cuileag	[kulag]	puist	[puʃdʲ]

STRESSED

U

U12	(-)ui +	lb(-), lbh(-), lch(-), lg(-), lgh(-), lm(-), lmh(-)	[ɯ-ɯ]
		nb(-), nbh(-), nch(-), ngh(-), nm(-), nmh(-)	[ɯ-ɯ]
		rb(-), rbh(-), rch(-), rg(-), rgh(-), rm(-), rmh(-)	[ɯ-ɯ]
		ml(-), mr(-), ms(-), mch(-)	[ɯ-ɯ]

When you have an **ui** in an environment where a helping vowel appears, this will give you [ɯ-ɯ]. Other letters may be in front of the whole group and/or follow. Should you have a case of **ui** being pronounced [u], then it behaves like rule U04 and you get [u-u].

STRESSED

Examples:

duilgheas	[dɯlɯjəs]	duirche	[dɯrʲɯçə]
duirgh	[dɯrʲɯj]	guirme	[gɯrʲɯmə]
luirg	[Lɯrʲɯrgʲ]	suirghe	[sɯrʲɯjə]

U13	(-)ui +	lb(-), lbh(-), lch(-), lg(-), lgh(-), lm(-), lmh(-)	[u-u]
		nb(-), nbh(-), nch(-), ngh(-), nm(-), nmh(-)	[u-u]
		rb(-), rbh(-), rch(-), rg(-), rgh(-), rm(-), rmh(-)	[u-u]
		ml(-), mr(-), ms(-), mch(-)	[u-u]

When you have an **ui** in an environment where a helping vowel appears, this can also give you [u-u]. Other letters may be in front of the whole group and/or follow. U12 and U13 are very hard to predict but fortunately it's not a mortal mistake to have the wrong one.

STRESSED

Examples:

cuilg	[kulugʲ]	buirbe	[burʲubə]
fuirmean	[furʲumən]	cuimsich	[kumuʃɪç]
cuirm	[kurʲum]	muinghinn	[munujɪNʲ]

U

U14	(-)u- ELSEWHERE		[u]

In a stressed syllable, both initially and following other initial letters and always followed by other letters, **u** will be pronounced [u] everywhere else.

STRESSED

Examples:

urram	[uRəm]	cus	[kus]
ugh	[u]	buntainn	[bundɪNʲ]
urchair	[uruxɪrʲ]	thuca	[huxgə]

U15	-u(-)		[ə]

The letter **u** in an unstressed position does not occur very often anymore in recent publications and if it does, it normally obeys the rules that say that unstressed vowels are boring, so you get [ə].

UNSTRESSED

Examples:

agus	[agəs]	MacCodrum	[maxˈkɔdrəm]
bu	[bə]	ud	[əd]
Calum	[kaLəm]	Sgùlamus	[sguːLəməs]

V.   Bibliography

Black, R.   *Cothrom Ionnsachaidh*
Edinburgh University, Dùn Éideann 1997

Borgstrøm, C.   *The Dialect of Barra*
Norsk Tidskrift for Sprogvidenskap, Oslo 1937

The Dialects of Skye and Ross-shire
in Norsk Tidskrift for Sprogvidenskap, Oslo 1941

The Dialects of the Outer Hebrides
Norsk Tidskrift for Sprogvidenskap, Oslo 1940

Brodick, G.   *A Handbook of Late Spoken Manx I-III*
Niemeyer, Tübingen, 1986

Buchanan, D.   *Gaelic-English English-Gaelic Dictionary*
Geddes & Grosset, Lannraig Ùr, 2004

Dorian, N.   *East Sutherland Gaelic*
Institiúid Ard-Léinn Bhaile Átha Cliath, Baile Átha Cliath 1978

Dubois, J. (ed)   *Larousse Dictionnaire d' Étymologie*
Larousse, Paris 2001

Frantz, D.   *Blackfoot Grammar*
University of Toronto Press, Toronto 1991

Hoad, TF.   *Oxford Concise Dictionary of English Etymology*
Oxford University Press, Oxford 1986

Holmer, N.   *The Gaelic of Arran*
Institiúid Ard-Léinn Bhaile Átha Cliath, Baile Átha Cliath 1957

The Gaelic of Kintyre
Institiúid Ard-Léinn Bhaile Átha Cliath, Baile Átha Cliath 1962
(reprint 1981)

The Irish Language in Rathlin Island
Acadamh Ríoga na hÉireann, Baile Átha Cliath 1942

Studies on Argyllshire Gaelic
Humanistiska Vetenskaps-Samfundet, Uppsala 1938

Klevenhaus, M.   *Lehrbuch der schottisch-gälischen Sprache*
Helmut Buske Verlag, Hamburg 2008

le Muire, A.   *Bunchúrsa Foghraíochta*
Oifig an tSoláthair, Baile Átha Cliath 1966

MacAlpine, N.   *Pronouncing Gaelic-English Dictionary*
Gairm, Glaschu 1975

Mac an Tàilleir, I. *Ainmean-Àite*
Pàrlamaid na h-Alba, Dùn Éideann 2003

MacGill-Fhinnein, G. *Gàidhlig Uidhist a Deas*
Institiúid Ard-Léinn Bhaile Átha Cliath, Baile Átha Cliath 1966

MacKone, K.   *Stair na Gaeilge*
Roinn na Sean-Gheailge Coláiste Phádraig, Maigh Nuad 1994

MacLagan, R.   *The Games & Diversions of Argyleshire*
Folk-Lore Society, London 1901

MacLeod, D.   *The Standardisation of Gaelic Pronunciation*
in Transactions of the Gaelic Society of Inverness,
Inbhir Nis 1932

MacNeacail, A.   *Oideas na Cloinne*
Colaiste Cnoc Iòrdain, Glaschu 1947

MacNeill, M.   *Everyday Gaelic*
Gairm, Glaschu 1999

MacPhàrlain, M.   *The Phonetics of the Gaelic Language*
J & R MacPhàrlain, Pàislig 1889

Oftedal, M.   *The Gaelic of Leurbost, Isle of Lewis*
Norsk Tidskrift for Sprogvidenskap, Oslo 1956

Ó Baoill, C.   *Lárchanúint don Ghaeilge - Tuarascáil Taighde*
Institiúid Teangeolaíochte Éireann, Baile Átha Cliath 1986

Ó Dochartaigh C. *Survey of the Gaelic Dialects of Scotland (Vol I-V)*
Institiúid Ard-Léinn Bhaile Átha Cliath, Baile Átha Cliath 1997

Ó Liatháin, A.   *Focloir Póca*
An Gúm, Baile Átha Cliath 1992

Ó Maolalaigh, R. *Scottish Gaelic in Three Months*
Hugo's Language Books Ltd., 1997

Scottish Gaelic in Twelve Weeks
Birlinn Ltd, 2008

Ó Murchú, M.   *East Perthshire Gaelic*
Institiúid Ard-Léinn Bhaile Átha Cliath, Baile Átha Cliath 1989

Ó Raithile, TF.   *Irish Dialects Past and Present*
Institiúid Ard-Léinn Bhaile Átha Cliath, Baile Átha Cliath 1988

Robinson, M.   *The Concise Scots Dictionary*
Clò Oilthigh Obar Dheathain, Obar Dheathain 1985

SCRE   *Aithris is Oideas: Traditional Gaelic Rhymes and Games*
London 1964

Ternes, E.   *The Phonemic Analysis of Scottish Gaelic*
Helmut Buske Verlag, Hamburg 1989

VI.   About the author

Michael Bauer was born into a trilingual family in Munich in 1974 and thus has had first-hand experience of the linguistic struggles encountered in a setting where one of the home languages was not the community language as well. Much later while still at school, the first Celtic language he encountered though was Irish, an event that triggered a long-standing fascination with Goidelic languages.

On leaving school in 1995, reality intervened though and Michael attended medical school for some time before he came to his senses and signed up for linguistics and phonetics at the Ludwig-Maximilians University in Munich.   A strange chain of events led him to switching not only courses but also countries in 1998 - to Edinburgh University for a degree in Linguistics and Celtic Studies.

Focussing heavily on phonology, language acquisition and modern Gaelic he won several prizes for his prowess and graduated in 2002. There followed some extra training to deepen his knowledge of the language.   Having moved to Glasgow he began working with the language professionally around that time and has been doing so happily ever since. In what remains of his "free time", he has also been behind many developments in and for the language such as Dwelly-d, the Faclair Beag, internet software including the Gaelic versions of Firefox, Thunderbird and Opera, a spellchecker and various other language technology projects. On a lighter note, his fascination and commitment to Gaelic has recently also led him to become the first person to sit the Life in the UK test in Gaelic en route to becoming a naturalised citizen.

His career in language teaching goes back a long time but started in the academic arena.   While at Edinburgh he had spotted the need for a better approach to the teaching of pronunciation to Gaelic adult learners.   After graduating he focussed on honing the methods and materials to suit this target audience. The first development was a Gaelic resource website. In light of the encouraging feedback from many users and learners in the global learners' community about the site, he embarked on the 8-year journey of producing this book.   Michael is genuinely indebted and grateful to his colleagues, friends, students and other guinea-pigs and sounding boards for their invaluable help, feedback and encouragement over the years.

He by no means believes that this will be the last word in improving the pronunciation of Gaelic learners and its teaching but he certainly hopes it will help everyone make a big step forward.

CPSIA information can be obtained
at www.ICGtesting.com
Printed in the USA
LVHW110923221020
669505LV00001B/3

9 781907 165009